Perspectives on the Russian State in Transition

Wolfgang Danspeckgruber
Editor

Liechtenstein Institute on Self-Determination
Princeton University
Princeton, New Jersey

Designed and produced by the Office of External Affairs, Woodrow Wilson School of Public and International Affairs, Princeton University.

WWS-LISD Study Series
Wolfgang Danspeckgruber, Editor-in-Chief
Beth English, Executive Editor

Telephone: (609) 258-6200
Facsimile: (609) 258-5196
Electronic Mail: lisd@princeton.edu
On the Web: http://www.princeton.edu/lisd

Liechtenstein Institute on Self-Determination at Princeton University
Woodrow Wilson School
of Public and International Affairs
Princeton, New Jersey 08544 USA

Contents

LIST OF TABLES

LIST OF FIGURES

INTRODUCTION
WOLFGANG DANSPECKGRUBER

Since the formal dissolution of the Soviet Union at the end of December 1991, Russia has gone through upheavals and has experienced inner turmoil. Through the early 1990s, the transition from communism to capitalism dominated much of the dialogue about Russia, its domestic economic and political stability, and its place in both a regional and global context. However, the imperial-style presidency of Vladimir Putin, Russia's vast energy reserves, and a cleverly conducted foreign policy have facilitated Russia's return to a position of power within the contemporary international system. With Russia's reemergence, increasing numbers of diplomats, policy-makers, and scholars began supplementing studies about Russia that focused largely on macroeconomic issues with ones highlighting the critical and interrelated issues of Russia's economic system, political and civil order, institutional infrastructure, geography, identity, national security, and global energy resources.

The chapters found herein evolved out of an ongoing international and interdisciplinary project, "Self-Governance in the Regions of the Former Soviet Union: Political Institutions, Property, and State Power," undertaken by the Liechtenstein Institute on Self-Determination at Princeton University's Woodrow Wilson School of Public and International Affairs. Contributing authors presented first drafts of their works at a project-related colloquium, "The Future of the Russian State," held in Triesenburg, Liechtenstein, 14-17 March 2002. The conference facilitated in-depth discussions about key developments in Russia and stimulated new thinking about the future of the Russian state and Russia's relationships with its regional neighbors, the European Union, and Asia. The resulting analyses written by leading authorities on the former Soviet Union offer an integrated picture of the institutions, economics, social trends, and geopolitics underpinning and resulting from transitions within the Russian state during the late 1990s and first years of the twenty-first century.

The overarching dynamics of continuity and change in Russian state institutions, in the Russian economy, and in Russia's foreign policy and national security frame much of the analysis in this volume. In the first three chapters, Dominic Lieven, Eugene Huskey, and Simon Clarke view this continuity and change paradigm through three different lenses: empire, the legal system, and trade unions. Lieven uses the construct of empire to understand the nature of the transitions that occurred as the communist-based USSR collapsed and the democratic-based Russian state emerged.

In doing so Lieven poses important questions about the relationship between the Russian state and its citizens, as well as about geography, identity, and governance. Huskey delves into the legal dimensions of the ongoing reconstruction of the Russian state, what he calls "the neglected actor in the drama of the Russian transition." As Huskey notes, Putin's reforms and the true motivations driving them have been a significant point of contention. But, they have the potential to alter relations within Russia's legal system and between the state and governing institutions, and to make a Russian legal system of the twenty-first century that is fundamentally different than any that have existed in the nation's history. Simon Clarke elaborates on the challenges faced by Russia's trade unions at the federal, regional, and branch levels in the transition from a planned to a market economy. This transition threatened to undermine trade unions' viability as unions, employers, and the government now, in theory, functioned independently from one another with often disparate agendas and goals. But in fact, Clarke illuminates how Russia's trade unions, rather than collapsing with the Soviet communist-party state, redefined their positions within the Russian state, survived, and in some instances provided a level of continuity in the administration of state power by performing functions for its members that the post-Soviet Russian state did not have the structures or capacity to undertake. Although it may be too soon to make a final judgment about the long-term ramifications of the legacies of empire, the remaking of Russia's legal institutions, and the role of Russia's trade unions in civil society, the keen insights of Lieven, Huskey, and Clarke provide a backdrop to understand the context and significance of ongoing institutional transformations.

Murray Feshbach, Richard Ericson, Rawi Abdelal, and Thane Gustafson, Simon Kukes, and Paul Rodzianko engage with Russia's economy and the changes and challenges the state has faced and continues to confront in this area. Murray Feshbach looks at demographics, health, and the environment in Russia to shed light on the problems facing the Russian economy of the future, especially relating to labor supply and to the quantity and quality of the country's human capital and potential military recruits. Environmental factors, disease, addiction, and the age-sex composition of the Russian population all place stresses on the post-Soviet economy, creating the likelihood of what Feshbach characterizes as "major negative changes" for the Russian state as a whole. Whereas Feshbach analyzes demographic and environmental factors to illuminate underlying threats to the stability and functioning of the Russian economy, Richard Ericson finds the nexus of the problems impacting Russia's economy in institutional and structural carryovers from the Soviet era. Ericson notes that vast and fundamental changes have occurred within the Russian economy since 1991, but he also argues that although the ongoing development program initiated by the Putin government looks to be promising, current domestic challenges may only exacerbate preexisting roadblocks to the country's market economy and, in fact, may derail meaningful future progress. Gustafson, Kukes, and Rodzianko expound upon the ways that the Russian oil industry has changed radically since the demise of the Soviet Union. These changes are exemplified by the restructuring of the industry and its operations, changes in corporate culture and management practices, and adaptations made for operating within a liberalized market. Yet, the legacy of the Soviet era continues to weigh heavily on the Russian oil industry. As an increasingly important player in the global energy supply network, Russia's oil companies must address Soviet-era vestiges to remain competitive and thrive in the twenty-first century.

Rawi Abdelal approaches the Russian economy from a broader regional perspective. He uses the ruble and monetary problems that Russia faced through the 1990s to highlight the role of currency in the restructuring of the Russian economy, and the ruble's importance in post-Soviet domestic and regional politics. Abdelal shows how the ruble is an important tool for understanding the complexities of economic reform and democratic institution-building in the former Soviet Union, while also analyzing how debates surrounding the ruble and the ruble's rejection by 14 of the Soviet-successor states brought to the forefront regionwide issues about national identity and political and economic relationships within post-Soviet Eurasia. As the Russian economy moves forward into its free-market future, the analyses of Abdelal, Feshbach, Ericson, and Gustafson, Kukes, and Rodzianko create a framework for a better understanding and appreciation of the next steps that must be taken by the Russian state and private industry to address both the legacies of the Soviet-era planned economy and challenges on the horizon.

Dale Herspring, Curt Gasteyger, and William Wohlforth round-out the volume by delving into issues of national security, foreign policy, and geopolitics. Herspring offers a frank and startling appraisal of the Russian military wherein morale is at rock bottom, soldiers are deserting, equipment is failing, and the situation in Chechnya looms large. Still, Herspring finds that in the midst of such crises within the Russian military, steps toward reform (although often tentative and slow) have been taken by Vladimir Putin. Putin's initiatives have proven positive and mark a turning point of sorts in the post-Soviet state because, for the first time since the break-up of the Soviet Union, a Russian leader is taking seriously the restructuring and reform of the

Russian military. Gasteyger argues that the demise of the Soviet Union also forced a fundamental reorientation of Russia's foreign policy and its association with the West. No longer a credible counterweight to the influence of the United States on the world stage, Gasteyger illustrates how Russia is now in a position of reappraising its relationships and strategic objectives within its own region, with the United States, and with the European Union as it seeks to reestablish its preeminence on the global stage. Finally, Wolhforth disputes the "heartland thesis" – a geopolitical theory ascribing Russia's global strategic significance to its size and location – and offers a counterargument that the heartland thesis is incorrect and its exaggeration of Russia's strategic importance has skewed analyses and perceptions of Russia's foreign policy interests and goals. His challenge to this body of geopolitical scholarship and to perceptions of Russia's place in the geopolitical system of the early twenty-first century speaks to forthcoming debates that will undoubtedly play out in the years to come among academics and, especially within the Russian state itself, among foreign policy strategists.

As a concluding note, I would like to thank the contributing authors for their commitment to seeing this volume come to fruition, and to the Princely House of Liechtenstein and the Woodrow Wilson School for their financial support. Also to Stephen Kotkin, Tyler Felgenhauer, Marc Berenson, and Dorothy Hannigan, I express my gratitude for their contributions and efforts during the early phases of the project. Thanks as well to Steven Barnes, Karyn Olsen, and Rebecca Dull at the Woodrow Wilson School for their parts in the design and production of the book, and to Ja Ian Chong and Natasha Gopaul for their work on the index. A key element of the mission of the Liechtenstein Institute on Self-Determination is to help inform and educate the next generation of policy-makers and leaders. It is in this spirit that LISD presents this volume.

LEGACIES OF EMPIRE
DOMINIC LIEVEN

Abstract

This chapter looks at the present Russian predicament from the perspective of empire. First, it discusses the various possible meanings and definitions of empire. Then it looks at empire and the ethnically-defined nation as viable types of polity in today's global order. The paper's final and longest section compares the aftermath of empire in contemporary northern Eurasia with the consequences of the collapse of empires elsewhere in the twentieth century.

In my first section I note that the dominant conception and definition of empire in today's world is drawn from the experience of the European maritime empires. But great land empires have existed since antiquity. As empires, both tsarist Russia and the USSR were hybrids which combined aspects of both land and modern maritime empires in interesting fashion. Though the similarities with great autocratic, military land empires legitimized by some universal religion may be most obvious, Russia was also an important participant in the expansion of Europe. It drew much of the ideological inspiration for empire as well as the technologies which made it possible from Europe.

My definition of empire is a broad one. I stress four factors: great territory, multi-ethnicity, rule without explicit consent of the governed, and (above all) very great power in international affairs.

Obviously, a polity defined in these terms is inappropriate in the contemporary world for many reasons. Empire contradicts basic tenets of democracy and nationalism, the dominant ideologies of the contemporary world. It tends to equate a polity's acquisition of territory and imposition on alien peoples of direct political rule with the maximization of the metropolitan society's power and wealth. Empire also usually entails an authoritarian government whose penetration of society nevertheless remains rather limited. None of this makes sense in the early twenty-first century. On the other hand, nor very often does empire's nemesis, the nation-state. The latter is in reality often ethnically defined, and may need to be so if it is to draw on the deep loyalty of its citizens. Turning Europe into a continent of polities so defined has been a bloody and destabilizing process. Most Asians (India, China, Indonesia) still live in polities closer to empire than to ethnically defined nations: should twenty-first-century Asia follow European patterns of ethnic nationalism then the result will be chaos. Meanwhile, the European Union is an attempt to transcend, or at least complement, the nation and is based on the belief that the traditional nation-state is inadequate to meet many of the challenges of today's world. Interestingly, the European Union faces many of the familiar dilemmas of modern empire: to be powerful requires continental scale, which in turn entails multi-ethnicity. How can continental-scale government be made legitimate and effective in a world dominated by ideologies of nationalism and democracy?

In the New World colonies of settlement, democratic nationalism had fateful consequences for indigenous populations who were always excluded from definitions of citizenship. Mass expropriation of property, ethnic cleansing, and even genocide were perpetrated by polities which could justifiably claim to be the most democratic countries of their era. This was in line with earlier comments by political theorists about the fatal consequences of being subject to a republic of citizens. In an increasingly interdependent global community, this alerts one to the point that democracy in the First World is no necessary guarantee of benevolence towards the Third, and could even lead in the opposite direction.

In comparing the post-imperial former USSR with the aftermath of previous empires, modesty is necessary. Circumstances differ, and so do eras and international contexts.

On the whole, the easiest comparisons are with great land empires' aftermath. In the case of both the Habsburg and Ottoman Empires, for example, one finds great difficulties in defining and legitimizing the core Turkish and Austrian nation-states which emerged from empire's ruins. It is also less easy in land empires for the former core to divorce itself from the chaos in former peripheral territories which the end of empire often brings. Even maritime empires did not altogether escape these dilemmas, however, above all when they sought to incorporate colonies into the metropolis (e.g. Ireland and Algeria).

During the decline and fall of empires, democracy can lead to competitive mobilization of rival ethnicities and ferocious battles over identity and territory. One reason why the collapse of the Soviet Union was in most areas relatively bloodless was the absence of democracy (compare e.g. Ireland after 1885 and India in 1935-47).

But in the longer run, democracy is not just valuable in itself but also often a source of stability (e.g. India as opposed to Indonesia). The rule of former colonial notables is temporarily more stable in the former USSR as has often been the case in other post-imperial contexts. But rigidity, corruption, and the denial of opportunities to new political and social forces can easily lead to chaos in the former Soviet "southern rim" as it has elsewhere, with growing instability linked to the advance of populist and nationalist groups and ideologies.

For the moment, however, the main lesson to be drawn from the comparative history of de-colonization is that the Soviet case has been relatively benign. The end of empire is usually linked to a host of wars even when relatively well-managed (N.B., for example, India versus Pakistan, the Arab-Israeli conflict, and other less devastating but still important conflicts in the British case). There are a number of reasons for this, of which the fact that the collapse of the USSR occurred in peacetime at a moment of international détente is perhaps the most important. Gorbachev himself was both partly responsible for the disintegration of the USSR and for the fact that it collapsed so peacefully.

But it is too early to rejoice. A little more than a decade is not long: the results of empire's collapse can take a generation or more to reveal themselves. Ten years after the collapse of the tsarist, Habsburg, and Ottoman Empires, Europe was basking in international détente (Locarno) and an economic recovery fuelled by a Wall Street boom. The Crash, Hitler, the Second World War, and the annihilation of the Jews (one of empire's great diasporas) was still to come.

* * *

The aim of this chapter is to look at the contemporary Russian polity from the perspective of empire.[1] The paper compares empire and the nation-state, and shows how both forms of polity have strengths and weaknesses when faced with the challenges of today's world. I then go on to look at the legacies of empire and the consequences of empire's collapse. This I do through a comparison between the current situation in northern Eurasia and the results of the collapse of other twentieth-century empires.[2]

To call any polity in today's world an empire is a term of abuse. Empire is taken to be the antithesis of democracy and nationhood, and these are the dominant legitimizing ideologies of the contemporary polity. In addition, empire and imperialism are seen as embodying political and cultural domination, and the economic exploitation of the Third World by the First.[3] For three main reasons "empire" is above all associated in contemporary consciousness with the West European maritime empires which existed from the sixteenth to the twentieth centuries. In the first place, West Europeans and their American heirs dominate the writing of history, so it is not surprising that it is their empires which are most frequently studied. More important, the debate over maritime imperialism went to the heart of the ideological struggles of the Cold War era. Finally, the history of these European empires was crucial to the creation of today's global economic and political order, and is therefore wrapped up in the heated disputes about relations between the First and Third worlds.[4]

In reality the history of empire is much more than just the story of West European overseas expansion and the origins of today's global economy. At the risk of gross simplification, it is possible to see two distinct strands of empire. One is the European maritime empires, some of which (above all the Dutch and to a lesser extent the British), were initially concerned in particular with the domination of global trade rather than the annexation of territory. But there is also a tradition of land empire which stretches from antiquity to the twentieth century. These land empires were usually ruled by theoretically autocratic monarchs in alliance with aristocratic or bureaucratic elites, and they were very often linked to some great high culture or universal religion.[5]

It is important to remember just how grossly simplistic this analytical distinction is. One could divide the land empires into a number of categories; nomadic or Islamic empire might, for example, be two sub-categories. The Habsburg Empire, rooted in a specific European feudal tradition and in the ancient historical identities of its separate provinces, is an example of how difficult it can be to subsume individual empires in larger categories. Nor is the distinction between the West European maritime empires and the rest at all clear-cut. The manner in which Spain ruled the Americas or the British ruled India, for example, had much in common with the traditional ways of autocratic land empire. Though the creation of the global, oceanic economy was indeed a unique product of the European maritime empires, these empires were far more than mere commercial ventures. At least as important as the global commercial networks they created was the mass colonization that transformed the Americas and Australasia into "new Europes," in the process changing the whole geopolitical and ideological map of the world. Despite its specific characteristics, European colonization can be compared to the colonizing activity which was of crucial importance to some other imperial traditions, most notably the Chinese.[6]

For an historian of Russia, one of the interesting points about empire was that tsarist Russia and the Soviet Union in many ways spanned the two imperial traditions I have defined. The fact that these polities to some extent fitted into the tradition of autocratic land empire linked to great universal religions is too obvious to require much argument. But Russia also played an important role in the expansion of

Europe, using European ideas and technologies to conquer the neighboring Muslim and nomadic societies in a manner very similar to European empires overseas. The last gasp of European territorial expansion at Asia's expense was Khrushchev's Virgin Lands scheme of the 1950s. Nowadays the demographic decline of the Slav population relative to that of its Muslim neighbors and the vulnerability of Russia's southern borders could be seen as part and parcel of the contraction of Europe and the First World's difficult relationship with formerly colonized Muslim peoples.

When I wrote my book on empire I deliberately defined the term in a way that would incorporate both the maritime empires and the tradition of autocratic land empire. In my definition an empire had four characteristics: It was a polity ruling over wide territories and many peoples without their explicit consent. Above all, it also was a very powerful polity, playing a major role in the inter-state relations of its era.

It seems to me rather clear that a polity defined by these four characteristics is inappropriate for today's world. In the first place, the contemporary international community is dominated by states which define themselves as nations and democracies, explicitly rejecting the legitimacy of empire.[7] To call oneself an empire is immediately to delegitimize one's polity and to render it liable to United Nations' resolutions calling for decolonization. Though, for instance, the People's Republic of China claims all the territories ruled by the Qing Dynasty (including Sinkiang, conquered 250 years after the Europeans arrived in the Americas), it is very careful not to call itself an empire. More important, historical empires generally ruled over largely illiterate populations, whose everyday lives in many cases were not greatly affected by the activities of government. Moreover a usual premise of empire was that the annexation of territory and populations increased the polity's wealth and power.

None of this makes much sense nowadays. No sane European believes that he or she would be richer or happier by taking responsibility for ruling Africa and coping with its problems. The logic of Algerie Francaise – in other words, the logic of integrating colonies into the metropolitan polity – is unrestricted non-White immigration into Europe. This is anathema to White electorates. Moreover, the open global economy makes it unnecessary to control alien peoples and territory. Non-European resentment of White rule, allied to the Kalashnikov and to the rocket grenade launcher, makes it very unadvisable. Contemporary Western society is much more sensitive to the loss of its soldiers' lives than used to be the case, and military technology puts cheap but destructive weapons in the hands of guerrilla forces.

Highly educated populations with large middle classes are not easily ruled by autocratic monarchs in alliance with irresponsible aristocratic or bureaucratic elites.

Government itself is far bigger and more intrusive than was the case in any traditional empire; because it matters more to its subjects, government also requires greater legitimacy and consent than was generally needed before 1800. When the Austro-Marxists devised schemes for cultural autonomy and ethno-national self-government on a non-territorial basis they were, consciously or not, following the tradition of religious-communal autonomy represented by the Ottoman millet.[8] But the Ottoman empire was a pre-modern polity which confined itself largely to preserving order and extracting sufficient resources to maintain its armed forces. Education, welfare, health, and a myriad of other duties of the modern state were deemed beyond its remit. At the beginning of the twentieth century the Habsburg state was far bigger and more intrusive than this, which is one reason why implementing the Austro-Marxists' ideas would have been difficult. In any case nationalism can answer the need of post-religious human beings for a sense of community, identity, and purpose in life. It can plausibly claim to offer some protection against the harsh demands of global markets and can clothe the unlovable and intrusive bureaucratic state in the ideology of the extended national family.

At the same time, it is obvious that empire's nemesis, the nation-state, also has major shortcomings which existed from its inception. In reality most nation-states are in part at least ethnically-defined; this is in general what gives them a hold on their citizens' emotions and loyalties. The aim to create a single homogeneous sovereign people with its own sacred territory has had devastating consequences in many parts of the world. The French republic of the 1790s, supposedly the harbinger of civic nationhood, in fact was ethnic to the core. It sought to crush rival provincial identities within France and then embarked on a career of conquest designed to exploit the rest of Europe in the cause of French power, plunder, and grandeur. The German nationalism which grew up partly in response to French domination was more explicitly ethnic and supplied a model for much of Central and Eastern Europe. In addition, however, in a region of intermingled peoples traditionally subject to empire the creation of ethno-territorial nation-states was bound to be far more traumatic than in France. It has taken two world wars and a multitude of ethnic conflicts, rising on occasion to the level of genocide, to turn most of Western and Central Europe into something approaching mono-ethnic nation-states. In today's Asia, most people live in multi-ethnic states that in many ways are closer to being empires than European-style ethno-territorial nations.[9] Should European history repeat itself in twenty-first-century Asia then the consequences would be appalling.

Meanwhile in Europe, partly in response to the disasters caused by ethno-territorial statehood, an attempt is being made to transcend the nation-state. The latter is seen as too small to meet some of the needs of contemporary capitalism. The European Union is not, can never be, and should not try to be an empire. Yet, it does attempt to provide many of empire's benefits such as a great internal market, external security and inter-ethnic harmony and co-operation. It also faces many of modern empire's dilemmas. Ever since the mid-nineteenth century it has seemed self-evident that a truly great power, capable of having a real voice in global councils, needs to be of continental scale. Continental scale almost always, however, implies multi-ethnicity. In an age whose dominant ideologies are still democracy and nationalism, how is government to be made legitimate and effective when exercised over a continent? This is the key dilemma for the European Union, as it was for modern empires generally.

Admittedly, the challenges faced by the European Union are in some ways less extreme than those confronting empire in Europe at the beginning of the twentieth century. The contemporary European polity does not need to conscript its young men and imbibe them with a loyalty so strong that they will die en masse in its cause. Therefore, one of the great *raisons d'etre* of the nation state since its inception in revolutionary France has disappeared. Given contemporary political and technological realities First-World conscript armies are useless. Professional armies have always been more effective instruments of empire than the male citizenry in arms. Two world wars and the horrors of Nazism have taken some of the shine off nationalism in Europe. The nation-state's overriding right to its citizens' loyalty no longer goes unquestioned. Regional identities have to some extent staged a comeback. Individualist, post-modern youth is on the whole less interested in politics than its grandparents and is certainly much less willing to sacrifice body and soul in the nation's cause. After the Reagan-Thatcher era even government's scale and aspirations are sometimes smaller than a generation ago. Central banks have been removed from the control of the democratic sovereign for the same reason that the Victorians tried to insulate finance from the vagaries of kings.

All these developments do not abolish the need for the European Union and its institutions to enjoy a degree of legitimacy among Europe's citizenry. But they do make some aspects of empire more attractive and more viable than was the case fifty years ago. A tolerant multicultural society, prosperous partly because of the scale of its domestic market, and living autonomously under powerful elected local institutions and a limited central government restrained by law and ethics; this has more in common with a modernized and civilized version of life under the later Habsburgs than with the Europe of Sacro Egoismo in which the peoples of the continent tore each other apart in the name of a supposedly national interest which recognized no higher law or morality. Moreover, the Union offers potential solutions to some deep-rooted dilemmas of European order and security. Under its flag, for example, German power can be mobilized for the cause of European stability without terrifying either Germany's neighbors or the German people themselves. This is especially important in Eastern Europe, where two world wars began and where Germany is fated by geography to be the leading actor among the states of Europe.

Outside of Europe, the history of the nation-state has been very checkered as well. When applied to the European overseas colonies of settlement, the principle of democratic nationhood had appalling consequences for the indigenous peoples. The latter often survived far better under more traditional forms of aristocratic or bureaucratic imperial rule. Only Whites were defined as part of the nation, indigenous peoples being subjected to ethnic cleansing on a grand scale, which in many local cases reached the level of genocide. The more local government and justice were in the hands of democratically elected White settlers, the greater the levels of ethnic cleansing and mass murder of natives were likely to be. White electorates voted for leaders whose support for ethnic cleansing and even local genocide was open and unequivocal. White juries refused to listen to native witnesses and turned a blind eye to mass murder. Though racialist and other ideologies were partly to blame, the roots of ethnic cleansing and genocide lay in economics. White farmer settlers desired native land and had no use for native labor.[10]

The fact that in the nineteenth century the most democratic polities in the world were also the ones most inclined to the exploitation and even mass murder of local peoples excluded from the body of citizens would not have surprised sixteenth-century Italian thinkers, who frequently insisted that it was better to be the colonial subject of a prince than of a republic. Francesco Guicciardini wrote that "it is most desirable not to be born a subject; but if it must be so, it is better to be under a prince than a republic. For a republic oppresses all its subjects, and shares out its benefits only among its citizens; whereas a prince is more impartial, and gives equally to one subject as to the other, so that everyone can hope to be beneficed and employed by him."[11] Guicciardini's statement and the history of settler democracy have possibly ominous implications for future global governance. First-World electorates will be crucial in determining responses to growing global ecological challenges, whose impact on the Third World is likely to be much harsher than on the First. History suggests that democracy is anything but a guarantee against these electorates defending their own interests and lifestyles at the expense of the Third World's devastation.

In the Russian case neither empire nor ethno-territorial nationalism is a sensible response to today's challenges. In many ways the Soviet Union itself was a modern form of empire.[12] Clearly it met my four criteria. It had other imperial characteristics too. On the good side the Soviet Union of the post-Stalin era sustained a considerable degree of inter-ethnic harmony and cooperation. Less admirable but also not untypical of empire was the ruthless sacrifice of its subjects' welfare in the pursuit of the state's external power and ambitions. The Soviet Union's declared aim to overthrow global capitalism and lead the socialist camp to a new world order was also imperial in the scale and grandeur of its ambition. The point is, of course, that this Russian attempt to sustain and extend its own anti-capitalist version of modernity vastly overextended Russian resources and failed disastrously. Any attempt to renew this challenge would be hopeless and fatal.

To embrace the cause of empire would once again be to challenge the world's most powerful countries and to cut Russia off from the global economy. To back a Chinese challenge to the West would risk Chinese domination of East Asia at a time when Russia is the only European country to rule territory which was once "Chinese" and which for the foreseeable future will be sparsely populated and weakly defended. To re-annex the former southern republics would make Russia responsible for solving their problems and accepting their immigrants. Even reabsorbing Russian-majority border areas would be hugely expensive in both financial and political terms, at a time when Russia needs to concentrate all its meager resources on economic recovery and when immigrants from the Russian diaspora might better be used to make up for demographic decline within the Federation.

But narrowly defined and exclusive ethnic nationalism is also no solution for Russia, if only because one-fifth of the Federation's citizens are not ethnic Russians. Russian identity has traditionally been imperial in ways which are by no means always bad. A sense of Russianness was linked to pride in a great language and high culture which people other than ethnic Russians often admired and absorbed. Such people were traditionally accepted as Russians. Moreover, drawing inspiration from all the cultures of Europe, the Russian pre-revolutionary intelligentsia was in some ways more cosmopolitan than its equivalents in Europe's nation-states. These traditions are useful for a still multi-ethnic federation. Following the post-imperial Turkish path of ethnically defined nationalism would ensure the eruption of conflicts similar to the one between the Turkish state and its Kurdish minority.

This brings me on to the second half of this paper, which is a comparison of Russia's post-imperial predicament with that of other former imperial peoples. In obvious ways the Russian position is different to that of the metropolitan cores of the European maritime empires. In many cases these empires collapsed amidst chaos and civil war in their former colonies. The Portuguese[13] and Belgian colonies in Africa are obvious cases in point but Britain departed the Indian sub-continent amidst war and ethnic cleansing on a massive scale. In Burma, civil war has continued almost without interruption since the British departure until today. The basic point is that the former metropolitan government can afford to take a rather relaxed attitude towards chaos in its former colonies when they are on the other side of the world. When, as in Chechnya, they are next door and the consequences of anarchy are felt on metropolitan territory it is less easy to be relaxed.[14]

In geopolitical terms Russia has the possibility to survive the loss of empire with a less dramatic decline in global status than the one suffered by the British and French. The latter, once deprived of their empires, became middle-sized, purely European states. The jewel in Russia's imperial crown, Siberia, remains Russian and gives Russia the long-term possibility of remaining a truly great power with a foot on the Pacific as well as one in Europe. In the short term, however, the burdens of empire are more apparent than the possibilities. A key to de-colonization was the shedding of responsibilities by the metropolis. Harold Wilson in 1968 could choose to retreat from east of Suez. Russia cannot and faces the daunting prospect of having to provide security for its Far Eastern possessions in a region where peace and security may well prove elusive in the twenty-first century.

The European metropoles of the maritime empires were also much closer than Russia to being nation-states during the last generations of empire. Their national identity was therefore not so severely threatened by empire's loss. The contrast is not a total one. The Anglo-Scottish union occurred a century after the founding of the English overseas empire and Scotland's allegiance to the Union was linked in part to the material and psychological advantages that the empire provided. The end of empire, therefore, to some extent did contribute to weakening the United Kingdom. In addition, both the British and the French attempted to absorb colonies into the metropolis; in the British case this meant Ireland, in the French, Algeria.[15] In both cases, this greatly increased the difficulties of escaping from empire. But most British and French colonies were beyond the oceans and were not defined as part of the metropolis or seen as integral to the nation by the metropolitan population. Moreover, and most important, Britain, France and the Netherlands were democratic polities, whose peoples had a sense of common citizenship. Even more than the geographical divide between metropolis and overseas colonies, this helped to give them a sense of national identity separate from the empire.

The Russian situation is more akin to that of the former core peoples of major land empires. Before 1918 neither Austrian-Germans nor Turks[16] were citizens of a nation-state. They were subjects of an empire whose internal borders were not defined by ethnicity. Historically, a common Russian ethnic identity was in fact far stronger than a common Austrian-German or Turkish one. Before 1918 an Austrian-German might identify with the Habsburg empire as a whole, with his or her province, with the whole German ethno-cultural community, or with German Catholicism. The one community with which virtually no one identified was that of all the German subjects of the Monarchy.

This led to major problems when it came to creating and legitimizing the post-imperial Austrian republic. Most Austrian-Germans probably would have chosen to merge with Germany. Given the choice, the Vorarlberg would have opted to join Switzerland, while Tyrolean identity was so strong that many Tyroleans preferred citizenship even of despised Italy to the partition of the province. The same geopolitical arguments that were used to bar an Austrian-German union were also utilized to divide the Austrian-German community between provinces that became part of the new republic and the Sudetenland, which went to Czechoslovakia. The breakup of the single imperial market damaged prospects of legitimizing the new republic through economic success, as was achieved after 1955. In addition, many Austrians, but in particular Austrian elites, hankered after empire. As subjects of a great empire many felt that they had counted in the world, and thereby acquired a certain additional sense of purpose and identity. This was a factor in reconciling even some anti-Nazis to the Anschluss. Only after the price of empire proved enormous in the Second World War did the charms of a small and neutral Austrian republic become evident, particularly since this was the best way to evade both Soviet rule and historical responsibility for Nazism.[17]

At first glance, the Turkish response to empire's loss looks more promising than the Austrian one. The new republic rejected the imperial tradition and defined itself against it. It accepted Western ideological and cultural hegemony. Islam and Ottomanism were blamed for Turkish backwardness and humiliation. The republic identified itself with progress and modernity, which it linked to capitalism, secular nationalism, and Western values. It is important not to forget, however, the costs of this strategy. A gap opened between the new regime and the Islamic values of most Turks. A narrowly ethnic definition of citizenship left no room for a distinct Kurdish political identity. Nor did Ankara altogether escape the legacy of empire in other ways. In time it became embroiled in the defense of the Turkish imperial diaspora in Cyprus.

In fact, it is the awful level of ethnic cleansing and mass murder which is the most striking feature of the decline and fall of the Ottoman Empire. Millions of Muslims were ejected or murdered in the empire's Balkan, Caucasian, and Crimean borderlands. The Turks responded in kind, the genocide of the Armenians and the ethnic cleansing of Anatolia's Greek community both occurring in the empire's final agony. Even the fate of the Ottoman Muslim diaspora was better than that of the Austrian-Germans and Jews, the two main diasporas of the Habsburg empire. The former were ethnically cleansed from virtually the whole former empire after the Second World War. The latter were exterminated by the Germans during the war's course, sometimes with assistance from the numerous communities of local anti-Semites.

In comparison to the end of empire in the Ottoman and Habsburg cases, developments in Russia have been surprisingly benign so far. It is quite true that Russia has never been a nation of citizens and that the ethnic boundaries between Russia and empire were traditionally uncertain. This was particularly so because of the situation of the Ukrainians[18] and Belarusians, who shared many common markers of identity with the Russians, but who emerged in the twentieth century as separate nations. In addition, a Soviet Russian identity was built on top of, and to some extent in conscious opposition to, the traditional pre-revolutionary Russian values and symbols. All this helps to explain the somewhat confused and conflictual sense of Russianness that reigned after 1991. Even so, by Turkish or Austrian standards the foundations of Russian identity were strong. Russians had traditionally lived in one state. All Russians could identify with Peter I, Borodino and the victory over Nazi Germany. Still more, they could identify with Pushkin and with a glorious and universally respected high culture. It is easier to build Russian statehood on these foundations than was the case in post-imperial Austria or Turkey.

In addition, the fate of the post-Soviet diaspora has been astonishingly benign by Ottoman or Austrian standards. Though many Russian civilians have left Central Asia and the Caucasus, none can truly be said to have been ethnically cleansed and very few Russian civilians have been murdered. In certain cases other migrant communities have fared worse in parts of Central Asia but by the standards of collapsing empires mistreatment of imperial diasporas has been low-key. The same is true of anti-Semitism despite its deep roots in Russian, Ukrainian, and Baltic popular culture, and despite the very prominent role played by Jews in the new business elite. No doubt awareness that, unlike between the wars, the Jews now have a powerful protector in the United States is one factor deterring overt anti-Semitic policies by the former Soviet republics. Even so, the relatively modest level of anti-Semitism is remarkable when one thinks of Russian and East European history or of the fate of other diasporas after the end of empire.

In the British case the key diasporas were the British themselves, the Chinese, and the Indians. In some cases the Chinese and even Indians played a similar commercial and financial role to the Jews in Central and Eastern Europe and acquired a similar odium.[19] Indians were expelled from post-independence Burma and Uganda; Chinese suffered pogroms and second-class status in Malaysia, and much worse pogroms in formerly Dutch Indonesia. On the other hand, the Chinese in south-east Asia and Indians in most of Africa remained far wealthier on average than the indigenous population. Unlike French or Portuguese settlers, the British diaspora was not ethnically cleansed after independence, even in colonies where they constituted a small but wealthy minority. This owed something to the skill with which London generally managed the process of decolonization. At present, however, the extinction of the White farming community in Zimbabwe appears to be underway, which is not at all surprising when one considers how this land was originally acquired or the emotions that landownership often arouses in the post-colonial setting.

In many ways the most interesting comparison with Russia is the situation in Ireland, however. Because Ireland was part of the United Kingdom and borders on England it is in any case easier to compare with Russia than are the overseas colonies. Had Russian-majority communities in frontier areas of Estonia, Ukraine, and Kazakhstan followed Ulster's example in seceding from the newly independent republics and rejoining their co-ethnics in the Russian Federation they would have destabilized the politics of the whole former Soviet region. In fact, by the standards of the Ulster Protestants and Pieds Noirs they have been politically very quiet.

The key to this was probably the absence of democracy. In the context of collapsing empires, competitive party elections in which rival political elites mobilize ethnic hatreds and challenge existing borders is extremely destabilizing. If this was true in Ireland before 1914, it was even more obvious in the last years of British India, where it led in time to war and ethnic cleansing on a catastrophic scale. Competitive democratic politics in no way excluded the creation of rival paramilitary forces or the resort to violence and blackmail in either the Irish or Indian cases. In fact, the very virtues of British rule, its relative restraint and legality, made this easier. In the Soviet case, none of this applied. No democratic tradition existed and communities had no experience of electing leaders or defining goals and identities for themselves.

Moreover, the collapse of the empire came so quickly and unexpectedly that it gave the Russian diaspora no time to organize in the Union's defense, even had it wished to do so. Once independent republics were established, organizing the diaspora against them faced many difficulties.

But simply to rejoice in the absence of democracy would be naïve. If India and Ireland suffered from democracy's vulnerability during the process of decolonization, they have subsequently benefited from its strengths. In the light of a small but dirty war of independence, and of a somewhat larger and more vicious civil war, the survival of democracy in inter-war Ireland was remarkable. Even more surprising was democracy's strength in poverty-stricken, huge, and multi-ethnic India. In both cases the tradition of representative and semi-democratic politics in the imperial era was a very important factor in democracy's subsequent survival. Quite apart from democracy's inherent value, it has also on the whole been a factor for stability in India. It is hard to imagine an authoritarian regime showing the flexibility and pluralism necessary to hold together so vast, varied, and changing a society. Certainly at present the survival of united India seems less threatened than is the case in Indonesia, to which Dutch rule bequeathed less democratic traditions and institutions.

All this is relevant to the former Soviet Union, in which democracy is only really secure in the Baltic republics. In most of the other republics, the key to relative stability has been the survival of the communist-era leaders and structures of power. Where these have broken down (Tajikistan) or nationalists have taken power (Georgia, Chechnya) war has usually followed. In comparative post-imperial terms none of this is surprising. Colonial-era notables frequently survived the end of empire and guaranteed (usually authoritarian) political stability in former colonies. Their replacement by more populist and nationalist leaders, who frequently mobilized ethnic nationalism in the majority community, seldom enhanced stability and in some cases, Sri Lanka for example, was the direct cause of civil war.[20]

But post-colonial notable-run regimes need to be at least minimally legitimate and effective if they are to survive. They also need to be open to new elites and currents which emerge in post-colonial society. These may be real problems in many of the post-Soviet republics. Their leaders are Soviet-era Uncle Toms, with no legitimacy derived from a struggle for independence. Their mechanisms for succession are inevitably much weaker than in post-imperial monarchies. They face the awful difficulties caused by the transition from socialism and the disintegration of the Soviet single "market." Nor is a flood of wealth from energy and mineral exports any guarantee of enhanced political stability. On the contrary, as frequently seen in the Third World, it can lead to the gross corruption of elites and regimes, and the collapse of effective government and any sense of political responsibility or patriotism.

For the moment, however, the main conclusion which emerges from comparing the Soviet case with the collapse of other empires is that we have been lucky. Most empires disintegrate in the midst of inter-state war, civil war, and ethnic cleansing on a grand scale. This was true in the Ottoman and Habsburg cases. The dismantling of the British Empire was better managed. It did not occur unexpectedly and overnight, and the British political elite was sophisticated and relatively liberal and benign. Nevertheless, the end of empire was by no means free of bloodshed. Moreover, some of the worst problems of the contemporary world are the products of the British Empire and its collapse. These include the rivalry between India and Pakistan, which has reached the level of nuclear confrontation, and the results of first creating and then abandoning the mandate in Palestine. By their standards, a plethora of other issues ranging from Northern Ireland to the consequences of mass Indian immigration into Fiji seem to be small beer. But some of these "lesser" crises are not merely inherently important but also offer an interesting sidelight on the problems of the post-Soviet world.

One enormously important reason why the collapse of the Soviet Union did not have worse consequences was that it occurred in peacetime. Miraculously too, barely a shot was fired in the empire's defense. This partly reflected the fact that the Soviet regime had lost legitimacy and the fact that few people were willing to die, or even kill, to preserve it. It reflected too the speed and unexpectedness with which events developed in 1990-1991. But Gorbachev's own unwillingness to take responsibility for shedding blood, his wavering but nevertheless remarkable respect for legality, were very important factors in the relatively peaceful demise of the Soviet Union. Power was devolved through elections in 1990-1991 to republican regimes, which thereby enjoyed both democratic and Soviet constitutional legitimacy. Not only the leaders but also the borders of the new republics were firmly established when the empire collapsed. Crucially, the Russian leadership under Yeltsin, far from defending the empire, played a major part in undermining and rejecting it.

The question now is whether a remarkably peaceful end of empire will be followed by lasting stability. Post-imperial comparisons provide some hints about the issues involved here.[21] In the Austrian case a key cause, of post-imperial instability lay in European geopolitics. In the last century, Russia and Germany very much have been the most powerful states in Europe. Only they have possessed the resources potentially to dominate the continent. The fall of one has generally therefore been mirrored by the rise of the other: this was true, for instance, in 1945 and 1990-1991. The two great European wars more than anything else revolved around their struggle to control Central and Eastern Europe. Whoever won would inevitably dominate Europe as a whole unless, as happened after 1945, an outside force (the Americans) intervened. By chance, in 1918 both Germany and Russia were in the ranks of the defeated and the peace settlement was constructed against both of them. That, in itself, guaranteed Europe's instability since it is not possible to create a stable European order to which neither Russia nor Germany are committed. When the Americans withdrew into isolation and the British retreated from European commitments, the Versailles settlement in Central and Eastern Europe became non-viable.

Instability was also greatly enhanced by the disappearance of the Habsburg Empire. Had it continued to exist, its rulers would have resisted Hitler tooth and nail. In its absence, Central and Eastern Europe was a power vacuum and a region of small and squabbling nation-states, which almost invited Hitler to intervene in its affairs. Moreover, very importantly, the Anglo-French-American version of modernity was not self-evidently superior to the German model of economy, culture, and society in 1914. Indeed in many respects, Germany had led Europe. Defeat in war did not necessarily delegitimize a specific German path to modernity. The Crash of 1929 and the subsequent decade of depression on the contrary challenged the legitimacy of the economic and political order which the victors of 1918 had created.

The Ottoman case was different. Turkey's new leaders accepted the hegemony of the victors' values. They blamed defeat on backwardness, and they linked the latter to the Ottoman tradition and Islam. Their whole-hearted rejection of the Ottoman tradition owed something to the fact that the last century of Ottoman rule had been a story of defeat and humiliation at the hands of the Christian powers. On the contrary, the republic was legitimized by victory in the war over the Greeks and over allied efforts to partition the Turks' Anatolian homeland. This also legitimized the new republican concept of an integral Turkish ethnic nation linked to a sacred territory. In addition, in the Middle East there was no geopolitical vacuum after the collapse of the Ottoman Empire. The British and French filled the gap. By enormous efforts Ataturk had expelled the allies and their clients from Anatolia but he knew that they were far too powerful to be challenged outside the Turks' own homeland. A supreme realist, Ataturk therefore had good internal and external reasons to turn his back firmly on empire.

By Turkish or Austrian standards, the loss of empire was far less traumatic for the West European former imperial metropoles, though it is worth pointing out even so that the war in Algeria brought down the Fourth Republic and threatened France with a military coup. To get the full measure of a British equivalent to the Soviet Union's collapse, one would have to imagine the disintegration of the British Empire in the 1920s, the simultaneous secession of Scotland (Ukraine) and Wales (Belarus), the fall of the monarchy and the parliamentary system of rule, and an economic depression much worse than the 1930s.

Even this would not be the complete story. Although British elites were wounded by the end of empire and the loss of international status, their demotion was relatively gentle. It was partly camouflaged by victory in the Second World War and by close alliance with the United States both then and in the subsequent Cold War. The transfer of power within the Anglophone bloc and the NATO alliance was sometimes painful for the British but it was greatly helped by the strong sense of ideological and cultural solidarity with the Americans and by the existence of a common external threat, first fascist and later Soviet. The other former imperial metropoles in Western Europe did not share the almost automatic British identification with American goals and values. But they did share a common anti-Soviet solidarity and a common interest in a booming, American-led post-war global economy. As members of NATO they were included in the camp of victors and the major Western security alliance. Even the French in practice always remained part of this grouping. Moreover, in their case the EU provided an opportunity to re-build a global role and influence on a new post-imperial basis.

To make exact comparisons between the present Russian situation and the response of other imperial metropoles to the loss of empire would be not only silly but also dangerous. Circumstances both in Russia and globally are different, and so is our era.

Clearly, however, the Russians are in a worse case than the post-imperial British. Though membership of the Security Council and the G8 may somewhat assuage pride, both in material and psychological terms the loss of empire has been a far greater shock. In a range of ways from the collapse of the integrated imperial market to the problems of identity and lost international status the Russian situation is much closer to the inter-war Austrian one. On the other hand the specific Russo-Soviet path to modernity has been delegitimized and the current geopolitical situation is far less favorable to Russian revanchism than was the case with inter-war Germany. Finally, from the Western perspective it may seem unfortunate that Russia does not follow the Turkish path of acknowledgement of Western ideological-cultural hegemony and wholesale rejection of all nostalgia for empire. On the other hand, when one remembers the devastating bloodshed and instability against whose background the Turkish elites came to this policy, one can only rejoice that by these standards Russia's fate has been so benign.

But of course a word of caution is in order. A little more than a decade is a short period and the results of empire's demise can take a generation or more to reveal themselves. Ten years after the collapse of the Habsburg and Ottoman Empires, Europe was reveling in the spirit of Locarno and in a post-war economic recovery fuelled by a frantic and speculative Wall Street boom. The Crash, Hitler, the Second World War and the full, terrifying implications of empire's collapse remained over the horizon.

It is true that today's global order under American hegemony looks more stable than the shrinking Anglo-French European and global condominium of the inter-war years. Nevertheless, elements of vulnerability are clear. The official ideology of the present global order is democratic and egalitarian, and this ideology is projected by modern communications into every Third-World province. Meanwhile, our world is in most respects more unequal than it was in 1500. Even in the First World there are great pockets of impoverished and alienated minorities, many of them non-Christian and non-White, who have causes to vent their hatred of the contemporary order. Previous societies and empires have been transformed and destroyed by revolutions in military technology. The advent of easily accessible pocket weapons of mass destruction could do the same to ours. All this applies even now, before the great conflicts between First and Third Worlds that environmental crisis may bring in a generation's time. The nature of First-World democracy, if anything, works against solutions to this possible crisis.

Though many twenty-first challenges are new, however, some are not. At the turn of the twentieth century the American naval thinker, Admiral Mahan, commented that the key to future global stability would be whether the West could win Asian societies for its values and the global order that underpinned them. We no longer speak in the clear tones of Victoria-era admirals but the problem Mahan outlined remains. Bringing China, India, and Indonesia into the First World is a vast task. Nor, for example, would a hugely powerful First-World China necessarily be a comfortable partner for the present members of the First-World club. But, given the immense problems that are likely to face the world in the twenty-first century, it seems hard to imagine that global order can be sustained by Americans and Europeans alone.[22]

NOTES TO CHAPTER 1

[1] This theme is covered in much greater detail in my book *Empire: The Russian Empire and its Rivals* (London: John Murray, 2000). The American edition came out in 2001 and is published by Yale University Press. See the notes and bibliography of these books for extensive references to sources. In this chapter, I will note only key texts and works read by me since my book was published.

[2] See Chapter 10 and the notes of Lieven, *Empire*. There are two useful works in English on this theme, Karen Barkey and Mark von Hagen, eds., *After Empire: Multiethnic Societies and Nation-Building: The Soviet Union and the Russian, Ottoman, and Habsburg Empires* (Boulder: Westview, 1997), and Karen Dawisha and Bruce Parrott, eds., *The End of Empire? The Transformation of the USSR in Comparative Perspective* (Armonk: M. E. Sharpe, 1997). See also, Alexander Demandt, ed., *Das Ende der Weltreiche* [*The End of the World-Empires*] (Munich: C.H. Beck, 1997).

[3] On these issues the literature is vast. A useful place to start is Anthony Brewer, *Marxist Theories of Imperialism: A Critical Survey* (London: Routledge and Kegan Paul, 1980). Wolfgang J. Mommsen, *Theories of Imperialism* (London: Weidenfeld, 1980) also remains valuable.

[4] D. K. Fieldhouse, *The West and the Third World* (Oxford: Blackwell, 1999) came out just as my book was being completed and is a good survey of debates on empire in the context of relations between the contemporary First and Third Worlds.

[5] The best place to start on these empires is Maurice Duverger, ed., Le Concept d'Empire [*The Idea of Empire*] (Paris: Presses Universitaires de France, 1980), followed by Michael Doyle, *Empires* (Ithaca: Cornell University Press, 1986). S. N. Eisenstadt, *The Political Systems of Empires* (New Brunswick: Transaction Books, 1992) is very scholarly but a touch indigestible.

[6] On comparative colonization, see above all Jurgen Osterhammel and Shelley L. Frisch, *Colonialism: A Theoretical Overview* (Princeton: Marcus Wiener/Ian Randle, 1997).

[7] On global ideological hegemony and democracy, see Francis Fukuyama, *The End of History and the Last Man* (London: Penguin, 1992).

[8] The great source on the millet is Benjamin Braude and Bernard Lewis, *Christians and Jews in the Ottoman Empire*, two volumes (New York: Holmes and Meier, 1982). On the Austrian nationalities issue, Robert A. Kann, *History of the Habsburg Empire: 1526-1918* (Berkeley: University of California Press, 1980), and R. A. Kann, *The Multinational Empire: Nationalism and National Reform in the Habsburg Monarchy 1848-1918*, two volumes (New York: Octagon Books, 1970) is still the place to start. For the non-German-reader, Uri Ra'anon, et al., eds., *State and Nation in Multi-Ethnic Societies* (Manchester: Manchester University Press, 1991) has useful articles on Austro-Marxism. But the great source on the "Austrian" nationalities is *Die Habsburger Monarchie: Die Volker des Reiches* [*The Habsburg Monarchy: The Peoples of the Empire*], vol. 1, part 3 (Vienna: Austrian Academy of Sciences, 1980).

[9] In addition to works cited in Lieven, *Empire*, Ian Talbot, *Inventing the Nation: India and Pakistan* (London: Arnold, 2000) brings out ethno-territorial diversity in the sub-continent and problems of nation-building.

[10] I made these points in *Empire*. They are made better and in more detail by Michael Mann, *The Dark Side of Democracy: Explaining Ethnic Cleansing* (Cambridge: Cambridge University Press, 2004), Chapter 4, "The Colonial Darkside."

[11] Stephan Epstein, "The Rise and Fall of the Italian City-States," in M. H. Hansen, ed., *A Comparative Study of Thirty City-State Cultures* (Copenhagen: Royal Danish Academy of Science and Letters, Copenhagen, n.d.), 290.

[12] The first edition of Paul Dibb, *The Soviet Union: The Incomplete Superpower* (Houndmills: Macmillan, 1986), is interesting on this point because it was written just before the cracks began to open under Gorbachev and looks at the Soviet Union from an imperial perspective.

[13] I failed to cover Portugal in my book. Norrie MacQueen, *The Decolonization of Portuguese*

Africa (London: Longman, 1997) is a useful survey. Anthony Clayton, *Frontiersmen: Warfare in Africa since 1950* (London: UCL Press, 1999) is only too graphic on post-colonial chaos.

[14] More than mere brotherly affection inspires me to draw the reader's attention to the excellent Anatol Lieven, *Chechnya: Tombstone of Russian Power* (London: Yale University Press, 1998).

[15] Two books by Ian Lustick are very worth noting in this context: *State-Building Failure in British Ireland and French Algeria* (Berkeley: Institute of International Studies, 1985), and *Unsettled States, Disputed Lands* (Ithaca: Cornell University Press, 1993).

[16] In addition to the numerous sources listed on this issue in Lieven, *Empire*, Kemal H. Karpat, *The Politicization of Islam: Reconstructing Identity, State, Faith and Community in the Late Ottoman State* (Oxford: Oxford University Press, 2001) is an extremely valuable and interesting addition.

[17] The key book on Austrian identity remains Gerald Stourzh, *Vom Reich zur Republik: Studien zur Osterreichsbewusstein im 20 Jahrhundert* [*From Empire to Republic: Studies in the Idea of Austria in the Twentieth Century*] (Vienna: ed. Atelier, 1990).

[18] Since Lieven, *Empire*, was written I have had the good fortune to read Andrew Wilson, *The Ukrainians: Unexpected Nation* (London: Yale University Press, 2000), and Roman Szporluk, *Russia, Ukraine, and the Breakup of the Soviet Union* (Stanford: Hoover Institution Press, 2000). I had already read some though not all of the articles contained in the latter but the volume remains very valuable.

[19] See also Robin Cohen, *Global Diasporas* (London: UCL Press, 1997), and Crispin Bates, ed., *Community, Empire and Migration: South Asians in Diaspora* (Houndmills: Palgrave, 2000).

[20] Michael J. Cohen and Martin Kolinsky, eds., *Demise of the British Empire in the Middle East: Britain's Responses to Nationalist Movements 1943-55* (London: Frank Cass, 1998) is a useful addition to sources cited in *Empire*. See in particular Chapter 10 by Michael Eppel on the Hashemite elite in Iraq.

[21] Aviel Roshwald, *Ethnic Nationalism and the Fall of Empires: Central Europe, Russia and the Middle East, 1914-1923* (London: Routledge, 2001) is a useful comparison of the consequences of the three empires' collapse, though in my view Roshwald is hard on empire and a little starry-eyed about the inherent virtue of modernity.

[22] Mahan's interesting essay, entitled "A Twentieth-Century Outlook" was published in A. T. Mahan, *The Interest of America in Sea Power* (London: 1897), 217 ff.

"SPEEDY, JUST, AND FAIR"?
Remaking Legal Institutions in Putin's Russia
EUGENE HUSKEY[1]

Abstract

This chapter approaches legal reform in Putin's Russia as a product of a peculiar set of legacies, circumstances, and interests. After assessing the reasons for the return of law to public prominence in Putin's first term, we examine in detail the most politically contested and legally significant elements of the current wave of law reform, emphasizing in particular changes that affect the financing, recruitment, privileges, procedures, and organization of the judiciary. The chapter concludes with reflections on the interaction of legal and economic reform and on the barriers to the development of a rule of law and constitutional order in Russia.

* * *

Introduction

Under Vladimir Putin, Russia has launched three ambitious and interrelated projects of state reconstruction. The targets of these reforms are the legal system, state administration, and relations between federal and provincial governments. After a decade in which Russia pursued new directions in specific policies of state, such as economics and diplomacy, the country's political leadership has at last turned to the more difficult challenge of remaking the state itself. As a result, law, the neglected actor in the drama of the Russian transition, is again finding an audience. Normally relegated to bit parts in Russian public affairs, law moved center stage during Putin's first year in office.[2] Building on the movement for a "law-based state" (*pravovoe gosudarstvo*) that was initiated in the late Gorbachev era and enshrined in the Conception for Court Reform in late 1991, contemporary Russian law reform has the potential under Putin to recast relations between legal institutions, between executive and judicial authority, and between center and periphery.[3]

Invoking the goals set out in the Judicial Reform of 1864, Putin remarked in a speech to judges in November 2000 that Russia must have a court system that is "speedy, just, and fair" (*skoryi, pravyi, i spravedlivyi*).[4] Whether the legal change advocated by Putin merits association with the Great Reforms of Alexander II is a matter of considerable controversy, however. While some regard the initiatives backed by Putin as part of a much-needed modernization of Russian law and legal institutions, others perceive them as a thinly-veiled attempt to strengthen presidential power and to erode hard-won professional privileges and immunities.

Why Law Matters to Putin

In the last century and a half in Russia, legal change has come in short and infrequent bursts of creative legislative energy unleashed by the country's rulers. The current episode of law reform is no exception. Traditionally, the institutional forces arrayed against legal change in Russia, most notably the Ministry of Internal Affairs (MVD) and the Procuracy, have been formidable. Given the absence of democratic pressures from below found in Western societies, no combination of reformist legal officials or legal scholars has been able to overcome the conservative opposition without the vigorous personal intervention of the tsar, general secretary, or president.[5] Thus, instead of the continual and incremental adaptation of law to its environment that one associates with modern states, one encounters in Russia episodic and radical upheavals in the legal order.

The window for legal reform that opened at the end of the twentieth century certainly reveals this penchant for *dirigisme*. After the better part of a decade in which proposals for serious law reform languished amid inconclusive legislative and scholarly debates, Putin ordered a white paper on economic reform from the Westernizing economist German Gref. Gref identified changes in the courts and legal procedure as essential components of a broad-based effort to shake Russia out of the malaise of the post-communist transition. Where Gref was the theoretician that placed law on Putin's policy agenda, the tactician responsible for shaping the legislative drafts and steering them through the parliament was Dmitrii Kozak, the head of the presidency's State-Legal Department in Putin's first term. Kozak chaired a drafting committee of forty legal scholars and officials that submitted to parliament new bills and amendments to existing legislation in the spring of 2001.[6] Among these were draft statutes relating to the status of judges, the organization of the courts, and the governance and responsibilities of members of the defense Bar (*advokatura*).

Putin's openness to the legal initiatives advocated by Gref and others appeared to follow from his perception that changes in the legal system would facilitate the reassertion of federal power, the further liberalization of the economy, and Russia's acceptance by, and integration into, the international community.[7] At least in the early stages of his presidency, Putin's central mission was the reversal of what he termed the "unraveling" (*raspolzanie*) of the Russian state. Put simply, he sought to reclaim political power for the center that had devolved to the country's eighty-nine provinces in the Yeltsin era. To claw back the vast patronage, budgetary, and lawmaking powers that had flowed from Moscow to the periphery, Putin began to put in place elements of a new ruling "vertical," one of which was a legal system whose laws and procedures would establish a single standard of justice throughout the country. To refederalize Russian law meant not just the elimination of provincial legislation that violated the Russian constitution and federal statutes, but also the establishment of new rules that would minimize localist or oligarchic influences on the investigation and disposition of criminal cases and the resolution of economic disputes. It was a project common to all modern states. In the early Soviet era, Lenin had campaigned for the introduction of a legal system where decisions would be similar "in Kaluga and Kazan."

The Russian president also launched an assault on what might be labeled the horizontal diffusion of legal authority in the central executive, whose ministries and agencies issue a steady stream of so-called substatutory acts (*podzakonnye akty*) that translate the general language of the statutes into the daily marching orders of the bureaucracy. As Putin noted, "the bureaucrat is used to acting according to written [ministerial] directives, which . . . often contradict the statute itself, yet remain unchanged for years."[8] Thus, Putin's much-publicized commitment to a "dictatorship of law" (*diktatura zakona*) signified in part a concern that law in the sense of statutes (*zakony*) would replace substatutory acts as the driving force in Russian legal behavior. By imposing "legal discipline" – another menacing sounding Russian term that essentially signifies "respecting the law" – one would tame departmental as well as localist and other sectional self-dealing.[9]

Moreover, for Putin legal reform was intimately connected with a need to restore the authority and legitimacy of the state in the minds of ordinary citizens. Where American politicians speak about the people as the repository of public virtue, Putin is no less comfortable invoking the state as the defining source of political wisdom and authority. To strengthen the state, Putin believed it essential to replace popular attitudes of legal nihilism with a respect for the courts and other state legal institutions. Citing the work of the nineteenth-century ethnologist, Vladimir Dahl, he lamented the absence in Russia of folk sayings that praised the courts. By reforming Russian law, Putin clearly hoped to enhance the prestige and vitality of the state. Seeking to mobilize the judiciary in this campaign for the revival of the state, Putin told a conference of judges that "the court is not simply the sphere of your professional activity. It is a state institution . . . ."[10]

Putin also understood law reform to be a precondition for the revival of the Russian economy. To be sure, there are occasional references in his speeches to law reform as a means of enhancing justice, especially for the thousands of suspects who have sat for more than a year in unspeakable conditions in detention cells awaiting trial.[11] But he has generally downplayed the human tragedy that is Russia's criminal justice system, a system that has sent a quarter of the current adult male population to jails or labor camps.[12] Instead, he has spoken most frequently and passionately about law reform as a means of achieving greater economic efficiency. Whatever the depth of his commitment to a market economy, Putin clearly came out of the gate championing the establishment of a legal infrastructure that could sustain radical economic reform, which meant expanding rights in real property, maintaining free capital flows, and simplifying business regulation. He appeared genuinely troubled by the parasitic role of the Russian state in business, which produced, in his words, a "rent-seeking rather than a productive economy." In his first State of the Union address, Putin adopted a decidedly neo-liberal tone, complaining that "rulemaking by government agencies (*vedomstvennoe normotvorchestvo*) is one of the main impediments to the development of entrepreneurial activity." He recognized that the unreliability of Russian courts as sources of remedies for businesses – foreign and domestic – was driving dispute resolution to overseas courts, such as arbitration tribunals in Stockholm, or underground within Russia, toward what Putin himself called "shadow justice."[13] In Putin's view, by reclaiming functions for the state that had devolved onto foreign institutions or private organizations, Russia would lower the transaction costs for business and thereby render it more competitive in the world market.

The international environment encouraged law reform in Russia in other ways as well. By Yeltsin's second term, foreign donors had realized that macroeconomics was not the master science and that democracy and markets would not follow inexorably from the privatization of property and control of the money supply. Without the requisite infrastructure of legal norms, institutions, and culture, rent-seeking "businessmen" and self-aggrandizing officials would continue their collaboration, which retarded and distorted economic reform. International financial institutions and Western governments began to encourage Russia, therefore, to give more attention to the legal preconditions for successful economic policies.

By becoming a signatory to international accords and a member of regional organizations, Russia also imported new norms and obligations into its legal system, which required revision and, at times, a broader reassessment of its laws and procedures. This integration of international and Russian municipal law, which began in earnest in the Gorbachev era,[14] created considerable controversy in the Yeltsin era because of the Council of Europe's insistence on the elimination of the death penalty, which had been in place for decades in Russia and enjoyed broad public support. In his first years in office, Putin appeared intent on moving expeditiously to bring Russia in line with imported international norms, even on the question of the death penalty. In a rare instance of insensitivity to public opinion, Putin made a forceful appeal for the elimination of capital punishment in the summer of 2001.[15] Only later, following the hostage tragedy in Beslan, in September 2004, did Putin entertain a proposal to reintroduce the death penalty in terrorist cases.

Finally, Putin's own biography may help to explain the renewed attention accorded to law in Russia. Understandably, most Western assessments of Putin's life emphasize his service in the KGB and the lessons derived from that institution. But one should also recall that the first five years of his *formation professionnelle* were spent in the law faculty of Leningrad State University, and that after losing his job as vice-mayor of St. Petersburg in 1996, he considered pursuing a career as a defense attorney. Thus, like Gorbachev, he was trained as a lawyer, pursued an unrelated career in state service, and then as leader of the country embraced law as an instrument of reform. It is evident from his discussions of legal policy that he has an insider's knowledge of legal affairs.[16] Whether out of a familiarity with, and respect for law, or a desire to project another professional persona besides that of a KGB officer, Putin has given law a visibility in public affairs that is rare in Russian history.

In keeping with Putin's political temperament and the correlation of political forces in the country, the current law reform proposals promise incremental rather than revolutionary change. In most cases, they seek to implement innovations formally adopted but never fully realized in the waning days of Soviet power and the early post-communist era. Russia is experiencing in many respects, therefore, the second installment of the law reform that began in the late 1980s. To recognize the debt that the current debates over legal change owe initiatives from the Gorbachev era should not diminish, however, their importance or ambition. Especially in Russia, the heavy lifting in legal reform comes not in the articulation – or even the adoption – of reformist ideas but in the creation of conditions that ensure their steady and faithful implementation. It is this mundane but vital side of legal development that is at stake in the proposals to pay judges a decent wage, to improve the physical conditions of the courts, to fund professionally produced court transcripts, to create a corps of bailiffs who can carry out judicial decisions, and to grant judges sufficient authority over criminal proceedings, especially at the investigative stage. Again invoking the hard lessons of Russian history, Putin pledged to put an end to a pattern in which "revolution was usually followed by counter-revolution, reform by counter-reform . . . . It's time to state firmly: this system has ended."[17]

The Contours of Russian Legal Reform

Judicial Recruitment, Rewards, and Discipline

The current campaign to reform the Russian legal system embraces a number of interconnected legislative and administrative initiatives. If fully implemented, their impact will be most evident in the judiciary, and it is here that we begin the analysis, proceeding from a consideration of sociological issues to more explicitly legal questions concerning procedure and jurisdiction. Judicial independence, a core value of all democratic legal systems, requires methods of selection, remuneration, promotion, and discipline that minimize the possibilities for executive or legislative interference in judicial decisionmaking. Although the Russian government took important steps in the early 1990s to erect a wall of separation around the courts – granting judges lengthy terms or life tenure, transferring the responsibility for the disciplining of judges from the executive to the judiciary, and raising judges' pay – judges have remained vulnerable to pressures that compromise their independence. These pressures have come from regional politicians, who top up the still meager salaries and budgetary outlays for the courts with in-kind payments; from parties to legal cases who tempt judges with bribes and intimidate them with violence; and even from the court leadership, most commonly the court chairmen, who at times use their influence in promotions or assignments to encourage deference to their wishes. While serving as a judge in a case involving the kidnapping of a Russian businessman, Sergei Pashin, an early champion of law reform, noted that he "began to receive unwelcome telephone calls and visits. There were calls from the public prosecutor, the organized crime squad, the FSB [Federal Security Service] and the vice chairman of the court, saying that I should pay serious interest [*sic*] to the case and that it should be decided in the 'proper manner'."[18]

The financial problems facing Russian judges are twofold. First, like other so-called *biudzhetniki* (public sector employees), who receive their pay from a woefully underfunded state budget, judges are at the mercy of the shifting moods of the parliament and the shifting fortunes of the Russian economy. In the Yeltsin era, to ensure that judges' living standards did not fall to the low levels of other *biudzhetniki*, such as doctors and teachers, the government introduced several substantial pay increases and brought the judiciary leadership into parliamentary budget discussions. But inflation and the financial crisis of August 1998 eroded the financial gains realized by the judges, and Putin introduced significant raises in pay to meet and exceed the doubling of salaries that German Gref believed was needed to strengthen the judiciary.[19] The federal program, "Developing the Judicial System," called for almost fifty billion rubles to be devoted to legal reform in the period from 2002 to 2006, with two-thirds of that amount devoted to increasing judges' pay, which is scheduled to reach $1,000 per month by 2006. Another 7.5 billion rubles is to be invested in the construction and remodeling of court buildings.[20]

However, solving the living standard problem, which makes recruitment and retention of talented judges more difficult and bribery easier,[21] will almost certainly require more than hefty pay increases. Because Russia is not yet a cash economy, at least for the vast majority of the population, state-provided perquisites, such as subsidized housing, private telephones, and access to affordable daycare and transportation, are essential elements of a "middle class" Russian existence.[22] According to one source, over 700 judges still did not have their own apartments at the beginning of the Putin presidency.[23] Judges' continued reliance on their judicial superiors to lobby for perquisites – and on executive agencies to provide them – impedes the development of a psychology of independence. Leading judges may complain that "we cannot allow the executive branch to put us in a situation where we are supplicants," but the reality is that many have no choice but to go hat in hand to executive agencies for many of the accoutrements of modern life.[24] In this respect, legal reform remains hostage to the broader socio-economic context in which it is imbedded.[25]

Problems of pay and conditions aside, recruitment policies introduced in the early 1990s represented a radical and progressive departure from Soviet traditions, in which the Communist Party nominated its own members to stand unopposed for election to five-year terms and then subjected judges to recall elections if their decisions disappointed the political authorities. In Yeltsin's first term, the president assumed responsibility for appointing the country's judges, though nominees to the highest courts required the confirmation of the upper house of parliament. According to the Law on the Court of 1996, judges at lower levels received a presidential appointment only after being vetted by a panel of judges, known as a judicial qualification commission, and approved by the legislature at the corresponding administrative level. In practice, however, regional executive leaders often selected the judges.

More importantly, following the extension of judicial terms from five to ten years at the end of the Soviet era, post-communist Russia introduced life tenure for judges in 1993, which vested after serving a three-year probationary term. Not only did Russian judges enjoy life tenure, they also received impressive protections against dismissal. Judges gained a blanket immunity from criminal prosecution, which could only be lifted by a judicial qualification commission, and they could only be dismissed for serious cause, which was again determined by a judicial qualification commission. In terms of the formal structure of incentives relating to questions of tenure, Russian judges were in an enviable position.

There were two sources of objections to the generous tenure and immunity provisions accorded Russian judges. Given the inheritance of a judicial corps socialized in the "accusatorial bias" of a communist legal system and frequently educated by correspondence courses or recruited from law enforcement institutions, some liberal jurists and policy makers believed that Russia was not yet ready to lock judges in place for life.[26] For their part, conservatives argued that the rules regarding tenure and immunities rendered judges unaccountable. In this debate, Putin adopted the conservative position. In a surprisingly harsh critique of Russian judges, Putin complained that the judges' "shortcomings and mistakes . . . encourage the growth of legal nihilism. . . . For the last three and a half years, 316 judges in courts of general jurisdiction have been removed from the Bench by judicial qualification commissions. The reasons are well-known: falsification of documents, inexplicable delays in court proceedings, and prejudice in the review of cases."[27] Where some would see this record as evidence that the judiciary has been willing to discipline its own, Putin apparently believed that the qualification commissions had been lenient. Noting that "these bodies are chosen by judges and consist exclusively of judges," he concluded that they therefore seek to protect fellow judges as a "corporate caste." The point was made even more directly by Putin's main legal advisor, Dmitrii Kozak. "If one believes court statistics for the year 2000, then 15 of 20,000 Russian judges took bribes. One of two things is going on here: either judges are angels or there's not a mechanism for fighting judicial corruption."[28]

To put in place such a mechanism, Putin championed proposals that eroded some of the privileges and immunities of Russian judges. The president's critics perceived these initiatives to be part of a broader strategy to eliminate pockets of autonomy in Russia, whether among oligarchs, governors, or judges. Putin's response has been that democratic societies must balance judicial accountability and independence, and in recent years, he would argue, the pendulum had swung too far in the direction of independence. It is curious, of course, that Putin has not exhibited a similar concern for the accountability of the Procuracy. Article 42 of the Law on the Procuracy provides that the investigation of any wrongdoing by a member of the Procuracy, or the launching of a criminal investigation against them, falls "within the exclusive competence of Procuracy organs."[29]

Under a new law on the judicial community of March 2002 and subsequent amendments, life tenure for judges was abandoned for a system in which judges, after a three-year probationary period, serve to age seventy. To reverse what Putin and others perceived to be the unhealthy trend in the courts' self-policing, the new legislation also expanded the membership of judicial qualification commissions – or collegia in the new wording – to include jurists from outside the judiciary. Thus, the law transformed the judge-only review boards into larger bodies with a broad representation of judges and other legally-trained citizens. The Supreme Qualification Collegium now includes twenty-nine members, with judges appointed by their own professional associations while other jurists – the so-called representatives of society – are selected by the upper house of parliament, the Federation Council. The twenty-one members of provincial-level qualification collegia (eleven in the case of small territories) are selected in similar fashion, with the judges in the respective republic or region selecting their own representatives and the legislative assembly on this level appointing the other jurists on the collegium.[30] Furthermore, the president has the right under the new legislation to appoint his own personal representative to each judicial qualification collegium. According to some judges, including on the collegia a sizable minority of members selected by non-judicial bodies will make it easier for them to discipline their own. Judges meting out sanctions will be less subject to the perception that they alone are betraying fellow judges.[31]

The new legislation also provides for the selection of all federal judges by the president on the basis of a recommendation of a judicial qualification collegium.[32] Legislatures at the regional or local level no longer review the candidates, and, in theory at least, regional executives are also excluded from the process, though their involvement continues in practice. Court chairmen also continue to enjoy considerable influence over the advancement of nominees to the Bench, in part through their ability to protest the appointment of new judges to their courts.[33] Besides the president and his staff, regional executives, and court chairmen, the FSB plays a role in the selection of Russian judges. Each judicial nominee is subject to a background check by the security organs, and a negative review will effectively scuttle a nomination. Because the grounds for the FSB's conclusions are neither transparent nor subject to appeal, the security services enjoy a de facto veto over all new Russian judges, which represents one of the most insidious elements of patronage politics in the Putin-era judiciary.[34]

Putin also supported legislation that limits judges' immunity from criminal prosecution and at the same time exposes them to administrative and disciplinary tribunals, which can issue sanctions for minor infractions and poor work performance.[35] Predictably, many in the judicial leadership expressed outrage at these proposals, arguing that they would return Russia to an earlier age, when the Procuracy and other state agencies could use threats of criminal prosecution or administrative hearings to intimidate judges.[36] As one district court judge explained, judges are vulnerable because, given the unbearable workload, "they have so many [unheard] cases in the safe that they are fearful of any inspection."[37] Although the judiciary was unable to scuttle the legislation subjecting them to greater scrutiny, they at least prevented the introduction of even more onerous restrictions on judicial independence that had been advanced by traditionalists on the presidency's legislative drafting team. Among these stillborn proposals were the removal of judges from the Bench while their relatives were under criminal investigation and a requirement that judges submit themselves to annual physical examinations to ensure their fitness for the Bench.[38]

Judicial Organization

The current legal reform promises to complete, and in some cases extend, the organizational changes in the court that were outlined, but never fully implemented, in legislation of the 1990s. In a controversial departure from previous structural reforms, the Putin team proposed the formation of a single Judicial Chamber (*Sudebnaia palata*) that would have united the country's three highest courts, the Supreme Court, the Supreme (*Arbitrazh*) Commercial Court, and the Constitutional Court. Putin's critics feared that a unification of the three judicial branches in Moscow would have made it easier for executive and legislative institutions to control the judiciary by having a single point of contact. They also pointed to the technical difficulties of creating an institution that would stand above three such large and disparate courts. The Supreme Court alone has well over one hundred members, the Supreme Commercial Court fifty, and the Constitutional Court nineteen.

The leadership of the three higher courts worried that their own visibility and influence would be diminished in a single Judicial Chamber.[39] One could also argue, of course, that the absence of a single supreme court has in fact hindered efforts to establish the judiciary as the political equal of executive and legislative authority. But the leaders of the judiciary retorted that there already existed a professional organization that unites all of the country's judges – the Council of Judges. This institution would have been the fourth potential loser in the proposal to establish a Judicial Chamber. The head of the Council of Judges, Iurii Sidorenko, who has been among the harshest critics of Putin's initiatives on the judiciary, went so far as to label the proposed organizational changes a "counter-reform" that "threatens to establish a police state."[40] In the event, the Council of Judges and the three highest courts were successful in stymieing Putin's attempts to simplify judicial organization by creating a single judicial chamber. By early 2006, the all-consuming issue in court organization was not the unification of the judiciary but whether the Constitutional Court, and potentially the other two supreme courts of the land, would be moved from Moscow to St. Petersburg.

One of the most widely debated issues of organizational reform, and the subject of much attention and commentary in the Anglo-American world, was the introduction of the jury trial. The legislative groundwork was laid for a jury system in the early 1990s, including a mention in the 1993 Constitution, but when Putin came to power in 2000 juries functioned in only nine of the country's ninety-one provincial-level courts. In a move reminiscent of the legal counter-reform of the 1870s, the expansion of the jury system had been effectively halted in the early 1990s because of the objections of powerful interests in the Russian executive, most notably the Ministry of Finance, the Procuracy, and the MVD. One line of attack against the jury system was financial. In a country in economic crisis, the government could not afford to fund the lengthy trials, the larger courtrooms, and the increased per diem expenses that jury cases required. The judiciary's own administrative department estimated that the costs of implementing the jury system would approach $1.5 billion.[41]

But the more passionate resistance to the jury grew out of political and not financial concerns.[42] State officials responsible for criminal investigation and prosecution did not want their work subjected to the scrutiny of a group of twelve laypersons, who were far more unpredictable and independent-minded than the judicial corps, with whom many investigators and prosecutors had worked for decades. Even now, the Constitutional Court chairman admits, "many judges quiver before the procurators *(drozhat melkoi drozh'iu pered prokurami)*."[43] In ordinary trials, Russian judges remain extraordinarily reluctant to acquit, and until recently, when poorly prepared cases were brought before the court by the prosecution, instead of finding the defendant not guilty, which reflected poorly on the investigators' and prosecutors' records, judges often returned the cases to the law enforcement officials for an open-ended "supplementary investigation." Although the new Criminal Procedure Code introduced under Putin prohibits this practice, judges are still finding ways to avoid embarrassing their colleagues in the Procuracy, whether through a scaled-down version of the supplementary investigation, which grants only a week recess to produce needed materials for the case, or through pretrial meetings in chambers with prosecutors, where the judge can ensure that his colleague is prepared to present a solid case.[44]

Even with these adaptations, the jury trial represents a direct challenge to the authority and flexibility enjoyed by law enforcement agencies. Dramatic evidence of this point came in August 2001 when a jury in the northern Caucasus acquitted a Chechen defendant and his Russian accomplice of a terrorist bombing, a verdict that the prosecution labeled "nonsense."[45] Estimates of the rate of acquittal in jury trials range from sixteen to twenty-one percent, whereas the figure is less than one percent in cases heard by a single judge.[46]

On the jury question, the reform introduced under Putin was a compromise between the liberal and conservative camps. Liberals were heartened that changes to legislation on the courts, and administrative orders issued to the Ministry of Finance, extended the jury to all of Russia's provinces in 2003. And where the conservatives had sought to limit jury trials to a very narrow band of cases, the final version of the Code of Criminal Procedure allowed defendants to seek a jury trial in all criminal cases heard in the first instance by provincial-level courts. The hurdle for convictions was set quite low, however, with only an absolute majority of the jury (seven of twelve members) required for a guilty verdict.[47] Of even greater import, Russian rules of criminal procedure allow prosecutors to appeal acquittals in jury trials, and appellate courts have returned the same case to a lower trial court on multiple occasions, which can subject defendants to double or even triple jeopardy. It is clear from the first few years of experience with nationwide jury trials that procurators and their allies will go to almost any lengths to prevent juries from acquitting defendants in cases where the authority and interests of important political and legal authorities are at stake.[48]

For years, legal policy makers have struggled to find ways to adapt Russia's courts to the heightened demand for law occasioned by the post-communist transition.

As Table 1 indicates, where the number of criminal, civil, and administrative cases increased several-fold during the 1990s, the size of the judicial corps grew by only fifty percent. This expansion in litigation led to an average caseload of nine criminal cases and thirty civil cases per month in 2001.[49] According to the chair of the commercial court in Moscow, "judicial reform isn't possible until we have a normal work load for judges. Judges are collapsing from overwork and they are carting them away to hospitals directly from the Bench."[50] Citing the comments of the eminent nineteenth century Russian jurist, A. F. Koni, Victor Pokhmelkin recently reminded his Duma colleagues that one may ask judges to be professional, or even above moral reproach, but not heroic.[51]

One method of addressing the workload problem is to hire more judges, as German Gref has advocated, and several thousand additional judges have been recruited to the Bench in the Putin era. But finding and funding so many new judges so quickly has been difficult. It takes over a year to bring a nominee through the nomination process, and already in some areas there has occurred a marked feminization of the Bench during the last decade, with the percent of women judges in St. Petersburg reaching eighty percent.[52] Unfortunately, in the Russian context, high percentages of women in a profession is an indication that it does not offer competitive pay or prestige. Highly qualified men in the legal profession continue to gravitate to better paying jobs in the private sector and to more prestigious posts in other state legal institutions.[53]

Given the difficulty of reducing the judicial workload through new hiring alone, policy makers began to look in other directions for solutions. One way of lessening the burden on judges is to reduce the scope of judicial responsibility, for example by decriminalizing certain behavior. But only the most radical voices in the legal community have advanced such proposals. The authorities are turning instead to two more traditional answers to judicial overload. For the first time, judicial clerks (sud'i assistenty) – several thousand in all – have been be hired to ease the judges' workload.[54] Second, Russia is reviving a pre-revolutionary institution, the justices of the peace, who now function at the base of the legal system to review minor criminal and civil cases that today overwhelm the courts of general jurisdiction. Although envisioned by the 1996 Law on the Court System, justices of the peace only began to appear in late 1999 – yet another example of a statute having to await specific enabling legislation and financing to be realized.[55] The government expanded the number of justice of the peace to approximately 5,000 in 2004 from a base of roughly 2,000 in 2001.[56] Because the justices of the peace handle less serious legal matters, their training and

Table 1: Basic Indicators of the Work of the Courts of General Jurisdiction in the Russian Federation

Source: Sudebnaia reforma v Rossii: predely I vozmozhnosti [Judicial reform in Russia: limits and opportunities] (Nikitskii klub. Tsikl publichnykh diskussii "Rossiia v global'nom kontekste," vypusk 5, Moscow, 2001), 109; O federal'nom biudzhete na 2006 god (The Federal Budget for 2006), *Rossiiskaia gazeta*, 29 December 2005.

Year	Number of Judges	Regional Courts (per 1000)	Completed Criminal Cases	Completed Civil Cases	Administrative Cases Reviewed	Percent of Verdicts Appealed	Percent of Decisions Appealed	Sentenced to Deprivation of Liberty	Sentenced to Deprivation of Liberty, Percent
1990	10,060	8,085	526,899	1,462,920	1,163,865	24.40%	6.00%	203,359	37.80%
1991	11,233	9,128	570,544	1,401,019	1,088,690	21.90%	5.70%	207,489	34.90%
1992	12,752	10,467	622,684	1,686,387	1,109,130	19.30%	5.30%	225,926	34.20%
1993	14,095	11,623	760,948	1,825,438	1,473,507	16.70%	5.10%	292,868	37.00%
1994	15,296	12,526	938,065	1,955,309	1,860,125	14.40%	5.20%	332,675	36.00%
1995	15,564	12,740	1,074,652	2,806,892	1,927,339	12.90%	4.00%	357,765	34.50%
1996	15,564	12,740	1,154,773	3,056,723	1,923,002	12.30%	4.30%	373,519	33.60%
1997	15,552	12,741	1,056,481	3,881,977	1,879,541	14.80%	3.70%	330,977	32.70%
1998	15,556	12,745	1,137,259	4,752,144	1,806,835	15.50%	3.60%	345,339	32.20%
1999	15,600	12,770	1,278,822	5,012,331	1,824,775	14.60%	4.00%	388,799	31.80%
2000	16,742								
2006	22,317								

remuneration can be less substantial than that provided to regular judges.

The justices of the peace reform is the rare proposal that appeared to enjoy support in all segments of the legal community. However, it is almost certain to create tensions between federal and regional authorities at the very moment when Putin is seeking to wrest power away from the periphery. Although subject to federal rules of procedure, the justices of the peace are the creatures of provincial governments. Where the president appoints all existing judges, the provincial assemblies select the justices of the peace on the basis of recommendations of the regional or republican courts.[57] This divergence in the method of selection raises the possibility of a rift between the two judicial corps, whose diverse backgrounds and orientations may make it more difficult to use justice of the peace courts as a training ground for a rising generation of regular court judges. Furthermore, it appears that whereas funding for the justices of the peace comes from both federal and provincial budgets, they must operate within budgetary guidelines established by the center, making it likely that the justices of the peace will find themselves torn between the interests of federal and provincial power.[58] Already certain regional officials are claiming that the Constitution grants to each "subject of the Russian Federation the right to create its own judicial system."[59]

Court bailiffs are another institution created legislatively in the Yeltsin era that only received substantial funding during the Putin presidency. In an attempt to enhance the protection of judges – who have been subject to rising levels of physical intimidation – and to improve the execution of court decisions in civil cases, the Russian government in 1997 replaced the old court executor (*sudebnyi ispolnitel'*) with a new institution of court bailiffs (*sudebnye pristavy*). In the view of many, the major reasons for the lack of confidence of the general population and the business community in Russian courts are the long delays in judicial proceedings and the inability of successful plaintiffs to collect on judgments. According to a Constitutional Court judge, "decisions are adopted by the courts but perhaps half of them are not implemented."[60] Essential to the rule of law is the ability to seek and receive remedies, and even if the court hands down fair and speedy decisions, justice will not be done until the will of the court is carried out.

The court bailiffs are certainly more visible and "muscular" than their predecessors and their collection rate appears to be higher. In 2000, they collected more than 100 billion rubles that were owed the state alone.[61] But the court bailiffs are not yet an effective and well-integrated component of the Russian legal system in the way that, say, local sheriffs or federal marshals have become in the United States.[62]

Despite the additional funding, power, and attention received by court bailiffs under Putin, they remain a subject of derision in some quarters. Even with the promised addition of 6,500 bailiffs to the existing corps of about 30,000, many believe that the institution will remain understaffed and unable to collect debts owed to successful plaintiffs or to the state. In 2000, the responsibility for the collection of tax arrears was transferred from the tax police to the court bailiffs, who allegedly collected only seventeen percent of the amount owed that year. However, the problems go beyond the quantity of cadres. According to some reports, the bailiffs inherited many of the "aunties in their 40s and 50s with a seventh grade education" who had served earlier as court executors.[63] With an average salary in 2001 of 1500-2500 rubles per month, or about thirty to forty dollars, it is not surprising that it has been difficult to attract talented personnel.[64]

Because of the meager pay and difficult assignments – bailiffs are the state equivalent of the repo man – there is a widespread perception that bailiffs are using their considerable discretion to cut deals on the side with those who face asset seizure. Allowing a debtor to keep some of his property can produce substantial and illicit financial rewards for the bailiffs.[65] But as Peter Hahn has pointed out in his exhaustive study of court bailiffs, the most serious shortcoming in the bailiffs' corps is not corruption but a structure of financial incentives that encourages bailiffs to favor certain collections over others, most notably those where the state is the judgment creditor or where private assets can be seized with little effort.[66]

Bailiffs are also subject to pressure from politicians to pursue their assignments in ways that may benefit the friends of officials and harm their enemies. As part of Putin's assault on the "family circles" surrounding republican presidents and regional governors in 2000, the Ministry of Justice – the agency to which the bailiffs are attached – fired one-tenth of all bailiffs in the provinces, allegedly for their excessively close connections to the regional political leadership.[67] But the bailiffs have also been involved in high-profile assaults at the national level on businesses perceived as critical of Putin. In the celebrated case of a national television network, NTV, court bailiff Evgenii Kurepov "arrested" twelve percent of the shares of the network, which facilitated its takeover by forces sympathetic to Putin.[68] The potential for abuse of authority by court bailiffs is a reminder that unless judges exercise sufficient supervision over the execution of court judgments, which means taming self-interested bailiffs and self-serving politicians, courts will never occupy a respected and defining role in Russian public life.

Procedure and Jurisdiction: The Courts and the Procuracy

The challenges facing Russian courts derive not only from the legacies of the Soviet era, or the unfavorable economic circumstances of the transition, but the very expansion of judicial authority that followed the collapse of communism. After 1991, the courts were no longer simply extensions of the party or executive authority but a relatively autonomous center of power that weighed in on many key political and economic issues of the day. Peter Solomon notes that "the gains in jurisdiction were dramatic," as judicial review extended for the first time to administrative acts, pretrial detention, and the constitution itself.[69] For example, in September 2001, the Military Collegium of the Russian Supreme Court ruled that the Ministry of Defense maintained an excessively broad definition of military secrets, a stunning challenge to one of the pillars of the Russian state.[70] As the deputy chairman of the Russian Supreme Court observed, "courts today deal not only with the issues they encountered previously, such as property settlements between spouses, but [through the resolution of electoral law cases] who becomes governor in a region or deputy in the parliament."[71]

This expanded scope of judicial activity posed problems for which the courts were ill-prepared. To borrow a phrase from Russian federal politics, the courts had a hard time digesting all the authority that they had swallowed. The issue was not simply the expansion of the workload or the adjustment to greater responsibilities – and the inevitable tension over jurisdictional boundaries between the several court systems – but the resentment and resistance toward judicial decisions by political and financial elites. Courts were gradually emerging as significant players in decisions concerning the partition of political and economic power, which began to mobilize forces hostile to the court.

Perhaps no institution stood to lose more from an expansion of judicial authority than the Procuracy. A jurisdictional issue that has become a *cause celebre* in the current reform debates is the division of labor between the courts and the Procuracy in criminal proceedings. Reforms of criminal justice in Russian history have generally involved a transfer of prerogatives to the courts from executive or quasi-executive institutions as well as a leveling of the playing field between prosecutors and defense attorneys. The Procuracy has consistently and vigorously fought such changes, and the current reform wave presents no exception to this pattern. Not only has the Procuracy maneuvered by stealth in behind-the-scenes attempts to block or weaken legislation, it has also sought to stir up the public against the courts by criticizing judges for corruption as well as liberality in dealing with criminals.[72]

In the Soviet era, the Procuracy's responsibilities for the investigation of criminal cases, the oversight of these investigations, the prosecution of cases in court, and then the reviewing of the legality of judicial decisions produced an "accusatorial bias" that was a central feature of Soviet criminal law. Seeking to eliminate this bias, legal reformers in the 1990s attempted to strip the Procuracy of all but the prosecutorial function by championing the formation of an independent investigatory committee and the granting to courts the exclusive right to review the legality of pretrial investigations as well as the soundness of lower-court decisions. But through passionate public campaigns to defend the honor and privileges of their institution, the Procuracy's leaders have managed to defeat, dilute, or delay these measures, which threatened to break up their unusual conglomerate. To mobilize support for retention of the status quo, the Procuracy has appealed to nationalist impulses, by emphasizing its pedigree as a distinctive Russian institution; it has appealed to the fear of ordinary Russians, by claiming that the relative liberality of judges would lead to an increase in crime;[73] and it has appealed to the self-interest of other "power institutions," such as the FSB, the MVD, and the Tax Police, who would lose their own investigative personnel and powers if an independent investigatory committee were formed. In parliamentary question time in April 2001, the Procurator-General, Dmitrii Ustinov, summarized his institution's objections to pending legislation on law reform. "'What today goes by the name of reform is not reform at all but instead a set of measures that they simply call reform. Reformers are just copying down Western models and saying this is something new . . . . only the Procuracy stands in the way of dishonest people, but they [the reformers] want to eliminate us'."[74] A year later, in a fiery speech before the full collegium of the Procuracy, with Putin and the heads of other legal agencies in attendance, Ustinov railed against the globalization of legal norms. "There are many dilettantes who cite the experience of Western democracies. But Russia is not the West. And the relations between 'the state and a concrete person,' between 'the authorities [*vlast'*] and the citizen' will develop for a long time on traditional Russian terms [*po traditsionnym otechestvennym merkam*]."[75]

In 2001, more than eight years after the Constitution granted the courts the sole right to sanction arrests or detention, and two years after the Constitutional Court confirmed the unconstitutionality of holding subjects without a court order, hundreds of thousands of Russian citizens sat in jails on the strength of procurators' decisions alone. Standing in the way of the implementation of the Constitution's provisions was a Criminal Procedure Code inherited from the Soviet era that did not grant courts such powers. The mere issuance of a ruling by the Constitutional Court did not guarantee that the Constitution's provisions would be implemented. In this case, as in many others, the offending legislation had to be changed by the parliament. In the summer of 2001, the chairman of the Constitutional Court, Marat Baglai, complained that "the Duma has to this point failed to introduce amendments to 11 laws whose norms the Constitutional Court has recognized as unconstitutional. Recently, I wrote an official letter to the lower house of parliament requesting it to work up appropriate drafts [to remedy this]."[76]

Thus, because of legislative inaction, the Criminal Procedure Code in effect trumped the Constitution for the better part of a decade. Given the requirement that the Code be passed by parliamentary supermajorities because it is a federal constitutional law, as well as the contentiousness of the issues raised by the Code, it was only at the end of 2001, as a result of Putin's personal intervention, that a new Criminal Procedure Code was passed by the parliament.

The maneuvers leading up to the bill's passage revealed the president's ambivalence on the appropriate division of labor between the courts and the Procuracy in criminal justice. They also illustrated the presence of diverse points of view within the presidential administration. In January 2001 the president proposed an immediate and complete transfer of responsibility for arrest, detention, and searches to the court, as the Constitution had envisioned. But several weeks later, Putin backpedaled and advanced amendments designed to satisfy many of the concerns of the Procuracy. One of these would have granted procurators the right to approve the launching of criminal investigations. In the event, this proposal was rejected by parliament, but revisions to the Criminal Procedure Code did postpone the transfer of responsibility for sanctioning arrests and searches from the Procuracy to the courts until 1 January 2004, allegedly to grant the judiciary time to prepare itself to assume the new responsibilities. In reality, the postponement accorded the Procuracy an additional two years to oversee the pretrial stage of the criminal investigation and to search for ways to halt or further delay the loss of their institutional prerogatives. Furthermore, the new version of the Criminal Procedure Code allows the Procuracy to issue search and arrest warrants without a judge's signature "in exceptional circumstances when the case won't allow for delay," and it extends the already lengthy time limits for holding suspects without arraignment and for holding the accused before trial.[77] It also includes rules relating to self-incrimination and the calling of witnesses that tend to place the prosecution in a more advantageous position than the defense.[78]

The new Criminal Procedure Code contained, however, an important change in the division of labor between the courts and Procuracy at the trial stage of the criminal process. Although legislative reforms in the late Soviet era made the participation of defense counsel mandatory in criminal trials, the law was silent on the participation of prosecutors. As a result, in approximately one-half of the trials, prosecutors have not been present. Instead of favoring the defendant, this practice usually disadvantages him by encouraging judges to assume the role of prosecutor in the case. Not only are Russian judges more active participants in the trial than their American counterparts, but, as Iurii Feofanov observed, "for many decades the court was not viewed as a referee in an adversarial process but as a instrument in the struggle against crime."[79] Even Dmitrii Kozak admitted that "in reality, few believe in the objectivity of the court. More often than not, the judge takes on the role of the accuser in the trial,"[80] an approach that may reflect in part the high percentage of Russian judges who come to the Bench from the Procuracy or the MVD rather than the defense Bar.[81] But the accusatorial bias of the Bench also derives from a basic principle of Soviet law, which held that judges were obligated to search for the "objective truth." If convinced of the guilt of the accused, judges felt justified in ignoring procedural violations at trial and in assuming de facto the role of prosecutor.[82] Formally, then, the new law requiring the presence of prosecutors as well as defenders at trial promises to move Russian courts toward the adversarial culture that reformists have long sought to introduce in legal proceedings.[83] It is unclear, however, to what extent this reform will reduce longstanding accusatorial bias or what many observers regard as the boorish behavior (*khamstvo*) of judges toward participants in the trial.[84]

The Defense Bar (Advokatura)

If the judiciary developed in the Yeltsin era with limited attention from lawmakers, the Bar escaped legislative reform altogether. But as with the court and other legal institutions, the broader changes in Russian society in the 1990s began to reshape the Bar even in the absence of new legislation. At the end of the Soviet era, virtually all advocates belonged to regional professional associations, known as colleges (*kollegii*), and practiced in the colleges' legal consultation bureaus. With the collapse of communism, the traditional colleges lost their monopoly, and new associations of advocates, known as parallel or alternative colleges, sprung up around the country. In addition, some advocates began to practice outside of colleges by receiving professional licenses from state institutions rather from the associations of advocates. By 1997, there were forty parallel colleges in addition to almost one hundred traditional ones, with two new parallel colleges in Moscow alone.[85] Advocates also began to flee the colleges' traditional vehicles for the provision of legal services, the legal consultation bureaus, for the greater autonomy and remuneration available in law firms or in individual practice.

The expanded jurisdiction of the courts, the rise in criminal activity, and the rapid growth of the private economic sector dramatically increased the demand for lawyers. With the traditional colleges no longer able to maintain caps on Bar membership, the number of advocates grew apace through the 1990s. By the end of the decade, Moscow had 7,000 advocates, compared with only 1,200 at the beginning of the Gorbachev era. The total number of Russian advocates approached 43,000 in 2001 and was well over 53,000 by 2003, an extraordinary increase over the Soviet era, though still a modest figure in relation to Western professions or to the total number of jurists in government service.

Not surprisingly, the most impressive transformation of the Bar came in the field of civil law, where some advocates were able to develop a vibrant business law practice focusing on transactions and contracts as well as litigation before the developing network of commercial courts (*arbitrazhnye sudy*).[86] If members of the parallel colleges dominated civil practice, their counterparts in traditional colleges, known as *traditsionshchiki*, were primarily devoted to criminal defense work, which had long been the most prestigious activity of the Russian Bar, owing to its political significance as a shield for the individual against state power and to the respect accorded oral advocacy in Russia.[87] Even before the adoption of the new Criminal Procedure Code, one could argue that Russian advocates were becoming more effective representatives of their clients in criminal cases through higher levels of participation at the pretrial stage, historically the defining phase of the criminal process, and through their appearance before juries in the nine regions that permitted such trials.[88] As we noted earlier, in jury trials advocates were unusually successful in procuring acquittals. Although numerous legacies from the Soviet era continued to limit the effectiveness of defense attorneys, including the tendency of judges to deny most defense motions while accepting those submitted by the prosecution, some restraints on criminal defenders were removed.[89] Among these was the requirement that defendants charged with sensitive political crimes select their attorney from a list of advocates pre-approved by the security services.

When the much-debated and oft-revised draft law on the Bar finally attracted the attention of the Russian president in 2000, it presented him with three especially divisive issues. The first was the future structure of the Bar. At various points in

Russian history, most notably the late nineteenth and late twentieth centuries, the government believed that a proliferation of Bar associations would render the profession less imposing and more malleable. But in keeping with his decision to simplify the presidency's relations with state and social organizations, Putin supported a draft law on the Bar that called for the reunification of the Bar into a single Advocates' Chamber (*advokatskaia palata*), based on the "traditional college" framework. It was a proposal that set off a firestorm of controversy, especially among the leaders of the parallel colleges, who viewed the traditional colleges as relics of the old order.[90]

Unlike the judiciary, which was able to unite in opposition to the formation of a single Judicial Chamber, and thereby remove it from the legislative agenda, the seemingly limitless egos and petty jealousies in the Bar prevented it from presenting a united front. Not only was the Bar deeply divided by competing national associations and by distinct regional colleges – for their part, the traditional colleges regarded the parallel colleges as havens for under-qualified refugees from the Procuracy and other state institutions – but individual colleges were at times rent by internal feuds.[91] The factionalization in the Moscow Interregional College, a parallel organization, led to one group seizing the college's headquarters by force on an early Sunday morning in August 2001.[92] As a result of these fissures, the provision on the creation of a single Advocates' Chamber remained a part of the new statute on the advocates when it was signed into law in May 2002.[93] Under the new legislation, defense lawyers in Russia became members of a single Advocates' Chamber in their home territory as well as a federal association of advocates based in Moscow.[94]

The presidency argued that a single Bar organization would facilitate the provision of legal assistance to less fortunate members of Russian society. Broad access to legal aid was, then, the second contested issue relating to the reform of the Bar. For decades, Russian advocates had been obligated under Article 49 of the old Code of Criminal Procedure to provide free or low-cost legal assistance to certain categories of citizens. This obligation did not disappear with the collapse of communism. Although advocates, especially those outside of the traditional colleges, sought to avoid or reduce to a minimum this poorly remunerated work, the chairman of the traditional college in Moscow claimed that his members spent approximately half of their time working on court-appointed cases, and that even the most prominent attorneys engaged in this service.[95]

Instead of creating a separate state-funded legal aid service, which had the disadvantages of being both expensive and politically suspect, given popular attitudes to state employees in the field of justice, Putin favored the retention of a system of legal aid based on modest payments to private attorneys for the handling of court-appointed cases. The issue for the Bar was not only ensuring that the obligations were minimal and the pay reasonable but that the structure of remuneration in such cases did not distort the provisions of legal aid by rewarding certain work, such as that in pretrial proceedings, at lower rates than appearances at trial or appellate hearings. Such had been the case since the late Soviet era.

Because the budget has not supported adequate pay in Article 49 cases, the state has offered the Bar other financial incentives, which raises a third area of controversy. In debates that bear an uncanny resemblance to those surrounding the law on the Bar introduced in the 1920s – when advocates were also seeking to adapt to a period of economic liberalization during NEP – the government offered benefits normally reserved for state employees if the Bar agreed to assume indigent cases for minimal pay.[96] Such benefits grant lawyers subsidized office space in buildings owned by local governments; assist them to locate affordable and decent private apartments; reduce tax rates below those normally applied to private businesses; and set contributions to the state pension fund at rates corresponding to those paid in by state workers rather than private employees.[97] Although an understandable compromise in Russia's current economic climate, such concessions to the advocates create the potential for political leverage that could limit the autonomy of the profession. Again, the absence of an authentic market economy in Russia prevents the purveyors of justice, in the first rank judges and advocates, from enjoying the kind of personal independence available to their counterparts in Western legal systems.

Finally, Russian lawyers operate in a legal culture that has refused to recognize the Bar as a genuinely private profession. Putin's deputy for legal reform, Dmitrii Kozak, revealed the extent to which Soviet legacies continue to color official thinking about this branch of the legal profession. "Within a year," he argued, "there will be an advocate's association that will carry out functions necessary to the advocates and to citizens [instead of] amassing money. This is a matter of principle – there must not be advocates' associations that are engaged in law as a business activity (*ne dolzhny organy advokatskogo soobshchestva zanimat'sia iuridicheskim biznesom*)." Even many advocates, including the head of the traditional college in Nizhegorodskaia region, regard the Bar as "part of the judicial system and therefore establishing it on a commercial basis would lead to a commercialization of not only the Bar but the whole court system."[98] To be sure, in the United States attorneys are referred to as "officers of the court." But the attachment of legal counsel to the state is far stronger in Russia. As one prominent judge observed, the advocate should not only be a representative of the client but "the first assistant of the judge [*pervyi pomoshchnik sud'i*]."[99] The cultural impediments to reform in Russia lie not only, then, in the much-discussed legal nihilism of its citizens but in the vestiges of statism in the thinking of political and legal elites.[100]

Conclusions

Instead of speaking of the primacy of legal or economic reform for Russia, it is essential to recognize the ways in which the two currents are mutually reinforcing, or mutually destructive. The absence of a reliable legal infrastructure retards and distorts economic development by raising transaction costs, discouraging investment, whether domestic or foreign, and rewarding businesses on the basis of their access to political power rather than their commercial acumen. As we have shown, however, the limited marketization of the economy also creates conditions that impede the emergence of a rule of law. Complicating the growth of an independent judiciary, for example, has been the scarcity of developed private markets for housing and other goods, which creates a dependence of the judiciary on executive agencies for the provision of essential goods and services. Moreover, besides limiting the state's ability to offer salaries commensurate with high levels of legal professionalism, the fiscal crises facing Russia have also encouraged forms of institutional self-financing that distort the pursuit of justice. Offering the Procuracy a ten-percent share of all awards collected in civil suits creates an incentive for state involvement in commercial litigation, which should remain a contest between private parties.

By the end of the 1990s, the political prospects for legal change seemed no more auspicious than the economic and financial conditions. Popular pressure for law reform was virtually nonexistent, and there was little sympathy for change even in the ranks of institutions that had in the past served as its champion: the Bar and the courts. Indeed, many judges and advocates exhibited an attitude to reform that Petr Barenboim reduced to the telling phrase, "just give us more money and don't bother us."[101] As one journalist noted, the struggle for reform legislation occurred "in the context of fierce opposition between . . . Dmitrii Kozak, heading the working group on legal and judicial reform, and the agencies and officials whose interests the reform directly affect."[102]

Much to the chagrin of many Western scholars and policy-makers, the attitude of the Russian business community to legal reform has also been ambivalent at best. As Kathryn Hendley has argued compellingly, when demand for law has come from economic actors, it has often been for laws that are "anti-market."[103] In theory, as Hendley notes, it may be in the interest of businessmen to lower transaction costs by seeking remedies in a sophisticated court system, but such a court system does not yet exist. In the absence of reliable judicial institutions, the old-fashioned *krysha,* or protection, is preferable to the "impersonal forces" of the law, which require the businessman to "cede power" to a third party – the court – whose authority and fairness is suspect. In this regard, the observation of the wizened Maine resident to the confused tourist seems apt: "you can't get there from here." Put in the scholarly language of Hendley,

> Shifting to a reliance on universalistic rules and institutions – submitting disputes to the courts – makes sense only if the shift is made almost simultaneously by a fair majority of economic actors. Absent such a collective shift, a director is naturally reluctant to risk his trading partner going outside the legal system and bringing political pressure to bear, thereby putting the director at a disadvantage. The safer course of action for a director is to forestall that risk by appealing to his patrons. It is a classic dilemma of collective action.[104]

If there is a group that may emerge as champions of more authoritative and independent courts, it is the smaller and less well-connected businesspersons, who lack the political clout or financial means to employ corrupt practices as an effective business tool. But unless these small businesspersons and women become better organized and political leaders become more responsive to their interests, they are unlikely to contribute much to the development of a legal infrastructure in Russia. Stephen Holmes may only slightly overstate the case, therefore, when he argues that "legal reform in Russia has no obvious political or social base." He is certainly correct to suggest that, at present, the president remains the primary engine of change in the legal system.[105] Put another way, Putin has trumped – at least temporarily – a remarkably unfavorable correlation of political forces in his bid to reform Russian law.

The guiding hand of the presidency in legal reform – so reminiscent of earlier episodes of Russian legal history – may well advance the country's development toward a constitutional order and the rule of law. But the *dirigisme* evident in the current round of law reform presents several dangers itself. First, with no potent constituency to rally behind him, save the enthusiastic sponsors of foreign legal assistance projects, Putin faces continuing resistance to change from the most powerful interests in the Russian legal bureaucracy. Now that the reform has moved from the public field of legislative battles to the deep recesses of the bureaucracy for implementation, the opponents of reform will be on more friendly and familiar territory. For all the arguments about democracy's inefficiency at the lawmaking stage, its emphasis on compromise, rather than *diktat*, has the advantage of creating stakeholders among the key actors in the state and society, including those charged with implementing change.

At the end of the current round of lawmaking in Russia, which was engineered by a narrow group of specialists attached to the presidency, few legal officials feel themselves "owners" of the reforms. Indeed, most appear to have agreed to legislative changes under duress. As Stephen Holmes has argued, "[t]o put through a reform of this magnitude, the Kremlin needs voluntary cooperation from the main actors in the legal system, including the Procuracy, who must accept the basic principles of the reform if it is to be successful."[106] Yet, the leadership of the Procuracy shows no sign of giving up a Russian way of justice for the universal values implicit in the rule of law. In many respects, then, legislative changes are to law reform what macroeconomic innovations are to economic reform: essential but by no means sufficient conditions. In both fields, Russia is now engaged in the tougher and more protracted business of nurturing institutions and not just establishing rules.

Second, Vladimir Putin's own commitment to legal reform is often ambivalent, witness the recent use of the courts to prosecute his political adversaries and to prevent them from standing for office. A willingness to allow courts to be used occasionally as instruments of political power will delay reform, or possbly derail it altogether. Unfortunately, a decline in the country's budgetary health or a worsening of terrorism or ordinary crime is seized on immediately by the opponents of reform as reasons to suspend recent innovations. In the wake of the Chechen hostage crisis in October 2002, for example, representatives of the military and security services pressed for new legal restrictions, some of which they received two years later in the wake of the tragedy in Beslan.[107] Moreover, the very indispensability of not just a Russian president but the current Russian president, Vladimir Putin, to the success of legal reform implies that a change of leadership could alter fundamentally the direction and pace of Russian legal development. Such is the disadvantage of reform movements that come from above rather than below.

The Russian presidency, therefore, is at once a patron of, and an impediment to, legal reform. Despite the expanding jurisdiction and confidence of the courts, judges remain unusually deferential toward the office of the president. This deference has its roots in both the Soviet and post-Soviet eras. It was Yeltsin, after all, who furloughed the Constitutional Court for months in 1993 when the chairman challenged presidential power. Even today, Constitutional Court justices remain dependent on the presidency for housing and other perquisites. But the sources of judicial deference toward the presidency lie most fundamentally in the cultural and institutional legacies of personalist rule. The very structure of the Russian constitution elevates the president, like the Communist Party before it, above the other branches of government – prime minister and Council of Ministers, the parliament, and the courts. The president appoints a personal emissary to the Constitutional Court to represent his interests, and when the president meets the chairmen of the country's highest courts in closed session, which would be an irregular occurrence in itself in the American tradition, it is always in the Kremlin, the seat of the presidency.[108] As long as Vladimir Putin and his successors remain comfortable with the personalism implicit in these arrangements, courts and justice in Russia will remain unduly influenced by the will of the executive, and a constitutional order and the rule of law will continue to serve as the goals of more "reform moments" in Russian history.

NOTES TO CHAPTER 2

[1] My thanks to Professors Robert Sharlet and Peter Solomon, and Judge Michael McDermott for their comments on an earlier version of this paper.

[2] According to Mikhail Krasnov, Yeltsin's counselor for legal affairs, "it took approximately ten years for the significance of judicial power and the justice system in general to become clear to the political and economic elite." "Is the 'Concept of Judicial Reform' Timely?" *East European Constitutional Review* nos. 1-2 (2002): 93.

[3] It is not that law reform disappeared altogether after the early 1990s, rather its progress slowed dramatically, in good measure because of the loss of the presidency as an institutional patron that could remove the innumerable barriers to law reform. For a discussion of what Russia did accomplish in the field of judicial change in the 1990s, see Peter H. Solomon, Jr., "The Persistence of Judicial Reform in Contemporary Russia," *East European Constitutional Review* (Fall 1997): 50-56.

[4] Vystuplenie Prezidenta RF V. V. Putina na V Vserossiiskom s'ezde sudei (Speech of the President of the Russian Federation, V. V. Putin, at the V All-Russian Congress of Judges), 27 November 2000. http://president.kremlin.ru/events/107.html.

[5] Eugene Huskey, "Judicial Reform after Communism," in Peter H. Solomon, Jr., ed., *Reforming Justice in Russia, 1864-1996* (Armonk: M. E. Sharpe, 1997), 325-347.

[6] On the work of this committee, see "Reforma osvobodit prokuraturu ot melochei" (Reform spares the Procuracy from trivial matters), *Strana.Ru*, 27 May 2001. http://www.strana.ru/.

[7] For an excellent assessment of the logic of Putin's legal reform, see Robert Sharlet, "Putin and the Politics of Law in Russia," *Post-Soviet Affairs* no. 3 (2001): 195-234.

[8] Vystuplenie Prezidenta RF V. V. Putina s poslaniem Federal'nomu Sobraniiu Rossiiskoi Federatsii (The State of the Union Speech of the President of the Russian Federation to the Federal Assembly), 3 April 2000. http://president.kremlin.ru/events/191.html.

[9] For a fuller treatment of Putin's use of the concept of "dictatorship of law," see Sharlet, "Putin and the Politics of Law," 203-205.

[10] Vystuplenie Prezidenta RF V. V. Putina na V Vserossiiskom s'ezde sudei (Speech of the President of the Russian Federation, V. V. Putin, at the V All-Russian Congress of Judges), 27 November 2000.

[11] Ibid. When justice was invoked, it was usually in regard to the victims of crime rather than suspects. Dmitrii Kozak commented that "the development of the state is not possible without a reliable defense of the rights and interests of citizens. This is even more important than the economy. Otherwise, we shall not defeat crime and corruption." Ol'ga Koltunova, "Dmitrii Kozak: v Rossii est' kasta neprikasaemykh" (Dmitrii Kozak: in Russia there is an untouchable caste), *Strana.Ru*, 5 June 2001. On Russian detention facilities and on the criminal procedural rules relating to their use, see the excellent work by Todd Foglesong, Sokrashchenie chislennosti naseleniia SIZO v Rossii: vybor strategii [Reduction in the jail population in Russia: strategic choice](Tsentr sodeistviia pravosudiiu pri regional'nom obshchestvennom fonde INDEM, 2001).

[12] Georgii Semenov, "Iz dvukh millionov evropeiskikh zakliuchennykh na Rossiiu prikhoditsia odin" (For every two million European prisoners there is one in Russia), *Surgutskaia tribuna*, 2 November 2001.

[13] Sergei Kashin, "Dmitrii Kozak ne boitsia obidet' prokuraturu. I sudei tozhe" (Dmitrii Kozak isn't afraid of offending the Procuracy. Or the judges), *Strana.Ru*, 27 April 2001. Court reform was a major subject on the agenda at a meeting between Putin and the country's leading industrialists in May 2001. See "Prognozy nedeli" (Outlook for the week), *Vedomosti*, 19 November 2001.

[14] George Ginsburgs, "The Relationship between International and Domestic Law and the Impact on Civil Law," in Ginsburgs, ed., *The Revival of Private Law in Central and Eastern Europe* (The Hague: Kluwer, 1996), vol. 46, Law in Eastern Europe Series, 431-497.

[15] Dmitrii Kozak was showing drafts of the laws on the judiciary to officials at the Council of Europe in Strasbourg as a means of illustrating to the Europeans Russia's serious commitment to legal reform and Russia's conformity with international human rights legislation. "Duma obidela sudei i banditov" (The Duma offended judges and criminals), *Izvestiia*, 9 February 2002, 2. By early 2002, the European Court of Human Rights in Strasbourg had already accepted two cases from Russia. Anna Zakatnova, "Pravosudie po-prezhnemu stoit dorogo" (Justice remains expensive), *Nezavisimaia gazeta*, 30 January 2002, 2.

[16] Putin claims that he "regularly" speaks with his classmates from law school who give him updates on development on the conditions in the courts, the Bar, and the Procuracy. Vystuplenie Prezidenta RF V. V. Putina na V Vserossiiskom s'ezde sudei (Speech of the President of the Russian Federation, V. V. Putin, at the V All-Russian Congress of Judges), 27 November 2000.

[17] Vystuplenie Prezidenta RF V. V. Putina s poslaniem Federal'nomu Sobraniiu Rossiiskoi Federatsii (The State of the Union Speech of the President of the Russian Federation to the Federal Assembly), 3 April 2000.

[18] Andrew Jack, "Russia: Intimidation and Corruption Persist," *Financial Times*, 9 April 2001.

[19] Vladimir Radchenko, the first deputy chair of the Supreme Court, observed that after the 1998 crisis, conditions deteriorated to the point that not only were there insufficient wage funds to hire desperately needed judges but the courts lacked money for stamps to send out essential correspondence. *Sudebnaia reforma v Rossii: predely i vozmozhnosti* (Judicial reform in Russia: limits and opportunities), vypusk 5, Tsikl publichnykh diskusii "Rossiia v global'nom kontekste" (Moscow: Nikitskii klub, 2001), 15. My thanks to Petr Barenboim for providing me with a copy of this exceptionally useful stenogram of a meeting of persons involved in legal reform, which was held at the Nikitskii Club on 26 April 2001.

[20] Natal'ia Melikova, "So stola Prem'era: $1000 na sud'iu k 2006 g." (From the desk of the Prime Minister: $1000 per judge in 2006), *Vedomosti*, 23 August 2001. Expenditures on the "judiciary" (*sudebnaia vlast'*) lines in the 2001 budget increased by fifty-nine percent over the previous year. Anna Zakatnova, "Reforma tret'ei vlasti oboidetsia nedeshevo" (Reform of the judicial branch won't be cheap) *Nezavisimaia gazeta*, 1 September 2001, 3. For the first examples of judges moving from squalid leased space to new, specially-designed facilities, see Aleksandr Ovechkin, "Sudebnaia

reforma: iz izbushki vo dvorets" (Judicial reform: from the hut to the palace), *Tiumenskie izvestiia*, 27 December 2001.

[21] The problem of recruiting able personnel is a serious problem facing all state legal institutions. In the MVD, for example, fifty-five percent of the criminal investigators have been on the job less than three years. The difficulty of attracting personnel has led to a lowering of education standards. If ninety percent of MVD investigators had a higher legal education in the late Soviet era, that number had fallen to forty-three percent by 2000. This decline in the quality of cadres in the criminal justice system makes even more important the heightening of judicial oversight of pretrial proceedings, discussed below. Reforma organov vnutrennykh del [Reform of the organs of Internal Affairs](Fond informatsionnoi podderzhki ekonomicheskoi reformy [hereafter FIPER], Moscow). http://www.fiper.ru/spr/2001/chapter-2-5.html.

[22] For a list of the many perquisites enjoyed by Procuracy officials, see articles 41, 44, and 45 of O vnesenii izmenenii i dopolnenii v Federal'nyi zakon 'O prokurature Rossiiskoi Federatsii' (On revisions and additions to the Federal Law 'On the Procuracy of the Russian Federation'), *Sobranie zakonodatel'stva* no. 7 (1999): st. 878. For the Constitutional Court, see Ob obespechenii deiatel'nosti Konstitutsionnogo Suda RF i o predostavlenii gosudarstvennykh sotsial'nykh garantii sud'iam Konstitutsionnogo Suda RF i chlenam ikh semei (On supporting the activities of the Constitutional Court of the Russian Federation and on granting state-sponsored social benefits to justices of the Constitutional Court and members of their families), *Sobranie zakonodatel'stva* no. 7 (2000): st. 795. To be sure, perquisites form an important part of the remuneration of government officials in most modern states, and even the classic Anglo-American *biudzhetniki*, the teachers, are having to rely on favors from the state, such as attractive mortgage rates, to make ends meet in areas as distinct as Southeast England and Central Florida.

[23] Filipp Sterkin, "Skol'ko stoit sudebnaia reforma, rasskazal Strana.Ru gendirektor Sudebnogo departamenta" (How much does judicial reform cost? The general director of the Court Department tells Strana.ru), *Strana.Ru*, 25 June 2001.

[24] *Sudebnaia reforma v Rossii: predely i vozmozhnosti* (Judicial reform in Russia: limits and opportunites), vypusk 5, Tsikl publichnykh diskusii "Rossiia v global'nom kontekste" (Moscow: Nikitskii klub, 2001), 37. Peter Solomon reports that "most court chairs sought and obtained supplementary funding from regional and local governments (sixty percent of those surveyed by Foglesong and me admitted this) and even from private sponsors (fifteen percent)." Peter H. Solomon, Jr., "Courts in Russia: Independence, Power, and Accountability," in Andras Sajo, ed., *Judicial Integrity* (Leiden and Boston: Martinus Nijhoff, 2004).

[25] Many in Russia and the West have criticized this paternalistic approach that, as Lawrence Lessig argues, "continues the communist practice of rewarding judges with perks allocated by state bureaucracies." Lawrence Lessig, "Redesigning the Russian Court: Introduction," *East European Constitutional Review* (Summer-Fall 1994): 73. But shifting to a cash-only payment system would be difficult to achieve quickly. Tamara Morshchakova, a former member of the Constitutional Court, believes that the financial vulnerabilities of judges continue to undermine judicial independence in Russia. See her "Printsip nezavisimosti i mekhanizma zavisimosti" (The principle of independence and mechanisms of dependency), *Gazeta.ru*, 31 March 2005.

[26] For a critique of the quality of judicial cadres, see Iurii Feofanov, "Zakon, sud, sud'ia" (Law, the court, the judge), *Izvestiia*, 12 April 2001, 4. As Wolf Heydebrand observed with regard to legal reform in Eastern Europe, "The reform and reconstruction of constitutions and positive laws, courts, and procedures . . . [do] not even begin to deal with the problems of continuity in office of judges and officials . . . let alone the persistence of legal judicial practices [and] patterns of decision-making." "The Dynamics of Legal Change in Eastern Europe," *Studies in Law and Society* 15 (1995): 291-292, as quoted in Pedro C. Magalhaes, "The Politics of Judicial Reform in Eastern Europe," *Comparative Politics* (October 1999): 45.

[27] Vystuplenie Prezidenta RF V. V. Putina na V Vserossiiskom s'ezde sudei (Speech of President of the Russian Federation V. V. Putin at the V All-Russian Congress of Judges), 27 November 2000. For the much softer tone Putin adopted in his meeting with the procurators several weeks later, see

Vystuplenie Prezidenta RF V. V. Putina na Vserossiiskom soveshchanii prokurorov (Speech of the President of the Russian Federation, V. V. Putin, at the All-Russian Assembly of Procurators), 11 January 2001. http://president.kremlin.ru/events/138.html.

[28] Iurii Feofanov, "Sudebnaia reforma na polovine puti" (Judicial reform at the halfway point), *Vremia MN*, 30 August 2001, 6. A newspaper in Sochi alleged that "in the South of Russia you can't buy a seat on the Bench for less than $50,000." Whatever the truth of the accusation, judges in that region brought a defamation case against the journal. Oleg Galitskikh, "Oskorblennaia Femida" (Themis Insulted), *Rossiiskaia gazeta*, 2 October 2002, 6.

[29] O vnesenii izmenenii i dopolnenii v Federal'nyi zakon 'O prokurature Rossiiskoi Federatsii' (On revisions and additions to the Federal Law 'On the Procuracy of the Russian Federation), *Sobranie zakonodatel'stva* no. 7 (1999): st. 878.

[30] Ob organakh sudeiskogo soobshchestva v Rossiiskoi Federatsii (On the organs of the judicial community in the Russian Federation), *Rossiiskaia gazeta*, 19 March 2002, 5. This law contains exhaustive detail on the formation and operation of the qualification commissions and on the congresses and councils of judges, which select them. Article 23 provides that decisions relating to judicial misconduct will be decided by an absolute majority of members present, except in cases where the judge's suspension or dismissal is at stake, when a two-thirds majority of those present is required.

[31] See Dmitrii Chernov, "Vremia politiki i ekonomiki. Komu na Rusi sudei sudit'" (The time of politics and economics. Who in Rus' will judge the judges), *Vremia MN*, 12 February 2002, 3.

[32] On the complex system of nominating and vetting judicial candidates, see Alexei Trochev, "Judicial Selection in Russia: Towards Accountability and Centralization," in Peter H. Russell and Kate Malleson, eds., *Appointing Judges in an Age of Judicial Power: Critical Perspectives from Around the World* (Toronto: University of Toronto Press, 2005).

[33] At present, such protests may be overridden by the qualification commissions. See "Khotite zaniat' dolzhnost' sud'i?" (Do you want to become a judge?), *Altaiskaia pravda*, 24 January 2002. For a detailed look at how judges are recruited to the Bench, see "Pravosudie stanovitsia dostupnym" (Justice is becoming accessible), *Altaiskaia pravda*, 7 November 2001. In providing shorter terms for court chairmen, new legislation was ostensibly designed to lessen the authority gap between the judiciary's leadership and its rank and file, but as Peter Solomon and others have noted, the reappointment of court chairmen makes them more vulnerable to the president, who is responsible for reappointments.

[34] For recent attempts to grant the president even more influence in judicial selection, see Peter H. Solomon, Jr., "Threats of Judicial Counterreform in Putin's Russia," in Kathryn Hendley, ed., *Remaking the Role of Law: Commercial Law in Russia and the CIS* (Juris Publishing, forthcoming).

[35] The legislation on the prosecution of judges represents a compromise. The original wording of the statute allowed judges to be brought to criminal responsibility on the basis of a procurator's complaint approved by three judges of a superior court. But the judges' resistance led to the inclusion of a further step in the process, the approval of the prosecution by a judicial qualification collegium. See Vladimir Nikolaev, "Zakon. 65 let vmesto pozhiznennogo" (The Law. 65 years old instead of life tenure), *Kommersant-Vlast'*, 22 January 2002, 18; Bulat Stoliarov, "Kozak skazal–Kozak sdelal" (Kozak said it—Kozak did it), *Vedomosti*, 23 November 2001.

[36] To the claims that administrative hearings will serve as another source of *kompromat* (compromising material) against judges, Kozak retorted that interested parties to cases already collect *kompromat* from diverse sources. Natal'ia Kozlova, "Dmitrii Kozak: Zakon dlia sudei. Sud'i dlia zakona" (Dmitrii Kozak: Law for the judges. Judges for the law), *Rossiiskaia gazeta*, 19 June 2001, 1. But surely the possibility of using of such *kompromat* at administrative hearings will make judges even more subject to influence from persons who seek to influence judicial decisions outside the courtroom. Vladimir Radchenko noted that "there have been well-known cases where the police have used the possibility of bringing judges to administrative responsibility to exert influence on them." *Sudebnaia reforma v Rossii: predely i vozmozhnosti* (Judicial reform in Russia: limits and opportunities), vypusk 5, Tsikl publichnykh diskusii "Rossiia v global'nom kontekste" (Moscow:

Nikitskii klub, 2001), 18. For other observers, the introduction of a disciplinary procedure is necessary to broaden the range of sanctions that can be leveled against wayward judges. The claim is that at present the qualification commissions tend to either dismiss the judge or the complaint. Ibid., 23, 27.

[37] Ibid., 72.

[38] Sergei Kashin, "Sud'i otsenivaiut idei administratsii Prezidenta" (Judges assess the ideas of the presidential administration), *Strana.Ru*, 30 January 2001. For Kozak's comments in support of removing judges when their relatives are under suspicion, see Sergei Anisimov, "Dmitrii Kozak: Opravdyvat'sia – znachit priznavat' sebia vinovatym" (Dmitrii Kozak: To be acquitted means to admit your guilt), *Obshchaia gazeta*, 2 August 2001, 4. Kozak's argument was that judges might be subject to blackmail from defendants or criminal investigators if their relatives were subject to criminal prosecution.

[39] In general, the commercial court judges were less openly critical of Putin's legal reform initiatives. For an explanation of the reasons for this tactic, see Aleksandr Privalov, "Raznoe. O sudebnoi reforme" (Various. On judicial reform), *Expert*, 19 November 2001, 12. For tensions between the Supreme Court and the Constitutional Court, see Alexei Trochev, "Implementing Russian Constitutional Court Decisions," *East European Constitutional Review* nos. 1-2 (2002): 99-100.

[40] Sidorenko's harshest criticism is reserved for the measures that would subject judges to administrative and disciplinary sanctions. Vladimir Tikhomirov, "Sud'i kritikuiut sudebnuiu reformu. Kozaka podozrevaiut v sozdanii sistemy politseiskogo gosudarstva" (Judges criticize judicial reform. They suspect Kozak of creating a police state), *Nezavisimaia gazeta*, 7 July 2001, 3. See also Anna Zakatnova, "Tret'ia vlast' nashla novogo soiuznika. Sud'i prodolzhaiut borot'sia s Kremlem za sokhranenie svoego statusa" (The judicial branch has found an ally. Judges continue to battle the Kremlin over a reduction in their status), *Nezavisimaia gazeta*, 11 July 2001, 3.

[41] Irina Dline and Olga Shwartz, "The Jury is Still Out on the Future of Jury Trials in Russia," *East European Constitutional Review* nos. 1-2 (2002): 106. The seminal work on early jury reform in Russia is Stephen C. Thaman, "The Resurrection of Trial by Jury in Russia," *Stanford International Law Review* no. 1 (1995): 61-274.

[42] There are also some who point to the Anglo-American world's disillusionment with the jury in recent years and whose subtext is often a profound suspicion of democratic institutions of all sorts. See, for example, the interview with Vladimir Zykov in "Nichemu ne prisiagaiushchie prisiazhnye" (Jurors taking an oath to nothing), *Rossiiskie vesti*, 5 September 2001, 10. Zykov claims that the first jury cases in Riazan region and Altai krai cost approximately one million rubles each (in mid-1990s rubles). One case in Krasnodar allegedly set the state budget back six million rubles. Ibid.

[43] Filipp Sterkin, "Marat Baglai: sudy, a ne prokuratura, iaviaiutsia glavnoi garantiei prav grazhdan" (Marat Baglai: the judge, and not the procurator, is the main guarantor of citizens' rights), *Strana.Ru*, 20 June 2001. An indication of the imbalance in power between the Procuracy and the courts is the practice of having representatives of the Bench occasionally attend meetings of the Procuracy's collegium. In a recent meeting of the Procuracy, the heads of the Constitutional Court and the Supreme Commercial Court were among the participants that discussed the legal policy laid out by the president. To my knowledge, representatives of the Procuracy's leadership are not present in meetings of the country's highest courts. Anna Zakatnova, "Ustinov stal glavnokomanduiushchim pravookhranitel'nykh organov. Prezident rasshiril polnomochiia Genprokuratury" (Ustinov became the commander in chief of law enforcement organs. The President expanded the powers of the Procuracy), *Nezavisimaia gazeta*, 12 February 2002, 1.

[44] For an analysis of the new Code of Criminal Procedure, see Peter Solomon, "The Criminal Procedure Code of 2001: Will it Make Russian Justice More Fair?" in William Pridemore, ed., *Ruling Russia: Crime, Law, and Justice in a Changing Society* (London: Rowan and Littlefield, 2005). The latest legislation on the jury may be found in O prisiazhnykh zasedateliakh federal'nykh sudov obshchei iurisdiktsii v Rossiiskoi Federatsii (On jurors in federal courts of general jurisdiction in the Russian Federation), *Sobranie zakonodatel'stva* no. 34 (2004): st. 3528.

[45] Liudmila Bel'diugina, "Gospodin sud'ia! Gospoda prisiazhnye!" (Your Honor! Members of the Jury!), *Rossiiskaia gazeta*, 28 August 2001, 2. The Procuracy appealed the verdict. One should note that a significant percentage of jury trial acquittals are reversed on appeal. "[I]n 1998 the Supreme Court reversed 36.9 percent of acquittals produced by jury trials." Dline and Shwartz, "The Jury is Still Out on the Future of Jury Trials in Russia," 108.

[46] "Ispoved' 'oblomka' sudebnoi reformy" (A confession of 'the wreckage' of judicial reform), *Rabochii put'*, 25 October 2002; Dline and Shwartz, "The Jury is Still Out on the Future of Jury Trials in Russia," 107. According to one source, the only acquittals in the Krasnodar Regional Court in the last three years have come in jury trials. Vladimir Zykov in "Nichemu ne prisiagaiushchie prisiazhnye" (Jurors taking an oath to nothing), *Rossiiskie vesti*, 5 September 2001, 10. Stanislaw Pomorski provides a first-hand account of the continuing strength of the no-acquittals policy in one Russian city in "In a Siberian Criminal Court," *East European Constitutional Review* nos. 1-2 (2002), 112.

[47] For an online version of the new Code of Criminal Procedure, see http://www.akdi.ru/gd/proekt/084513GD.SHTM.

[48] The most serious challenge to powerful state interests came in an acquittal in a case of treason. Ekaterina Butorina, "Ne delo prisiazhnykh. Vstupil v silu prigovor fiziku Danilovu" (Not a matter for the jury. The sentence of the physicist Danilov has gone into effect), *Vremia novostei*, 30 June 2005, 3. On this and related cases, see Peter H. Solomon, Jr., "Threats of Judicial Counterreform in Putin's Russia," in Hendley, ed.

[49] Nikolai Smirnov, "Sud'iam ne dali razgruzit'sia. Prokuratura podelitsia chast'iu polnomochii" (They didn't allow judges to unburden themselves. The Procuracy will share part of their responsibilities), *Nezavisimaia gazeta*, 21 June 2001, 3. Some reports put this workload even higher. See "Tselevaia programma sovershenstvovaniia sudebnoi sistemy RF potrebuet bolee 44 mlrd rublei" (The complex program for improving the judicial system of the Russian Federation will require more than 44 billion rubles), *Strana.ru*, 12 February 2002.

[50] *Sudebnaia reforma v Rossii: predely i vozmozhnosti* (Judicial reform in Russia: limits and opportunities), vypusk 5, Tsikl publichnykh diskusii "Rossiia v global'nom kontekste" (Moscow: Nikitskii klub, 2001), 48.

[51] Evgenii Mal'kov, "Priamaia rech'. Sudeiskoe soobshchestvo ne gotovo k peremenam" (Straight talk. The judicial community is not prepared for changes), *Novgorodskie vedomosti*, 12 February 2002.

[52] *Sudebnaia reforma v Rossii: predely i vozmozhnosti* (Judicial reform in Russia: limits and opportunities), vypusk 5, Tsikl publichnykh diskusii "Rossiia v global'nom kontekste" (Moscow: Nikitskii klub, 2001), 33.

[53] The chief bailiff of the Smolensk region, when asked about the share of men and women in his offices, noted that there was an obvious gender tracking, with women serving as court executors, which required "tedious, exacting, and assiduous" work, while men were in the security details for the court buildings. "Sudebnyi pristav – eto vlast'" (The court bailiff – that's power), *Rabochii put'* (Smolensk), 4 December 2001.

[54] It appears that these clerks will be more involved with administrative tasks than the legal research normally associated with their American counterparts. Previously, only higher court judges had the support of clerks.

[55] According to Putin, by the end of 2000, justices of the peace were working in only thirty-three of Russia's provinces and even there less than one-fifth of the planned number had been hired. Vystuplenie Prezidenta RF V. V. Putina na V Vserossiiskom s'ezde sudei (The speech of the President of the Russian Federation at the V All-Russian Congress of Judges), 27 November 2000.

[56] Pavel Dzygivskii, "Dmitrii Kozak: Administrativnaia iustitsiia prizvana zashchitit' cheloveka ot proizvola gosudarstva" (Dmitrii Kozak: administrative justice is asked to defend the individual from the tyranny of the state), *Strana.Ru*, 8 July 2001.

[57] V. Aleksandrov, "A sud'i-to mirovoi" (But it's a justice of the peace), *Sovetskii Sakhalin*, 23 January 2002.

[58] The contradiction is evident in *O povyshenii dolzhnostnykh okladov sudei RF i rabotnikov organov i uchrezhdenii prokuratury Rossiiskoi Federatsii* (On increasing the base salary of judges of the Russian Federation and Procuracy personnel), *Sobranie zakonodatel'stva* no. 48 (2000): st. 4664. Another institution certain to complicate relations between the center and periphery is the recently-established constitutional or charter court (*ustavnyi sud*), which has been established in each republic and region to interpret the laws of that province.

[59] Filipp Sterkin, "Marat Baglai: sudy, a ne prokuratura, iaviaiutsia glavnoi garantiei prav grazhdan" (Marat Baglai: the judge, and not the procurator, is the main guarantor of citizens' rights), *Strana.Ru*, 20 June 2001.

[60] *Sudebnaia reforma v Rossii: predely i vozmozhnosti* (Judicial reform in Russia: limites and opportunities), vypusk 5, Tsikl publichnykh diskusii "Rossiia v global'nom kontekste" (Moscow: Nikitskii klub, 2001), 36.

[61] The bailiffs fund themselves in part through a seven percent commission on all tax arrears collected. Petr Netreba, "Sudebnye pristavy perekhodiat na samofinansirovanie" (The court bailiffs are shifting to self-financing), *Kommersant Daily*, 16 February 2001, 2.

[62] The same Constitutional Court judge cited above complained that because the court bailiffs are part of the executive, and do not fall within judicial administration, "there's no way to check them." According to Kozak, attempts to subordinate the bailiffs to the Supreme Court were unworkable because they would also have served the commercial courts. Bailiffs are also not subject to minimum educational standards. Ibid., 36, 79.

[63] Evgenii Chubarov, "Glavnyi sudebnyi pristav otkryl kinofestival'" (The Chief Bailiff opened the film festival), *Izvestiia*, 25 April 2001, 1. Only twenty percent of bailiffs currently have a higher legal education. Sergei Kashin, "Arkadii Mel'nikov khochet naiti kak mozhno bol'she obrazovannykh pristavov" (Arkadii Mel'nikov wants to find as many educated bailiffs as possible), *Strana.ru*, 25 January 2002. This figure is not surprising in light of the fact that over a quarter are essentially security guards for judges and court buildings. Ibid.

[64] Elena Bekhchanova and Galina Liapunova, "Sudebnye pristavy ne dali strane rublia" (Bailiffs didn't give the country a ruble), *Kommersant Daily*, 12 January 2001, 2. For a detailed description of a bailiff corps in one region, Smolensk, see "Sudebnyi pristav – eto vlast'" (The bailiff – that's power), *Rabochii put'* (Smolensk), 4 December 2001.

[65] Bekhchanova and Liapunova, "Sudebnye pristavy ne dali strane rublia" (Bailiffs didn't give the country a ruble), 2. For the hazards of work as a bailiff, who can be caught between not just diverse business interests but also different courts, see Dmitrii Samartsev, "IuVZhD srazhaetsia s sudebnymi pristavimi" (The Southeastern Railway is battling with the bailiffs), *Strana.Ru*, 1 August 2001; and Nikolai Mikhailov, "Moskva i moskvichi. K chemu pristavlen sudebnyi pristav" (Moscow and Muscovites. Whom is the bailiff pitted against), *Trud*, 4 July 2001, 6.

[66] Peter L. Kahn, "The Russian Bailiffs Service and the Enforcement of Civil Judgments," *Post-Soviet Affairs* no. 2 (2002): 148-181. Kahn's article is at once an empirically rich investigation of the bailiff's corps and a compelling case study of how well-intentioned legislation is distorted during implementation.

[67] Viktoriia Sokolova, "Zdraviia zhelaiu. Miniust izmenit printsip konsensusa" (I wish you well. The Ministry of Justice changes the basis of consensus), *Izvestiia*, 25 January 2001, 4. For a revealing case of the pressures brought to bear on bailiffs by regional political elites, see Konstantin Chaplin, "Obladministratsiia–Voronin. Poka–nich'ia" (Regional administration vs. Voronin. So far a tie), *Bereg* (Voronezh), 16 November 2001.

[68] Al'mira Kozhakhmetova, "Liuboi pristav mozhet 'nazhat'' na chetvertuiu knopku" (Any bailiff can 'push' on the fourth button), *Novye Izvestiia*, 27 January 2001, 4. In contrast to NTV, which was part of the media empire of Vladimir Gusinsky, an enemy of the Kremlin, ORT, which had close ties to the presidential administration, received favorable treatment from the bailiffs' service in its attempts to fight off creditors. Kahn, "The Russian Bailiffs Service and the Enforcement of Civil Judgments," 176-179.

[69] Solomon, "Courts in Russia: Independence, Power, and Accountability." This is the best

general introduction to the issues surrounding the current judicial reform. See also Solomon's "Putin's Judicial Reform: Making Judges Accountable as well as Independent," *East European Constitutional Review* nos. 1-2 (2002): 117-124, and his "Judicial Power in Russia: Through the Prism of Administrative Justice," unpublished paper delivered at the 2002 Annual Meeting of the American Political Science Association, Boston, 29 August-1 September 2002. For an authoritative analysis of the state of the Russian judiciary and criminal justice at the end of the 1990s, see Peter H. Solomon, Jr. and Todd S. Foglesong, *Courts and Transition in Russia: The Challenge of Judicial Reform* (Boulder: Westview Press, 2000). See also the useful study by Pamela Jordan, "Russian Courts: Enforcing the Rule of Law?," in Valerie Sperling, *Building the Russian State* (Boulder: Westview Press, 2000), 193-212. On the question of constitutional interpretation, and the tensions between the Constitutional Court and the courts of general jurisdiction on this question, see Peter Krug, "The Russian Federation Supreme Court and Constitutional Practice in the Courts of General Jurisdiction: Recent Developments," *Review of Central and East European Law* no. 2 (2000): 129-146; Peter Maggs, "The Russian Courts and the Russian Constitution," *Indiana International and Comparative Law Review* no. 1 (1997): 99-117; and Tamara Morshchakova, "The Competence of the Constitutional Court in relation to that of other Courts of the Russian Federation," *Saint Louis University Law Journal* 42 (Summer 1998): 733-742.

[70] "Russian Supreme Court makes Cuts to List of Military Secrets," BBC Monitoring, Ren TV, Moscow, in Russian, 1500 GMT, 13 September 2001, as translated in Johnson's List, 14 September 2001.

[71] *Sudebnaia reforma v Rossii: predely i vozmozhnosti* (Judicial reform in Russia: limits and opportunities), vypusk 5, Tsikl publichnykh diskusii "Rossiia v global'nom kontekste" (Moscow: Nikitskii klub, 2001), 55. Among the many controversial court decisions on electoral issues was the ruling of the Republican Supreme Court of Sakha (Yakutia) allowing the sitting president to run for a third term, which went against a ruling of the Supreme Court of the Russian Federation. "TsIK RF gotovit obrashchenie v Genprokurataturu po povodu deistvii Verkhovnogo suda Iakutii" (The Central Election Committee of the Russian Federation has appealed to the Procurator General concerning the actions of the Supreme Court of Yakutia), *Iakutiia* (Iakutsk), 2 November 2001.

[72] "V ozhidanii sudodnia" (In the expectation of a judge's day), *Obshchaia gazeta*, 9 August 2001, 4.

[73] Though in fact Russian judges appear to deal with defendants with unusual harshness given the sentencing guidelines. See Iurii Feofanov, "Po vnutrennemu ubezhdeniiu" (According to internal conviction), *Izvestiia*, 25 August 2001, 4.

[74] Svetlana Smetanina, "Vladimir Ustinov: Reformatory perepisyvaiut zapadnye obraztsy i govoriat, chto eto novoe" (Vladimir Ustinov: reformists copy Western models and say that it's new), *Strana.Ru*, 25 April 2001. For an equally venomous defense of the Procuracy's powers, which combines Russian chauvinism with a disdain for the 1993 Constitution, see the interview with Ustinov's advisor, Vladimir Kolesnikov. Marianna Rozova, "Zabrat' funktsii u prokuratory – eto znachit ne meshat' grabit' stranu" (To take functions and the procuracy – that means not to interfere in the theft of the country), *Strana.Ru*, 16 February 2001. A deputy Procurator General, Badir Kekhlerov, argued that the Procuracy's unique position was justified because "our people's mentality is different . . . our perception of justice is different . . . the respect of the law is not the same [as in the West]. Why shouldn't we demand that these standards should first be attained and only then introduce the rest [judicial reform]." Sophie Lambroschini, "Russia: Judiciary Reform Meets with Resistance-I," RFE/RL, 24 April 2001, as printed in Johnson's List, 25 April 2001. For an excellent introduction to the Procuracy, see Prokuratura (FIPER, Moscow). http://www.fiper.ru/spr/2001/chapter-2-3.html. The powers of the Procuracy are in fact far more extensive than this brief account suggests. Not only do they retain the right to exercise "general supervision" of legality, but they have become active litigants in civil cases, often on the side of commercial plaintiffs. Stimulating that activity is a 26 January 2000 directive that orders ten percent of any judgment supported by the Procuracy to be deposited in the Fund for the Development of the Procuracy. Irina Granik, "Zakonodatel'naia vlast' vzialas' za sudebnuiu" (The legislative branch engages with the judicial

branch), *Kommersant-Daily*, 23 June 2001, 2.

[75] This speech also contained a remarkable set of personal attacks on the heads of other legal agencies, many of whom were in attendance. "Vladimir Ustinov: Prokuratura, k kotoroi vse privykli, uzhe ne budet" (Vladimir Ustinov: A Procuracy that everyone has gotten used to won't exist any longer), *Strana.ru*, 11 February 2002. Despite its venom, the speech recognized that law reform was a fait accompli, and that the Procuracy would have to make certain concessions. The loss of authority in certain areas was at least partially compensated for by Putin's designation of the Procurator-General as the lead figure among Russian legal officials. According to Ustinov, "the primary strategic task of the Procuracy is now the supervision of the entire law enforcement system [pervoocherednaia strategicheskaia zadacha prokuratury teper'–nadzor za vsei pravookhranitel'noi sistemoi]." Anna Zakatnova, "Ustinov stal glavnokomanduiushchim pravookhranitel'nykh organov. Prezident rasshiril polnomochiia Genprokuratury" (Ustinov became the commander in chief of law enforcement organs. The President expanded the powers of the Procuracy) *Nezavisimaia gazeta*, 12 February 2002, 1. See also, Grigorii Punanov, "Iavka obiazatel'na. Parol' – General'naia prokuratura" (Attendance is mandatory. Password – Procurator General), *Izvestiia*, 12 February 2002, 1.

[76] Filipp Sterkin, "Marat Baglai: sudy, a ne prokuratura, iaviaiutsia glavnoi garantiei prav grazhdan" (Marat Baglai: the judge, and not the procurator, is the main guarantor of citizens' rights), *Strana.Ru*, 20 June 2001.

[77] Dmitry Pinsker, "Case for Legal Reform Looks Far from Watertight," *The Russia Journal*, 13-19 July 2001. For a forceful critique of the draft Code, see Igor Petrukhin, "Novyi UPK: Duma vozrozhdaet atributy inkvizitsii" (The New Code of Criminal Procedure: The Duma is reviving features of the inquisition), *Nezavisimaia gazeta*, 16 August 2001, 3.

[78] Ibid. Sergei Pashin, "The Vertical Takeoff of Reforms," *Moscow Times*, 2 July 2001. According to one source, under the new rules the courts only rarely deny procurators' requests for an arrest warrant, accepting their argument that almost all suspects are flight risks. "Sud'ia dopustila pobeg. I otpravila pod arest liudei, opravdannykh prisiazhnymi" (The judge allowed a victory. And placed under arrest persons acquitted by jurors), *Novaia gazeta*, 4 August 2005.

[79] Iurii Feofanov, "Po vnutrennemu ubezhdeniiu" (According to internal conviction), *Izvestiia*, 25 August 2001, 4.

[80] Leonid Nikitinskii, "Sud ogranichivaet vlast'" (The court limits political power), *Vremia MN*, 26 June 2001, 1.

[81] One Duma deputy claimed that ninety-eight percent of the judges had backgrounds in the law enforcement organs, though this figure is almost certainly high. Evgenii Mal'kov, "Priamaia rech'. Sudeiskoe soobshchestvo ne gotovo k peremenam" (Straight talk. The judicial community is not prepared for changes), *Novgorodskie vedomosti*, 12 February 2002. Peter Solomon believes that only "a substantial minority of judges, including new ones, worked previously in the procuracy and police." See Solomon, "Courts in Russia: Independence, Power, and Accountability," unpublished paper delivered at the 9th Annual Conference on the Individual vs. the State, Central European University, Budapest, 4-5 May 2001, 17.

[82] Irina Dline and Olga Shwartz note that, even now, "[t]he legal provision that requires mandatory exclusion of inadmissible evidence in any trial is, in reality, practiced only in jury trials. In traditional trials, judges routinely overlook 'minor' procedural violations and such supposedly insignificant formalities as missing signatures and dates. In jury trials, inadmissible evidence is mercilessly excluded, ruining a prosecution's case." "The Jury is Still Out on the Future of Jury Trials in Russia," 108.

[83] If implemented, such a reform will occasion requests by the Procuracy to expand its numbers to meet the heightened demand for prosecutors. For just such a request by a regional procurator in Cheliabinsk, see "Ia chasto govoriu 'net'" (I often say 'no'), *Cheliabinskii rabochii*, 12 January 2001. But the institution's critics will object that Procuracy is already one and a half times its size in the Soviet era, with 50,000 personnel as opposed to 34,000 as decade earlier, even though it serves a population that is half that of the USSR. Prokuratura (FIPER), http://www.fiper.ru/spr/2001/chapter-2-3.html. Moreover, it now performs inspections that many regard as unnecessary or

redundant, and with the Procuracy's oversight of the pretrial stage scheduled to disappear in two years, it should soon have plenty of personnel reserves.

[84] See for example, Valerii Abramkin, "Prezident dolzhen protivostoiat' davlenii kazennykh struktur" (The President should resist pressure from bureaucratic structures), *Strana.ru*, 15 February 2002. That the implementation of the Criminal Procedure Code is likely to be slow and distorted is indicated by the fact that six months after the law's adoption, most criminal investigators, prosecutors, and judges did not yet have a copy. Aleksandr Novikov, "Sudebnuiu reformu tormozit Miniust. Novyi UPK, okazyvaetsia, eshche nikto ne chital" (The Ministry of Justice is slowing down judicial reform. It seems no one has read the new Criminal Procedure Code yet), *Nezavisimaia gazeta*, 23 July 2002, 2.

[85] These figures come from Pamela Jordan, "The Russian Advokatura (Bar) and the State in the 1990s," *Europe-Asia Studies* no. 5 (1998): 765-791, who has written the best introduction in English to the contemporary Bar, *Defending Rights in Russia: Lawyers, the State, and Legal Reform in the Post-Soviet Era* (Vancouver: University of British Columbia Press, 2005).

[86] A vital area of legal reform that lies beyond the scope of this paper is the commercial courts. For excellent discussions of developments in the area of economic dispute resolution through the end of the 1990s, see Kathryn Hendley, Peter Murrell, and Randi Ryterman, "Law, Relationships and Private Enforcement: Transactional Strategies of Russian Enterprises," *Europe-Asia Studies* no. 4 (2000): 627-656; Hendley, "Remaking an Institution: The Transition in Russia from State Arbitrazh to Arbitrazh Courts," *American Journal of Comparative Law* (Winter 1998): 93-127; and Hendley, "Temporal and Regional Patterns of Commercial Litigation in Post-Soviet Russia," *Post-Soviet Geography and Economics* no. 7 (1998): 379-396. New legislation is reshaping the organization and jurisdiction of the commercial courts, granting them new institutions at the federal district [*federal'nyi okrug*] and interdistrict level and granting them wider authority over cases previously heard by the courts of general jurisdiction. See the draft law now before parliament, O federal'nykh administrativnykh sudakh v Rossiiskoi Federatsii (On federal administrative courts in the Russian Federation), at http://www.akdi.ru/gd/proekt/084950GD.SHTM.

[87] According to Jordan, members of the traditional colleges "handle over 90 percent of criminal cases but only 2.5 percent of civil cases." Jordan, "The Russian Advokatura (Bar) and the State in the 1990s," 765-791.

[88] Ibid.

[89] Iurii Feofanov, "Debaty vokrug UPK v Dume i na publike" (Debates concerning the Criminal Procedure Code in the Duma and in the public), *Vremia MN*, 27 June 2001, 6.

[90] The Bar was already feeling increasing pressure from the Ministry of Justice, which had been effectively removed as a supervisory organ over the Bar at the beginning of the 1990s, but by the end of the decade was seeking to reprise its role as the institutional monitor of the Bar. New legislation allows the Ministry's local justice departments to maintain the register of practicing advocates and to call for a special meeting of the advocates' chamber. See Prikaz Ministerstva iustitsii RF 29 iiulia 2002g N 211 g. Moskva, Ob utverzhdenii Poriadka vedeniia reestra advokatov sub'ektov RF (Order of the Ministry of Justice of the Russian Federation of 29 July 2002, no. 211, City of Moscow, On the confirmation of the rules on the registration of advocates of the territories of the Russian Federation), *Rossiiskaia gazeta*, 15 August 2002, 6, and Ob advokatskoi deiatel'nosti i advokature v Rossiiskoi Federatsii (On advocate's practice and the Bar in the Russian Federation), *Rossiiskaia gazeta*, 5 June 2002, 11. For a critique of the Ministry's interventionist approach to the Bar, see Mariia Viktorova, "'Augustovskii putch' v kollegii advokatov" (The August coup in the colleges of advocates), *Rossiiskaia gazeta*, 3 August 2001, 12.

[91] In a typical complaint against the parallel colleges, the prominent Moscow attorney Genri Reznik alleged that "more and more advocates' associations were becoming a collection point (*otstoinik*) for the worst personnel from the police, the Procuracy, and other organs that only had a foggy understanding of advocates' work." Leonid Berres, "Sud'iam ustanovili srok" (They established a term for judges), *Kommersant-Daily*, 29 June 2001, 3.

[92] Leonid Berres, "Advokaty zakhvatili vlast'" (The advocates seized power), *Kommersant-Daily*,

7 August 2001, 7; Dar'ia Guseva, "'Pokazatel'naia' ssora" (An exemplary quarrel), *Vremia MN*, *11 August 2001*, 2. For a criticism of the "self-serving" leadership of the traditional colleges, see Sergei Zapol'skii, "Advokaty: zakon dlia generalov" (Advocates: a law for generals), *Vedomosti*, 21 June 2002. The Bar's internal disputes also contributed to the adoption of legislation that eroded more of the Bar's autonomy than that of the courts. Whereas the judicial qualification commissions do not allow advocates to be members, two members of the thirteen-person advocates' qualification commission are drawn from the Bench. Moreover, the commission includes two persons selected by the local justice department, the bete noire of the Bar. See Article 33 of the *zakon ob advokatskoi deiatel'nosti* (law on advocate's practice). Some advocates fear that this composition of qualification commissions will result in political litmus tests for admittance to the Bar in some regions. See "Iurii Mashkin: my ne dolzhny toptat'sia na meste" (Iurii Mashkin: we mustn't march in place), *Vostochno-sibirskaia pravda* (Irkutsk), 7 September 2002.

[93] Ob advokatskoi deiatel'nosti i advokature v Rossiiskoi Federatsii (On advocate's practice and the Bar of the Russian Federation), *Rossiiskaia gazeta*, 5 June 2002, 11.

[94] On the forming of a new Bar under Putin, see Eugene Huskey, "The Bar's Triumph or Shame? The Formation of Chambers of Advocates in Putin's Russia," in Ferdinand Feldbrugge and Robert Sharlet, eds., *Public Policy and Law in Russia: In Search of a Unified Legal and Political Space* (Leiden: Martinus Nijhoff, 2005), 149-167.

[95] Alla Malakhova, "Advokaty zhdut prigovora. Ot gosudarstva" (Advocates await a verdict. From the state), *Novye izvestiia*, 23 August 2001, 4.

[96] On lawyers' relations with the state in late Imperial and early Soviet history, see Eugene Huskey, *Russian Lawyers and the Soviet State: The Origins and Development of the Soviet Bar* (Princeton: Princeton University Press, 1986).

[97] A 1997 law had increased the percentage of advocates' salaries subject to deductions for the state pension fund from five percent to twenty-eight percent, though a Constitutional Court decision a year later held the law to be unconstitutional because the law did not consider the advocates' public service as a provider of legal aid to the population. Jordan, "The Russian Advokatura (Bar) and the State in the 1990s," 765-791. Jordan also discusses the attempts by the state to re-establish licensing of advocates as a means of monitoring the profession.

[98] "Predlozhenie uchastnikov 'kruglogo stola'," Predlozhenie k zakonoproektu "Ob advokature v Rossiiskoi Federatsii" (The proposal of participants of the round table [suggestion for the draft law 'On the Bar of the Russian Federation']) (Gosudarstvennaia Duma, 2001).

[99] *Sudebnaia reforma v Rossii: predely i vozmozhnosti* (Judicial reform in Russia: limits and opportunities), vypusk 5, Tsikl publichnykh diskusii "Rossiia v global'nom kontekste" (Moscow: Nikitskii klub, 2001), 79, 52.

[100] On these categories, see Eugene Huskey, "A Framework for the Analysis of Soviet Law," *Russian Review* no. 1 (1991): 53-70.

[101] *Sudebnaia reforma v Rossii: predely i vozmozhnosti* (Judicial reform in Russia: limits and opportunities), vypusk 5, Tsikl publichnykh diskusii "Rossiia v global'nom kontekste" (Moscow: Nikitskii klub, 2001), 11.

[102] Viktor Semin, "Dve pravdy odnoi reformy" (Two truths of a single reform), *Obshchaia gazeta*, 2 August 2001, 4.

[103] Kathryn Hendley, "Legal Development in Post-Soviet Russia," *Post-Soviet Affairs* no. 3 (1997): 237. Regarding what many have argued is a low "demand for law" in Russia, Pistor notes that "[l]aw simply may not be in great demand because it imposes unwanted constraints during the 'great snatch.' The weakest are least able to voice their demand for law in such a situation." Katharina Pistor, "Supply and Demand for Law in Russia," *East European Constitutional Review* (Fall 1999): 107.

[104] Hendley, "Legal Development in Post-Soviet Russia," 243. The findings of Timothy Frye are somewhat less pessimistic than those of Hendley. Surveying 500 firms on their attitudes to the courts, Frye found that, at least with regard to the commercial courts, businessmen and women had reasonably favorable views of their work. Attitudes to the courts of general jurisdiction and the court

bailiffs were less positive. Timothy Frye, "The Two Faces of Russian Courts: Evidence from a Survey of Company Managers," *East European Constitutional Review* nos. 1-2 (2002): 125-129.

[105] In his thoughtful essay, Holmes admits that this lack of a base "is the deep and massive problem with which foreign-funded legal-development projects must grapple." Stephen Holmes, "Can Foreign Aid Promote the Rule of Law?," *East European Constitutional Review* (Fall 1999): 70.

[106] Stephen Holmes, "Simulations of Power in Putin's Russia," *Current History* (October 2001), as printed in Johnson's List, 11 October 2001.

[107] For a penetrating assessment of attempts to undermine the law reform movement in Putin's second term, see Peter H. Solomon, Jr., "Threats of Judicial Counterreform in Putin's Russia."

[108] According to the chairman of the Constitutional Court, Putin meets approximately every quarter with the heads of the country's highest courts, though he insists Putin does not interfere in their work. Filipp Sterkin, "Marat Baglai: sudy, a ne prokuratura, iaviaiutsia glavnoi garantiei prav grazhdan" (Marat Baglai: the judge, and not the procurator, is the main guarantor of citizens' rights), *Strana.Ru*, 20 June 2001.

SOCIAL PARTNERSHIP, CIVIL SOCIETY, AND THE STATE IN RUSSIA
SIMON CLARKE

Abstract

In this chapter I consider the role of the traditional trade unions (organized in the Federation of Independent Trade Unions of Russia – FNPR) in the constitution and reconstitution of structures of state power in Russia as well as in the consolidation of democratic institutions.

Soviet trade unions were an integral part of the party-state apparatus. Their functions were primarily state functions, in the formulation and administration of state social and welfare policies and in monitoring the performance of enterprise management in relation to the policies of the party-state. The collapse of the party-state threatened the very survival of the trade unions by removing their primary functions from them and by removing the principal support for their authority.

The strategy adopted by the trade unions as the party-state disintegrated was a strategy of "social partnership." Social partnership was in principle tripartite, but the system of social partnership was constructed at a time at which the state was still the dominant employer. In practice social partnership was initially bipartite, involving negotiation between trade unions and state bodies as well as the collaboration of the trade unions with state structures, with only the symbolic participation of employers, at branch, regional, and federal levels, and negotiation between trade unions and employers at the level of the enterprise.

For the trade unions, the strategy of social partnership provides a means of retaining or reconstituting their traditional functions on a new foundation, with political and legal guarantees replacing their former endorsement by the party. During 1991-93, the trade unions oscillated between confrontation and conciliation with the government, but following Yeltsin's confrontation with parliament in September 1993, the trade unions have taken a consistently conciliatory position, with their regular days of action playing a purely symbolic role.

For federal, branch, and regional state structures, the continued performance by the trade unions of their traditional functions facilitated the maintenance of a degree of continuity in the administration of state power, in the absence of alternative state structures able to perform the functions which had traditionally fallen to the trade unions. Although their social insurance and health and safety functions were formally taken away from the trade unions in 1994, the new state bodies could not perform those functions without relying on the army of voluntary trade union officials who administered the distribution of social insurance funds and monitored adherence to labor and health and safety legislation. Similarly, the regional administration was able to use the trade unions for the implementation and administration of large parts of its social and welfare policies and to draw on the support of the trade unions in lobbying the federal government as well as to legitimize its claims to represent the interests of the population of the region. Branch structures were similarly able to use the support of the trade unions for lobbying their branch interests against or within the government.

The system of social partnership has provided an important element of the retention and reconstitution of traditional structures of political power at federal, branch, and regional levels. The system also has allowed the trade unions to retain or reconstitute their own traditional state functions and their traditional identification with the authorities at all levels. While this might have proved functional for the trade union apparatus and for state structures, it has produced very few benefits for ordinary trade union members. The trade unions have had very little influence on falling living standards, widespread redundancies, and the pervasive violation of labor and health and safety legislation. It should not be surprising that most trade union members do not regard the trade union as a membership organization, reflecting the collective strength of its members, but as just one of the less significant power structures to which they are subordinate and to which they can, on occasion, appeal for assistance.

The participation of the trade unions in the system of social partnership has also played a major role in the consolidation of democratic institutions in Russia, which is a necessary, if far from sufficient, condition for the constitution of a democratic political system. The trade unions have remained the only mass membership civil society organization in post-Soviet Russia, still representing the majority of employees and almost a third of the adult population. Although the trade unions have only a limited mobilizational capacity, they have the membership and the financial and organizational resources to constitute a powerful opposition force. Yeltsin's primary objective throughout his period of office was to ensure that these resources could not be deployed by the radical opposition. From 1991-93 the presidential administration repeatedly let it be known that the trade unions retained their property and privileges on sufferance. Following Yeltsin's confrontation with parliament in 1993, the unions were progressively incorporated into bureaucratic structures of social partnership and focused their efforts on peaceful lobbying of the government and the Duma, distancing themselves from the radical opposition and declaring their unequivocal commitment to the constitution and the rule of law. This commitment has been a very important element in the stabilization of the democratic constitutional order and the trade unions have provided powerful support for the attempt to establish a legal state.

In 2001, the FNPR leadership came under attack from the left and the right in the run-up to its fourth Congress in November. On the one hand, the Communist Party, having lost its parliamentary leverage, launched a campaign to win the presidency of FNPR with a view to mobilizing FNPR as an extra-parliamentary oppositional force. On the other hand, the presidential administration maneuvered to secure the election of a more congenial leader of FNPR, in conformity with the KGB conception of social order, in which the tentacles of the state should extend into every institution of civil society. In the event, the latter initiative was thwarted and the presidential administration withdrew from the fray, leaving the incumbent, Mikhail Shmakov, to trounce the Communist candidate, Anatolii Chekis, in the presidential election. Nevertheless, Chekis's derisory vote by no means reflected the degree of dissatisfaction in the ranks of FNPR with the conciliatory approach of the leadership, nor did the withdrawal of the presidential administration from the contest reflect a loss of interest in domesticating the trade unions.

Having been a powerful force for democratization through the 1990s, under Putin's presidency FNPR succumbed to the pressures to play its assigned role in the president's "managed democracy" as a subordinate part of the state apparatus. Whether FNPR can find ways more forcefully and effectively to represent its members in the future remains to be seen.

* * *

Although the traditional trade unions have seen a substantial decline in membership since the collapse of the Soviet system, they remain by far and away the largest non-governmental organizations in contemporary Russia, claiming almost thirty-two million members at the beginning of 2004 (Table 1), almost half the employed population, and almost a third of the entire adult population, a figure roughly supported by survey data.[1] Of course, the vast majority of trade union members do not participate actively in their trade union organizations, and public confidence in the trade unions is low and has been declining, although it is higher than public confidence in political parties. Nevertheless, the trade unions constitute one of the most important institutions mediating the relation between the state and civil society.[2]

Table 1: Membership of FNPR Trade Unions

Source: FNPR Reports

Date	Membership	Density
I Congress: September 1990	54 million	70%
II Congress: October 1993	60 million	86%
III Congress: December 1996	45 million	69%
June 1999	37 million	58%
November 1999	34,637,700	54%
IV Congress: November 2001	>38 million	52%
January 2004	31.8 million	48%

The Russian trade unions have constituted their relations with the state within the framework of the ideology of "social partnership." In this paper I want to look behind the rhetoric to ask what is the significance of social partnership for the construction of relations between the state and civil society. In particular, to what extent does social partnership introduce an element of public accountability into a political process which is notoriously unresponsive to the direct electoral expression of the public will? The central argument of the paper is that, far from introducing such public accountability, social partnership in Russia has provided a framework for the corporatist reconstitution of Soviet political structures and practices at federal, branch, and regional levels.

Russian Trade Unions: From Transmission Belts to Independent Social Actors

Soviet trade unions, as the "transmission belts" between the party and the masses were deeply embedded in the structures of the party-state. The organizational structure of the trade unions mirrored that of the party-state, the majority of their functions were party-state functions, and their authority derived from the party-state. As an integral part of the ruling apparatus, performing a variety of party-state functions, the position of the trade unions was undermined by the processes of *perestroika* and *glasnost* and their very existence was threatened by the collapse of the Soviet system.

A number of factors seriously weakened the trade unions in the period of *perestroika*. First, the trade unions were by-passed by Gorbachev's thwarted attempts to introduce industrial democracy to the Soviet workplace, which in 1987 established the Labor Collective Council (STK) rather than the trade union as the representative body of the labor force in its interaction with management. Second, at the nineteenth Party Conference in June 1988 Gorbachev proclaimed a clear division of labor between the party, soviets, and executive bodies, with the party assuming its role as political vanguard with priority being given to ideological work. This removal of the party from interference in economic life threatened to remove the most important prop supporting the authority of the trade unions. Third, the botched wage reforms introduced by Gorbachev, followed by the growing dislocation of the economy, provoked increasing unrest among workers and sporadic strikes from 1987, culminating in the great strike wave of July 1989 which swept across the coal-mining regions and in which the trade unions notoriously sat at the negotiating table alongside party and government representatives, opposing their own members.

The trade unions were not immune from the economic and political reforms introduced by Gorbachev, but in the growing conflicts within the leadership over the course of reform they generally aligned themselves with the conservative opposition. The Soviet All-Union Central Council of Trade Unions (VTsSPS) asserted its "independence" from the party and state as early as 1987, distancing itself from the project of *perestroika* and government plans to introduce market reforms, insisting on very substantial social guarantees, high levels of unemployment pay, etc., as preconditions for any agreement to new legislation. This rearguard action was extremely ineffective, and simply meant that the unions lost what little impact on policy they had once enjoyed.

VTsSPS came under growing pressure to decentralize and democratize its structure in response to the changes of *perestroika* and *glasnost*. The second half of the 1980s saw a steady increase in the role of collective agreements, which required that more initiative and responsibility be shown by trade union primary groups. The urgency of encouraging more grass roots initiative in the trade unions was increased by the challenge posed to their authority by the new Labor Collective Councils and by the growing unrest among workers which was expressed outside trade union channels. The second and third Plenums of VTsSPS in December 1987 and August 1988 recommended the democratization of trade union primary groups and removed many of the regulations which limited their independence and initiative. In September 1989, following the miners' strikes in the summer, the Plenum decided to grant much greater independence to primary groups, endorsed the principle of delegation as the basis for the election of higher trade union bodies, and increased the accountability of the apparatus to elected bodies. The Plenum also adopted a new statement defining the tasks of the trade unions which put their role of social protection unambiguously in first place, emphasizing this by freeing trade union committees from their responsibility to participate directly in economic management. However, even the unions' official history acknowledges that changes on the ground were few and far between as officials continued in their habitual ways.[3]

These structural reforms culminated in the replacement of VTsSPS by a new General Confederation of Trades Unions (VKP) in October 1990, which was formed as a federation of independent trade unions in which the branch and republican union organizations had a greater degree of autonomy. The formation of VKP marked the formal separation of the trade unions from party and state bodies, a separation which was confirmed by the USSR Law on Trade Unions of 10 December 1990. VKP declared that the unions should be the government's "constructive opponents," opposing the government's plans for privatization. At the same time, it was decided to establish a Republican trade union organization in Russia, the only Union Republic which had hitherto not had its own organization.

The Federation of Independent Trade Unions of Russia (FNPR) was established in 1990 as a voluntary association of trade unions "independent of state and economic bodies, political and social organizations, not accountable to them and not under their control." Igor Klochkov, a Deputy President and formerly Secretary of VTsSPS, was elected President of FNPR.

The declaration of independence by the Russian trade unions was an acknowledgement that the principal prop of their authority had been removed, while the devolution of power to their workplace organizations was a reflection of the fact that the terms and conditions of labor were now to be determined at the workplace rather than being imposed from the center. However, if the trade unions were to establish a new basis for their authority and give substance to their independence it was essential that primary trade union organizations should become the independent representatives of the labor force in their negotiations with management.

In the workplace the Soviet trade unions had served as the eyes and ears of the party, monitoring the implementation of the party's economic and social policies at the point of production. Although the trade union was supposed to provide an independent check on management, in practice the trade union was the subordinate member of the troika of director, party secretary, and trade union president. The formal tasks of the trade union were to encourage the maintenance of labor discipline and the growth of productivity, organizing socialist competition, rationalization and innovation, unpaid overtime and Saturday working, and distributing honors and awards, but in practice the bulk of the trade union's work involved the administration of the social and welfare infrastructure of the workplace and providing material assistance to trade union members. As far as most trade union members were concerned, the production functions of the trade union were risible formalities that had to be undergone and the trade union was rightly regarded as a branch of the enterprise administration. Even in its social and welfare functions the trade union rarely got any credit for its beneficence. Since the main role of the trade union was to allocate resources in short supply, it bore the brunt of complaints about the inadequacy of both the quantity and quality of provision and was always suspected of privileging managers and its own officers in allocation. The close identification of the trade union with management in the workplace meant that it was ill-prepared to take up a new role as representative of the employees in the conditions of a market economy.

Although the "administrative-command" system was rapidly displaced by a market economy, so that enterprises and organizations had, at least in principle, to confine their costs within the limits of their revenues rather than delivering planned output targets at any price, the internal structure of the post-Soviet enterprise changed little, so that within the enterprise the trade union remained, as it always had been, primarily the social and welfare department of an authoritarian-paternalist enterprise administration, distributing the shrinking supply of social and welfare benefits among the workers. The primary organizations of the trade unions expressed the dependence of the employees on their employers and so were in no position to articulate any conflict that could be expected to arise as employers chose or were forced by market pressures to cut costs by intensifying labor, cutting wages, and reducing employment. As in 1989, so through the 1990s, conflict in the workplace tended to arise spontaneously and was often directed as much against the trade union as against management, workers often turning to the new alternative trade unions for support. Only when such conflict could be turned to the advantage of the director by exerting pressure on higher authorities to provide resources, as in the budget sector or the subsidized coal-mining industry, did the trade unions actively organize their members to press their demands, reproducing the traditional soviet pattern of lobbying in which the trade union president would accompany the enterprise director to Moscow or to the regional party apparatus to plead for resources.

In the absence of significant pressure for a "renewal from below," the process of change in the Russian trade union movement was orchestrated primarily from above. Without a foundation in independent workplace organization, the trade union leadership could not transform the trade unions overnight into representative bodies articulating the collective strength of organized labor. The priority of the trade union apparatus, which had been completely dominant over elected trade union bodies in the Soviet period, was to preserve the trade unions as institutions by preserving, as far as possible, their existing functions and this could only be achieved by restoring their former relationship with the state. This aspiration was expressed in the trade unions' commitment to the principles of social partnership, which they saw as providing the institutional framework that would underpin their new role.

"Social Partnership," Post-Soviet Style

The commitment to social partnership as the framework for the activity of the Russian trade unions was established at their inception. The 1990 Founding Congress of FNPR adopted a resolution defining the basic tactics of the trade unions as involving the negotiation of general, tariff, and collective agreements, to be backed up by demonstrations, meetings, strikes, May Day celebrations, and spring and autumn days of united action in support of the unions' demands in negotiations as well as to enforce the subsequent fulfillment of the agreements. With a changing balance between confrontation and collaboration, this has been the basis of trade union strategy ever since the signing of the first agreement with the Russian government in February and the first trade union "day of unity" in March 1991. Social partnership with government and employers promised to provide the trade unions with a new prop, enabling them to retain or reconstitute their traditional functions on a new foundation, the state and the law replacing the party as the guarantor of their authority.

For the post-Soviet trade unions, social partnership built on the traditional bureaucratic structures of participation of trade unions in management: the collective agreement at the level of the enterprise; collaboration of branch trade unions with the structures of economic management in relation to such issues as "socialist competition," "rationalization and innovation," norm setting, wage and bonus scales, health and safety, certification, training and retraining, and the recruitment and retention of labor; and the collaboration of regional trade union organizations with regional government in considering issues of economic, housing, social and welfare policy. In the past, the participation of trade unions in these structures had been guaranteed by party control. Following the removal of the party from its economic management role under Gorbachev and the destruction of the party-state by Yeltsin, tripartite institutions of social partnership promised to preserve the trade unions' functions by substituting legal and political guarantees for party control.

The interest of the trade unions in the formation of such tripartite structures to replace the old apparatus of party-state control was shared by parts of the state bureaucracy. In branches of the economy which remained state-controlled, such as health and education, or state-managed (and subsidized), such as coal-mining, the support of the branch trade union could provide additional leverage for the relevant ministries in lobbying for funds within government. Even in privatized branches, tripartism could give a *raison d'être* for the residues of the old ministerial apparatuses, which otherwise risked losing their role (and jobs) in the transition to a market economy.

Tripartism was also attractive to regional and federal government, which had an interest in establishing a framework within which they could integrate the trade unions into democratic institutions in order to maintain social peace. Despite the weakness of the trade unions, their mass membership and organizational and financial resources meant that they were the organizations best equipped to mobilize popular opposition to the government. Tripartism had an ideological as much as a political significance. The weakness of the party system and the dominance of the executive over the legislative branches of government at federal and regional levels meant that the executive appealed over the head of the legislature to base its legitimacy on claims to represent the interests of the population as a whole, on behalf of which the trade unions also claimed to speak. Ideologically, particularly at the regional level, the participation of the trade unions in the framework of social partnership supported the claim of the executive to serve the interests of the people.

As corporatization and privatization advanced rapidly, employers had a more equivocal relation to tripartite structures. To the extent that tripartite bodies might provide employers with a corporatist structure through which to press their individual or branch interests on government with trade union support, mimicking the traditional forms of lobbying through ministerial structures, such bodies could serve a useful function. On the other hand, to the extent that such bodies might take binding decisions regarding the terms and conditions of employment, the employers had a much more qualified interest in participating in tripartite structures. Similarly, at the level of the enterprise the employers had an interest in the trade union continuing to perform its traditional role of encouraging workers to achieve production plans, managing the social and welfare apparatus of the enterprise, and supporting management in its lobbying with higher authorities (particularly in relation to lobbying for state funds or the struggle for control of the enterprise in the privatization process), but had no interest in the trade union establishing an alternative basis for its authority as representative of the interests of the labor force in opposition to management.

Establishing the legal and institutional framework for social partnership and implementing the strategy in meaningful tripartite agreements was, therefore, no easy matter. The priority of the trade unions has been to create the legal, normative, and administrative framework of social partnership through which they would be able to secure the passage of favorable trade union and labor legislation and negotiate binding collective, branch, and regional agreements with employers and state bodies. Although the priority has been set from the top, the development of such tripartite structures has also relied on the initiative of branch and regional trade union organizations, who have had to identify the appropriate social partners and persuade them to enter into meaningful negotiations as well as encouraging and supporting their affiliated primary groups in developing the infrastructure of enterprise collective agreements. The main barriers to the development of these institutions have been the absence of representative employers' associations, the reluctance of employers and state bodies to make meaningful commitments, and the lack of any means of enforcing the obligations entered into in tripartite agreements. The trade unions, therefore, campaigned for federal and regional legislation on employers' associations and on social partnership, the principal purpose of which is to impose obligations on employers to participate in tripartite structures and to give legal force to tripartite agreements.

The primary object of tripartism in practice has not been for the unions to extract concessions from the employers, with the state serving as mediator and guarantor of the agreement, but for the unions and the employers to extract concessions from the state. Tripartism has, therefore, built upon and reinforced the identification of trade unions with employers at the enterprise, regional, and branch levels on the basis of common interests in evading the strictures of the market, and it has been on this basis that the trade unions have encouraged the formation of what are more like producers' associations than employers' associations to participate as social partners. The development of tripartite structures has correspondingly accelerated the fragmentation of the trade union movement as branch unions have been oriented more to the particular interests of their branch (and regional organizations to the interests of their regions or the dominant branches in their regions) than to the common interests of their members as workers. Thus, it has been divisions of branch interest, rather than, for example, political differences, which have been predominant within the trade union movement.

Without the cohesion imposed by party rule, the state apparatus is no more monolithic than are the trade unions or the employers, and tripartism has also built upon and reinforced the fragmentation and sectionalism of the state apparatus, providing a means by which parts of the state apparatus are able to strengthen their hands in the constant battle for resources. This is most obvious in the case of public services and those branches which remain heavily dependent on state subsidies or state orders, where tripartite structures reinforce the demands for resources of the appropriate ministries or quasi-ministerial bodies, but even where the state no longer distributes resources there are residual state and quasi-state bodies responsible for all manner of monitoring, servicing, and regulation of the branch. The role of tripartism in reconstituting the traditional structures of lobbying is equally apparent in the use of regional tripartite agreements to strengthen the hand of regional authorities in their negotiations with Moscow.

As in the traditional troika, the trade unions are the junior partner in tripartite structures, dependent on the goodwill of the relevant political authorities to negotiate and implement a meaningful agreement. Although there is an objective basis for collusion between trade unions, employers, and parts of the state apparatus in negotiating tripartite agreements, it is the regional or federal government which is called on to provide the resources, introduce the regulations, or pass the legislation that is required to meet the obligations embodied in the agreement, so it is the government which is the principal barrier to the achievement of agreement. Trade unions have sought to increase their bargaining power by holding pickets, demonstrations, and days of action and calling or endorsing warning or full-scale strikes, but such attempted displays of strength have more often than not backfired by attracting very limited support, undermining the unions' claims that rising social tension threatens widespread social unrest (large-scale strikes of coal miners, teachers and health workers, aimed at extracting money from the government to pay wages, have been the exception, but even they have been on the wane). The dependence of the trade unions on the goodwill of federal and regional governments for the realization of the strategy of social partnership has severely restricted their ability to participate in serious political opposition. The trade unions' political restraint has been reinforced by their vulnerability in a situation in which they depend for their existence on rights and privileges which are embodied in legislation and administrative practices which the state has given and the state can just as easily take away.

The Development of Social Partnership at the Federal Level

FNPR's primary declared aim was to protect the interests of the mass of the working population in the transition to a market economy. It sought to achieve this aim in two principal ways. First, by pressing for a change in the direction of macroeconomic policy in order to reverse the trajectory of economic decline unleashed by the radical reform program introduced in January 1992. It sought to achieve this aim through collaboration with the "industrial lobby" and participation in attempts to establish a center-left opposition, reinforced by the organization of mass protests and demonstrations. The strategic aim of this collaboration was to secure the formation of a center-left government committed to a corporatist program of economic regeneration, while the tactical aim was to secure guarantees from the government to be included in the tripartite General Agreement. Second, FNPR sought to defend its members in the transition to a market economy not on the basis of their collective organization, which was probably unrealistic in a context in which workplace trade unions were under the thumb of the employers, but by preserving and augmenting the legal guarantees of the terms and conditions of labor inherited from the Soviet period, which defined a framework in which the trade unions could defend their members through judicial and political intervention. FNPR sought to achieve this aim by lobbying legislative bodies to resist the dismantling of the legal guarantees of the Soviet era and for the passage of legislation appropriate to new economic and political circumstances, and by seeking to incorporate legally enforceable guarantees in general, branch, regional, and enterprise agreements.

Despite its rhetorical commitment to the defense of its members, FNPR's primary strategic aim was to secure its own institutional survival by ensuring that it retained the property and the legal privileges which had guaranteed the trade unions' role in the Soviet period. The principal threats to FNPR in this respect were, first, that the alternative trade unions, which initially had considerable support in Yeltsin's entourage, would secure the redistribution of trade union property, the re-registration of trade union membership and legislative support for trade union pluralism. The second threat was that the government would transfer the state functions, and corresponding resources, which the trade unions had performed in the Soviet period to state bodies. This concerned, most particularly, the administration of the state social insurance fund, which comprised the vast bulk of the trade unions' income, and the enforcement of health and safety legislation, which was a primary function of the regional trade union apparatus.

FNPR sought to reestablish its authority and secure its strategic objectives by all the means at its disposal. During the 1990s the tactical emphasis of FNPR's activities changed quite radically, the watersheds being the three Presidential *coups d'état* of August 1991, September 1993, and December 1999.

FNPR and the Struggle for Constitutional Power in Russia

The first stage in the development of social partnership at the federal level was dominated by the attempt of FNPR to secure its own institutional survival against the attempts of the presidency to neutralize FNPR as an oppositional force. This stage culminated in Yeltsin's dissolution of parliament and the defeat of the center-left in the December 1993 elections to the new Duma.

From the autumn of 1991 FNPR adopted a strategy of confrontation with the Yeltsin administration, combining rhetorical denunciations of the government's reform strategy with periodic attempts to organize mass demonstrations which proved the weakness rather than the strength of FNPR as the turn-outs were derisory. The government initially tried to intimidate and marginalize FNPR, threatening the disbandment of the FNPR trade unions and the nationalization of their property, and giving a blocking minority of seats on the newly established Russian Tripartite Commission (RTK) to the tiny alternative trade unions. In the course of 1992, however, FNPR established an alliance with the industrial lobby in the form of Arkadii Vol'skii's Union of Industrialists and Entrepreneurs, with whom it established a united front in the negotiation of the 1992 General Agreement, joining Vol'skii's "Assembly of Social Partnership" in July 1992 and jointly publishing a newspaper. The alliance of trade unions and industrialists, with their supporters in the Supreme Soviet, presented much more of a threat to Yeltsin than had FNPR's attempts at popular mobilization, and the presidential apparatus began to pursue a much more conciliatory line with FNPR, while marginalizing the alternative trade unions which had been the president's loyal supporters.

FNPR's alliance with the industrial lobby appeared to be paying off when it managed to secure the annulment of a Presidential decree nationalizing the Social Insurance Fund in September 1992, despite the protests of the alternative trade unions, and with the replacement of Gaidar by Chernomyrdin as Prime Minister in

December 1992, in what turned out to be a false dawn. Meanwhile, the government bypassed the RTK, with its representatives of the alternative trade unions, in favor of occasional bilateral talks with FNPR, and threw most of the representatives of the alternative unions off the RTK for 1993.

Social partnership was overshadowed through 1993 by Yeltsin's confrontation with the Supreme Soviet, where FNPR had been actively lobbying its interests. In the confrontation between Yeltsin and the Congress of People's Deputies in March 1993, FNPR stood on the side. As the confrontation developed over the summer, FNPR moved into more active opposition to the government, but a planned autumn campaign of meetings and warning strikes was cut short by Yeltsin's suspension of parliament on 21 September, which was accompanied by dire warnings to FNPR to stay out of politics. Nevertheless, the FNPR Executive Committee called for workers to use all available means, including strikes, to protest against Yeltsin's anti-constitutional actions. Klochkov, meanwhile, called on the Moscow regional organization to strike and to join the defenders of the White House.[4] However, the Moscow Federation of Trade Unions (MFP) opposed Klochkov's radical stand, warning trade unionists "not to be drawn into bloodshed while all means of defending the constitutional order have not been employed."[5]

The government was equally sharp and rather more effective in its response to FNPR, cutting off its telephones and freezing its bank accounts, announcing a ban on the check-off of union dues (never implemented), the transfer of the Social Insurance Fund to the state and the removal of the trade unions' responsibility for health and safety, in addition to the loss of their right of legislative initiative under Yeltsin's new Constitution. As a result of this debacle, Igor Klochkov was replaced as president of FNPR, reportedly on the demand of the government, by Mikhail Shmakov, president of the Moscow Federation. Shmakov immediately emphasized the need to go beyond the question of survival to address the strategy for the development of the unions in new economic conditions, arguing that open pressure on power structures without considering economic realities undermined the mechanisms of social partnership from within. He also stressed the need to take account of different branch and regional interests in formulating demands and the need to maintain political neutrality.

The replacement of Klochkov by Shmakov marked the recognition by FNPR of the failure of a confrontational strategy which had already created severe internal tensions since its member organizations were by no means united in their opposition to the course of the reforms, the metallurgists having withdrawn from FNPR in

October 1992. Shmakov's election marked a turn from confrontation to the social partnership that Shmakov had developed with the Moscow City government, a turn which was reinforced by the results of the December 1993 Duma election in which Vol'skii's centrist Civic Union was thrashed, while the Communist Party and their Agrarian allies had put up a strong showing.

From Confrontation to Social Partnership

After the December 1993 election, there was a fear within the presidential apparatus that FNPR would use its considerable funds and organizational resources to support the resurgent Communists, and the presidential apparatus again let it be known in February 1994 that a decree appropriating the unions' assets had been drawn up and only awaited Yeltsin's signature. However, the development of social partnership was renewed when, on 10 March 1994, Yeltsin launched his "Memorandum of Civic Accord" at a meeting to which all the significant trade union leaders were invited, calling on all social partners to commit themselves to the peaceful resolution of their differences, the main political purpose of Yeltsin's initiative being to draw a line between the center and the left-right extremes. FNPR welcomed the initiative, which they signed on 28 April, although the Accord was only signed by thirty-one of FNPR's forty-two constituent branch unions. FNPR held a peaceful May Day demonstration in 1994 around the theme of reconstruction and reconciliation as part of the new strategy of "passive protest," which included the symbolic picketing of government buildings by representative delegations, but no longer the attempt to organize mass demonstrations.

The reconciliation between the trade unions and the government in 1994 laid the foundations for the incorporation of the trade unions into a bureaucratized system of social partnership within which the trade unions negotiate the General Agreement with government, while lobbying the Duma for the passage of favorable legislation and continuing to pursue the chimera of the installation of a center-left government in which they could play a leading role. FNPR was not able to remain entirely passive, particularly in the face of the escalating non-payment of wages and continuing decline of employment and living standards, and so backed up its bureaucratic politics with periodic days of action and participation in the traditional May Day demonstrations.

The Russian Tripartite Commission and the General Agreement

The Tripartite Commission resumed in March 1994, as though nothing had happened, under a new co-coordinator, Yuri Yarov. The alternative trade unions had hoped to be rewarded for their support of Yeltsin in the allocation of seats on the Commission, but their hopes were disappointed as the government resumed its conciliatory approach to FNPR. While FNPR strengthened its position on the Tripartite Commission, the Commission was fairly inactive through 1994-95 as Yeltsin relied on his Memorandum of Civic Accord and occasional bilateral meetings with FNPR. However, under Yarov's chairmanship the RTK was developed into a self-sufficient quasi-governmental organization, its apparatus rooted in the apparatus of the Vice-Premier. From 1995, its meetings became much more regular and its proceedings more bureaucratized. The RTK established a series of working groups, which were responsible for the preparation and monitoring of the General Agreement and the consideration of government policy and legislative proposals, with *ad hoc* working groups sometimes being set up to deal with particular issues.

The trade unions and the government played the dominant role in the RTK because although there were about sixty registered All-Russian employers' associations, none had much representative status so that any commitments entered into by the employers' side were meaningless and unenforceable. The dominant employers' association, Vol'skii's Union of Industrialists and Entrepreneurs (whose origins lay in the industrial departments of the Central Committee apparatus), was in close alliance with FNPR between 1992 and 1995, and in general the trade unions and employers at that time formed a united front in the RTK, confronting the government with their common demands. As FNPR President Mikhail Shmakov noted, "in preparing the tripartite General Agreement we find that we have much more in common with the employers than with the government."[6]

A Coordinating Council of Employers' Associations (KSOR) was established in November 1994 as an umbrella organization and reconstituted on a more substantial basis as the Coordinating Council of Employers' Associations of Russia (KSORR), initially dominated by Potanin's InterRos, in March 2000 (KSORR is a member of the International Employers' Organization, and as such represents Russian employers at the ILO). The majority of employer representatives still represented producer rather than employer interests, with little interest in labor and social issues, using their position to get access to government and to press their individual and sectional interests. It is indicative of the status of KSORR that its formation had to be cleared by the anti-monopoly commission.

In 2001, Vol'skii's organization was taken over by the "oligarchs" who control the commanding heights of the Russian economy, who intended to turn it into a more effective body for the representation of employers' interests, initially in the debate over the reform of the Labor Code. However, the law "On Employers' Associations" of November 2002 confined recognition to those organizations whose sole purpose was to represent employers, which sealed the dominance of KSORR at the federal level, and undermined the former collaboration between FNPR and the employers on the basis of common sectoral interests, although seven sectoral associations which were not members of KSORR were still represented on the RTK in 2004.

With the routinization and bureaucratization of the RTK it increasingly came to resemble the traditional Soviet form of consultation of the trade unions with the party-state, which in the past was mediated through their collaboration with the State Committee for Labor and Social Policy (Goskomtrud), and of course some of those involved in the activities of the RTK had participated in many such meetings in the past. As in the past, the government would decide what to refer to the RTK and whether to take any account of its proceedings. The trade union side continued to complain that important issues were not referred to the RTK and that the Commission lacked teeth, but such complaints were mostly voiced behind closed doors rather than being taken onto the streets.

The difference from the Soviet period was that the government no longer controlled many of the features of economic and social life, such as levels of wages, prices, and employment, which had been under the firm control of the party-state. Nevertheless, such features were routinely the object of discussion in the RTK and were incorporated into the General Agreement, despite the fact that in the new market economy the government could realistically do no more than express its aspirations, without having the means to realize its commitments. Corresponding to the limited powers of the government, the Agreements tended to be declaratory and very general, laying down the broad lines of the government's economic and social policy and the aspirations of government and employers, with no means of enforcing the agreements reached. Although successive agreements have become more detailed and specific, they still express aspirations rather than guarantees. Despite the largely rhetorical and unenforceable character of the General Agreement, the fact that negotiations can be quite tough and the government has become increasingly resistant to making substantial and unrealizable concessions indicates that it has at least some ideological and political significance.

Lobbying the Duma

The rights of the trade unions and the social protection of their members were embodied in the labor legislation of the Soviet period. The trade unions have attached considerable importance to their lobbying activity in the legislature, particularly after they lost their right of legislative initiative in 1993, even holding out hopes that they might be able to restore the social insurance and health and safety functions that Yeltsin had withdrawn by decree at the beginning of 1994. The weakness of the Duma and the small size of the trade union faction limited what could be achieved, but FNPR claimed credit for successive increases in the derisory state minimum wage and Duma representatives of the branch trade unions had some impact as defenders of their branch interests. The crowning achievement of FNPR's lobbying was the passage of a raft of trade union and labor legislation in 1995-96 which not only consolidated most of the trade union and labor rights inherited from the Soviet Union, but also heavily favored FNPR, as a national trade union federation, over the more fragmented alternative trade unions. FNPR was able to find sufficient allies to obstruct government attempts radically to reform the soviet-era Labor Code until the Third Duma, elected in 1999, in which the government was able to command a substantial majority and FNPR accordingly had to take an increasingly conciliatory line.

The Electoral Dream

Despite the resounding defeat suffered by Vol'skii in the 1993 Duma election, the FNPR leadership continued to harbor the hope of participating in the formation of a center-left party which could constitute an effective parliamentary opposition, or even command a parliamentary majority. This aspiration was not shared by many of the branch and regional trade union organizations, which had their own political preferences and priorities linked to their branch and regional interests. Nevertheless, the trade unions did share a common interest in securing the election of trade unionists as Duma deputies in order to strengthen the trade union and/or relevant branch and regional lobbies.

The electoral dreams of FNPR's leadership were put to the test in the 1995 and 1999 Duma elections. Despite considerable internal opposition, the FNPR leadership resurrected the alliance with Vol'skii for the December 1995 Duma elections, with humiliating results as their party, *Profsoyuzy i promyshleniki Rossii – Soyuz truda* (Trade Unions and Industrialists of Russia – Union of Labor), secured only 1.59

percent of the party list vote, well below the threshold required to secure Duma representation (even less than was polled by Viktor Anpilov's revanchist *Komunisty – Trudovaya Rossiya – za Sovetskii Soyuz* (Communists – Working Russia – For the Soviet Union). Although nine trade unionists were elected to the Duma from the constituencies, only one had been endorsed by *Soyuz truda*. Underlying the lack of commitment of trade union organizations to FNPR's electoral strategy lay the fact that the "industrial lobby" had lost any coherence that it might once have had. Privatization had intensified the fragmentation of interests so that in place of a single industrial lobby, enterprise directors looked to their own efforts or to more narrowly branch or regionally-based organizations in lobbying for their interests.

For the 1999 Duma election, the FNPR leadership again sought to forge a center-left coalition, again despite strong internal opposition. The ally in this case was not Vol'skii but the mayor of Moscow, Yurii Luzhkov, who had developed a strongly corporatist form of social partnership in Moscow in which the trade unions had become virtually an arm of the city government. When Luzhkov and former Prime Minister Yevgenii Primakov merged their parties to establish *Otechestvo – Vsya Rossiya* (OVR) [Fatherland – All Russia] it looked for a time as though FNPR was participating in an unbeatable coalition which would take control of the Duma in December 1999 and the Presidency in the subsequent presidential election. However, the hopes that many trade union representatives would vault into the Duma on the OVR list were destroyed by the collapse of the OVR under intense pressure from the presidential apparatus in the later stages of the campaign. In the end only four trade unionists were elected to the Duma on the OVR list, three were elected on the KPRF lists and one on the list of Yedinstvo, the presidential party. A further nine trade unionists were elected in single-mandate constituencies, one nominated by OVR, two by the KPRF, one by the Union of Right Forces and the remaining five as independents. The fact that the successful candidates chose a wide range of routes into the Duma reflects the extent to which branch and regional trade union organizations ignored the commitments of FNPR and went their own way, just as they had done in 1995.[7]

Although social partnership had made slow progress at the federal level, with successive governments showing little sympathy for the trade unions and the annual General Agreement offering no more than vague promises and empty declarations of intent, at branch, regional, and enterprise level the institutions of social partnership had put down much more solid roots and the trade unions had established their own allegiances, which did not necessarily coincide with those of the FNPR leadership.

Social partnership had integrated the trade unions into the emerging political system, but at the cost of their political subordination and of reproducing divisions of branch and regional interest within their own ranks. The result was that branch and regional trade union organizations subordinated themselves to diverse sectoral and regional interests and it was impossible to organize a concerted trade union election campaign. In recognition of this limitation, FNPR did not even try to participate in the 2003 Duma election.

Popular Mobilization – Days of Action

FNPR could not confine itself entirely to bureaucratic interaction with the government and lobbying the Duma while popular discontent with the government's reform program mounted and spontaneous strikes erupted, mostly against the non-payment of wages. FNPR continued to attempt to mobilize its members in successive days of action which, it claimed, attracted ever-increasing numbers of participants. Although it continually insisted that its demonstrations were making purely economic demands and it made every effort to impede the participation of communist and "national-patriotic" parties in them, it could not prevent the organizers of its regional demonstrations from putting forward political demands, including the resignation of the government and the president.

The demonstrations each spring and autumn acquired an increasingly ritual character, allowing the critics of the government to let off steam and FNPR to demonstrate to the government that it was a significant force for social peace in being able to channel such criticism into harmless protest, but they were never part of a concerted FNPR campaign of opposition. On 1 June 1995, Shmakov declared to the General Council, "Today it is clear that a decisive, open confrontation with the regime would throw our trade unions into the backwaters of public life, would deprive them of all of the constitutional means of defending the interests of the toilers, and would be a real threat to the existence of the Federation and of FNPR unions as a whole."[8] The largest day of action, apart from the traditional May Day demonstrations, was on 7 October 1998, in which FNPR claimed twenty-five million people participated, but mass demonstrations were suspended for 1999 as FNPR focused on its electoral activity. Subsequent events have been mere token demonstrations in support of FNPR's lobbying activities. For example, FNPR claimed the participation of only 230,000 people in its pickets in support of social rights and guarantees on 10 June 2004. Meanwhile, the traditional May Day demonstrations were embraced by an increasingly wide political spectrum, even United Russia coming to play a leading role.

Social Partnership under Putin

Between 1994 and 1999 FNPR had sought to defend its own interests and those of its members through the constitutional process, participating in the bureaucratic structures of the Tripartite Commission and quietly lobbying in the State Duma, while doing its best to discourage any more militant actions on the part of its members or member organizations. While the Duma was controlled by the opposition, such restraint was all that the government and presidential apparatus could ask, but following the collapse of OVR the political framework was transformed. The Duma election, followed by Yeltsin's resignation, had unexpectedly resulted in a consolidation of the existing "party of power" and left FNPR with the task of redefining its stance.

In January 2000, Shmakov had a long meeting with Putin, with whom FNPR had established what it saw as good partnerly relations during his time as Prime Minister, Putin having expressed his desire to listen to the trade unions. In the middle of February, FNPR declared its support for Putin's presidential candidacy, following his address to the General Council in which he declared that "the trade unions should have a worthy place in society." There was strong opposition in the General Council to FNPR making a hasty decision, particularly from those who favored other candidates but, as in the Duma elections, the commitment of the General Council was not binding, and branch and regional trade union leaders made their own decisions whom to support.

With Yeltsin's resignation the trade unions had believed that the principal barrier to the consolidation of social partnership at the federal level had been removed. However, the trade unions were disabused of their belief that the election of Putin would mark a step forward soon after the election, when the government introduced a Unified Social Tax, which had been vigorously opposed by all the trade unions (apart from Sotsprof) and was in clear violation of the 2000 General Agreement,[9] introduced its draft of a new Labor Code into the Duma without any consultation with the unions, and nominated former tax minister, Aleksandr Pochinok, who had a reputation as a hard man, as Minister of Labor. Although the RTK continued to meet regularly, in May its staff was reduced to one person. Finally, in his speech to the Federal Assembly on July 9, Putin paid special attention to the claims of the trade unions, insisting that there was no longer any call for the trade unions to perform state functions in the distribution of social benefits. The role of the trade unions should be confined to defending the rights of hired labor by studying the market, organizing legal training, and determining the priorities for retraining.

Although the government forced the Unified Social Tax through the Duma against the opposition of the trade unions, it eventually took a more conciliatory line with FNPR with regard to the long-postponed revision of the Labor Code. Both FNPR and the alternative unions had independently launched campaigns against the government draft of the Labor Code although, while the alternative unions organized small but militant pickets and demonstrations, FNPR's actions were largely confined to propaganda work among its members and lobbying Duma deputies. When the government proposed the establishment of a Commission to work out a compromise draft Labor Code, FNPR decided to participate in the Commission, while the alternative unions stepped up their campaign of protests and demonstrations. The variant of the Labor Code agreed to between the government and FNPR, eventually adopted by the Duma and signed into law in December 2001, removed some of the benefits and protections accorded to workers in the Soviet-era Labor Code that it would replace, but it also considerably strengthened the position of FNPR against the alternative unions, which would effectively be deprived of bargaining rights and of the right to strike. The debacle came to a head at the first reading of the new Labor Code, when the Duma was militantly picketed by a demonstration from the alternative unions, which faced a counter-picket in favor of the new Code organized on behalf of FNPR by the Moscow Federation of Trade Unions.

While Putin proclaimed his continued commitment to social partnership, there were increasing indications that he was not content merely for FNPR to confine its activity to constitutional channels. Having exploited his constitutional powers and his powers of patronage to neutralize opposition from the regional governors and to consolidate his control of the State Duma, he turned his attention to FNPR, which was the only remaining potential source of opposition to his unchallenged rule, his target being the FNPR Congress due to be held in December 2001 at which the President, Mikhail Shmakov, was to stand for reelection. The communists were already mobilizing in support of the candidacy of Anatolii Chekis, Duma deputy and former leader of the FNPR trade unions in the Kuzbass mining region, but rumors grew increasingly strong in the course of 2001 that Shmakov's candidacy would be opposed by a candidate endorsed by the presidential administration. The pressure on FNPR was gradually stepped up and criticisms of Shmakov's leadership were voiced in a number of quarters, from the left as well as from the right. One particularly powerful lever was the threat of establishing a new trade union federation, which would be centered on the trade unions of the Russian transnational corporations, primarily in the oil and gas and metallurgical industries. The formation of such a federation would deal a critical blow to the relevant FNPR trade unions, particularly the metallurgists, chemical workers, and the oil and gas trade union, by depriving them of their largest and richest branches. It was reported that this lever was used to persuade FNPR to agree to the government draft of the Labor Code, on condition that the new federation not be formed, and rumored that the threat was also being used as a lever to secure the support of the affected unions for the opposition to Shmakov. FNPR did back the government over the Labor Code, but in August 2001 the new federation was established all the same, with the active participation of Vladimir Shcherbakov, president of the former Soviet Trade Union Confederation, VKP.

The initiative, and Shcherbakov's participation in particular, was denounced by FNPR and the two alternative trade union federations, VKT and KTR, on 10 September in a joint appeal to the international trade union movement. The hopes of the leaders of the new Association that they would achieve some international recognition were dashed when ICFTU and ICEM both sent strong protest letters to Putin, condemning the involvement of government and the employers in the formation of the Association and referring to the relevant ILO Conventions. In reaction to these letters, on 1 October, the leaders of the new Association were summoned to a meeting with the presidential administration and informed that the presidential administration regarded any attempt to replace Shmakov as being unrealistic. Nevertheless, Shcherbakov undertook what was clearly a pre-election campaign, with the backing of the leaders of the Transnational Association, but was unable to find any body to forward his nomination and withdrew his candidacy the week before the Congress, at which Shmakov beat Chekis convincingly by 659 votes to eighty, with thirteen abstentions.

Meanwhile, the absorption of OVR into United Russia in the Duma meant that FNPR's deputies, headed by Andrei Isaeev, found themselves incorporated into the party of power. This turned out not to be a purely bureaucratic maneuver, but one embraced by the FNPR leadership as a means of consolidating its partnerly relations with the presidential administration. The collaboration of FNPR with United Russia culminated in the signing of an "Agreement on collaboration and interaction between the United Russia fraction in the State Duma and the Federation of Independent Trade Unions of Russia" on 27 July 2004. One outcome of this accommodation of FNPR with United Russia and the presidential Administration has been the systematic consultation of the government with FNPR, directly and through the RTK, on all items of labor and social legislation, including the notorious Law 122 of August 2004 on the monetization of social benefits. FNPR prided itself on its constructive collaboration with the government, which had amended the legislation, supposedly in response to the demands of FNPR expressed in its day of action on

10 June, and FNPR opposed the demonstrations against the law which erupted in 2005, endorsing the government position that various political forces were exploiting deficiencies in the implementation of the law for their own purposes. For many observers this indicated the definitive incorporation of FNPR into Putin's "managed democracy" as the price of its (provisional) institutional survival. Although there were reports that the presidential administration was once again considering the creation of a new "loyal" trade union organization to displace FNPR, such an initiative would seem unnecessary and so most unlikely.

Social Partnership at the Branch Level

The Soviet trade unions were constructed on the branch principle, with the branch organization more or less paralleling the structures of ministerial control so that each branch trade union collaborated with its appropriate branch ministry in developing the branch social and economic development plans, and lobbying within the government and party for the interests of the branch. The collapse of the administrative-command system was not immediately accompanied by the liquidation of the branch ministries. In the first instance, the bulk of the economy remained under state ownership and, although the ministries had lost many of their direct powers of intervention, remained under ministerial control. Even with mass privatization these ministerial structures retained some of their regulatory, technical and advisory functions and, in some cases, distributed government funds to enterprises in the branch in the form of subsidies, grants, and investments. In many of the privatized branches, former state functions were devolved to formally private but quasi-state bodies and producers' associations were spun out of the state and Central Committee structures which formerly had responsibility for the branch.

One of the functions of these state, quasi-state, and former state bodies was to negotiate tariff agreements with the relevant branch trade unions. In the early 1990s, before mass privatization, the state figured in the negotiation of branch tariff agreements as both the employer, represented by the appropriate branch ministry, and the government, represented by the Ministry of Labor. This provided considerable scope for the trade union and branch ministry to collaborate in order to extract more resources from the government, much as they had done in the Soviet period, particularly as the Ministry of Labor was not responsible for resourcing any agreement reached. In the latter half of the 1990s the government brought the negotiation of branch tariff agreements more firmly under control, confining the negotiation of tariff agreements within the limits of budgetary allocations, but even with privatization the scope for trade unions and branch structures to use the tariff agreement to lobby for branch interests remained.

Around sixty branch tariff agreements are signed covering virtually all branches of the economy. The majority of tariff agreements are bipartite, involving only the government and the trade union, with only about one-fifth being signed by private employers' representatives, and the proportion of the latter has been in decline, although many bipartite agreements, such as those covering education and the health service, are signed with government departments which represent the employers. In other cases, such as the defense industry, the tariff agreement is signed with government agencies which have no role as employers. Tariff agreements apply to all those employers who have authorized the employers' association to negotiate the agreement on their behalf, so the very limited coverage of employers' associations severely limits the coverage of branch tariff agreements.[10] Thus, tariff agreements still tend more to reproduce the traditional interaction between branch trade unions and the appropriate ministerial structures than the outcome of collective bargaining between employers and employees.

The absence of employers' organizations is a reflection of the weakness of trade unions, which do not have the collective strength to induce the employers to combine. In an attempt to find social partners, the branch trade unions, sometimes with government support, have been very active in sponsoring the formation of branch employers' associations. The role of the government side in tariff agreements is also ambiguous. The Ministry of Labor is a signatory of about half the tariff agreements concluded, but it plays the role of consultant in the negotiation process rather than that of a representative of the government ready to assume the appropriate obligations and, in particular, to guarantee the financing of the tariff agreement in those branches which are budget-funded or rely on government subsidies.[11]

Social Partnership at the Regional Level

The pattern of social partnership at the regional level is very similar to that at the federal level, but regional social partnership has developed much more smoothly, and in many cases to a much greater extent, than at federal level. Participation in the regional institutions of social partnership is the principal function of the regional trade union federations, which comprise representatives of the regional committees of the branch unions, and is the principal justification for their existence.

Regional agreements are concluded in virtually all the regions of the Russian Federation. Although all regional agreements are tripartite, there is often a problem in identifying an appropriate organization to sign on behalf of the employers, despite the efforts of the trade unions and regional administration. In some regions a single association signs on behalf of the employers and in others a number of different organizations are identified, but the coverage of these associations is often very small and, as at the federal level, it is difficult to enforce any commitments entered into by the employer representatives so that regional agreements are essentially between the trade union and the regional administration and relate to the economic, social, welfare, and employment policies and aspirations of the regional administration.

The core of regional agreements, like the General Agreement, consists of pious aspirations to encourage the growth of the regional economy, to protect jobs and increase employment, to see a rising level of wages, and often an aspiration to increase the minimum wage towards the regional subsistence minimum. The substantive terms of regional agreements often do no more than repeat the terms of the General Agreement and of branch tariff agreements, but in some regions they provide additional concessions, although there are often doubts that such concessions will be delivered. For example, the Sverdlovsk regional agreements since 2000 have defined the regional minimum wage as equal to the regional subsistence minimum. Although the regional trade union federation recognizes that this is completely unrealistic in a situation in which even the average wage in some branches is below the subsistence minimum, and will not be realized, they see it as an important symbolic expression of a shared aspiration, which is how they approach the agreement as a whole.

The most important substantive content of regional agreements for the trade unions is that they frequently include provision for the collaboration of the trade unions in the conduct of state functions, reinforcing or restoring their traditional role. Thus, for example, regional agreements often include specification of social and welfare benefits to be provided by the regional administration, in particular using the resources of the Social Insurance Fund and often in collaboration with the trade unions. Other forms of collaboration between the regional trade unions and the regional administration include joint action to monitor health and safety. Regional and sub-regional agreements are often of particular significance for the budget sector trade unions whose members are government employees; in some regions the agreement includes provision for increases in budget sector wages to be paid from the regional budget.

While the regional agreement defines the common aspirations of the regional trade union federation and the regional administration, everyday collaboration between trade unions and the regional government is extensive. Social partnership at the regional level reinstates the traditional relationship between the regional party committee and the regional trade union federation; Eduard Rossel', governor of Sverdlovsk oblast, reportedly referred to his regional trade union federation as the "trade union obkom." The trade unions often participate in the consideration and implementation of labor and social policies by executive and legislative bodies and lobby for the passage of regional legislation to complement and supplement federal laws. Before the passage of federal laws on social partnership and employers' associations, regional trade union federations were successful in pressing for the passage of regional legislation in the majority of Russia's regions. The regional administration often collaborates with the trade unions in inducing employers to recognize trade unions and sign collective agreements. For example, in Khabarovsk and Moscow oblast, registration as an entrepreneur is conditional on membership of the employers' organization and signing a collective agreement, while the Moscow City administration gives priority in distributing state orders and a range of other benefits to enterprises which have a collective agreement. Under Mayor Luzhkov, the Moscow Federation of Trade Unions has largely retained and even reinforced its traditional functions, administering the social and welfare policy of the city administration and monitoring the performance of employers on behalf of the administration. Moscow is by no means an exception: it provides the model to which all regional trade union federations aspire.

Summary and Conclusion

The development of trade unions in post-Soviet Russia has been subject to two contradictory pressures. On the one hand, the transition to a market economy dictated that the trade unions should transform themselves from an integral part of the party-state apparatus into institutions which could articulate and represent the interests of their members in relation to the newly independent employers. On the other hand, the first priority of the Russian trade unions had to be to secure their own institutional survival, which dictated that they should attempt to retain their traditional functions by preserving or reconstituting traditional structures.

These contradictory pressures were expressed in the contradiction between the rhetoric and the reality of social partnership. On the one hand, the ideology of social partnership expressed the participation of the trade unions in tripartite structures as the representatives of the employees. On the other hand, the practice of social partnership embraced the construction of bureaucratic structures within which the trade unions could retain their state functions and maintain their traditional practices.

Within the enterprise the trade union retained its traditional role as the branch of the enterprise administration responsible for the social welfare of employees. The reduction in the resources of the trade unions, and particularly the loss of control of social insurance funds, meant that the trade unions were more dependent than ever on the enterprise administration for resourcing their social welfare activity. Rather than representing the interests of employees in opposition to the employers, the trade unions retained the traditional Soviet conception of a commonality of interest of management and employees in the development of production, helping to enforce labor discipline and supporting management's attempts to lobby government for resources.

The collaboration of trade unions and management in the workplace was reproduced at the branch level, where the branch trade unions sought to represent their members' interests primarily by representing the interests of the branch in lobbying ministerial and quasi-ministerial bodies at regional and federal levels. In order to do this effectively, the branch trade unions played a very active role in encouraging the formation of employers' associations at regional and federal levels, so as to reproduce or reconstitute the traditional Soviet forms of branch lobbying through new corporatist structures.

In the absence of independent trade union activity in the workplace, the regional trade union organizations sought to represent the interests of the population of the region as a whole, speaking not only for workers but also for their families, for pensioners, and students, as well as for the unemployed and the disadvantaged. This led them to negotiate with the regional administration and lobby the regional legislature not only over labor issues, but also over social and welfare issues more generally. At the same time, the regional trade union organizations played an important role in the retention or recovery by the trade unions of their state functions, participating in the formulation and implementation of social and economic policy by the regional administration and the regional legislature, and coordinating the collaboration of branch and enterprise trade unions with the regional organizations of the Social Insurance Fund, the Ministry of Labor and the State Labor Inspectorate, so that the trade unions were able to draw on state powers and resources to retain their traditional state functions. The trade unions and regional administration collaborated closely to persuade employers to establish branch and regional employers' associations with which they could negotiate and collaborate in the formation and implementation of regional economic, social, and welfare policies. Thus the trade unions again played an important role in securing the continuity of state power by reconstituting the traditional troika at the regional level.

In the workplace and at regional level, there was a fairly smooth transition from Soviet to post-Soviet structures and practices of power so that it was not too difficult for the trade unions to retain their traditional functions and practices. The tension between the trade unions' role as defenders of their members and their own priority of survival was most acute at the federal level. The vulnerability of the trade unions, most dramatically expressed in the wake of Yeltsin's putsch in September 1993, made them very wary of participating in active opposition to the government so that they concentrated their efforts on quietly lobbying the State Duma and participating in the bureaucratized semi-governmental structures of the Tripartite Commission, while politically the FNPR leadership shied away from constituting the trade unions as an independent political force, pinning its hopes instead on playing a role in a center-left coalition with the industrial lobby and its successors before being absorbed into Putin's statist project.

The trade unions have played a very important role in the reconstruction of corporatist state structures at the federal, branch, and regional levels which reproduce many of the traditional forms of Soviet governance. The trade unions would not have been able to achieve this ambition if there had not been a parallel aspiration on the part of the state to reconstitute effective forms of governance and a prior disposition on the part of state officials to fall back on traditional practices and traditional connections in order to do so. This is not to say that the trade unions have sought to reconstitute Soviet power, for the new corporatist structures exist within a formally democratic constitutional framework, and the trade unions have played a very important role in consolidating democratic institutions and processes in their insistence on pursuing their aims through constitutional channels. Moreover, the emphasis placed by the trade unions on defending their members by reference to the law and collective agreements has meant that the trade unions have been among the strongest advocates of the strengthening of the rule of law – it is trade union members who have been the principal victims of the systematic violation of labor legislation by employers in not paying wages on time, failing to pay for overtime and weekend working, putting workers on short-time without the due compensation, sending workers on compulsory unpaid leave, denying workers their holiday entitlements, and dismissing them without the compensation due under the law.

The trade unions' contribution to the development of a stable democratic system in Russia has been at the expense of the unity of the trade union movement.

The collaboration of the trade unions with the employers and their integration into corporatist state structures has proved very corrosive of the unity of the trade union movement, since branch and regional trade union organizations identify primarily with their distinctive branch or region rather than their common trade union interests. Branch and regional trade union organizations seek to represent their members' interests primarily through lobbying the interests of the branch or region directly in government, in collaboration with the employers and appropriate state bodies, rather than through common action within the framework of the trade union movement as a whole. This lack of trade union unity has repeatedly been displayed in the relative failure of FNPR's attempts at mass mobilization and, most conspicuously, in the lack of unity displayed in the Duma election campaigns of 1995 and 1999.

The trade unions' contribution to the development of democracy has not been matched by their contribution to the well-being of their own members either, as it has impeded the constitution of the trade unions as an independent channel of representation of their members' interests. The price that they have paid for their institutional survival and a very limited amount of influence on enterprise management and on regional and federal government has been their incorporation into bureaucratic management and administrative structures at the expense of the effective organization of their own members, distancing the union organizations from the members and demobilizing and demoralizing the latter. The trade unions do not provide any channels through which trade union members can articulate and express their own interests and participate in the resolution of their own problems, and attempts on the part of ordinary members to do so are seen as a threat to the orderly conduct of industrial relations rather than an opportunity for the development of the trade union organization.

The trade union leaders are aware of the problems that the trade unions face, but are not sufficiently aware of their own responsibility for those problems. FNPR, branch and regional trade union organizations patiently negotiate General, Branch Tariff, and Regional Agreements and lobby for the passage of laws and the adoption of policies which will benefit their members, but they lament the fact that their primary trade union organizations do not show the independence and initiative that is needed to realize these achievements at the workplace. Provisions of higher level agreements are routinely ignored or negated in enterprise collective agreements. Employers violate the provisions of the Labor Code with impunity because the primary trade union organizations do not react. Regional trade union organizations arrange to collaborate with the State Labor Inspectorate to enforce health and safety legislation, but complain about the ineffectiveness and the difficulty of recruiting voluntary workplace health and safety inspectors who can monitor compliance with protective legislation. FNPR and the branch and regional trade union organizations call for demonstrations and days of action in defense of their members, but the members fail to respond and pickets and demonstrations are dominated by the trade union apparatus "representing" their members. Yet, the "passivity" of the trade union members derives primarily from the fact that they are treated as passive by the leadership. They are not called on to defend their own interests by developing their collective organization, but only to activate the instruments provided by the state by pursuing individual labor disputes through the courts. Trade union members do not identify themselves as "members" of the trade union, the overwhelming majority seeing the trade unions as just another of the apparatuses of power which stands over them, an impression which is not entirely unjustified.

The conclusion should not be entirely negative. The survival of the trade unions is a considerable achievement which means that there are channels available through which workers are, in principle, able to articulate and express their collective interests. Moreover, there are some courageous trade union officers and activists who do play a more active role, even if they are often isolated and intimidated and even if many ultimately withdraw demoralized from the fray. As Russian enterprises adopt capitalist practices of production and human resource management, the fiction of a common interest of employer and employee will be harder to maintain, and independent trade union activism will become more common, providing the regional, branch, and federal levels of the trade unions with a base on which they will be better equipped to assert their own independence of the state. On the other hand, the presidential and regional administrations have been very successful in bringing the trade unions under their wings and reducing them to a simulacrum of the Soviet trade unions, as subordinate partners in a state apparatus that is seeking to extend its tentacles into every pore of civil society. Whether the trade unions will be able to recover their role as a force for the democratization of Russian society remains to be seen.

NOTES TO CHAPTER 3

[1] Richard Rose, "Getting Things Done with Social Capital: New Russia Barometer VII" (Glasgow: Centre for the Study of Public Policy, University of Strathclyde, 1998).

[2] This paper is based on a program of research on the "development of trade unionism in Russia" conducted in collaboration with the regional affiliates of ISITO in Kemerovo, Sverdlovsk, Perm, Samara, Ulyanovsk, and Leningrad oblasts, the Komi Republic, and the cities of Moscow and St. Petersburg. The research has been funded by the EU's INTAS program and the British ESRC. Project reports and working papers are available from the project website at go.warwick.ac.uk/russia/trade. An overview of the findings is presented in Sarah Ashwin and Simon Clarke, *Trade Unions and Industrial Relations in Post-Communist Russia* (Basingstoke and New York: Palgrave, 2002).

[3] N. N. Gritsenko, V. A. Kadeikina, and E. V. Makukhina, *Istoriya profsoyuzov Rossii* [*History of the Russian Trade Unions*], (Moscow: Akademiya truda i sotsial'nykh otnoshenii, 1999), 316-320.

[4] Walter D. Connor, *Tattered Banners: Labor, Conflict and Corporatism in Postcommunist Russia* (Boulder: Westview Press, 1996), 130.

[5] K. Buketov, "'Osen' 1993: profsoyuzy v period krizisa'" [Autumn 1993: Trade unions in the period of crisis], *Rabochaya politika*, (1995): 20, cited in Rick Simon, *Labor and Political Transformation in Russia and Ukraine*, (Aldershot: Ashgate, 2000), 131.

[6] *Obshchaya gazeta*, 27 July-2 August 1995.

[7] Simon Clarke, "Russian Trade Unions in the 1999 Duma Election," *Journal of Communist Studies and Transition Politics* 17, no. 2 (2001): 43-69.

[8] Quoted in D. Mandel, "The Russian Working Class and Labor Movement in the Fourth Year of 'Shock Therapy'," (Montreal, 1995), mimeograph.

[9] The Unified Social Tax consolidated the dues paid by employers to the various non-budget funds and reduced the overall rate, justified by the claim that more effective collection would increase the overall tax take. However, the trade unions saw this as a means to reduce the amount allocated to the Social Insurance Fund. Although the trade unions no longer controlled the Fund, they still played a major role in distributing the social and welfare benefits that it financed among their members, this being one of the principal attractions of trade union membership. Trade union fears have been justified by the steady reduction in allocations to the Social Insurance Fund and the withdrawal of most of its benefits.

[10] The law also prescribes that where a tariff agreement covers more than half the employees in the branch, the Ministry of Labor can extend its coverage to all employers who do not notify their refusal to be covered in writing within thirty days.

[11] Any tariff agreements which presuppose government funding have to be signed by the Ministry of Finance. Details of branch tariff agreements are taken from an unpublished FNPR document, "Informatsiya o tarifno-dogovornoi kampanii 1999-2000 godov" (Information on the tariff-agreement campaign, 1999-2000).

THE DEMOGRAPHIC, HEALTH, AND ENVIRONMENTAL SITUATION IN RUSSIA

MURRAY FESHBACH[1]

How Has Russia Been Attempting to Confront the Soviet Legacy in the Environment?

The clearest possible signal of the Russian government's attempts to drastically reduce the significance of the environmental issue is the abolition of the State Committee on Ecology. Its functions, in part, were transferred to the Ministry of Natural Resources. Not only did the June 2000 administrative decree eliminate the principal environmental agency solely devoted to associated issues and problems, but also it gave the "responsibility" to an organization that is overtly oriented toward the economic exploitation of mineral resources. The ministry's purpose is to dig out natural resources from the ground and to earn foreign currency. In March of 2001, I was told that the transition team in the Institute formerly headed by German Gref, the new head of the Ministry of Economic Development, had a staff of some 400 persons preparing policy papers, but did not have a single environmentalist participating in the discussions and preparation of such policy papers. This lacuna is not very helpful if one wishes to reduce the burden of the legacy of ecological disasters carried over from the Soviet period, or those of more recent vintage.

The elimination of the separate Forestry agency also was part and parcel of such negative attitudes towards preserving the natural environment, if not repairing the legacy. While nominal ecological monitoring is to be carried out by the Ministry of Natural Resources, I doubt that it will make a major effort to reduce the level of pollution. The expanded assignment of monitoring given to the Rosgidromet (the Russian Federation's Hydrometeorological Agency) and the Sanepidnadzor (Sanitary-Epidemiological Surveillance) Directorate of the Ministry of Health is necessary to retain at least minimal efforts to monitor the situation. Whether this will be sufficient remains to be seen. Moreover, Victor Orlov,[2] the president of the Russian Geological Society and first Minister of Natural Resources,[3] reportedly warned that the increased extraction of oil during a period of high world prices in the last few years (which contributes more than half of the Russian budget hard currency revenues) will be the main economic problem in coming years. "Industry, coming out of its state of collapse, will require increased extraction of raw materials. But to achieve this will be very difficult." To me, this is the perennial economy vs. ecology issue, and the former can be expected to emerge victorious in the permanent battle between the two in Russia. The website of the Ministry,[4] however, contains numerous rationalizations by the Minister and by the organization about the need to reorganize activities. Whether it is true or not, though it likely is true, that sixty-one of the ninety-five member states of the United Nations' Environmental Program (UNEP) do not have an independent ecological organization (called EPA or what have you), they also may not have the level of environmental disasters that Russia does.[5]

Some progress can be said to have taken place if one looks solely at the officially reported quantities of pollutants emitted into the atmosphere, and the amount of pesticides used on the farm. However, these "improvements" are based not on true reductions, but on the statistical artifact resulting from major reductions of industrial production activity, and therefore emissions from smokestacks not yet retrofitted, and the fact that farms cannot afford to purchase pesticides and similar materials designed to increase yields. Its human health impact is described later.

Another signal of the government's worry that organizational efforts by environmental NGOs to prevent the import of nuclear waste was too constraining for the economy and the nuclear industry, was the elimination of over 500,000 signatures collected by NGOs to put the issue on a referendum. With a minimum of 2,000,000 signatures required to have a referendum question on the "illegality" of such nuclear waste imports banned by the Constitution of the Russian Federation, the Federal Election Commission decided that over twenty percent of the signatures were incorrect and therefore an insufficient number for a referendum were certifiable. Recent indications show that the NGOs have not been totally unsuccessful in demonstrating the importance of this matter. The Duma may be more of a player than hitherto expected, and it has delayed sanctioning such waste to be imported.

If it holds beyond the current delay, which I doubt will be permanent, this would be a serious setback to the Ministry of Atomic Industry, and the economic policymakers who hope to earn significant funds from this activity. Complicating this matter is the firing of Adamov, the successor to the hardliner, Viktor Mikhaylov, as the Minister. In his first interview, the new Minister, Alexander Rumyantsev, seemed to be more circumspect, but he indicated that he expects to continue this program for importing nuclear waste. He would do this, he added only "if we can ensure safety [and therefore] the project deserves support."[6] Nongovernmental environmentalists so far seem to be in a wait and watch period, but do express themselves when they feel it necessary. One can hope for more realistic evaluations of the impact on the environment, especially health hazards, but much remains to be seen.

Of course, the FSB (the successor organization to the KGB) calling in all local environmental NGOs throughout the country in 2000 for a review of their activities was not an encouraging sign; nor were the past and current trials of Nikitin, Pasko, Sutyagin, and the raid on the American Joshua Handler's apartment, searching for potentially incriminating environmentally related matters (most of which has been returned to him) conducive to more democratic, civic society approaches. The rejection of charges against Nikitin and Pasko by the courts, however, are encouraging.

What is the Environmental and Health Picture in Russia: Continued Disaster or Possible Turnaround?

The situation regarding the health status of the population of Russia is so negative that it is difficult to present, or perhaps more so to overcome, Western cultural mindsets about the depth of the reality. Speaking during the Government Hour to the Duma in June 1999, Viktor Danilov-Danilyan, the head of the State Environmental Protection Agency, noted that about fifteen percent of Russian territory, where most of the population and manufacturing capacity exists, is designated as "ecologically unfavorable." As was true ten years earlier, even before the change in the government, average air pollution levels exceed maximum permissible levels in more than 1,200 towns and villages. Water quality has not improved; treatment of industrial and household waste has not improved. In detailing environmental health hazards in military-chemical cities, Danilov-Danilyan admitted that where such weapons are stored, toxic levels are "frequently 1,000 times over the maximum permissible level."[7] The environmental health hazards to the population, especially children, pregnant women, and people in the older age groups, persists and may be even worse than before. With some exceptions, it seems that most problems continue in part due to insufficient attention or investment in environmental remediation.

One of the most terrible issues relates to pollution in military-chemical cities. Of 160 such cities, we now have data for some locations, as well as for the country as a whole, on the percentage of pregnancies which end in spontaneous abortions. This is a notably difficult measure to collect because it is not always reported by women who have miscarriages, that is, spontaneous abortions. New data reported late in the year 2000, in the environmental newspaper *Zelennyy mir* (*Green World*), shows that in the cities of Dzerzhinsk and Chapayevsk, miscarriage rates are above fifteen percent. This point is a direct public health "pathway" measure indicating that chromosomal aberrations (due to chemical mutagens) lead to fetuses being aborted naturally and/or artificially terminated after appropriate medical examination of the pregnant woman. Thus, in both Dzherzhinsk and Chapayevsk, the environmental health hazard of chemical pollution leads to extraordinary rates of spontaneous abortion, ranging up to over thirty-four for every 100 pregnancies in Chapayevsk (in Samara oblast) and as high as eighteen percent in Dzherzhinsk (in Nizhegorodskaya oblast) during the period 1989 to 1998. The national rate of about five percent spontaneous abortions may be too low given other information about rates of miscarriages in other countries, but this does not detract from the incredibly high rates in these former military-chemical cities and their impact on the local populations.[8]

One of the major health hazards deriving from environmental pollution involves poor quality water. Most of the water consumed by the population is from surface water rather than aquifers below ground; surface waters are highly polluted (fifty to seventy-five percent of water is reported to be non-potable throughout Russia). Virtually the entire water pipeline system is unlined and deteriorating, and additional contaminants are injected into the water supply from this source. Danilov-Danilyan stated several years ago that it would take $400 billion over twenty years to correct the water quality issue. Further pollution by heavy metals, chlororganic compounds, runoffs of mineral fertilizers from farms, discharges of waste water from plants, and multiple other sources make the likelihood of water as a vector of illness very prominent in public health hazards in the former Soviet Union, not just Russia alone.

Air pollution has been referred to earlier when describing the likely source of spontaneous abortions, but this is not the entire spectrum of underlying problems. Before the dissolution of the Soviet Union at the end of 1991, it was officially reported that of the 3.1 million smokestacks in the country, only one-half had environmental pollution abatement equipment, and only one-third of those worked. Moreover, when they worked, it was mostly solid particulates such as ash and dust that were caught, and most lesser proportions of the gases and liquids emanating from these stationary sources of pollution. There has been a dramatic increase in the number of motor vehicles in Russia, and most do not have catalytic converters or the equivalent to reduce emissions. In addition, unleaded gas has only recently become available in sufficient quantities. As a result, the share of air pollution from vehicles in the city of Moscow, for example, is not significantly more than half of the total air pollution from all sources. Clearly the decline in industrial production and the lack of retrofitting to older, worn-out plants and factories has contributed to the growing share of pollution from vehicles relative to stationary sources. When industrial production fully recovers, we can expect that not only will the total amount of pollution increase, but that the share of vehicular pollution will fall. Nonetheless, it is not healthy to breathe in many places throughout the Federation.

Land pollution has been slightly reduced due to the lack of purchasing power by farms to acquire previous quantities of fertilizers, pesticides, herbicides, etc. As a result, not only is there less pollution of the arable land, but also there is less contamination of the food chain from this source. Putting aside any issue of the poor quality of the water table, which enters into farmlands throughout the country, the quality of the soil has improved markedly in the regions surveyed and for the pollutants checked by the Russian Federal Service for Hydrometeorology and Environmental Monitoring. In its yearbook for 1999, the data from their examination of 37,000 hectares, in 517 locales, in which 154 farms of 101 districts in thirty-four "subjects" (administrative-territorial units) of the country, plus children's camps in two oblasts (Kurgan and Novosibirsk) are provided. They found toxic substances such as Total DDT, 2, 4-D, and others almost everywhere. Total DDT, for example, was found in the range of 1.1 to 11.0 times the official Maximum Pollution Concentration level.[9] Detailed data for Total DDT shows a peak multiple of maximal usage in the longitudinal study between 1990 and 1999, in the year 1994.[10] In 1994, 45.3 times the maximum allowable concentration (PDK) was found during the summertime in all crops or cultivated areas surveyed. It had been "only" 10.1 times the maximum in 1990. A major change occurred and during the summer period of 1997-99, the level had been sharply reduced to 0.15 and 0.20 times the PDK. The changes are impressive, even if these are from a selected sample whose representativeness is not known. But granting this, it does show progress and likely is the reason for claims of improvement in land amelioration.

Data and other information on heavy metals had been rarely if ever published until recently. This grouping is another major source of human health hazards that occur everywhere, but the Russian scene perhaps is worse than could have been expected. A joint Russian-American publication on the effort to determine the amount of lead contamination in the country and its human health impact, particularly on the young, shows that the load rates far exceed the Russian PDK. The direct impact on mental retardation of children (zero to fourteen years of age, inclusive) ensuing from such levels is noted to be as much as 75.7 percent in Krasnoural'sk, a town where lead car batteries were produced. The average content of lead in the blood of children was 13.1 +/- 0.5 micrograms per deciliter (mcg/dl, hereafter.) Apparently if one utilizes a broader definition of retardation in the nerve system and psychological development, the share increases to 82.5 percent of all children in Krasnoural'sk. This is an unbelievable level, and devastating for the future of the city.[11] Hopefully, serious attention will be devoted to this issue, and a different production line not using lead in car batteries at least will save some future youngsters from such hazards.

The most striking information for this paper is from the newest report that provides bar charts (without precise numbers) on the "Percentage of children with elevated blood lead levels in selected Russian cities." From these charts, we can determine (roughly) that in Krasnoural'sk, the city referred to above, 78 percent of all children were severely contaminated: sixty-three percent of all children zero to fourteen years of age had elevated blood levels of 9.9-14.9 mcg/dl and sixteen percent had 15.0 or more mcg/dl. For other cities, Belovo was the next worst, with fifty-one percent of all children affected, the figures were thirty-six percent in Gus-Khrustal'nyy, twenty-three in Saratov, twenty-eight in Volgograd, and so forth.[12]

Using the survey of forty-three city Lead Project Sites, it was estimated using this same U.S. Environmental Protection Agency Biokinetic Model, that 1.9 million children throughout urban Russia were likely to have behavior and learning problems because the lead content of their blood was between 10 and 19 mcg/dl; 400,000 other children had 20-44 mcg/dl of lead in their blood and needed a medical check-up and a subsequent test for lead. And 90,000 more children with 45-69 mcg/dl lead content were in immediate need of therapy "within 48 hours."[13] Hopefully, treatment and other measures were properly undertaken. A number of appropriate steps were initiated, including adoption of a national program to decrease lead contamination; very high priority was set in both the 1999 National Environmental Action Plan and the 2000 National and Environmental Health Action Plan. Leaded gasoline production is expected to continue to decrease.[14] However, the national plans may be aborted by the new "environmental administration" if it sets other priorities.

On a more positive note, it appears that the Ministry of Health and its Sanepidnadzor Department, are becoming more active in environmental health activities. That a number of major articles on this topic were published in the March-April 2001 issue of the Ministry of Health's public health journal, *Zdravookhraneniye Rosssiyskoy Federatsii*, can be construed as a serious reformation of their activity and concern. While the article "O natsional'nom plane deystviy po gigiyene okruzhayushchey sredy Rossiskoy Federatsii," (On the National Action Plan on Environmental Hygiene in the Russian Federation) is but one of three such items in this issue, the specific details are important for our purposes. Written by V. Chiburayev of the Russian Ministry of Health's Federal Sanepidnadzor Center and

Boris A. Revich of the Center for Demography and Human Ecology of the Russian Academy of Sciences' Institute for National Economic Forecasting, the first ever analysis (in print) of morbidity and mortality attributed to various environmental hazards is very pertinent, as well as enlightening. For example, atmospheric pollution by solid particulates and nitrogen dioxide emission is estimated to cause between 270,000 to 340,000 cases of respiratory ailments and about 22,000 to 23,000 deaths from solid particulates alone each year.[15] Pollution of the atmosphere of cities by lead is estimated to lead to "deviations in the nervous and psychological development of children" of up to 400,000 children per year, or 1.5 percent of all children zero to fourteen.[16] If this human health impact has continued for ten years and will continue for another ten years (hopefully no more), then the share of all children that have been and will be affected so negatively can be devastating for the country and its future. This only reinforces what has been said about health here and elsewhere.[17]

Does AIDS Challenge Pose a More Serious or Specific Problem?

It is now clear that the rate of increase in new cases of HIV/AIDS infection in the Russian Federation is the fastest growing in the world.[18] Moreover, the prevalence of HIV/AIDS among the population is over one percent. The situation certainly is not yet as "bad" as in certain sub-Saharan African countries, but it will not only deteriorate in the near term, but also possibly be devastating to economic, social, and political expectations of the national and many local governments in Russia.

The reported official rate of HIV/AIDS infection in Russia during the year 2000 was announced as fifty-seven per 100,000 population. Regional differentials portray the significance of the issue to local authorities. In Irkutsk oblast, the rate is more than five times as high as the national rate, i.e., 301 cases per 100,000 population. Between 1 September 2000, and 1 April 2001, the absolute numbers of cases was much higher for both national and region-specific areas. Again, in Irkutsk oblast, the number of registered cases (the word "registered" is a clue to major undercounts, of which more below), increased by almost eighteen percent in these six months, from 7,507 to 8,842, respectively. For the city of Moscow, the numbers registered changed from 9,375 to 10,881, or sixteen percent, over the same period.[19] The total number registered was 103,024 on 1 April, up from 86,259 at the end of 2000.

In the nation and, to a greater and lesser degree, in the constituent units of the country, the putative numbers and rates are ten times higher if Dr. Vadim V. Pokrovskiy (the head of the Federal HIV/AIDS Prevention and Treatment Center of the Russian

Ministry of Health), the First Deputy Minister of Health, Onishchenko, the World Health Organization, and leading epidemiologists are correct in their frequent assertion in articles, interviews, and speeches. The reported figure of 55,157 new cases in the year 2000 is double the number of cases from 1987 to 1999, inclusive;[20] one month later, Pokrovskiy gave a higher figure for the year 2000, as 56,471.[21] Moreover, if we look at the level of new cases and the rate per 100,000 population of new incidence, Russia is now higher than, for example, the United States. Recent figures for new incidence of HIV/AIDS in the United States hovers around 40,000 – twenty percent lower than in Russia. However, it is also quite noteworthy in any assessment of the impact that the total population of Russia is only slightly above half (51.6 percent at the beginning of 2001) of the American figure; thus, comparing official incidence figures, the Russian figure should be almost doubled to standardize it by the relative size of the total populations in each country.

At his press conference on 3 April 2001, Pokrovskiy projected a figure of three million HIV-positive persons in five to six years, and by 2010, hundreds of thousands, according to the Vansovich report on the press conference, will "simply die of AIDS." This presumably is based on his multiplier of the true number of HIV patients. New figures, for instance, and his estimate that they will begin to die twelve years after initial infection is part of his calculation. He further noted that, beginning in 2010, the number of newly infected and the number of deaths will be about the same.[22] If he is correct, and I believe that he is not exaggerating just to get additional funding (even if it is on his agenda, as well), the changes in the structure of deaths from the current pattern to incorporate those who will die from AIDS and associated illnesses, such as pneumococcal pneumonia, and/or tuberculosis, or other epidemiological synergies, will be devastating for the country and its potential development.

The precursors to the rise in HIV/AIDS are the increases in injecting drug abuse, increasing rates of syphilis (the current official figures which show a decline in incidence are incorrect due in part to changes in the law in 1998), increasing rates of prostitution, especially among very young females in and out of the country, perhaps insufficiently tested blood donations, and increases in the rate of pregnant women with HIV infection, in prison and among the population in general. The recent large amnesty of prisoners likely will contribute to an even greater epidemiological synergy of the two diseases. There has been an explosion of positive HIV cases among pregnant women, increasing from three HIV-positive cases recorded in 1994 up to 378 in 2000. This is a small increase in absolute number but a horrific increase in relative terms.[23]

In terms of rates of HIV-positive status per 100,000 persons examined, the most remarkable is that among drug addicts, increasing from zero in 1994 to 3,315.14 in the year 2000. The next highest rate per 100,000 persons examined is among prisoners, increasing from 0.587 in 1994 to 520.49 in 2000. Again, these rates are only for persons examined. How many were not examined? Are the rates among the non-examined persons with venereal diseases (principally syphilis) even higher than among those who were recorded? In all of these comments, the underlying issue is the potential, as well as likely impact on the country's economy, society, military, and stability in the near term and not too distant future. How will they cope? Not very well, I expect.

The large regional numbers in the incidence of HIV/AIDS within Russia extend beyond the city of Moscow and Irkutsk oblast referred to earlier, with the higher numbers in Moscow oblast, Kaliningrad, Krasnodarsk Kray, Tyumen oblast, Khanty-Mansiyskiy District, Rostov oblast, Tverskaya oblast and Samarskaya oblast (in descending order). Local authorities in each have to be concerned with the demands for funds, for costs of health services, the impact on labor productivity, the reduction in healthy conscripts, premature mortality among the fifteen to twenty-nine year olds, and other issues which will divert them from funding other priority projects.

With the federal budget allocating only ten million rubles in the year 2000 (which, when divided by 28.5 rubles per dollars, equals about $350,000 and when further divided by $10,000 per patient per year – current costs according to Pokrovskiy) it allowed for the treatment of thirty-five (sick) patients. If so, this is 0.06 of one percent of the new registered cases (55,157 or 56,471, see above) in 2000. However, if the "real" number of cases is some 550,000 (using Pokrovskiy's multiplier of ten to provide for a more accurate number of cases), then the funding potential from the federal budget for treatment is so minuscule as to be not worth trying to calculate. It is more than doubtful that the local budgets can or will be willing to make up for this enormous shortfall from their own funds. Thus, many more will die. A loan of $150 million from the World Bank announced early in 2001 was to go to illness prevention, or only to treat TB patients, HIV/AIDS or hepatitis C, or other demands. It is not clear because the actual allocations are not stipulated or recorded up to the present time. However, it was later rejected by the Russian government.

Figures for 2001 confirm the likelihood that very large numbers of people will die within the next decade. Of the current official prevalence figure of 180,000 for the beginning of 2002, the last two years represent more than 150,000 new cases. This is slightly less than ninety percent of all the prevalence figure, again as officially recorded. Perhaps in eight to ten years, when they begin to die in large numbers, the state will finally take serious actions to deal with this tragedy. An earlier death than projected will ensue as the co-infection with tuberculosis becomes rampant. In one country, Swaziland, this co-infection rate is thirty percent. And as Russia comes closer to African rates of illness as the explosive rate shown here continues, then the analogy may not be far-fetched at all.

By 2000, the Russian government provided funding for treatment for only a grand total of 550 persons (excluding monies for prevention and education of the public). This also is a minuscule "drop in the ocean" of needs. The official figure of 180,000 cited above, should be multiplied by three, five, seven, or ten times (maybe even more). Thus, 550 out of 750,000 to one million persons with HIV/AIDS means the nation is very far from meeting any serious level of funding need. Very useful and valuable unpublished estimates by Dr. Nicholas Eberstadt of the American Enterprise Institute – which while I expect may understate the likely numbers because of the co-infection issue referred to earlier – show annual AIDS deaths by 2010 of 163,000 and by 2020 of 360,000. With current mortality for the entire Russian population from all causes of death numbering about 2.2 million, this would be disastrous. An alternative scenario prepared by Dr. Eberstadt projects 230,000 deaths in 2010 and 397,000 in 2020. (These are average number of deaths over a five-year period.) The projections are for adults only. While this should be overwhelmingly the correct population group involved, there might well be some deaths among youngsters as the proportion of drug addicts at earlier and earlier ages continues into the future. Economic costs will be high not only for treatment (if funded by Russia or by other countries and international organizations fearful of the spread of disease) but also for output foregone because these persons clearly would not be available for economic activity. For Ukraine, projections prepared for the United Nations' Development Program, UNAIDS, and the British Council in 1997, provide a "slow" and a "fast" scenario of deaths to 2016. By 2010, the projected number of deaths in Ukraine from the "slow" variant is 478,000 and from the "fast" variant, almost 850,000.[24] No matter which number is correct, the impact will be very significant in Ukraine as well as in Russia.

It must be noted that the threat to the health of the population is due not only to environmental human health hazards and to HIV/AIDS, but to other extremely important issues which must be very briefly mentioned at least. Included in this rubric must first of all be tuberculosis morbidity and mortality in its own right having increased to almost 29,800 deaths in 2000 (the comparable U.S. figure is 1,100); hepatitis C, which is increasing sharply in Russia and is expensive to treat and very frequently mortal; as well as the explosion in drug abuse and addiction. Alcoholism and smoking are far from benign issues and affect heart illness and death, as well as other illnesses. There is virtually no end to this litany of illnesses other than those specifically addressed here. Stress, mental illness, and disability of the population add to all of these burdens. Exogenous causes of death due to alcohol poisoning, other poisons, accidents, murders, suicides, and the like contribute very seriously also to problems of management of the health of the population and its consequences on a local as well as national level.

Education

Payment for entry into higher educational institutions has both a formal tuition as well as a room and board component. But much also is paid in a so-called "grey economy" form, that is, bribery. This bribery was estimated in an article published in the first week of March 2002, at between two and five billion U.S. dollars. This is not a minor sum.[25] However, not all can afford to pay for entry either above or below the table, but many do based on these figures. The newspaper also estimates that paid higher education encompasses about 350,000 students, or nine percent of total higher education enrollments. These data are for the beginning of the 1999-2000 school year. In the 2000-01 school year, enrollment is reported by Goskomstat as 4,270,800 in State VUZy (higher educational institutions) and 470,600 in pay-for-education VUZy. This latter figure represents eleven percent of all enrollment, a growth of two percentage points over the period. Admissions in the fall of 2000 to State Higher Educational Institutions numbered 1,140,300, and to so-called Non-State (Private) Institutions, 152,200, or over 13.3 percent of new admissions.[26]

More disturbing is the number of children under sixteen years of age who do not go to school at all. According to Kondorsky, about two million do not attend school. More and more information is accumulating about this relatively new phenomenon, or at least on its unprecedentedly massive scale. Whether this number also includes a reasonably good estimate for the homeless and/or unsupervised children is not known. However, it is not just an issue of human capital formation and preparation for working, but also about the ability of individuals to make reasoned choices during elections.

Afterword

In 1993, UNICEF's International Child Development Centre in Florence, Italy, issued a publication on social stability, entitled *Public Policy and Social Conditions*. The report stated that if the figures they then had available were correct, then one could look toward "social disintegration" in Russia.[27] This evaluation was made before the demographic decline became fully apparent, and the continued health deterioration, especially the explosive trends in HIV infection. And despite the decline in industrial production, a less than proportionate decline in atmospheric pollution, indicating that when production returns to its previous (1991) level, pollution will be even greater and have an impact on the very young and the elderly even more so and add to the burden of other phenomena.

Other issues involve the poor infrastructure of the health sector. In an earlier study conducted in 1988 by Goskomstat, with its results being repeated ever since by Soviet and Russian commentators and myself, showed that fifty percent of hospitals did not have any hot water, twenty percent had no sewage and ten percent had no water at all. No more recent national data are available, but I would expect some (but not major) improvement in these surrogate measures of elementary sanitation and health provision. Again, where the funds will come from is far from clear or certain, especially given competing demands for scarce capital.

The demographic issue in Russia, however, is a "national security threat" as is health, not only to an outside observer such as myself, but also to political, military, and medical authorities in Russia. It can affect the geopolitics of the Far East border with China; it can affect the stability of the society as the overall population, and the numbers, let alone the health (read "quality") of children decline.

The legacy of environmental hazards remain largely unremitting in their effect, with only some improvement because of reduced half-lives in levels of radiation in the Cesium-137 Chernobyl impact area in the sixteen years since the accident in 1986. It can and will affect the overall issue of reproductive and child health – which bodes ill for the country and its stability in many ways. Whether it be the labor force, the armed forces, the economy, the social structure, or costs associated with any major improvements in the environment, there will be competing claimants for scarce resources. The picture is not hopeful, neither in the short run nor in the longer time horizon. A more positive expectation seemed to be engendered in the first year of the Putin presidency, but whether it can be preserved so that the psychological underpinning for a society can be maintained is still moot. If the situation is as described here, and elsewhere in some of my recent writings is correct, then much remains to be done and if so, it must be done very soon.

NOTES TO CHAPTER 4

[1] This report on the demographic, health, and environmental trends in Russia follows the sequence of specific questions appertaining to these issues as set by the organizers of the 2002 Liechtenstein Colloquium.

[2] Cited by Yekaterina Vasil'chenko, "Ekonomika. Skol'ko stoit posledniy neftedollar?" (Economics: How Much is the Last Petrodollar Worth?), *Rossiyskaya gazeta*, 30 March 2001, 12.

[3] The current Minister is Boris Aleksandrovich Yatskevich.

[4] See http://ministr.mnr.gov.ru/pressa/.

[5] The reference to the UNEP is given in the interview of the Minister by Yekaterina Pavlova, "Yedinstvo i bor'ba protivopolozhenostey" in *Okhrana dikoy prirody* no. 4 (2000), and reproduced at http://ministr.mnr.gov.ru/pressa/22.html.

[6] Published in *Izvestiya*, 6 April 2001, conducted by Sergey Leskov.

[7] ITAR-TASS news agency, Moscow (in Russian), 1430 gmt, 11 June 1999, transcribed in BBC, *Monitoring Former Soviet Union – Economic*, 12 June 1999.

[8] *Zelennyy mir* nos. 27-28 (2000): 16; and Boris Revich, Center for Human Ecology and Demography, Institute of National Economic Forecasting, Russian Academy of Sciences. Data in the newspaper are reduced from the numbers and rates shown per 1000 pregnancies.

[9] Federal'naya sluzhba Rossii po gidrometeorologii i monitoringu okruzhayushchey sredy, Nauchno-proizvodstvennoye upravleniye 'Tayfun,' Institut eksperimental'noy meteorologii, *Monitoring pestitsidov v ob'yektov prirodnoy sredy Rossiskoy Federatsii, Yezhegodnik, 1999* (St. Petersburg: Gidrometeorizdat, 2000). Only 100 copies of this report were issued. It contains very valuable additional details and information about the various regions under survey.

[10] Ibid., 15-16.

[11] State Committee for Environmental Protection of the Russian Federation, *Doklad o svintsovom zagryaznenii okruzhayushchey sredy Rossiskoy Federatsii i yego vliyanii na zdorov'ye naseleniya* (Moscow: 1997), 124. A follow-up summary of the activity was published for USAID by MEASURE Communication, *Lead in the Environment and Public Health in Russia: Five Years of American-Russian Collaboration, 1995-1999* (n.p., n.d. but likely is Washington, D.C.: 2000). The original summary report in English, was published in Moscow in 1997, under the title *White Paper: Lead Contamination of the Environment in the Russian Federation and its Effect on Human Health.* Issued by the State Committee for Environmental Protection of the Russian Federation, the Russian-language full report, also issued by the State Committee, is *Doklad o svintsovom zagryaznenii okruzhayushchey sredy Rossiskoy Federatsii i yego vliyanii na zdorov'ye naseleniya* (Moscow: 1997), 200 copies.

[12] Ibid., 13.

[13] Ibid., 12.

[14] Ibid., 16.

[15] From *Zdravookhraneniye Rossiyskoy Federatsii* no. 2 (March-April 2001): 11, 10.

[16] 400,000 divided by 26,604,113, from *Demograficheskiy yezhegodnik Rossii, 2000* [*Demographic Yearbook of Russia, 2000*] (Moscow: Goskomstat RF, 2000), 33.

[17] See, for example, my article on "Soviet Population Meltdown," *Wilson Quarterly* (Winter 2001): 15-21.

[18] According to UNAIDS latest reports.

[19] See *Epidemiologiya i infektsionnaya bolezn'* no. 1 (January 2001): 14; and Yelena Vansovich, "Obshchestvo. SPID nepobedim," *Kommersant-Daily*, 4 April 2001, 9.

[20] From information supplied by Aleksandr Golyusov, head of the HIV/AIDS Department, Sanepidnadzor, broadcast by the Russian News Agency, RIA, on 8 February 2001, in FBIS, CEP20010209000029.

[21] ITAR-TASS news agency (in English), 3 April 2001.

[22] Vansovich, "Obshchestvo. SPID nepobedim," 9.

[23] The data are from V. V. Pokrovskiy et al., "Razvitiye epidemii VICh-infektsii v Rossii," *Epidemiologiya i infektsionnaya bolezn'* no. 1 (January-February 2001): 11.

[24] "Epidemiya VICh/SPIDa v Ukraine: sotsial'no-demograficheskiy aspekt," 3. http://vyavorsky.narod.ru/dir_paper/aids/part6.htm.

[25] Alexzander Kondorsky, "Knowledge Costs," *The Russia Journal*, 1-7 March 2002.

[26] Goskomstat Rossii, *Rossiyskiy Statisticheskiy Yezhegodnik 2001, Statisticheskiy sbornik* (Moscow: 2002), 233, 237.

[27] Russia was not alone. Albania also was included in this apocalyptic prognosis. UNICEF, *Public Policy and Social Conditions* no. 1 (November 1993): 44.

THE RUSSIAN ECONOMY
RICHARD E. ERICSON

Abstract

This chapter surveys the state and structure of the Russian economy at the beginning of the twenty-first century. The nature of the economic system is characterized in terms of the inherited institutional and structural legacies, and the efforts to overcome these since 1991. Despite the vast changes that occurred during the first decade of transition, many of these legacies still stand in the way of developing a well-functioning market economy. The size and structure of the economy is analyzed, together with prospects for further development. The Gref development program of the Putin regime is argued to be promising, if appropriately implemented, but faces domestic challenge that may derail progress, and indeed appears stalled at the beginning of Putin's second term.

* * *

Introduction

The Russian economy in the new millennium was still very much a reflection of its Soviet predecessor. Indeed, despite vast changes in the organizational, institutional, and production structures of the economy, there has been a feeling that ten years of reform had been wasted, and only now can real reform begin.[1] While macroeconomic performance has bottomed out, and we are witnessing a continuing strong and rather broad growth of economic activity, the dead hand of the Soviet economic system still lies across the economy, stifling new initiative, dragging resources into wasteful activities and structures, and obstructing a clear view of what still needs to be done for a true modernizing and globalizing revival of the Russian economy. Yet, a new spirit is struggling against this legacy, embodied in new entrepreneurs and managers, and some political agents, who are fighting to break through with new business activities, resuscitating and restructuring old industrial objects, and exploiting opportunities presented by the fluid situation.[2]

The result is that Russia has an unevenly marketizing – hence partially marketized, but not yet fully market – economic system. While making money is a primary motivation, and virtually anything – political, social, or economic – can be bought,[3] the nature of economic interaction and the structural incentives and opportunities built into the system, are often quite different from those typical of a functioning and functional market economic system. This distorts both policy impacts and performance statistics, rendering economic analysis and policy formulation more difficult and raising questions of the suitability, or indeed ability, of Russia to effectively and fruitfully integrate into the global economy, other than as a resource appendage to the developed market economies. But there is a tremendous amount of turbulent economic activity – experimentation, adjustment, success, and failure – that is pressuring the economic system to adjust toward more market-friendly institutions and structures. Thus, the future is far from determined, or even predictable. The Russian economy stands at a crossroads where policy choices can make a critical difference.

Nature of the Economic System

The Russian economy is typically referred to as a distorted or quasi-market economy. It is market as the private sector is predominant, everything carries a price, profit is an incentive, and most economic activity is formally connected with markets for both acquiring means and disposing of product, as indeed were the Soviet contractual supply (*snabzhenie*) and disposal (*sbyt*) systems. It is quasi or distorted as necessary markets are often severely restricted or missing, activity is often legally unprotected and/or subject to bureaucratic or criminal caprice or extortion, and non-economic factors (personal ties and/or traditional links) are often determinant of the activities allowed or pursued. The transactional, banking and legal institutions that undergird a market economy are in Russia weak, personalized, and often dysfunctional in their intermediating roles. Yet, prices arise from market-like decentralized interaction. This combination of market and non-market forces and institutions, capitalism Russian style,[4] is largely a consequence of inherited structures, institutions and behaviors (or understandings) coming out of the Soviet system and its pseudo-market forms, or from its autocratic Russia predecessor. These legacies have provided much of the content of the new market forms introduced during transition.

Structural Legacies

The structure of economic activity in the Russian Federation – its location, capital and other factor use, and output portfolio at the beginning of transition – was the consequence of seventy years of mal-development of production and distribution capacities in the Soviet Union. The resulting Soviet structure of production was fully consistent with the planned priorities of the Soviet state, but was, and is, inconsistent with any coherent pattern of economic cost accounting.[5] The plans and prices toward which economic activity was oriented were seriously distorted with respect to true economic costs and opportunities. Hence, virtually every production operation was economically inefficient, and highly wasteful in its use of resources, materials, energy, labor, and capital.

Developed without consideration of economic (opportunity) costs or valuation, this overall structure of production is fundamentally non-viable in a decentralized market environment. Further, much of the distortion was systematically hidden by arbitrary and economically irrational Soviet pricing that failed to reflect economic (market) valuations.[6] That implies, after price liberalization, serious problems of cost recovery in the operation of much of the industrial structure, vast unmeasured amounts of waste in its operation, and the need for massive cross-subsidization and further waste in any attempt to operate it in a decentralized, non-command, mode.

This distorted structure is currently reflected in patterns of:

- Crumbling infrastructure, irrationally and sparsely built, always poorly maintained, and now often without a clear owner responsible for preservation of its useful parts;[7]
- Location of industrial and other economic activity, built for planners convenience and security and defense considerations, and innocent of real transportation, location, and other opportunity costs;[8]
- Structure and location of employment and factor use, reflecting wasteful "extensive" growth and excessive factor and input stocks as a buffer against disruption in the absence of market redundancy; and
- Use of technology, both inappropriate and obsolete from the perspective of producing economic value, due to the absence of economic criteria for its evaluation.[9]

To facilitate planning, and based on a misplaced belief in (engineering) economies of scale, production activity was concentrated in massive facilities with sole suppliers and users ("technological chains"), eliminating the redundancy inherent in market competition. The absence of any economic criteria of relative value or obsolescence led to the maintenance of virtually all installed capital and all enterprises and facilities, resulting in an age structure and employment of the capital stock that is undesirable, and indeed unsustainable, when market based costs must be covered by earnings from its use.

As a consequence, there remains a need for extensive cross-subsidization of important economic activity, that, in the absence of direct government control, has been implemented indirectly through the acceptance of payment arrears, tax offsets, and generously priced barter. This is substantially driven by non- and anti-market survival strategies of inherited production organizations and enterprises (recourse to virtual economy behavior), accepted, and often encouraged, by government at all levels.[10] And it has the serious consequence of the preemption of critical resource flows (e.g. energy, real estate services) by existing enterprises and operations, starving new activity of resources and placing a substantial barrier in the way of *de-novo*, market-based economic activity.[11]

Institutional Legacies

Much of the institutional structure and patterns of interaction remain an inheritance from the command economy. Where new organizational forms and rules have been introduced, their content and the nature of their functioning have been defined more by the attitudes and understandings, the economic culture, inherited from the Soviet Union than by the market models from which they were adopted. This can be seen in the absence of key institutional arrangements required for the proper functioning of a market economy.

Economic

One of the key economic legacies of the Soviet Union is the lack of a dense and redundant set of networks for economic and financial intermediation. Planning rationality dictated sole suppliers and users, unique transportation links and wholesaling organs, and minimal output inventory holdings. Furthermore, the fundamental irrelevance of money for economic, and in particular production activity meant that there was no proper intermediating banking or financial system. Thus, the demise of the central planning and allocation system, the disappearance of the hierarchical controlling structures of Gossnab and the Party, and the breakup of the monobank left economic agents without the trading and financing options essential to the functioning of the market, and hence subject to opportunistic exploitation by individuals and groups with personal connections and networks derived largely from positions in the Soviet political apparatus or the Soviet criminal underground.[12] The result is a highly personalized and politicized intermediation, aimed in large part at overcoming political barriers and extracting rents for insiders. Markets are thus highly segmented, and quite dependent on the goodwill and facilitation of local and regional political authorities.

Another critical institutional legacy is the incompleteness and ambiguity of property rights. Given the chaotic, and both legally and socially questionable means of acquiring productive property, there remains much doubt as to its security.[13] There has been a lack of free and clear ownership, questionable enforceability of property rights except perhaps by private means,[14] and a general lack of contract protection and enforcement. This generates extremely short behavioral horizons, and subsequent efforts to minimize investment and realize gains as soon as possible. It also means that economic agents must fall back on stronger ties, on personal connections and networks, with extra-economic and extra-legal means of enforcement, in order to engage in complex economic activity.[15] Hence, there is a tendency for existing organizations to rely on inherited networks, and maintain inherited ties and activities, rather than engaging in entrepreneurial restructuring and market exploration.

These tendencies are reinforced by the lack of disinterested adjudication of disputes.[16] Just as Soviet First Secretaries, administrative and Party functionaries could dictate the terms of resolution of conflict, the interpretation and implementation of plans, so political agents now influence regulatory bodies, civil and arbitration courts, making the outcome of property and contract disputes as much a function of political relations and influence as of the content of the dispute. This is particularly clear in the implementation of the recent bankruptcy law, expressly based on Western models and practice. The influence over bankruptcy judges by political authorities has led bankruptcy to become an instrument for redistribution of property to the politically connected and for the extraction of rents by regional and local political authorities.[17] This is to a large extent just a continuation of Soviet telephone justice.

Political

Much of this economic institutional environment is derivative of the post-Soviet nature of governance and political power. In the Soviet system, vast discretionary authority, unchecked by law or institutional constraint other than the power of higher Party organs, resided in political and administrative organs. Pleasing them became the ultimate criterion of economic (and political) success, and hence their whim (interpretation of plans, and of their superiors' intentions) became law for all subordinates.[18]

This personalization of economic authority, political power, and governance has largely survived the demise of the Soviet Union. Indeed, it was enhanced by the elimination of the authority and power of the Communist Party and its discipline and controls, leading to an extraordinary intertwining of economic and political authority and decisions. It allows personal gain and political consideration to dominate economic choices, disemboweling markets of their economic content by systematically distorting pricing and other market signals of economic value. By intertwining the personal and the public, the political and the economic, it has fostered at all levels ubiquitous corruption, rule by decree rather than law and contract, the predominance of patron-client relations, and the domination (trumping) of formal institutions by personal relations.[19]

Such a personalized, fealty-based system is the antithesis of one based on rule of law so essential to the functioning of a modern market economy. While its roots are undoubtedly historically and culturally deeper than the Soviet system,[20] that system by its very nature amplified and strengthened the personalized, pre-modern, and anti-market aspects of the inherited structures of political and economic relations. This absence of the rule of law, of effective constraints on both the strong and the state, was most clearly visible in Yeltsin's Russia and its autocratic, elite (insider) dominated governance, its exercise of arbitrary discretion at the top, with obsequious submission at the bottom, and the resort at all levels of government to the use of secret instructions, orders and decrees that operated above all laws.[21] It was also clearly visible in the ubiquitous predation against new, unauthorized (outsider) activity and initiative, particularly reflected in the difficulties of small business and family farming.[22]

Social

This arbitrariness of political and economic power is reinforced by another central legacy of the Soviet system, the absence or weakness of autonomous social institutions, and the extreme vulnerability of those that have been formed in the post-Soviet period. Soviet labor unions were house pets of the state management, and functioned largely as transmission belts for information gathering and dissemination, and for the management of state guaranteed workers' benefits.[23] While a number of independent labor unions in the European mold have arisen during the transition period, the large successors to the official Soviet unions remain the dominant labor union structures. They also remain weak and unable to, or uninterested in, upholding workers' rights; they appear to be more rent-seeking agencies working in collusion with management to maintain as much of the old structures and prerogatives as possible. The Orthodox Church in Russia has always been an arm of the state, and remains very much such. Other religious organizations either remain disengaged as they reassert themselves in their spiritual domain, or are struggling to survive as they are subject to increasing political pressure, sometimes provoked by the Orthodox church. In neither case are they capable of effectively articulating or representing alternative social interests to those of the ruling elite.

Until high *perestroika* in the late 1980s, all other organizations that might constitute civil society were either illegal or strictly subordinate to, and directly controlled by, Party organs or organizations such as *Komsomol*. For example, all musical, theater and artistic groups, all chess and sports clubs, and all forms of recreational activity outside the immediate family were subject to organization, approval and control by some responsible organ of the Party or (by delegation) the State. Such control extended to all forms of legal civic association and all political and/or discussion clubs and organizations.

In the late Gorbachev period we saw a flowering of such civil society under the protection of official *glasnost*. Its roots, however, were extremely shallow and weak, as evidenced by its steady marscesense under both Yeltsin and Putin.[24] Hence, there remains a systematic lack of any countervailing social power to the arbitrary discretion of the elite and its governmental tools, facilitating the personalization and idiosyncrasy, and hence, self-serving nature, of economic and political decisions and interactions.

This stimulates and rationalizes the general lack of initiative among the mass of the population, and the failure of society to insist on and assert it rights against the authorities. Instead, authority is looked to for initiative and problem solving; the elite decides for all, with democratic formalisms a cover for legitimacy, just as market forms are a cover for political power. Finally, the absence of vigorous civil society leads to the search for individualized, special relation based solutions to economic and social problems, and in particular to a family-based striving for maximum possible self sufficiency.[25] This seriously undercuts the development of generalized, trust and law-based, interaction and support that characterizes properly functioning market systems.[26]

Legacies of Understanding and Behavior[27]

These economic, social, and political legacies reflect deeper patterns of behavior, and their associated understandings of, and attitudes toward, the economy and markets. These understandings and attitudes are inherited from the Soviet period or perhaps the deeper Russian past, and inhibit market development and market-functional behavior. They comprise an economic culture and understanding of how an economy works that are profoundly destructive of the necessary relations and proper functioning of a modern market economy.[28] While this topic deserves an entire monograph, I can only touch on a few general misunderstandings obstructing the path of proper marketization and development of the Russian economy.

One critical attitude is the reification of value in physical structures. There is no understanding of the economic concept of opportunity cost, or indeed of the meaning of sunk costs. This is seen in the general belief that value is determined by expenditures (sunk cost), and a subsequent faith in the value and utility of inherited structures. These attitudes are supported by the Soviet misunderstanding of the role and functioning of markets, prices, and financial constraints. There is very little understanding of how market value is determined, and in particular of the informational role of price levels and, more significantly, their changes in determining what should be done in a market system. Rather, there is a belief that connections, influence payments, and *blat* determine (and should determine) activity undertaken, and the acceptance of subordination of economic activity to political authority; government as player rather than referee.

This is closely related to the managerial and bureaucratic belief that activity and payment are not necessarily related; that failure to cover costs is a problem with prices, not the activity.[29] Thus, there is a lack of acceptance of budget constraints; as in the Soviet Union money should follow clear economic need rather than limiting and forcing choice among possible alternatives. These attitudes are reinforced by the acceptance of different rules of the game for insiders and outsiders, a general hostility toward outsiders, and possessive managerial and governmental attitudes to their enterprises and operations.[30] Thus, only trusted insiders, or those who make special arrangements with the authorities, are allowed to operate, undercutting the competition so essential to the proper functioning of markets and the proper determination of prices and valuations. Finally, there is a critical misunderstanding of the meaning and function of property rights in a market economic system. Hence, privatization is largely understood as the seizure and redistribution of existing property rather than the creation of secure, tradable property rights facilitating the generation of new value.

Is Russia a "Market Economy"?

In view of these legacies, I have argued at length elsewhere[31] that the Russian economic system under Yeltsin was better characterized as feudal in structure, than as a market economy. Four general systemic characteristics stood out: the politicized and personal-connection based economic decision making; the disintegration of the state, with parcelization of its sovereignty and privatization of its functions; a fragmentary market structure without effective complex intermediation; and, widespread market non-viability of economic organizations and institutions, leading to survival strategies of autarky and virtual economy networking.

Of these characteristics, three continue to be important, if of diminishing significance since 2003, to the current Russian economic system; only the second has apparently been reversed under Putin, albeit frequently through compromise with regional and business magnates. These legacies and characteristics cast doubt on the claim that Russia has a market system, despite being recognized in mid-2002 as a market economy by both the U.S., and the European Union. For markets, market motivations, financial constraints, and the ability to cover costs and produce value at market prices are the essence of any system that can claim to be market based and driven. Rather than being built on idiosyncratic personal and traditional networks, a market system is non-hierarchical and functions within an established political and legal framework providing rules of the game, constraining behavior regardless of the political or social position of the agent. In a market economy, sovereignty resides in an autonomous state outside, and in some respects, above the market system, rather than being parcelized among various political and economic actors, as was the case in Yeltsin's Russia. And the rule of law provides constraints on the state, as well as private agents, in the economic and political spheres. Thus, there is a clear separation of political and economic roles, of the public and private spheres, with rules and limits applicable equally to all regardless of rank or status. Similarly, property and contractual rights in a market system are clearly defined and socially protected, regardless of the status of the agent.

Interaction and networks in a market economy are thus primarily based on the perception of opportunity and mutual benefit from cooperation and/or exchange, and are perpetually changing in pursuit of new opportunity and/or cost avoidance.

Ties are contractual, specific, and subject to voluntary renegotiation and third-party enforcement, rather than traditional, general, and based of personal commitment and obligation. And incentives derive from the rewards to meeting the needs and desires of other market participants, to creating new products, services and wealth. Hence, investment in the pursuit of opportunity, and of the wealth to develop further opportunities, is a primary reflection of market economic motivation. In a market economy, economic power is clearly differentiated from political power and/or political and moral authority, and is based on success on markets rather than social or political legitimacy and power.

These modern characteristics of a market system still stand in sharp contrast to those of the coalescing Russian system. And they lie behind the growth of active, complex systems of factor, product, service, and financial markets, operating independently of direct political and social controls, that are at the heart of a market economic system and provide the basis for investment and economic growth. In Russia, however, we see few of the deep structural characteristics of a modern market economy, and less the functioning of an integrated system of complex markets fostering investment and growth. Rather, feudal characteristics seemed to have developed under Yeltsin, and still hold some influence, albeit diminished and perhaps fading, under Putin. Despite dramatic differences in technologies and capabilities for communication, for information processing, and for control of economic activity, a feudal, fealty-based parcelization of sovereignty,[32] a devolution of much economic activity to quasi-autarchic networks, a fragmentation of markets, and a personalization of rule and interregional interaction seem to continue to hold.

At the base of this system remain industrial, agricultural, and construction enterprises, whether privatized or not, regional and local governments, and some of the more important, as they are politically connected, new commercial and financial structures (FIGs). Most of these organizations are legitimated by tradition, having been derived from Soviet economic and political entities or built on connections from that period, and many of the new commercial and financial structures have acquired the status of the industrial enterprises over which they have taken control.[33] Personalized power is exercised through overlapping networks of personal ties and obligations, replicating to a large extent Soviet and traditional patterns of coordination and control.[34]

Markets and market relations seem predominant only in dealing with strong outsiders, e.g. foreign firms and markets, and in areas outside the core interests of the major institutions surviving from the Soviet era. Even there, markets are locally regulated or monopolized where possible, often by informal, extralegal organizations. And, as under feudalism, property and contract rights are diffuse, circumscribed by Soviet tradition and the increasingly assertive (under Putin) state apparatus, and encumbered by conflicting claims of multiple stakeholders, rendering them often unenforceable through regular legal channels. Hence, there was very little investment beyond that required to maintain current, reduced levels of activity until the post-crash boom of 1999-2001. During that boom, much of that investment outside the energy sector seems to have been aimed at resuscitating Soviet industrial structures, rather than at restructuring or developing new market-viable operations.[35] Finally, the sources of political and economic power are localized and relational, unencumbered by moral or overarching institutional constraint, although now increasingly circumscribed by the power of Putin's center.

Thus, the structure and functioning of the Russian economy seem to be fairly inconsistent with a market system, despite the fact that, as Anders Åslund demonstrates, the command economy has been destroyed.[36] Despite radical decentralization, the lack of ex-ante planning and coordination, and the absence of vertical integration and control of information, markets cannot play the role that they must in a true market economy. Essential institutions for the proper functioning of markets and market relations are weak or lacking, including: transparent, uniformly enforced laws, rules, and regulations; enforcement of property rights; contractual commitment with third party enforcement; and hence, institutions supporting complex physical and financial intermediation.

There has been virtually no complex market intermediation, except when dealing with foreign entities, but rather spot markets and networks based on personal connections and mutual dependence. The domain of impersonal, horizontal relations, characterizing much market interaction, is severely restricted even if currently expanding, and there remains a substantial lack of equivalence in exchange that is reflected in the continuing, if less wide-spread, non-uniformity and personalization of prices, depending on the status of and relationship between the agents. Factor markets are still degenerate, and full market relations predominate only when dealing with foreigners, basic localized non-durable goods, and some advanced and luxury products. Most economic behavior has not been oriented toward the creation of wealth and minimization of opportunity cost, but rather toward the redistribution of property, the seizure of wealth for consumption and political power, and their insurance through political connections (relational capital).[37] Survival and autarchy have become primary objectives. Incentives beyond personal still derive largely from your network or clan, and stimulate supporting its organizations and leadership, not creating market value.

Size and Structure

The Russian economy is undergoing substantial and turbulent change. The ambiguity of rules and variance in behaviors, the mixing of inherited and new patterns of activity and interaction, and the absence of well established, stable market institutions and structures, render any measurement of the size of the Russian economy rather questionable. Yet, certain broad trends and developments seem clear.[38]

Issues of Measurement

The classical problems of incomplete, incoherent statistics, and index number relativity continue to haunt the measurement of the Russian economy.[39] Reporting channels are largely those developed in the Soviet period, and the accounting methodology of most existing firms, whether privatized or not, remains oriented toward material product and physical production indicators, poorly measuring economic value and cost. High and variable inflation undercuts the reliability of measures of economic aggregates and their changes. Base prices in which economic activity is measured and aggregated are frequently distorted by both regional and national price controls on basic inputs, and regional segmentation of markets. Price information for measuring both inputs and output is often further distorted by the use of quasi-monetary instruments or barter, rendering the measurement of real economic activity less reliable than it appears,[40] and raising questions about the reliability of the balances in the system of national accounts (*natsional'nye scheta*).

Among the problems with official economic statistics, five deserve to be particularly highlighted:

- only the activity of large and medium enterprises is directly measured (reported), a legacy of the Soviet data base; the activity of small scale and individual enterprises is estimated from a survey based on a stratified sample from tax records;[41]
- the guesstimate of unofficial economic activity, raised from twenty percent through twenty-three percent (1998) to twenty-five percent (2001) of reported activity;
- the lack of adjustment of official statistics for reported activity

supported by black cash payments, generating deductible costs for fictitious economic activity (usually construction, repair or other services);[42]

- economic activity is not fully market determined or driven, hence the meaning of Western accounting concepts is not the same when applied to Russia; the economic value of activity measured in national accounts is not necessarily the same as it would be were those numbers generated by a fully functional market economy – errors occur both in measuring waste as real activity and in ignoring valuable economic activity;[43]

- the use of un- or poorly-explained methodology, particularly with respect to revisions of statistical series, preventing consistent updating and comparison.[44]

A further problem has recently arisen in the economic statistics of the post-crisis period due to tax avoidance strategies of the profitable resource and energy sectors. As a recent World Bank analysis pointed out, those industries most profitable in the period of high world energy and resource prices have systematically hidden their value-added in production from the tax authorities through transfer pricing, thereby shifting profits to their controlled trade intermediaries subject to lower taxation. This distorts reported value-added (sectoral GDP), exaggerating the output share of services (especially trade), and depressing the reported share of industry, and in particular the fuel industries, in GDP.[45]

Despite these continuing problems, substantial progress has been made in adopting standard international SNA methodologies, and in attempting to get clean, reliable data. A significant recent development has been the introduction, extending over two years to 1 January 2005, of the international system of classification of economic and industrial activity (SIC; NACE). This should make economic data provided in national income accounts and input-output tables fully comparable with the corresponding data available in Western statistical reports, and more reliable for use in economic analyses in the future. But the task is extremely difficult, due to the level of understanding, and the inherited mind-set of most of the managers and administrators at the basic reporting levels in the economic system. Western accounting concepts and understanding of the cost and value categories being measured are only vaguely understood, if at all, by the vast majority of Russian managers and bureaucrats, leading to inevitable mistakes in measuring and reporting real economic activity.[46] Where real progress has been made is in the statistical accounting organs at the center (*Goskomstat*, now *Rosstat*) where substantial training and aid has been provided by international assistance programs.[47] As a result, we have apparently conscientious and honest processing of rather unreliable data, subject to substantial errors on both the positive and negative side.

The Aggregate Economy

Official *Goskomstat* (GKS) statistics placed GDP at 4,545.5 billion rubles, or 34,068 rubles per capita, in 1999. At official exchange rates, this makes GDP about $175 billion, or $1,320 per capita, indicating an economy about the size of Denmark despite its vastly larger population at an apparently Third-World level of development. That, however, seriously understates the size and strength of the economy, for reasons discussed below.

A better relative measure, taking account of many of the pricing distortions in the Russian economy is in terms of purchasing-power parity (PPP) prices. GKS has estimated 1996 Russian GDP at PPP prices as $996.1 billion, or $6,742 per capita, placing Russia at the level of development of Thailand, Turkey, or Mexico in that pre-crisis, pre-recovery year when GDP was still some two percent above its level in 1999. A more recent estimate by the World Bank in 2000 corroborates that estimate for 1999: $948 billion or $6,500 per capita, making the Russian economy the tenth largest in the world.[48]

The macroeconomy grew between 7.7 and 8.3 percent in 2000 when output was weighted by the 1995 sectoral structure, but that was revised in 2001 to ten percent, due to a reweighting in terms of the 1999 sectoral structure and a revaluation of value added in the unofficial economy. The aggregate economy grew at a slower rate of 5.1 percent during 2001, giving a 2001 annual GDP of about 9,040.8 billion rubles (about 62,350 rubles per capita), or about $288 billion ($1,984 per capita) at the then-current exchange rate (♦30 RUR per U.S. dollar).[49] The 2001 lull in growth continued into 2002, as the growth in oil and metals prices stalled during world economic slowdown following 9/11, with GDP increasing by only 4.7 percent, but still raising PPP-valued GDP per capita to $7,961, or twenty-one percent of the U.S. level, in 2002. However, with the strong continuation of the liberal (Gref) reforms in 2003, the evident political stability and confidence in its continuation, and a strong rise in oil, gas and metals prices, the Russia macroeconomy rebounded strongly, growing at a rate of 7.3 percent and 7.1 percent in 2003 and 2004. Despite this growth, initially consistent with Putin's proclaimed objective of doubling GDP by 2010, the Russian economy remains at best at the level of upper tier developing economies, and well behind the less developed countries of southern Europe.[50]

The Shadow and Virtual Economies

Beyond the marketized and officially measured economy, there is a substantial unofficial, shadow or second, economy. Excluding activities which are criminal and hence not measured anywhere (e.g. drugs, extortion, theft), the statistical organs estimate now that this activity adds about twenty-five percent to the levels of measured activities. Some scholars, and some statements by the tax authorities and prosecutor general, place the size of this shadow economy at forty percent, although this estimate is not used in calculating official performance statistics.[51] This twenty-five percent adjustment tries to capture small-scale activity missed by the inherited statistical measurement systems, as well as tax avoiding and unregistered, but otherwise legal, activity. This adjustment is included in official measures of macroeconomic and sectoral performance above.

A phenomenon which is ignored in official statistics, but indirectly influences them, is that of the virtual economy.[52] This encompasses a range of activities, largely in the traditional industrial sectors, whose reported performance is exaggerated by the use of quasi- and non-monetary instruments of exchange, such as barter, offsets, and promissory notes, that allow wide variation and idiosyncrasy in transaction prices, generally exaggerating the reported value of industrial output and understating the costs (particularly fuel and energy) of its production.[53] This exaggerates both gross output and value added in industry to an unknown degree. If properly accounted for, and we have no evidence that it is, it will also reduce the estimated size of the value adding sectors (e.g. fuel and energy, intermediate materials and metals, services) with an ambiguous impact on the measured size of the overall economy.[54]

Thus, the virtual economy has a significant impact on the measurement of the sectoral structure of the Russian economy, and its changes over the last decade. In particular, it reduces the measured relative size of the fuel and energy and basic metals and materials sectors, while exaggerating the size of a number of the manufacturing and engineering sectors. These non-market driven activities cloud our measurement of the market structure of the economy, raising questions about its economic coherence.

Sectoral Structure

The Soviet Russian structure of production activity was strongly tilted toward heavy and military industry and the inputs critical to their expansion, and quite weak in the production of consumers' goods and services. It focused on physical product and the production of the means of further production as the key to economic, and hence, military power, downplaying unproductive if necessary activity that only provided goods and services to the civil population. Thus, the resource, fuel, and energy sectors, and the manufacture of industrial inputs and machinery, dominated the structure of industrial activity, while industry, agriculture, construction, and industrial transportation accounted for almost three-fourths of GDP, with all consumer services, including housing, a portion of the remaining quarter.[55]

This structure underwent substantial change in the mid-1990s, particularly after the first real shock of stabilization set in during 1995, amid the general and deep contraction of all economic activity.[56] Tables 1 through 4 show the shift in the structure of both employment and output by macroeconomic sector and industrial branch from 1990 to 1999, and then through the post-crisis recovery to 2002. These data show that most of the structural change had taken place by 1999, although new industries continued to grow disproportionately thereafter. As was to be expected from the substantial, if incomplete, marketization of the economy, industry, construction, and agriculture shrank in relative size, while services expanded substantially. Within industry, manufacturing and processing contracted substantially, while new sectors, particularly business and financial services, arose where the Soviet state had placed low priority or had forbidden activity (e.g. financial intermediation). Finally, the resource, energy, and fuel sectors appeared to grow dramatically in terms of relative output share, leading to claims of deindustrialization and becoming a resource appendage of the capitalist world.

The changes in the structure of output have been much greater than those in employment. This is partly a reflection of the unwillingness of management, now often the controlling private owners, to release workers. This arises from the confluence of strategic, paternalistic, and political motives, and the pressure of local and regional governments.[57] But it is also partly the consequence of the dramatic changes in sectoral prices following the liberalizations of 1992, and the succeeding gradual adjustment of the still regulated (in particular, energy and transportation) prices.

In the Soviet Union, priority inputs for industrial development, and military

Table 1: Employment Structure: Totals and Shares

Source: For 1990 and 1999 data, Goskomstat Rossii, *Rossiiskii Statisticheskii Ezhegodnik* (Moscow, 2000), 112, and author's calculations. Last three columns are from Rosstat, *Rossiiskii Statisticheskii Ezhegodnik* (Moscow, 2003,) 137, and author's calculations.

Branch	1990	1990s	1999	1999s	99/90	99s/90s	2002	2002s	02s/99s
Industry	22,809	30.3	14,297	22.4	.6268	.7393	14,534	22.2	.9911
Agriculture	9,727	12.9	8,495	13.3	.8733	1.0310	7,683	11.8	.8872
Forestry	238	0.3	245	0.4	1.0294	1.3333	264	0.4	1.0000
Construction	9,020	12.0	5,080	7.9	.5529	.6583	4,982	7.6	.9620
Transportation	4,934	6.6	4,060	6.3	.8229	.9545	4,137	6.3	1.0000
Communication	884	1.2	859	1.3	.9717	1.0833	882	1.4	1.0769
Trade and Food	5,869	7.8	9,320	14.6	1.5880	1.8718	10,837	16.6	1.1370
Housing, Cmnl Svcs	3,213	4.3	3,361	5.3	1.0461	1.2326	3,208	4.9	.9245
Health, Sport, Soc Spt	4,238	5.6	4,496	7.0	1.0609	1.2500	4,591	7.0	1.0000
Education	6,066	7.9	5,935	9.3	.9784	1.1772	5,887	9.0	.9677
Culture, Art	1,165	1.7	1,129	1.8	.9691	1.0588	1,200	1.8	1.0000
Science	2,804	3.7	1,209	1.9	.4312	.5135	1,181	1.8	.9474
Finance,Insurance	402	0.5	744	1.2	1.8507	2.4000	816	1.3	1.0833
Government	1,602	2.1	2,858	4.5	1.7840	2.1429	2,965	4.5	1.0000
Other	2,350	3.1	1,875	2.8	.7979	.9032	2,192	3.4	1.2143
Total	75,325	100	63,963	100	.8502	1.0000	65,359	100	1.0000

Measurement is in thousands of employees. After a year, "s" indicates "share" of sector. The final two columns indicate ratios (proportional change) of shares.

Table 2: Output Structure: Total and Shares

Source: Goskomstat Rossii, *Rossiiskii Statisticheskii Ezhegodnik* (Moscow, 2000), 252, 257, and author's calculations. 2002 data from Rosstat, *Rossiiskii Statisticheskii Ezhegodnik* (Moscow, 2003), Table 12.17, and author's calculations.

Branch	1990	1990s	1999	1999s	2002	2002s	99s/90s	02s/99s
Industry	585.4	.4861	2,995,200.4	.3866	7,116,743.8	.3720	.7953	.9573
Agriculture and Services	159.1	.1321	634,318.0	.0819	1,077,514.1	.0563	.6200	.6874
Forestry	0.9	.0007	8,136.1	.0011	18,655.6	.00098	1.5714	.8909
Construction	108.4	.0900	471,553.7	.0609	1,438,740.7	.0752	.6767	1.2348
Other Goods Production	12.9	.0107	33,083.7	.0043	103,511.5	.0054	.4019	1.2558
Transportation	70.2	.0583	563,998.8	.0728	1,384,538.8	.0724	1.2487	.9945
Communication	8.0	.0066	108,703.0	.0140	297,641.9	.0156	2.1212	1.1143
Trade and Food	45.2	.0375	1,034,228.4	.1335	3,331,854.7	.1742	3.5600	1.2971
Zagotovki (procurement)	4.3	.0036	6,200.0	.0008	←	←	.2222	←
Computer Services	2.1	.0017	4,800.0	.0006	20,213.2	.00106	.3529	1.7667
Real Estate	0	0	116,119.4	.0150	443,630.0	.0232	∞	1.5467
Market Operations	0	0	53,062.1	.0068	371,887.2	.0194	∞	2.8529
Geology/Exploration	0	0	21,342.8	.0028	58,142.4	.0030	∞	1.0714
Housing, etc., Services*	27.8	.0231	340,994.1	.0440	648,453.5	.0339	1.9048	.7705
Finance, Insurance	6.0	.0050	83,813.3	.0108	352,440.7	.0184	2.1600	1.7037
Science	34.4	.0286	78,697.1	.0102	290,875.0	.0152	.3566	1.4902
Health, Sport, Social Spt	26.6	.0221	242,094.2	.0312	545,547.4	.0285	1.4118	.9135
Education, Culture, Art**	43.1	.0358	232,771.9	.0300	564,693.8	.0295	.8380	.9833
Defense Gov't [+ Def (after '97)]	55.1 / 9.4	.0457 / .0078	→	.0510	→	.0514	→	1.0078
Social Organizations	5.5	.0046	53,954.7	.0070	82,732.1	.0043	1.5217	.614
Total	**1204.4**	**1.0000**	**7,748,038.1**	**1.0000**	**19,130,330.3**	**1.0000**	**1.0000**	**1.0000**

Measurement is in current million-ruble units. After a year, "s" indicates "share" of sector. The final two columns indicate ratios (proportional change) of shares.
* Four categories in 2003 yearbook: roads services; housing services; communal services; non-production services to population.
** Two categories in 2003 yearbook: education; art and culture.

Table 3: Employment in Industry

Source: Goskomstat Rossii, *Promyshlennost.Rossii* (Moscow, 2000), 20-27, and author's calculations. The 2002 figures are from Rosstat, *Rossiiskii Statis-cheskii Ezhegodnik* (Moscow, 2003), Table 6.25, and the author's calculations.

Branch	1990	1990s	1999	1999s	99s/90s	2002	2002s	02s/99s
Electric Power	545	.0260	880	.0662	2.5489	928	.0720	1.0876
Fuel	801	.0381	738	.0555	1.4544	774	.0601	1.0829
Ferric Metals	785	.0374	676	.0508	1.3594	695	.0539	1.0610
Non-Ferrous Metals	487	.0232	503	.0378	1.6304	570	.0442	1.1693
Chemical	755	.0360	761	.0572	1.5911	866	.0672	.9168
Petro-Chemical	294	.0140	214	.0161	1.1490	←	←	←
MBMW	9,639	.4590	4,688	.3524	.7677	4,510*	.3500*	.9932
Woodworking-Paper	1,792	.0853	1,057	.0795	.9311	1,010	.0784	.9862
Construction Materials	1,097	.0522	718	.0540	1.0331	667	.0518	.9593
Glass-Porcelain	135	.0064	100	.0075	1.1693	-	-	-
Light	2,288	.1090	863	.0649	.5954	765	.0594	.9153
Food	1,545	.0736	1,439	.1082	1.4703	1,492	.1158	1.0702
Microbiology	36	.0017	21	.0016	.9208	-	-	-
Feed and Grain	128	.0061	163	.0123	2.0102	-	-	-
Medical	105	.0050	116	.0087	1.7439	*	*	-
Poligraphic	143	.0068	114	.0086	1.2584	-	-	-
Other	423	.0201	251	.0189	.9367	-	-	-
Total	20,998	100	13,302	100	1.0000	12,886	.9528	0.9528

Measurement is in thousands of employees. Note that, for 2002, 4.72 percent of employment in industry is not detailed; – indicates missing numbers in the Goskomstat table. After a year, "s" indicates "share" of sector. The final two columns indicate ratios (proportional change) of shares.

* medical equipment included in MBMW.

Table 4: Output in Industry

Source: Goskomstat Rossii, *Promyshlennost.Rossii* (Moscow, 2000), 20–27, and author's calculations. The branch "unclassified" is the residual from the total reported and the sum of all reported branches of industry. The 2002 figures are directly from Rosstat, *Rossiiskii Statischeskii Ezhegodnik* (Moscow, 2003), Table 14.4.

Branch	1990	1990s	1999	1999s	99s/90s	2002s	02s/99s
Electric Power	21	.0359	269,551	.0900	2.5087	.119	1.3222
Fuel	40	.0683	452,686	.1511	2.2119	.199	1.3170
Ferric Metals	29	.0495	223,356	.0746	1.5053	.081	1.0858
Non-Ferrous Metals	32	.0547	269,527	.0900	1.6462	.077	.8556
Chemical	27	.0461	126,103	.0421	.9128	.063	1.0570
Petro-Chemical	12	.0205	52,346	.0175	.8526	←	←
MBMW	168	.2870	509,742	.1702	.5930	.201*	1.1810
Woodworking-Paper	31	.0530	128,670	.0430	.8112	.044	1.0233
Construction Materials	20	.0432	77,096	.0257	.7534	.033	1.2840
Glass-Porcelain	2	.0034	9,826	.0033	.9602	.005	1.5152
Light	66	.1127	45,041	.0150	.1334	.015	1.0000
Food	73	.1247	392,599	.1311	1.0511	.139	1.0603
Microbiology	1	.0017	3,430	.0011	.6704	-	-
Feed and Grain	19	.0325	49,614	.0166	.5104	.012	.7229
Medical	3	.0051	22,888	.0076	1.4911	*	-
Poligraphic	1	.0017	13,714	.0046	2.6803	-	-
Other	9	.0154	29,796	.0099	.6471	-	-
Unclassifed	31.4	.0536	319,215.4	.1066	1.9869	-	-
Total	585.4	1.00	2,995,200.4	1.00	1.0000	0.988	0.988

Measurement is in current million-ruble units. Note that 1.2 percent of the current value of output is missing in the source. After a year, "s" indicates "share" of sector. The final two columns indicate ratios (proportional change) of shares.
* medical equipment included in MBMW.

priority resources, were priced artificially low, giving the appearance of lower output in those sectors and limited input use in downstream sectors.[58] If relative world prices are used, rather than current Soviet prices, to explore the structure of production in pre-transition Russia, the branch structure of industry appears to have changed much less since 1990, and indeed, the relative shares of the energy, fuels, and metals sectors may have fallen in the transition, as can be seen from Table 5 which shows the output structure of industrial branches in world prices of 1991. However, their share may still be understated due to the continuing regulation of prices and the operation of the virtual economy which exaggerates output in inherited manufacturing and processing industries. However, as the last column shows, there may be a countervailing distortion through tax-avoiding transfer pricing, as discussed under measurement issues above.

Table 5: Industrial Branch Output Structure (percent): 1991, 2000

Source: OECD (1995), 4; World Bank (2/2004), 15, where wbtp indicates output structure at prices with World Bank adjustment for transfer pricing.

Branch Output	1991dp	1991wp	Branch Value Added	2000dp	2000wbtp
Electric Energy	4.0	12.4	Electric Energy	8.8	5.4
Fuel	7.3	25.7	Fuel	29.3	51.1
Metallurgy	11.2	7.9	Metallurgy	17.7	11.2
Chemistry	6.5	2.2	Chemistry	6.0	5.6
MBMW	24.9	19.0	MBMW	16.0	10.3
Wood and Paper	5.8	13.5	Wood and Paper	4.7	3.9
Construction Materials	3.7	5.4	Construction Materials	2.8	2.3
Light Industry	16.2	2.9	Light Industry	1.6	1.0
Food Industry	14.4	8.2	Food and Industry	10.7	7.8
Other	5.9	2.8	Other	2.2	1.4
Total	**100**	**100**	**Total**	**100**	**100**

Thus, the actual change in the structure of output has been less than it appears from the output data in current prices, and the sectoral structure still remains rather far from that of a modern market economy, despite some substantial movement in that direction.

Performance and Prospects

To 2002, the Russian economy was still experiencing a strong, if diminishing, recovery from the great depression of the 1990s.[59] As can be seen in Table 6, there was slowdown in growth rates, as some of the advantages of the devaluation and default of 1998 faded, limits to the restoration of old capacities were approached, and Putin began pushing, both rhetorically and in legislative initiatives, a renewal of the radical reform agenda. This paid off in a dramatic improvement in overall economic performance, with a 7.3 percent rate of GDP growth and a 12.5 percent increase in investment in 2003. That performance was largely sustained through 2004, although it is showing signs of a dramatic falloff in 2005. The overwhelming victory of Putin and his political supporters in the elections of 2003 (Duma) and 2004 (Presidency), have guaranteed continued political stability at the center, and given Putin a relatively free hand to move forward on his political agenda. But that agenda appears increasingly to have veered from modernizing and marketizing economic reform to further enhancing the power of the Federal center, strengthening and centralizing the power vertical, and subordinating key economic sectors and social institutions to the will of the Kremlin.[60] Thus, the economic reform process appears to be stalling, although domestic political and economic stability promise, in the

Table 6: Macroeconomic Performance Indicators

Source: BOFIT, *Russian Economy: Month in Review* (June 2005); eop = end of period.

Indicator	1999	2000	2001	2002	2003	2004
GDP growth, percent	6.4	10.0	5.1	4.7	7.3	7.1
Industry growth, percent	11.0	11.9	2.9	3.1	8.9	7.3
Fixed Investment growth, percent	5.3	17.4	10.0	2.6	12.5	10.9
Unemployment level, percent eop	12.4	9.9	8.7	9.0	8.7	7.6
Consumption growth, percent	-14	11	9	9	7.6	11.8
Current Account, $bil	24.6	46.8	33.9	29.1	35.4	60.1
FDI, $bil eop	4.26	4.46	3.4	3.9	8.0	11.9
Budget Balance, percent GDP	-4.2	0.8	3.0	1.4	1.7	4.4
CPI-twelve month growth, percent	36.5	20.2	18.6	15.1	12.0	11.7

These figures are based on the 2001 reweighting of sectors reflecting the 1999 sectoral structure, rather than that of 1995 (in which GDP grew 7.7 percent in 2000 and 4.3 percent in 1999). Further adjustments in 2001 raised GDP growth in 2000 from 8.3 percent to 9.0 percent, while still further adjustments of figures in 2003 and January 2005 have raised growth estimates to the reported levels.

absence of serious shocks from the external economy, to maintain this fading recovery in the near future. Further, renewed reform offers the prospect for renewed rapid and sustained growth, realizing Russia's economic potential over the longer term. But to realize that potential, reform must be sufficiently comprehensive and sharp to break the grip of remaining Soviet legacies, some of which have been reinforced by Putin's centralization of authority and decision making, and thus transform the economic system into a truly market one capable of thriving in the globalized economic environment.

The Post-Crisis Recovery

Since bottoming in out in April 1999 following the financial crisis and default of August 1998, Russian GDP has rebounded, surpassing its level of 1995 by three percent at the end of 2000, and achieving that of 1993-94 by the end of 2001. While still below pre-transition levels (about ninety percent of 1990 levels, in official measures), it reflects a qualitatively different performance and structure, better reflecting true value produced than did the arbitrary and inflated measurements of the Soviet period.[61]

This somewhat surprising, if long awaited recovery arose on the coincidence of a favorable economic environment and the hitting of an economic bottom. The preceding economic collapse, beginning under *perestroika* in 1990, had been so deep and extensive that there was little room for further contraction by early 1999; the contraction of industrial activity by the end of 1996 far exceeded that of the U.S. Great Depression and was beginning, in some sectors to resemble that of the 1919-21 Civil War collapse.[62] The August 1998 default and devaluation, after a sharply negative impact on the new (especially financial) sectors of the Russian economy, and the subsequent dramatic rise in international fuel, energy, and resource prices, opened new easily profitable opportunities for the un- and under-employed factors and resources of the Russian economy. Russian industrial and resource capacities, particularly in the manufacturing and processing sectors, which had been unable to cover basic operating costs, never mind turn a profit, suddenly became viable as producers for markets. And the easy transfers, credits and subsidies through governmental and quasi-governmental organs came to a halt in the collapse of government finances, forcing producers to turn, in ways that they had hereto been able to avoid, to the market in order to survive.[63]

This recovery was based on substantial, but fundamentally short-run, favorable shocks:

- an over four-fold devaluation of the ruble, which priced competing foreign products out of the market and dramatically lowered domestic, in particular labor, costs;
- maintained price controls over energy, utility, and transportation input costs, further enhancing the competitiveness of Russian industry; and
- a dramatic rise in international basic commodity and energy, in particular oil, prices in 1999, greatly enhancing the relative value of Russia's primary exports.

Each of these appeared to be fading (the first and third), or slated for removal (the second), by 2003. The ruble had recovered more than half of its real value against the dollar, energy and resource prices have dropped substantially following 9/11 in association with a spreading world recession, and the need for reform of the natural monopolies has led the government to begin slowly raising energy, utility, and railroad transportation prices to final users in 2002. Yet, they remain important factors, as international fuel prices recovered in 2003, and accelerated to unprecedented heights by the end of 2004 (around fifty dollars per barrel), first under first OPEC action and then under disruptions in supply (e.g. the Iraq war, Venezuelan turmoil) and rapidly growing demand in both China and the U.S., while political pressures and the fear of inflation led the government to slow the rise in natural monopoly prices, and maintain tight control over the exchange rate. Finally, their impact was enhanced by the new-found fiscal rectitude of the Primakov government in 1998-99, the monetary conservatism of Viktor Gerashchenko on his return to head of the Russian Central Bank (1998-2002), and the continued conservatism of his successor, Sergei Ignatiev.[64]

Thus, we have seen substantial import substitution in both consumers' and producers' goods markets, a significant strengthening of businesses bottom line, and a strong improvement in the current account as imports collapsed and the price of exports rose in 1998-2001. These factors substantially improved the government's liquidity position, and set into motion a remonetization of economic activity and an improvement in enterprise cash flow, as witnessed by a drop in wage and tax arrears and a decrease in the role of barter in the economy. Payments arrears are now stable at less than twelve percent of GDP (down from fifty percent in 1998), barter is now used in less than nine percent of industrial transactions (down from fifty to seventy percent in 1997-98), and business profits were up more than twenty-five percent in

2000, declined slightly in real terms in 2001-02, and accelerated again in 2003-04. This improvement in enterprise cash flow, together with improved tax collection, higher excises on oil and gas exports, and initial mandatory turnover of seventy-five percent of foreign exchange earnings to the Russian Central Bank for rubles, despite being reduced to fifty percent in 2001 and twenty-five percent in 2003, has further aided the recovery of state finances to the point where the budget runs a substantial surplus (over 2.5 percent of GDP through 2004). Russia is current in all its international financial obligations, in 2001 refused further IMF loans despite being in substantial compliance with the budgetary and macroeconomic performance conditionality earlier imposed by the IMF, in 2003 renegotiated its London Club debt reducing it by forty percent, and in 2004 began accelerated repayment of all its outstanding (Soviet and Russian) international debt.[65]

This positive dynamic was aided by what would generally be considered negative factors. First, the maintenance of controls holding down domestic energy price increases contributed substantially to the economic viability of manufacturing, while not damaging the energy and resource firms whose primary earnings were, and remain, based on exports; windfall profits in the energy and resource sectors are being transferred to support weak manufacturing and other industrial sectors.[66] The general default also played a role in facilitating these transfers and husbanding financial resources for domestic industrial recovery by preventing the transfer of new earnings to foreign creditors, albeit at the cost of disrupting access to foreign borrowing. Fortunately for Russia, foreign borrowing has not been, and still largely remained until 2004, an insignificant factor; indeed FDI shrank through 2002, only recovering to 1996 levels in 2003-04. And finally, the lack of a functioning financial intermediation (banking) system played a role in limiting the potential damage from financial disruption following default; a credit crunch and crisis was avoided as Russian industry has never had access to normal credit.

Some credit for the recovery must also be attributed to the strengthening of Federal executive authority under Putin and the stability that this has imparted to the political-economic environment. This has helped ensure that the Russian government has shared in the increased prosperity of business brought about by the recovery, and has given business the stability required for effective planning of activity and the initiation of structural change. It has brought greater order to both tax collection and budget implementation, has increased collection and payment discipline of Federal organs, and has induced greater caution on the part of regional and local lords in their extraction of rents from business activity. Thus, a more favorable and predictable business environment has been fostered by the strengthening of the center, and the ensuing predictability of the economic environment, that has encouraged new managerial behavior and entrepreneurship.[67] This environment has lengthened decision horizons, thereby encouraging businessmen and managers to implement new initiatives and undertake serious restructuring, improving the efficiency and viability of many, if not most, businesses in Russia.[68]

The improvement in macroeconomic performance in 2003-04 was also driven by substantial structural reforms, in effect renewing the economic transformation begun in the early 1990s. Announced by Putin in each of his first three State of the Nation addresses,[69] framed in the reform program of Putin's Minister of Economic Development and Trade, German Gref, systematically accept by the Duma, and actively implemented in 2001-2003, these reforms gave new life and direction to the private economy, stimulating a burst of real restructuring and growth in the final two years of Putin's first presidential term.

Restructuring

The decade of disintegration of Soviet economic structures has also had a positive effect in this recovery. Much of the obsolete capital stock and many non-profitable activities have been abandoned, and substantial shifts have taken place in the allocation of labor throughout the economy. Thus, much Soviet low to negative value-added activity has withered away during the prolonged depression of the 1990s, in principle freeing resources for new and restructured economic activities.[70] Those sectors, such as engineering (MBMW), processing, and agricultural, whose logic of Soviet development left their enterprises least likely to be viable, have shrunk the most, while new (e.g. financial and consumer services) and resource sectors have shown greatest growth in both output and employment. As a result of this reallocation, labor productivity in Russian industry, which shrank through 1994, has been broadly increasing since then. This has been the result largely of the elimination of low productivity jobs and a rise in intra- and inter-sectoral job reallocation, focused through privatization and market competition on the lowest productivity jobs, rather than new job creation in *de-novo* or restructured firms.[71]

However, in spite of the improved allocation of labor and activity, there was surprisingly little strategic restructuring among inherited production activities prior to 2003, although defensive restructuring in pursuit of survival did yield efficiency gains. But much more could be expected through appropriate restructuring of technology, factor use, market relations, and management practices and structures.[72] Here, continuing Soviet institutional and behavioral legacies, their anti-market and feudal character, have blocked or distorted new activities and initiatives, undercutting the incentives for and returns to true restructuring. Indeed, privatization per se has been found in Russia to have little impact on restructuring and productivity, except in cases of truly new, in general outside and/or foreign, owners.[73]

Yet, despite the less than hospitable socioeconomic and political environment, new activity appears to be taking root under the Putin stabilization and Gref reforms. There is increasing anecdotal, and now some official,[74] evidence of new and revived economic activity, of serious strategic restructuring, beginning to occur in industry. It is part of the burst in economic activity created by the favorable post-crash conditions discussed above, although by now Russian companies have lost over half of the cost advantage they gained in 1998. It is hard in such conditions, however, to know how much of this activity involves real restructuring, and how much is just patching up and resuscitating old Soviet capacities that can now temporarily cover their production costs. That judgment is further clouded by the substantial move toward reagglomeration in industry, as rich resource and energy companies plow their new earnings into acquisitions instead of investing in themselves, presumably engaging in restructuring of other industrial operations. Thus, we see consolidation in the oil industry, Alfa Group moving into telecoms, Interros adding food processing and a naval shipyard to its core nickel-mining interests, Severstal buying automotive, engine and locomotive factories, Siberian Aluminum purchasing Gorky Automotive, and Russian Aluminum consolidating most of the rest of the aluminum industry.[75]

The crisis of 1998 appears to have marked the beginning of qualitatively new, market-based and driven economic activity, with qualitatively different managers and entrepreneurs, as this new economic activity and growth has been, to 2004, resilient in the face of the evanescence of the favorable external conditions behind the 2000-01 recovery. After a pause for the passage and assimilation of market-supporting reforms in 2001-02, economic activity and growth accelerated in 2003 and maintained a strong pace in 2004, despite signs of increasingly illiberal political and social changes imposed by the Putin regime. This growth was supported through 2004 by strong, and indeed increasing fuel and resource prices, with oil moving to above fifty dollars per barrel by the end of 2004,[76] raising a question as to exactly how much of this growth can be attributed to fundamental restructuring. If broad restructuring has taken place, we should see a strong continuation of growth and new activity even after the price of oil falls below twenty-five dollars per barrel, internal energy and transportation prices are raised to near market-clearing levels (WTO standards), and the ruble completes its reappreciation against the dollar and euro. If, under such conditions, strong growth resumes after a brief adjustment period, then substantial restructuring in 1999-2004 will be revealed.

Performance Trends[77]

At the end of 2000, the Russian economy appeared to sputter and stall. Investment plummeted almost six percent, GDP and industrial growth all but ceased, and inflation spiked (twenty-one percent) in the December 2000-February 2001 period, although all output figures showed positive growth relative to those twelve months earlier. Beginning in March 2001, however, new growth appeared to kick in, although its pace remains far below that of the previous year. The result is that economic performance remained approximately on the track anticipated in the 2001 budget. Real wages continued to rise (4.4 percent in six months; eighteen percent for the whole year), despite stronger than anticipated inflation (18.6 percent), while the underlying rise in producers' prices is slowing, having dropped from a forty-seven percent annual rate in mid-2000 to a twenty-six percent annual rate in mid-2001. The output of key sectors was up six percent to October 2001, but then stalled in October-November resulting in a 5.7 percent increase for the year, and a rise in GDP of about five percent.[78]

This performance pattern has repeated in 2002, with growth in all major aggregate indicators dipping sharply before the beginning of the year and through the first quarter, with a rebound, albeit weaker than in 2001, occurring in the second and third quarters, yielding GDP growth of 4.7 percent for the year. Real investment took a particularly steep dive in the first quarter (only one percent above the low investment of the first quarter of 2001) but then recovered to some 3.5 percent growth over investment in quarters two and three of 2001. It, however, plunged again in the fourth quarter, only growing 2.6 percent for the year over 2001. This performance led to the expert consensus forecast for GDP growth in 2003 to be below four percent, consistent with the fading of the advantages spawned by the crisis of 1998. On the other hand, this steady, albeit slowing, growth resulted in the recovery of aggregate real disposable income to its pre-crisis 1998 level.

2003 however, turned out to be a banner year for economic welfare and growth. After the pause of 2002, strong, broad-based economic growth took hold. While still largely based on strong and rising fuel and resource prices, this growth showed signs of new development beyond the pure recovery phenomenon of the 1999-2000 expansion. GDP grew by 7.3 percent, industrial output by 8.9 percent, and investment by 12.5 percent! Real household incomes increased by over eleven percent, real wages by 26.8 percent (dollar terms), unemployment dropped 3.3 percent, and inflation fell to a twelve percent annual rate. This strong performance continued in 2004, although it appeared to be tailing off in the second half, until a change in the statistical reporting system (from the Soviet to the Western industrial classification system) led to a final estimate of 7.1 percent for GDP, 7.3 percent for industry, and 10.9 percent for investment, as well as a downward revision in 2003 industrial output growth to seven percent.[79] Thus, the economy showed continuing strength, reflecting prior reform and restructuring as well as still growing fuel prices (rising to forty-five to fifty dollars per barrel near the end of the year), despite increasing uncertainty about the policy direction of the Putin regime and growing strain in government-business relations in 2004. Other basic performance indicators can be seen in Table 6.

Beginning in 2001, new growth was most rapid in the core industrial sectors – MBMW (up over ten percent in six months), Defense Industry, Chemicals, and Petro-Chemical products – although food and light industry were still showing import substitution strength; it was not oil, gas, or metals exports that drove the Russian economy in 2001-02.[80] But this growth was not accompanied by the sort of investment boom, including foreign direct investment, that would have been reliable evidence of sustainable economic recovery. Hence, the growth in these industrial sectors slowed in 2002, outside of those firms servicing the resource and energy industries, while housing, telecoms, and consumer services (especially retailing) showed continuing strength in 2002. Indeed, foreign direct investment (FDI), was running just about four billion dollars per year, remained far below its peak of six billion dollars in 1997. On the other hand, capital flight, which exceeded twenty-four billion dollars in 2000, ran at about sixteen billion dollars in 2001, and had fallen to somewhere around eight billion dollars in 2002,[81] and there was renewed and growing interest in investing in Russia by U.S. firms following the visit of Secretaries O'Neill (State) and Evans (Commerce) in July 2001.[82] Fixed capital investment grew 8.7 percent to 1.6 trillion rubles, some 17.7 percent of GDP or twenty-seven percent of the value of industrial output in 2001, but that growth slowed substantially in 2002. Further, investment in capital formation remained overwhelmingly self-financed and concentrated in those resource and energy industries which have benefited most from the favorable circumstances behind the recovery, despite an increase in bank financing to 4.5 percent of the total. Indeed, those domestic industries that lead early in the increase in industrial output, in particular MBMW, food and consumer durables, are the only industries, outside of coal, investing less than they did in 1998![83] Finally, as noted above, many those firms with an investable surplus were using it both to acquire foreign assets (some $15.8 billion in 2000) and to diversify through the purchase of existing companies in Russia, rather than restructuring to insure future viability.

The positive structural trends of 2001-02 strengthened and deepened in 2003-04. Overdue payables (arrears) decreased from almost thirty percent of sales in 2002 to just over ten percent by the end of 2004, and non-cash settlements shrank from over eighteen percent of sales in 2002 to about eleven percent in the same period. Capital flight shrank to $1.9 billion in 2003, having vanished by mid-year but then again growing in the wake of the legal and political assault on YUKOS,[84] and grew to $9.4 billion in 2004. Average enterprise profitability grew to 20.7 percent of sales in 2003, and to twenty-six to twenty-seven percent of sales in 2004, but the number of loss-making firms remained stubbornly above forty percent, showing a sharp divergence between winners and losers in the overall growing economy.[85] The liberalizing structural reform program legislated in 2001-03 began to take effect, and business, in particular big business, took advantage of these changes, and the opportunities offered by ever stronger fuel and resource prices, to invest, acquire assets, and expand production, albeit at a slower rate in 2004 than in 2003. This investment and expansion appears to have been driven by factor productivity growth leading to strong earnings growth, and the need to maintain it, on the supply side, and demand growth by both consumers and businesses. They were reflected in the structure of the expansion: continuing strong growth in manufacturing (9.2 percent), and in particular machine building (14.2 percent), even as growth in the energy and extractive industries tailed off (6.8 percent) in 2004. Factor productivity increased from 128 percent of its 1997 level in 2002 to over 150 percent in 2004, somewhat offsetting the strong rise in real wages, and slowing the rise in unit costs in industry until late in 2004. However, price competitiveness of manufacturing continued to decline through 2003-04 as the impact of devaluation dissipated, leading to import growth that was substantially faster (fifteen to twenty percent per year in volume) than either domestic production (7.5 percent) or domestic demand (ten percent).[86]

State finances remained strong in 2001 and 2002, allowing Russia to not only remain current on payments to international financial organizations, but to also buy back debt lowering its future burden, without additional support from the IMF. Russia maintained a strong current account surplus of thirty-four billion dollars for 2001, if down over twenty percent from 2000, ran a current account surplus of about $29.1 billion in 2002, expanded it dramatically to $35.4 billion in 2003 and $60.1 billion in 2004. This allowed it to get ahead on its international obligations, increase its FOREX reserves to $36.6 billion in 2001, $47.8 billion in 2002, $76.9 billion in 2003, and $124.5 billion in 2004, with no sign of diminishing growth, and to reduce the amount of mandatory turnover of foreign exchange earnings from seventy-five percent to fifty percent to twenty-five percent.[87] The federal budget ran a primary surplus of about three percent of GDP in 2001, 1.4 percent and 1.7 percent in 2003 and 2003 respectively, and 4.4 percent in 2004, and even the consolidated regional and federal budgets are running a slight surplus. This gave the Russian state flexibility in dealing with its creditors, eliminating the 2003 problem of repayment, allowing renegotiation of its London Club debt and accelerated repayment of its Paris (government creditors) debts.[88] It also gives the Russian state greater flexibility in dealing with its vast investment and restructuring needs, although it has yet to begin using these funds for such purposes. Rather, the Russian government has created a Stabilization Fund of over eighty-six billion dollars in 2004. This fund is providing insurance against a potential drop in oil and other export earnings should energy and resource prices drop substantially, while domestic energy, labor, and social costs rise with the implementation of further economic and social reforms. Finally, both accelerated debt repayment and sequestration of export earnings in the stabilization fund are playing a role in holding down inflation, and hence, production costs, by reducing the demand for money that use of these earnings for investment of consumption would generate.

Prospects for Development

On the basis of aggregate performance trends, the prospects for development are now the most encouraging of at least the past decade. As noted by U.S. Secretaries Paul O'Neill and Don Evans in their July 2001 visit to Russia, and repeatedly emphasized by Vladimir Putin in his annual state of the nation addresses, the Russian government appears committed to developing investment and investor-friendly institutions and environment by stressing structural reform and political stability. It is hoped that this will attract foreign capital and business expertise, and Russian domestic and flight capital, to the task of transforming and rebuilding infrastructure, restructuring production activity and economic interactions, and hence, exploiting the vast opportunities for developing a modern, high technology, and consumer oriented economy in place of the crumbling, old-industry, and resource extraction oriented remains of the Soviet economic system. The concrete reform agenda was outlined in the Gref Program and in Putin's 3 April 2001 address to the legislature.[89] And its economic liberalizing thrust was repeated tirelessly throughout 2001-03 by Kasyanov, Kudrin, Gref and the other economic Ministers of Putin's government. However, beginning with Putin's 2003 address to the Federal Assembly, a different strain appeared, emphasizing more enforced growth and state-driven solutions to the development problem, and an increasingly authoritarian and security oriented polity. Steps in this direction, particularly in the political and legal spheres, raise questions about the commitment to, and prospects of liberal economic growth.

Putin/Gref Program

In its economic content, this program is a continuation of the liberal reforms of Gaidar and Chubais (1992-95), and as such has stimulated some vocal opposition.[90] It hopes to stimulate private initiative under the oversight and protection, but not direction, of the state. It directly addresses a number of the institutional and structural problems discussed above, beginning in 2000 with reasserting the role and powers of the central government, in particular Federal fiscal authority, and with initiating budgetary and tax reform.

The initial focus has been on strengthening the executive vertical, enforcing the superiority and uniformity in application of Federal law, and taming the legislative organs at both the central and regional levels. Thus, the Federation Council has been reorganized, reducing the direct role of the regional governors, and seven new supra-regional districts have been set up to coordinate and control activity of federal organs and to ensure the observance of federal law and decrees. In addition, a number of highly visible steps were taken to tame the oligarchs, including a number of prominent tax raids and the opening of criminal cases against those too vocally in opposition, and in a set of moves to ensure a compliant mass media.[91]

Tax reform has been one of the top priorities. It has included a rationalization of tax structure and a redivision of revenues, largely to the detriment of the regional and local governments,[92] as well as simplification: a reduction in exceptions and loopholes and in the profit tax (from thirty-five percent to twenty-four percent) for businesses, a reduction in top personal tax rates to thirteen percent while raising the tax and withholding on lower incomes to the same rate, and a unification of payments to off-budget (e.g. medical insurance, pension, unemployment, road, and utility, etc.) funds. This has led to a budget that has been successfully implemented in every year since 2000, and the dramatic improvement in the Federal fisc that was noted above. Similarly, customs and import regulations and tariffs have been simplified – made more uniform and transparent – in an attempt to limit corruption and to introduce more meaningful competition for Russian manufacturers. Toward the same end, the Putin administration is also pushing hard for early admission to the WTO, although they are bargaining hard for favorable accession conditions.[93] Discussions on admission are still continuing into 2005, with admission being announced as imminent at the beginning of every year.

Other aspects of the reform program have been moving more slowly and, as it has turned out, somewhat less surely.[94] A compromise land code, which still leaves the issue of agricultural land sales in abeyance (subject to local and regional determination and discretion), allowing full title and resale of urban and industrial property even by foreigners, finally passed the Duma in July 2002, albeit over strenuous objections of the Communist and Agrarian Parties and many of the regional leaders. A money laundering law, albeit one lacking significant teeth, became law in 2001, and met international anti-money-laundering standards with the establishment of a Financial Monitoring Committee in October 2002. And currency liberalization continued, cutting the repatriation requirement for foreign currency earnings from fifty percent to twenty-five percent in 2004, with prospect of its complete elimination in 2006. Approval has also been given by the Duma to eleven bills reforming the legal system, aimed at reducing the arbitrariness and discretion of prosecutors and judges and imposing some new competency standards.[95]

The extremely contentious issues of social reform were also raised in legislation introduced in 2002, but final legislation and implementation were delayed through 2004. These reforms aim at making benefits promised commensurate with the means of the state, and by focusing them on the truly needy, thus eliminating them for most Russians. Proposals have been made with respect to unemployment, housing and utility pricing, and pension reform, involving shifting greater burden to households. They also involve the (gradual) elimination of state subsidies to industry for social purposes, with the transfer of social obligations from industry to local governments. These proposals, and a new, more market-oriented labor code, eliminating many formal protections promised by the Soviet system but no longer delivered in practice, have provoked vociferous opposition, as neither households nor local governments appear to have the necessary means to take on such responsibilities. As a result, most of these reforms are still delayed in the political process, although the Federal Government appears intent on pushing some version of such reforms through to implementation.[96]

The reform of the banking and financial intermediation systems is also moving very slowly, largely due to opposition of the Russian Central Bank which has subsided, if not disappeared, after Sergei Ignatiev replaced Gerashchenko as its Chairman on 20 March 2002. Indeed, beyond raising capital standards and some tightening of oversight, there have been no reforms in the banking sector to the end of 2004. This is also the case with the structural reform of natural monopolies (UES, Gazprom, railroad system, etc.) that is to separate true natural monopoly from other business activities. The latter is true despite Rem Vakhyrev's removal as head of Gazprom and the (modified) acceptance of Chubais' proposed restructuring of UES.[97] In fact, much of 2002-04 has been spent developing a weak consensus on Chubais' reform plan for UES, taking account of the demands of local political powers, major industrial energy users, and foreign minority investors.[98] As of the end of 2004, only the corporatization of the railroads, a preliminary step to partial privatization, has been accomplished in the area of natural monopoly reform.

One further area in which some real progress has been made is in debureaucratization, in reducing regulatory burden by simplifying and/or eliminating registration, licensing, and regulatory requirements on (in particular, small) business. This was indicated by Gref to be a priority of the 2001-03 period, and is an important early step in addressing the institutional and behavioral legacies of the Soviet period. Indeed, as noted above, it has generated the first real growth in the number of new small business since the mid-1990s. Finally, the program includes further measures to: enhance regulatory efficiency; improve corporate governance (new Joint-Stock Company Law and Corporate Governance Code in 2003); improve bankruptcy procedures to reduce their abuse for seizing property (2003 Bankruptcy Law); introduce international accounting, fiduciary, and transparency standards;[99] and lift administrative curbs (often locally and/or regionally imposed) on the movement of goods, capital, and labor. Since mid-2004, however, administrative reforms have stalled out, with much of the laws unimplemented, or perverted, due to bureaucratic opposition and foot dragging.[100]

Thus, overall, the Putin/Gref program provides important initiatives in addressing a number of the legacies of the Soviet Union that are restraining modern market development of Russia. The reforms under this program, largely legislated in 2001-2002, together with high international energy and resource prices, appear to be behind the renewal of robust growth and restructuring in 2003-04, despite the apparent rise in political risk stimulated by the assault on YUKOS.

Alternative Programs

While the Gref program was the driving force behind the Kasyanov government's legislative program, Putin seems to have also encouraged the development of a number of alternative programs of a much more *dirigiste* nature, perhaps for insurance in case of an economic downturn. The most substantial of these is the Ishaev Report of 22 November 2000 prepared largely by Academy of Science and opposition economists under the auspices of Khabarovsk governor Viktor Ishaev.[101] Supposed to complement the Gref program, it essentially negates it in proposing: a massive, state directed mobilization of resources involving forced mobilization of investment, particularly in MBMW, through a Russian Development Bank; forced modernization and development of domestic manufacturing and processing through state orchestrated and controlled financial intermediation; new state institutions to evaluate debt quality and investment projects, to absorb investment risk and guarantee credits; an emphasis on dual-use technologies with direct state control of the defense, agricultural, and transportation complexes; and state control of wages, credit, and financial flows between regions to preserve equity and the desired directions of industrial development. While there has been no attempt to systematically implement this program, its underlying assumptions and logical thrust appear to lie behind much of the economic thinking of the *siloviki* who are increasingly influencing government policy as Putin's second presidential term begins.

Another anti-liberal program was also developed in an interdepartmental working group of the Security Council headed by V. Soltaganov.[102] Called a State Strategy for National Economic Security, it emphasizes strengthening of the military and its supporting industries, and focuses on developing self-sufficiency and limiting international dependence, by developing state priority activities and enforcing threshold levels of international contacts. Further, there remains in the background the pseudo-Keynesian program of the Russian Academy of Sciences Institute of Economics.[103] This program emphasizes reviving the Soviet industrial structure through massive monetary emission and deficit financing of state orders to bring un- and under-used capacity back on line. It involves an incomes policy, reinforcing social guarantees through industry, state control of resource industries, emphasis on investment in manufacturing and high-tech (largely military) industries, import substitution, and state directed industrial policy. It appears an attempt to return to the policies of *perestroika* and do them right this time! And both of these programs provide a justification for the recent state policy of taking direct control of the oil and gas industries, allowing only minority stakes for private owners and some subservient private firms.[104]

Finally, we see the continuing, and perhaps growing, influence of these *dirigiste* ideas in a series of think-tank reports throughout 2003-04 criticizing Gref and his Ministry for focusing on liberal reforms for their own sake, and ignoring Putin's imperative to double the size of the economy in ten years. The most recent of these is a report of the Council on National Strategy on 17 February 2005, entitled "The State and Business: A Union for National Modernization." It argues that the state, led by Putin, must mastermind the nation's economic development and consolidate all responsible public forces, capable of insuring the country's dynamic economic advancement. The state must control redistribution, and run a robust industrial and investment policy, eschewing doctrinaire liberalism. There appears a real possibility that this organization and its program will replace Gref's in providing the vision for future economic policy and development in Russia.[105]

As should be clear from prior discussion, none of these alternative programs can facilitate the development of a modern market economy in Russia. They are rather themselves products of the Soviet legacy of economic understanding which fall back on precisely those aspects of that structural and institutional legacy which are so debilitating for the modern economic development of Russia. Although these programs do not appear to have had much influence to mid-2002, they remained in play due to the slowing of the process of reform development and implementation, and apparently have some growing, if still small, influence as Putin begins his second term.

Growth Prospects

At the end of Putin's first term, the Russian economy was riding a wave that was apparently fading away.[106] The special conditions following the crisis of August 1998 have largely withered away; only the high and rising price of oil remains. In the near term, and in the absence of serious negative shocks, the prospects are quite good for moderate (three to five percent) annual rates of economic growth, although not Putin's demanded seven to eight percent, even without further substantial systemic reform. We have already witnessed a resurrection of the mid-1990s economic and industrial base and a renewal of confidence, leading to new economic activity and development, albeit largely in the fuel, resource and trading sectors and among their upstream suppliers. These developments are largely a result of the politically stable economic environment and the vast flow of wealth from the export of mineral and energy resources. The reforms now in place, and those proposed – now more credibly than ever before – have provided new incentives and an increased confidence in the future that could be the basis for a prolonged spurt of real investment and growth. With the state, regional and local governments increasing efforts to shore up inherited infrastructure, and increasingly recognizing the value of new economic activity, the stage is set for a full recovery from the great depression of the 1990s.

But whether this recovery turns into true modern market growth, whether it leads to Russia playing a leading role in the world economy, depends very much on the choice of policy and its proper implementation. The window of opportunity that opened following the crisis of August 1998 has been used to stabilize the economy and set the stage for dramatic economic growth. And the reforms of that period have, at least in some sectors of the economy, allowed the development of a market base on which to build that growth. But much more needs to be done in order to lay a firm foundation for sustained market growth. Continuing strong economic growth (seven to eight percent per year), with increasing integration into the world economy, will require at least:[107]

- substantial progress toward disentangling political power and economic activity, including
    - building and strengthening institutions of outside intermediation and adjudication;
    - separating the personal and public spheres in administration, regulation, and business;
    - extending Putin's dictatorship of law to all levels of government, including Federal organs, thereby protecting individuals and businesses from political predation;
    - withdrawing the state from direct market activity and intervention, to allow it to effectively enforce the legal and regulatory framework of modern market activity;
- further substantial progress on the structural reform agenda, particularly relating to banking, debureaucratization, legal and judicial reform, and financial market and natural monopoly regulation – social reform is less critical, although a gradual focusing of support and shifting of responsibility is ultimately needed;
- substantial investment in both production and social infrastructure;[108]
- a broader and deeper, truly radical restructuring of industrial

structure and capacities, moving beyond resource extraction, and their related, sectors;

The first set of these is perhaps the most critical. It is required not only to remove substantial distortions in incentives faced by economic agents, but also to allow the price system to begin playing its proper role as a source of determining information for economic decisions. This would allow institutional and structural reforms to have the desired impact on economic behavior and decisions, leading to true value-creating investment and other value-creating economic activity. In particular, it will foster economically rational investment in infrastructure and rational restructuring of economic capacities, by allowing true market prices and valuations to inform those decisions. True modernization and growth will be fostered by such changes, undercutting the non- and anti-market foundations of much of the current economic system discussed above.

There is, however, nothing inevitable about such success, although its likelihood increases with the duration of the present reform regime. Without further sufficiently vigorous and comprehensive reform, the feudal and virtual aspects of the current system might still emerge triumphant, particularly if an economic security oriented version of directed market development is chosen. Such an approach would overemphasize the protection of existing activities and agents, and foster ignorance and avoidance of new economic opportunities and initiatives. It would seriously undercut opportunities and incentives for market exploration and experimentation, protect incumbents, both political and economic, from challenge, and hence, foster re-stagnation, and continuing de-integration of economic activity within Russia and with respect to the global economy. It would direct investment resources into state projects of national significance selected by an economically ill-informed bureaucracy, reducing the capability of market agents to pursue economic development, and deepening the backwardness of most of the economy.[109] It would likely generate highly uneven, regionalized development, with oases of (resource exporting; state priority) strength amid vast stagnation and decay, and limited, particularized integration of some activities into the world economy, with little feedback into Russian development. While such a policy could maintain a certain amount of aggregate physical growth for a time, it would inevitably stifle new economic activity, except in the shadow economy, and eventually reduce true economic (value) growth back toward zero, just as the Soviet system did.

Conclusion

As 2002 drew to a close, the Russian economy appeared to be poised on the threshold of relaunching and completing the radical systemic transformation envisioned by the optimists of 1992. A new set of institutional and governance reforms were proclaimed as objectives, substantial reshuffling and streamlining was launched in governmental institutions, corruption was targeted, and raising living standards through doubling GDP was proclaimed the immediate objective of state policy and continuing reform. 2003 was to be a breakthrough year, removing dependence on foreign financial support and goodwill by meeting and exceeding all international financial obligations, and launching second-stage institutional reform. Yet, virtually nothing happened in structural reform implementation, despite phenomenal economic performance, driven by soaring energy and metals prices, strongly growing tax revenues, and a renewed investment boom, including the highest levels of FDI ever seen in Russia, following the 2002 slowdown. Reform of the bureaucracy and public administration, a centerpiece of the new policy thrust, created growing operational chaos within the government, perhaps due to self interested bureaucratic foot-dragging and obstruction, leading to an almost total stalling of new implementing legislation.[110] This was aggravated by active lobbying, including vote-buying, by interested parties and, in particular, the so-called oligarchs. Mikhail Khodorkovsky, head of YUKOS – the largest and recently most transparent oil conglomerate in post-Soviet Russia – was particularly active in spreading his wealth politically, buying politicians and votes in the Duma, supporting opposition political parties and a number of liberal NGOs and educational and research funds organizations.[111] Thus, political gridlock seized all serious reform and policy initiatives as Russia, as in 1996, focused all political effort on the upcoming Duma (December 2003) and Presidential (March 2004) elections.

Economic performance, on the other hand, after a pause in 2002 during which the Russian economy appeared to digest, and adjust to, the reforms that Putin had pushed through with such determination in the prior two years, took off. As those liberal policies began to be fully implemented in 2003, new economic activity bloomed, and growth accelerated to over seven percent, maintaining that pace through 2004. This growth was accompanied by consolidation of industrial control under major industrial-financial groups and conglomerates (oligarchs) and the beginning of serious micro-level restructuring in the firms acquired and/or controlled by those groups. Thus, investment growth rose from 2.6 percent in 2002 to 12.5 and 10.9

percent in 2003 and 2004 respectively, enterprise profitability increased by nineteen percent in 2003 and ninety-four percent in 2004, while state revenues fell from over twenty to about nineteen percent of GDP, despite a dramatic growth in absolute terms. And big business became increasingly confident, ever more openly flexing its political muscle to influence legislation and policy implementation. The increasingly clear evidence of state capture by the oligarchs led both to warnings about the negative efficiency and equity impacts of excessive concentration of ownership and control and to warnings by the statist oriented elite of an oligarch coup.[112] Thus the direction of social and economic development, over which Putin had struggled to gain apparent control, appeared to be slipping away from state influence, driven by a logic of capitalist development and concentrated private power.

This situation seems to have been intolerable to Putin and the *siloviki*. In mid-2003 the state moved decisively against the largest and most successful private company, YUKOS, whose head, Mikhail B. Khodorkovsky, had been most active among the oligarchs in pursuing independent political objectives. Beginning with massive armed "tax inspection" raids on units of the company and the arrest on 2 July 2003 of a co-owner, Platon Lebedev, on charges associated with an unrelated 1994 privatization, continuing with the arrest of Khodorkovsky on 25 October 2003, and ever broader, deeper, and more violent raids on YUKOS and its affiliates through 2003 and 2004, the State Prosecutor and tax services coordinated a legal and financial attack, launched 29 December 2003, that led to a nine year prison term for Khodorkovsky in late May 2005 after an eleven month show trial, and the dismemberment of YUKOS in December 2004 to the benefit of the state oil company Rosneft.[113] The way the attacks were managed, and the Prosecutor's and court's unwillingness to consider any compromise offers, settlements or defense motions, clearly highlights the political motivation of the assault, and raises questions about the security of property and the autonomy of economic agents, both essential components of a properly functioning market system, in Russia.

As many analysts have noted, Putin and the *siloviki* whom he has placed in key government, bureaucratic, and business positions, began in 2003 systematically moving to eliminate any independent (autonomous) sources of political and economic power. Building on the earlier successful taming of the independent media and the elimination of the most active of Yeltsin's oligarchs, Vladimir Gusinsky and Boris Berezovsky, aggravated by what he considered the misuse of Russian resource wealth by the remaining oligarchs, and exploiting the general antipathy of the population toward wealthy businessmen, the oligarchs in particular, Putin had his government pursue aggressive collection of back taxes, and selective criminal cases relating to the privatizations of the early 1990s.[114] And he urged businessmen in his Federal Assembly addresses on 16 May 2003 and 26 May 2004, to focus their efforts on the proper development of Russia, rather than the pursuit of private interests and profit, with appropriate activities clearly subject to approval, if not determination, by the state. After a few weak initial protests in late 2003, the oligarchs fell into line, abandoning Khodorkovsky and any pretense of independent economic initiative. Sales of large assets, particularly if involving Western companies, and major industrial development projects became clearly subject to Kremlin approval, support for NGOs and educational projects without Kremlin approval dried up, and tax collections rose dramatically beginning in the second half of 2004. And the control over productive property began shifting out of the hands of the original oligarchs and into those of a new class of *silovik-oligarch* taking state companies (e.g. Gazprom, Rosneft) or representing the state on the boards of (partially) privatized companies.

Thus, Russia, while still formally espousing the liberal Gref program, is reasserting state, or at least bureaucrats, control over the commanding heights of the marketizing economy. Following a Third-World model, the oil and gas industry has been substantially renationalized, energy export capability and exports have been brought under tighter state control, the liberalization and privatization of the banking sector has been partially reversed, electronic mass media and communications are subject to ever tighter controls, railroads, pipelines, and most shipping and air transport remain under government control, the government has begun selecting and funding special technology development zones, and large private companies clear their development plans with the government before making important moves. Private profit and wealth, even at extraordinary levels, is allowed and even encouraged, as long as the will of the state is not flouted and that wealth, at least at the margin, can be exploited by agents of the state for their own, ostensibly official, purposes. As long as economic agents remain subservient to the interests of (the agents of) the state, and in particular avoid challenging the decisions of the political authorities, they can run and develop their own businesses, exploit market opportunities, and enrich themselves. But they may not pursue major, unauthorized initiatives or projects which conflict with the interests of some higher state agent. Thus, the economic system is beginning to resemble the stunted market economy of the Tsarist patrimonial system of the beginning of the twentieth century.[115]

Such a system cannot long be competitive in the twenty-first century. Yet, it appears socially and politically appealing to many Russians as a path to regain lost glory and national strength. Thus, there remains for Russia a real danger of drifting into a third way, a peculiarly Russian path, where state guidance, and the perceived social and personalized political constraints it fosters, fetter private initiative and market development, resulting in fitful, slow economic growth and development, and leaving Russia increasingly far behind the leading market economies. On the other hand, there is also a real prospect of renewed liberal reform after the Putin shock effectively reins in private excesses, rebuilds effective state sovereignty, and puts all, including itself, under the effective rule of law. This could bring about the completed transformation to a truly market-based economic system with sustained growth and market-oriented development.

The consequences for globalization of the Russian economy are diametrically opposed. Modern market development, unleashing Russia's substantial potential, should make Russia a leading player in the world economy, bridging and enhancing development in Europe and Asia to its own great benefit. This is the hope engendered in Russia's acceptance into G-8, and driving its accession into WTO. Because of its uneven resource, physical, and human capital endowments, Russia can be expected to become one of the most open economies in the world, despite its vast size, and to reap among the greatest gains to trade and globalization. On the other hand, settling for a patrimonial Russian-style capitalism, with its inherited distortions of market institutions and activities, is likely to render globalization increasingly painful and humiliating for Russia. Russia would increasingly become what it appeared to be in the mid-1990s: an industrial backwater and resource appendage to the world market system, supplying low value-added basic inputs to, and absorbing excess production from, the advanced capitalist world. Which path Putin's Russia will ultimately take is currently very much an open question.

NOTES TO CHAPTER 5

[1] This feeling has been expressed, for example, by Sergei Karaganov, Deputy Director, Institute of Europe RAN, in an interview published in *Trud,* 29 June 2001. In fact, Vladmir Putin has started a structural reform of Russian society which former leaders tried to carry out in the early 1990s. Russia tried to reform its economy and finances but failed and lost ten years.

[2] Some evidence of this is seen in a 3 August 2001, conference in Volgograd, "Business and Power: A Strategy for Interaction, sponsored by local entrepreneurs with support of the Presidential Administration." See Johnson's Russia List, 7 August 2001. Also, the entrepreneurial group Russia Club-2015 has been active in pushing to improve the business environment. See Carnegie Endowment, "Private Sector Initiative for Russia Meeting Report," 3, no. 14 (3 May 2001), available at http://www.ceip.org.

[3] This everything-is-for-sale characteristic of the first decade of transition is less so at the beginning of Putin's second presidential term. With the growing authoritarianism, and growing state control over economic activity in key sectors, it is increasingly only the "right" people, with

the "right" positions and connections, who have this capability. See the conclusion below, written during the spring of 2005.

[4] See Thane Gustafson, *Capitalism Russian-Style* (Cambridge: Cambridge University Press, 1999); Rose Brady, *Kapitalizm* (New Haven: Yale University Press, 1996); or Stefan Hedlund, *Russia's "Market" Economy: A Bad Case of Predatory Capitalism* (London: UCL Press, 1999).

[5] The argument is developed in Richard E. Ericson, *The Soviet Union: 1979-1999* (San Francisco: ICS Press, 1990), and "The Classical Soviet-Type Economy: Nature of the System and Implications for Reform," *Journal of Economic Perspectives* 5, no. 4 (Fall 1991): 11-28.

[6] This problem of pricing and its implications are discussed in Richard E. Ericson, "The Structural Barrier to Transition Hidden in Input-Output Tables of Centrally Planned Economies," *Economic Systems* 23, no. 3 (September 1999): 199-224.

[7] This is nicely illustrated in the special report on Russia by Edward Lucas, "Putin's Choice," *The Economist*, 19 July 2001.

[8] Examples include unsustainable regional and local autarky in food production, interior and northern locations in extremely hostile and costly environmental conditions, and manufacturing concentrations that ignored costs of procuring inputs and disposing of outputs. Some of these are elaborated in recent work of Clifford Gaddy, "The Cost of Cold," Brookings Paper (2001); and in Fiona Hill and Clifford Gaddy, *The Siberian Curse* (Washington, D.C.: Brookings Press, 2003).

[9] Many of these legacies, and others regarding household behavior, are discussed in Sergei Guriev and Barry Ickes, "Microeconomic Aspects of Economic Growth in Eastern Europe and the Former Soviet Union, 1950-2000," *NES Working Paper* (Moscow: The New Economic School, 2001).

[10] See the discussion in Clifford Gaddy and Barry Ickes, "To Restructure or Not to Restructure: Informal Activities and Enterprise Behavior in Transition," WDI Working Paper No. 134 (February 1998); Clifford Gaddy and Barry Ickes, *Russia's Virtual Economy* (Washington, D.C.: Brookings, 2001); and Richard Ericson and Barry Ickes, "A Model of Russia's 'Virtual Economy'," *Review of Economic Design* 6, no. 2 (2001): 185-214. David Woodruff, *Money Unmade* (Ithaca: Cornell University Press, 1999) shows how this was a natural response of local and regional governments attempting to preserve local substantive economies in face of the shock of marketization. The political dimension is also found to be empirically significant in the work of Simon Commander and Christian Mummsen, "The Growth of Non-Monetary Transactions in Russia: Causes and Effects (chapter 5)," in P. Seabright, ed., *The Vanishing Rouble* (Cambridge: Cambridge University Press, 2000), 114-146; and Commander, Irina Dolinskaya, and Mummsen, "Determinants of Barter in Russia: An Empirical Analysis," EBRD and IMF Discussion Paper (December 2000).

[11] This economy has become less visible in the cash rich environment of high oil and resource prices and a devalued ruble, making even highly inefficient producers solvent and allowing more open cross-subsidization through price controls. See the working paper of Clifford Gaddy and Barry Ickes, "A Virtual Economy View of Russia's Oil Economy," prepared for the VII World Congress of ICCEES, 2005.

[12] On the traditional roots of the Russian *mafiya*, see Peter Reddaway and Dmitri Glinsky, *The Tragedy of Russia's Reforms* (Washington, D.C.: U.S. Institute of Peace Press, 2001), 109-113. Also see Stephen Handelman, *Comrade Criminal: Russia's New Mafiya* (New Haven: Yale University Press, 1995).

[13] How institutional and behavioral legacies perverted the privatizations process and its outcome is nicely discussed in Stefan Hedlund, "Property Without Rights: Dimensions of Russia's Privatization," *Europe-Asia Studies* 53, no. 2 (March 2001): 213-237. Their continuing influence is visible in the systematic destruction of Khodorkovsky and YUKOS in 2003-05.

[14] See Vadim Volkov, *Violent Entrepreneurs* (Ithaca: Cornell University Press, 2002) for a discussion and analysis of the origins and development of private protection and enforcement of property and contractual rights.

[15] See the discussion in Ericson, "The Post-Soviet Russian Economic System: An Industrial Feudalism? (chapter 6)," in Tuomas Komulainen and Iikka Korhonen, eds., *Russian Crisis and its*

Effects (Helsinki: Kikimora Publications, 2000): 133-166, for some detail and references. Examples in retailing in three Russian cities are analyzed in Timothy Frye and Ekaterina Zhuravskaya, "Rackets, Regulation, and the Rule of Law," *Journal of Law, Economics, & Organization* 16, no. 2 (October 2000): 478-502. The use of contract killings in enforcement was recently highlighted in the *Jamestown Foundation Monitor*, 10 August 2001. See "From Moscow to Vladivostok, Contract Killings are Common."

[16] The arbitrage courts have been improving, and, unless government is involved, generally fair in adjudicating contract and property disputes. They, however, lack reliable means of enforcement, leading firms to ignore them, or pursue private enforcement of their decisions. See, among others, Randi Ryterman, and B. Weber, "The Role of Attitudes in the Performance of the Legal System: Evidence from a Survey of Russian Firms," The World Bank (October 1996); Katherin Hendley, Ickes, Peter Murrell, and Ryterman, "Observations on the Use of Law by Russian Enterprises," *Post-Soviet Affairs* 13, no. 1 (1997): 19-41; V. Radaiev, "On the Role of Force in Russian Business Relationships," *Voprosy ekonomiki*, no. 19 (October 1998); and S. Lambroschini, "Russia's Judiciary: The Arbitration Courts' Problems," *RFE/RL Newsline*, 26-27 April 2001.

[17] For a theoretical and empirical analysis, see Ariane Lambert-Mogiliansky, Konstantin Sonin, and Ekaterina Zhuravskaya, "Capture of Bankruptcy: Theory and Evidence from Russia," CEFIR Working Paper (September 2000). Also see S. Tavernise, "Using Bankruptcy as a Takeover Tool," *New York Times*, 7 October 2000, C1, for a discussion of the case of the profitable Novokuznetsk Aluminum Plant.

[18] See Ericson, "The Classical Soviet-Type Economy" on the economic logic of this.

[19] While in many respects resembling east Asian and Latin American crony capitalism, the phenomenon in Russia is much more pervasive and destructive of market economic activity, as it is unencumbered by tradition, moral constraint, and pre-existing markets, both domestic and foreign.

[20] For some discussion of roots and their impact on reform, see the articles in Jeffrey D. Sachs and Katherina Pistor, eds., *The Rule of Law and Economic Reform in Russia* (Boulder: Westview Press, 1997).

[21] This is nicely discussed in Reddaway and Glinski, *The Tragedy of Russia's Reforms*, although the discussion is scattered throughout the volume due to its primary focus on political and social developments.

[22] See the discussion in Andrei Shleifer, "Government in Transition," *European Economic Review* 41, no. 3-5 (1997): 385-410; and Anders Åslund, "Observations on the Development of Small Private Enterprise in Russia," *Post-Soviet Geography and Economics* 38, no. 4 (1997): 191-205.

[23] See Blair Ruble, *Soviet Trade Unions* (New York: Cambridge University Press, 1981).

[24] For a wonderful discussion of the origins, growth, and gradual cooptation and destruction of the democratic movement and its associated civic organizations under the Yeltsin regime see Reddaway and Glinski, *The Tragedy of Russia's Reforms*, especially chapters 3, 4, 6, and 7. Putin has attempted to systematically bring civic associations and NGOs under direct state influence, organizing annual conferences of civic organizations that each year show less independence and spontaneity.

[25] This is much of the basis for Russia's historical and continuing economy of favors. See Alens V. Ledeneva, *Russia's Economy of Favors* (Cambridge: Cambridge University Press, 1998).

[26] Of course, this is a matter of degree. Personal ties and networks play an important role in well functioning market systems also, but they do not comprise its central, driving component. Rather they are embedded in impersonal networks and markets which provide a rich, heavily redundant, set of "outside options" ensuring that voluntarily entered special relations are value adding for the individuals, and not stifling or exploitative.

[27] This section is based on my general reading of Soviet and Russian economic and business literature, and not on any specific sources.

[28] This is emphasized in Stephan Hedlund, *Russia's "Market" Economy*. See also Kathryn Hendley, "Rewriting the Rules of the Game in Russia: The Neglected Issue of the Demand for Law," *East European Constitutional Review* 8, no. 4 (Fall 1999): 89-95, where the author argued that this

lies behind the lack, on the part of Russian business and society, of a sufficient "demand for law" to enable the reform of both laws and the legal system to become effective.

[29] This can be seen in the repeated claims that energy and/or utility prices are too high, despite their below market-clearing levels, or that subsidies are necessary for operations in the North or to preserve some enterprise of sector in a specific region. Instead of questioning the value of operations that are apparently non-viable at market prices, the call is for prices to be fixed so that the operations appear viable. This is one of the fundamental roots of the virtual economy, or indeed the Siberian Curse of Hill and Gaddy, *The Siberian Curse*.

[30] This can be seen in the revealed attitudes of managers, businessmen, and politicians in their statements quoted in Joseph R. Blasi, Maya Kroumova, and Douglas Kruse, *Kremlin Capitalism: Privatizing the Russian Economy* (Ithaca: Cornell University Press, 1997); or Woodruff, *Money Unmade*, for example.

[31] Ericson in Komulainen and Korhonen, eds., *Russian Crisis and its Effects*.

[32] This parcellization is now more to bureaucrats and "*siloviki*" than oligarchs.

[33] For example, Menatep evolved from a "bank" through and industrial holding company, Rosprom, to an energy company based on YUKOS, although it has recently been substantially dismantled in the politically motivated assault on Khodorkovsky. Similarly, Bank Rossiiskii Kredit has become a holding company in the metallurgical industry, and Oneximbank has combined Noril'sk Nikel with Sidanko oil, before losing the latter through a manipulated bankruptcy to TNK. This trend accelerated following the crisis of 1998, with new energy and resource-based conglomerates taking center stage. Three of the most important are Interros, based on Noril'sk Nikel, Millhouse Capital, and the Alfa Group, each controlling three to five percent of the GDP of the Russian Federation. For an introduction to these, see V. Korchagina, K. Koriukin and A. Startseva, "The New Face of Russia's Oligopoly," *The Moscow Times,* 1 November 2001, 1.

[34] Ledeneva, *Russia's Economy of Favors*. A number of the new commercial structures and their oligarchs have moved in 2002 to break with this pattern and introduce greater transparence and regularity into corporate governance, thereby improving their access to Western capital and their capitalized value on financial and equity markets. Most noticeable among these has been YUKOS owner, Mikhail Khodorovskii. See the *Wall Street Journal*, 24 June 2002, article on his announcement of wealth to meet U.S. disclosure standards, or *The Times* (London), 23 June 2002.

[35] There were some indications that this is changing as 2001 drew to a close, and new, broad-based manufacturing investment appeared to grow in 2003-04 supporting both rapidly growing consumption and the investment needs of the resource (especially energy) extraction and processing industries. Indeed, as we noted above, resource and energy firms began diversifying into conglomerates, through investment in unrelated Russian industries, rather than exporting their earnings in this period.

[36] See Anders Åslund, *How Russia Became a Market Economy* (Washington, D.C.: Brookings Press, 1995).

[37] Gaddy and Ickes, "To Restructure or Not to Restructure: Informal Activities and Enterprise Behavior in Transition."

[38] The basic sources used for official statistical data on the Russian economy are Goskomstat Rossii, *Maloe predprinimatel'stvo v Rossii [Small Enterprise in Russia]* (Moscow: GKS, 2000); *Natsional'nye scheta Rossii v 1992-1999 [National Accounts of Russia in 1992-1999]* (Moscow: GKS, 2000); *Promyshlennost' Rossii 2000 [Industry of Russia 2000]* (Moscow: GKS, 2000); *Rossiiskii statisticheskii ezhegodnik 2000 [Russian Statistical Yearbook 2000]* (Moscow: GKS, 2000); and Roskomstat, *Rossiiskii statisticheskii ezhegodnik 2003 [Russian Statistical Yearbook 2003]* (Moscow: GKS, 2003), and more recent press reports on performance since 2001. Note that in 2004, the state statistical organ was renamed *Federal'naia sluzhba gosudarstvennoi statistiki [Federal Service for State Statistics] (Rosstat)* in Putin's administrative reorganization for his second term; the State Committee became a Federal Service.

[39] On some of the problems, and the early progress in addressing them, see Vincent Koen, "Russian Macroeconomic Data: Existence, Access, Interpretation," *Communist Economies &*

Economic Transformation, 8, no. 3 (1996): 321-333.

[40] This is related to the maintenance of the virtual economy as seen in Gaddy and Ickes, *Russia's Virtual Economy*; or what Woodruff in *Money Unmade* calls local substantive economies inherited from the Soviet period.

[41] See Goskomstat Rossii, *Maloe Predprinimatel'stvo v Rossii* (*Small Enterprise in Russia*), 3-4.

[42] The use of black cash for tax evasion and "rents" and cost shifting is analyzed in Andrei Yakovlev, "'Black Cash' in the Russian Economy," *Europe-Asia Studies* 5, no. 1 (January 2001): 33-55. This clearly leads to an exaggeration of levels of economic activity, particularly by small and medium-sized firms.

[43] There is an interesting discussion of this problem in Gaddy, "The Cost of Cold," related to issues of measuring the virtual economy. See also Gaddy and Ickes, *Russia's Virtual Economy*.

[44] A nice summary if this, and some other problems, with examples, can be found in the BOFIT report *Russian Economy: Month in Review* (October 2002).

[45] The impact of this bias can be seen in Table 5. For a thorough analysis, see World Bank, Russia Country Department (2/2004), *Russian Economic Report*, no. 7, on the web at http://www.worldbank.org.ru. There is some controversy regarding this critique. See Paul Gregory and Valerii Lazarev, "Structural Change in Russian Transition," Economic Growth Center Discussion Paper No. 896, Yale University (October 2004).

[46] This situation had changed by mid-2003 in the Westernized oil, metals, and exporting companies, which had turned to Western accounting and managers in order to get access to Western capital markets. Unfortunately, the more transparent accounting data has apparently been used against YUKOS, the leader in this process, in the government's effort since July 2003 to crush Khodorkovsky and take operational control of the oil industry.

[47] A concise, but incomplete, summary of methodology and assumptions behind Russian National Income Accounts can be found in Goskomstat, *Natsional'nye scheta Rossii* [*National Accounts of Russia*] (Moscow: GKS, 2000), 16-26. Recent changes are discussed in the introduction and methodological appendices to the international comparisons section of *Rosstat*, 2003.

[48] See the World Bank's *World Development Report: 2000*. RosKomStat's International Comparison Program, Roskomstat, *Rossiiskii statisticheskii ezhegodnik* [*Russian Statistical Yearbook*] *2003* (Moscow: GKS, 2003), Tables 26.30-31, put 1999 GDP at $891 billion in PPP terms, giving $6,090 per capita, or eighteen percent of the U.S. level. PPP estimates for 2000, 2001, and 2002 are $1.003 trillion, $1.077 trillion, and $1.146 trillion total GDP respectively, giving about $6,892, $7,438, and $7,961 per capita in those years.

[49] These are the final revisions in a long series of efforts to estimate economic performance accurately. A further re-weighting of sectoral shares in January 2002 raised estimated 2000 GDP growth to nine percent, and allowed *GosKomStat* to claim five percent GDP growth for 2001. See V. Korchagina, "Government Rewriting the Stats," *St. Petersburg Times*, 19 February 2002. By mid-2002, growth for 2001 had been further revised to 9.1%. The final revision reported here was set at the end of 2003. See S. Nikolaenko, "Problems of economic statistics in Russia," in BOFIT report *Russian Economy: Month in Review*, October 2002, 4; and the statistics in the June 2005 BOFIT *Russian Economy: Month in Review*. Also, see GosKomStat report on *Itar-Tass*, 22 February 2002.

[50] Putin, in his first State of the Nation address, 8 July 2000, claimed that it will take Russia over fifteen years of annual growth of seven to ten percent per year to surpass Portugal in GDP per capita. Putin set the national objective of doubling GDP in ten years in his fourth annual State of the Nation address on 26 May 2004, and made it a central theme of his 2004 presidential election campaign. Full texts of these addresses are available at http://www.president.kremlin.ru.

[51] See Simon Johnson, Daniel Kaufmann, and Andrei Shleifer, "The Unofficial Economy in Transition," *Brookings Papers on Economic Activity* no. 2 (1997): 159-239. Also see Kaufmann and Aleksandr Kaliberda, "Integrating the Unofficial Economy into the Dynamics of Post-Socialist Economies: A Framework of Analysis and Evidence," *World Bank Policy Research Working Paper No. 1691* (Washington, D.C.: The World Bank, 1996) for some Western estimates of its size. The larger figure is regularly repeated in statements of the legal authorities and in the Russian press. See the

Introduction in Dolgopyatova, *Neformal'hyi sektor v Rossiiskoi ekonomiki* [*The Informal Sector of the Russian Economy*] (Moscow: ISARP, 1998).

[52] See Gaddy and Ickes, *Russia's Virtual Economy*.

[53] See in particular the Guriev and Ickes, and Simon Commander papers in the conference volume of Paul Seabright, ed., *The Vanishing Ruble: Barter and Currency Substitution in Post-Soviet Societies* (Cambridge: Cambridge University Press, 2000).

[54] This bias may be partially compensated for by the above noted bias introduced by transfer pricing in the fuel sectors.

[55] Ericson, *The Soviet Union*; IMF, World Bank, EBRD, and OECD, *A Study of the Soviet Economy* (Paris: OECD, 1991); OECD, *OECD Economic Surveys: Russian Federation 1995* (Paris: OECD, 1995) for more detail.

[56] The beginnings of this structural change are analyzed in some depth in Masasuki Kuboniwa and Evgenii Gavrilenkov, *Development of Capitalism in Russia: The Second Challenge*, (Tokyo: Maruzen, 1997).

[57] These constraints are emphasized in the empirical studies of labor and its adjustment in the Russian transition. See, in particular, Harry Broadman and Francesca Recanatini, "Is Russia Restructuring? New Evidence on Job Creation and Destruction," preprocessed, (Washington, D.C.: World Bank, 2001); Guido Friebel and Sergei Guriev, "Should I Stay or Can I Go?: Worker Attachment in Russia," CEFIR Discussion Paper (November 2000), available at CEFIR web site http://www.cefir.org/papers2.html; and Padma Desai and Todd Idson, *Work without Wages* (Cambridge: MIT Press, 2000).

[58] The implications of this for understanding the Soviet structure of production and some of the difficulties of the early transition are explored in Ericson, "The Structural Barrier to Transition Hidden in Input-Output Tables of Centrally Planned Economies." In particular this pricing hides wasteful use of basic inputs such as energy, metals, and industrial and construction materials.

[59] Statistics on most recent performance are derived from the current Russian press, *Russian Economic Trends*, and the Bank of Finland's Institute for Economies in Transition, *Russian Economy: The Month in Review*, issues through April 2005.

[60] This is most clearly seen in his response to the Beslan tragedy, 1-4 September 2004. To strengthen the war against terrorism, he proposed replacing elections for governors and independent legislators with presidential appointment of the former and party-list election of the latter. See the presidential address of 13 September 2004 at http://www.kremlin.ru. All these changes had received full legislative approval by June 2005.

[61] Soviet performance measures captured the use, and indeed the massive waste, of fundamental resources and industrial capacity, rather than the value of output produced, giving a substantially false picture of real economic performance. See Anders Åslund, "The Myth of Output Collapse after Communism," Working Paper No. 18, Post-Soviet Economies Project, Carnegie Endowment for International Peace (March 2001); Ericson, "The Structural Barrier to Transition Hidden in Input-Output Tables of Centrally Planned Economies;" and G. I. Khanin, *Sovetskii ekonomicheskii rost: analiz zapadnykh otsenok* [*Soviet Economic Growth: Analysis of Western Evaluations*] (Novosibirsk: EKO, 1993), among others.

[62] On the dimensions of the collapse, see the EBRD (1999), chapter 3 and 258-261. The civil war collapse can be seen in the statistics of chapter 3 of Paul Gregory and Robert Stuart, *Russian and Soviet Economic Performance and Structure*, sixth ed. (Reading: Addison-Wesley, 1998).

[63] This is a point emphatically made by analysts at the Gaidar Institute of the Economy in Transition (IET), and the businessmen of the 2015 Club. It is also argued by Anders Åslund, *Building Capitalism: The Transformation of the Former Soviet Bloc* (Cambridge: Cambridge University Press, 2001).

[64] Yevgenii Maksimovich Primakov was Prime Minister from September 1998 to May 1999, when Yeltsin appointed Vladimir Putin to that position.

[65] By mid-2001 Russia had already paid one billion dollars of the $2.07 billion due that year, out of a total debt owed to the IMF of $8.8 billion. See *RFE/RL Newsline*, 7 August 2001. By the

end of the year, Russia had begun buying back debt, reducing the need for payments in 2003, and continued accelerated payments eliminating its IMF debt by 2005. The figures in the text are from the *Russian Economic Trends* monthly update, July 2002, and from the monthly issues of *Russian Economy: The Month in Review* of the Bank of Finland (BOFIT), through June 2005.

[66] This transfer process was made much more transparent in 2004 with the dramatic increase in excise and export taxation on oil. See *Kommersant*, 6 May 2004.

[67] A nice discussion of the changed management ethos appeared in *Rossiiskaia gazeta*, 21 March 2001.

[68] Over thirty-five percent of business firms, however, remained unprofitable, despite the highly favorable macroeconomic environment. See *Russian Economic Trends,* July 2001. This illustrates the continuing need for deep restructuring of many enterprises. That number remained stubbornly high, at thirty-seven to forty percent, right through the end of 2001 and even appears to have gone up in the first half of 2002. Indeed, some forty percent of all industrial enterprises remain money-losers to the end of 2004. See respectively, http://www.strana.ru, January 30, 2002; *Russian Economic Trends,* July 2002; and *BOFIT Russia Review*, April 2004.

[69] These are the annual addresses to the Federal Assembly (*Poslaniia Federal'nomu Sobraniiu*) which can all be found on the web site http://www.president.kremlin.ru. They have taken place in 8 July 2000, 3 April 2001, 18 April 2002, 16 May 2003, 26 May 2004, and 25 April 2005.

[70] This process is empirically investigated in David Brown and John Earle, "Gross Job Flows in Russian Industry Before and After Reforms: Has Destruction Become More Creative?," *Journal of Comparative Economics* 30, no. 1 (March 2002): 96-133.

[71] See Ibid. Aspects of its regional dimension, and constraints on the process, are discussed in Harry Broadman and Francesca Recanatini, "Is Russia Restructuring?: New Evidence on Job Creation and Destruction," preprocessed, (Washington, D.C.: The World Bank, February 2001).

[72] This point is eloquently made by the 1999 Report on Russian Economic Performance of the McKinsey Global Institute. There the particularly destructive role of inherited social and political relations and elite behaviors discussed above is highlighted.

[73] Simeon Djankov and Peter Murrell, "Enterprise Restructuring in Transition: A Quantitative Survey," preprocessed, Department of Economics, University of Maryland (April 2000); and John Earle and Saul Estrin, "Privatization, Competition, and Budget Constraints: Disciplining Enterprises in Russia," preprocessed, SITE (March 1998). The impact of privatization is clearer and positive in market economies, and even in east central Europe where the institutional environment was not distorted by seventy years of Soviet socialism. See Jozef Koenings, "Firm Growth and Ownership in Transition Economies," *Economic Letters* 55 (1997): 413-418; G. Pohl, R. Anderson, S. Claessens, and Djankov, "Privatization and Restructuring in Central and Eastern Europe," *World Bank Technical Paper*, No. 368, (Washington, D.C.: World Bank, 1997); and Roman Frydman, Cheryl Gray, Marek Hessel, and Andrzej Rapaczynski, "When Does Privatization Work?: The Impact of Private Ownership on Corporate Performance in the Transition Economies," *Quarterly Journal of Economics*, 114, no. 4 (November 1999): 1153-1192.

[74] Finance Minister, Alexei Kudrin has claimed that reforms liberalizing business licensing and regulation have resulted in the creation of 400,000 new small businesses. See *Reuters,* 26 February 2002. If so, that would have been a forty-five percent increase in total number over the last two years. Their impact, however, turned out to be more modest: a rise of 36,000 in the year to 1 July 2002 (*Vedomosti*, 3 October 2002). This trend, however, continued during the growth acceleration of 2003-04 as small business felt a lessening burden of bureaucratic intervention. See the CEFIR study summarized in the World Bank publication, *Beyond Transition*, 16, no. 1 (January-March 2005); and *BOFIT Russia Review*, no. 4 (April 2004).

[75] For anecdotal evidence on these trends, see for example P. Starobin, "Russia's Big Get Bigger," *Business Week* (International Edition), 16 July 2001; and R. Cottrell, "Consumer Goods Shake Off a Bad Reputation," *Financial Times,* 25 July 2001. Also see V. Korchagina, K. Koriukin and A. Startseva, "The New Face of Russia's Oligopoly," *The Moscow Times,* 1 November 2001, 1.

[76] Indeed, the Ministry of Economic Development forecasts for 2004-07 assumed a price of

oil in the low to mid $20s, with the 2004 price at $28.50/bbl. (Urals loading). See *Ekspert*, no. 6 (2004).

[77] The data in this section, unless otherwise noted, are derived from July *RET Monthly Update*, 6 July 2001, and the monthly reports of BOFIT, *Russian Economy: Month in Review*, September 2001-July 2005.

[78] These figures are from the *Goskomstat* reports in *The Moscow Times*, 23 July 2001 and 24 January 2002.

[79] See Section "Issues of Measurement" above. This change essentially involved defining sectors as a group of products, independent of who produced them, rather than a group of firms (as in a Soviet industrial ministry). For a clear discussion of the impact of these statistical changes, raising the GDP growth estimate by 0.8 percentage points, see World Bank, *Russian Economic Report*, March 2005, 3-5, at http://www.worldbank.org.ru.

[80] Otto Latsis, "The Glass Today is Half Empty," *Russia Journal*, 3-9 August 2001.

[81] The Ministry of Finance reported 1H02 capital flight at $2.1 billion, while estimates of private financial services run around $8.5 billion. All agree that there has been a substantial drop. See *Moscow Times*, Capital Flight Drops by eighty percent, 17 October 2002.

[82] See the August 2001 edition of the JFK School's newsletter, Russian Investment Symposium.

[83] Overall, these industries are investing at only 91.5 percent of their 1998 levels, and the food industry is investing at only a 71.7 percent rate. See V. Fedorin, "Lokomotivy promyshlennogo rosta katiatcia po inertsii (The Locomotive of Industrial Growth Rolls by Inertia)," *Vedomosti*, 15 February 2002.

[84] Platon Lebedev, a co-owner of YUKOS, was arrested on 2 July 2003, and the head of YUKOS, Mikhail Khodorkovsky was seized at gunpoint from is private jet at a refueling stop on October 25, 2003. See Elena Chinyaeva and Peter Rutland, "The YUKOS Affair: Politics Trumps Economics," *Russia & Eurasia Review* 2, no. 15 (22 July 2003); and Michael McFaul, "Vladimir Putin's Grand Strategy," *The Weekly Standard*, 17 November 2003, for some insightful early analysis.

[85] See World Bank, *Russian Economic Review*, no. 8 (June 2004): 3-7; and no. 10 (March 2005): 21.

[86] See *BOFIT Russia Review*, no. 10 (October 2004): 1; and World Bank, *Russian Economic Report*, no. 10 (March 2005): 2-6, 21.

[87] The government has proposed, and the Duma is on the verge of approving, the elimination of this turnover requirement, and placing a thirty-five percent upper bound of future imposition. See the discussion in the *RFE/RL Business Watch* 2, no. 31 (22 October 2002). The turnover rate was reduced to twenty-five percent in 2004 by the December 2003 Currency Regulation and Control Law. See the OECD analysis, *OECD Economic Surveys: Russian Federation* (Paris: OECD Publications, 2004), 91.

[88] In early 2005 Russian public sector external debt stood at $100.8 billion, of which $40.6 billion was owed to the Paris Club creditors, $10.1 remained of debt to private creditors, and all IMF debt had been repaid in full with a final $3.3 billion payment in January. See Seija Lainela, "Russia's Financial Situation," *BOFIT Russia Review*, no. 7 (2005): 4.

[89] See Vladimir Putin, Annual Address to the Federal Assembly, on Russian TV, 11:00 am, 3 April 2001, reproduced in *Johnson's Russia List*, no. 5185 (3 April 2001), for the primary directions being pursued in 2001. The original Gref Program, published 15 July 2000, is available at http://www.kommersant.ru. The state of the program and current tasks had earlier been elaborated in a press briefing by German Gref, Minister for Economic Development and Trade, on 2 March 2001. See http://www.fednews.ru for that date. The original program was published in July 2000 after receiving support at the G-8 meeting, and is most clearly outlined and analyzed in Roland Nash and Yaroslav Lissovolik, "Putin's First Six Months – An Assessment of Economic Reforms," *Renaissance Capital Economics*, November 2001, at http://www.rencap.com.

[90] For a recent example, see M. Zimin, "Putin's Choice: Cabinet Dismissal or Social Upheaval," *Novaya gazeta*, no. 56 (9 August 2001). An even more strongly worded attack by forty-three leading

opposition figures, warning of impending disaster, was published as an open letter to Putin, "Stop the Lethal Reforms!" in *Sovetskaya Rossiya*, 14 August 2001.

[91] Before 2003, the most prominent case was that against Vladimir Gusinsky, resulting in his exile and the destruction of his media empire, concluding with the take over of NTV by Gazprom-media and the assault on Ekho Moskvy in July 2001. The establishment of Federal Media Center, the role of the Lesin's Press Ministry, and the use of *strana.ru*, and the FSB requirements on all web access providers for direct access to content, all fit the pattern of attempting to control the commanding heights of public information, in the interests of security of the state. A new level of assault on independent wealth striving for political power took place in 2003-04, in jailing of the top management, and the systematic dismantling, of the perhaps most successful private company in Russia, YUKOS. See the discussion of the YUKOS affair below.

[92] Indeed, there was some indication of an impending crisis in financing local governments, with numerous complaints voiced by regional leaders. A good source for following these is the *EWI Regional Report,* available on line at http://www.iews.org.

[93] For some discussion, see, for example, the articles in the weekly *Ekspert,* no. 47 (17 December 2001), and no. 4 (4 February 2002). On the continuing division within the Russian business community see Evgenii Arsukhin, "Stepped Up Lobbying," *Rossiiskaia gazeta,* 13 May 2005.

[94] The Duma session ending in July 2001 passed 130 new reform bills. See *The Moscow Times,* 16 July 2001. While the pace slackened significantly in 2002, some two dozen significant reform bills passed in the areas of tax simplification, civil procedure, pensions, trade in agricultural land, bankruptcy, state enterprises, the central bank, energy tariffs, etc. See the June, July, and October issues of *RFE/RL Russian Political Weekly,* 2 (2002).

[95] These reforms have had some impact on improving the legal environment for business, as long as the interests of the state or sufficiently important political figures are not involved. They are, however, widely flouted in high profile and/or political cases, such as that of Mikhail Khodorkovsky in 2004. See the October 2004 report of the London think-tank, Russian Axis, entitled "Judicial Authorities in Russia: A Systemic Crisis of Independence," at http://www.russianaxis.org.

[96] A major social reform monetizing privileges, e.g. free transportation for veterans and invalids, was clumsily implemented in early 2005, generating massive protests against the government and the weakening or reversal of the reform in a number of regions, including Moscow, despite being overwhelmingly approved in both the Duma and the Federation Council in Early August 2004. See Jamestown Foundation, *Eurasia Daily Monitor* at http://www.jamestown.org, 15 June 2004 and 3 August 2004 on prior protests and passage of the law. The protests filled the Russian press through January 2005. One summary can be found in Jamestown Foundation, 2, no. 15. For translations of dozens of Russian articles on the protests, and the local compromises they induced, see *Johnson's Russia List,* nos. 9003-9034 (3-25 January 2005) at http://www.cdi.org/russia/johnson.

[97] Indeed, much of the discussion of these reforms seems focused on consolidation to insure profitability rather than on fostering competition and efficiency. Thus, the new head of *Gazprom,* Alexei Miller, is moving to reacquire assets that had been alienated to relatives and friends of "insiders" under Vakhirev, but is much less keen on accounting and governance reform and a rationalizing restructuring of *Gazprom's* operations.

[98] A package of six bills on reform of the electric power sector was accepted by the Duma on a first reading on 9 October 2002. *RFE/RL Russian Political Weekly* 2, no. 34 (2002).

[99] Financial market regulation currently provides insufficient oversight and protection of commoners and weak enforcement mechanisms, fostering insider manipulation and undercutting the development of financial intermediation. For an interesting empirical study of this, see Bernand Black, "Does Corporate Governance Matter?: A Crude Test Using Russian Data," Working Paper No. 209, Stanford Law School (December 2000). A new Corporate Governance Code took effect in 2004, including a requirement that Boards be elected by cumulative voting to improve minority representation.

[100] See Aleksandr Bekker, *"Peretriaska vmesto reformy"* (Reshuffling Instead of Reform), *Vedomosti,* 15 October 2004.

[101] For an outline and analysis of the report see J. Tannenbaum, "The Ishaev Report: An Economic Mobilization Plan for Russia," *Executive Intelligence Review* 28, no. 9 (2 March 2001).

[102] This is discussed a in A. Nadzharov, "Backing Up?," *Novye Izvestia,* 9 August 2001.

[103] Its fullest statement is in the May 1997 booklet, RAN, *Guidelines of the Programme for Medium Term Social and Economic Development of Russia* (Moscow: RAN, 1997).

[104] This became a dominant theme in 2004 with the dismemberment of YUKOS, the political-legal assault on its owners and top managers, the building of Rosneft on the seized assets of YUKOS, the taking of a state majority ownership of Gazprom, the reassertion of state control over the transportation of energy resources, and new restrictions on foreign ownership of energy assets in Russia. See Carola Hoyos and Arkady Ostrovsky, "Kremlin Tightens its Control Over the Russian Economy," *Financial Times,* 5 August 2004; Andrei Panov, *"Za razresheniem – v Sovbez"* (For Permission – to the Security Council), *Vedomosti,* 30 June 2005; and Robert Coalson, "A Privatization Deal to Create a New State Oil Giant," *RFE/RL Russian Political Weekly* 4, no. 36 (16 September 2004). For a clear analysis of the logic of these developments, see A. Radygin, "Russia in 2000-2004: On the Way to State Capitalism," *Voprosy ekonomiki,* no. 4 (19 April 2004).

[105] See Valerii Vyzhutovich, "Will Putin Have a Think-Tank Coup," *Moskovskie novosti,* 23 February – 1 March 2005.

[106] This was reflected in numerous press reports and commentary in late 2004 and early 2005, and both the EBRD and IMF reports in mid-2005. See, for example, the RosBusinessConsulting analytic report, "Russia is Losing 'Steam' for Growth," 17 January 2005; Boris Grozovskii, *"Rost pochti prekratilsya"* (Growth Has Almost Stopped), *Vedomosti,* 14 April 2005; Boris Grozovskii, *"Nadezhdy taiot"* (Hope is Melting), *Vedomosti,* 24 May 2005.

[107] Much of this was officially recommended in the World Bank country memorandum, *Russian Economic Report* of June 2004, which can be found at http://www.worldbank.ru.

[108] For a discussion of some of the needs here, see the conference report, National Intelligence Office, "Russia's Physical and Social Infrastructure: Implications for Future Development," *Seminar Series Report CR 2000-06* (Washington, D.C.: NIC, 2000).

[109] Those sectors targeted for state priority support would become more technologically advanced and capable, but are apt to remain economically maladapted to the changing market environment, due both to the absence of real market feedback and to their protected status.

[110] This claim is made in numerous Russian analyses. See, for example, Vladimir Mironov, *"Adminreforma: Udvoenie apparata* (Admin Reform: Doubling the Apparatus)," *Vedomosti,* 16 June 2005.

[111] For an indictment of this activity, see Stanislav Menshikov, "The Kremlin Plays with Oligarchs Instead of Harassing Oligarchs," *Slovo,* 11-17 July 2003.

[112] On the former, see the World Bank, *Country Economic Memorandum* (April 2004) for Russia, *Russian Economic Report* (June 2004), at http://www.worldbank.ru. An early and clear expression of the latter was contained in the May 2003 report of the Council on National Strategy, The State and the Oligarchy.

[113] The timeline and content of the parallel attacks on Khodorkovsky and YUKOS can be seen on their respective web pages: http://www.supportmbk.com and http://www.yukos.ru. For a discussion of the sale that dismembered YUKOS, see Jamestown Foundation, *Eurasian Daily Monitor* 2, no. 1 (3 January 2005); or E. Derbilova, "$6 Billion was Found," *Vedomosti,* 2 February 2005.

[114] Indeed, Lebedev and Khodorkovsky were accused of criminal activity and conspiracy in relation to the 1994 privatization of a small fertilizer factory *Apatit.*

[115] On traditional Russian patrimonialism see Richard Pipes, *Russia Under the Old Regime* (New York: Penguin, 1974), especially 23-24, 84; and Nicolas Spulber, *Russia's Economic Transitions* (Cambridge: Cambridge University Press, 2003), 28.

ENERGY ACROSS EURASIA
The Place of Russian Energy in the Former Soviet Union and Central Europe

THANE GUSTAFSON, SIMON KUKES, AND PAUL
RODZIANKO[1]

Abstract

A new, privately-owned oil industry is rising from the ashes of the Soviet oil industry. Having survived the challenges of the 1990s the companies that have emerged are better managed and more commercial than before. From its beginnings as an isolated, domestic industry, the Russian oil sector is poised to become international as Western oil companies reevaluate opportunities in Russia and Russian oil companies prepare to move overseas.

The Soviet oil industry had many unique characteristics, having developed in isolation from the industry in the West. It was multinational and well-adapted to its environment. By the last decade of the Soviet era, the industry was in trouble: it was unable to develop the necessary technologies required to meet annual targets. At the same time, the declining Soviet economy relied more than ever on oil as a resource.

Perestroika destroyed the Soviet command economy. By 1991, virtually no central authority remained, and both oil production and consumption went into sharp decline. However, the structures of the Soviet era survive in the form of the infrastructure created in that era. These structures provide both challenges and opportunities for the leaders of the Russian oil industry. These leaders come from diverse backgrounds, some from the oil industry itself and others from the world of Russian finance. During the past decade, they have restructured the industry, vertically integrating their enterprises, radically changing management cultures, improving corporate governance, and making businesses more efficient. They now operate in a liberalized market.

Despite these successes, the Russian industry still must operate with the legacy of the Soviet era. Most current production is derived from fields developed in the Soviet era. Efficiency still suffers from short planning horizons as a result of the past instability in the sector and the unresolved tensions between owners and managers.

The challenges for the second decade of this post-Soviet oil industry include reversing the consequences of significant under-investment during the 1990s and the need to raise their market valuations to levels closer to that of their Western peers. Only then will the companies be in a strong position to build on their domestic base and create a truly international industry. A new, privately owned oil industry is rising in post-Soviet Russia. The Russian oil companies have a long and rich history dating back to the very beginnings of the industry. They have survived unique challenges in the 1990s and have emerged strengthened, with renewed skills and self-confidence. They are now ready to reach for new opportunities, at a time when the world needs diversified oil supplies as never before. This chapter tells the story.

* * *

The Way It Was: Energy in the Soviet Union and Its Continuing Legacy

Four Generations of Russian Oil, 1900-90

The Soviet oil industry was unique in ways that continue to mark its Russian successor today. First, it was uniquely a *homegrown* industry, which grew up largely independently of the West, yet by the 1980s was the world's number-one producer of crude oil. Second, it was *multinational* in its own distinctive way, drawing on the many nationalities of the Soviet Union: its geology was Russian; its equipment was Azerbaijani and Ukrainian; and its drillers were Tatars and Bashkirs – while its mosquitoes, one might add, were homegrown Siberian. Third, the Russian oil industry was heavily *shaped by the Soviet era*, particularly by the central planning system's indifference to economics and its unremitting pressure for fast results. Fourth, it was *well adapted to its environment*: over the decades, by trial and error, it had developed the appropriate techniques and equipment for dealing with the climate and geology, the long distances, and the challenging conditions of the Russian oil patch. The Russian oil industry was a rugged, tough, and resourceful group of people.

At its start, the Russian oil industry had not been isolated from the West. At the turn of the last century, the booming Caspian city of Baku, then a part of the Russian Empire, was the world's largest producer of crude oil. Western capital from leading financial families such as the Nobels and the Rothschilds catalyzed the first generation of Russian oil. Even after the Russian Revolution, Western companies played a role in Baku through the end of the 1920s, notably in laying the basis for the Soviet oil tool industry, which remained centered in Azerbaijan over the following six decades.

In the 1930s and 1940s the Russian oil industry began a second generation, with the discovery and development of the oil fields of the Volga-Urals, and in the 1960s, the oil industry crossed the Urals into West Siberia, entering a third generation. During this period, the Soviet Union was largely cut off from the world economy, and the Russian oil industry made its own discoveries and developed them with its own science, technology, and skills. From this period of high achievement, Russian oilmen retain a sense of pride, but also deeply entrenched practices and traditions.

After World War II, Soviet geologists and engineers also ventured into the Caspian offshore. Although they soon realized the enormous geological potential of the Caspian, both north and south, the region was effectively placed on hold for forty years, while the oil industry pursued the more glittering and immediate opportunities in central Russia and West Siberia. Russian oilmen spoke of the Caspian as the coming "fourth generation," and as the oil resources of West Siberia began to fade at the end of the 1980s, they began focusing more attention on the south.

But by that time the Soviet Union was disappearing, and the oil and gas resources of the Caspian would henceforward be shared by five sovereign nations. Thus, by the end of the twentieth century the Russian oil industry had in a sense come full circle – not only back to the Caspian, but also back to something like the wide open international environment of early Baku. The Russian oil industry will have a major role to play in this fourth generation, but two things are already quite different:

- The Russian companies are rapidly evolving into something quite new under the sun – into integrated, private-sector majors, equipped with leading-edge technologies, modern business practices, and a renewed entrepreneurial spirit. The Russian companies working in the Caspian today are rapidly becoming the equals of the other international companies there.
- Their mental map has also changed. The "fourth generation," as it is perceived in Russia today, is located not only in the Caspian, but also in a host of new opportunities: in the Russian northwest and east, in the Arctic offshore, and indeed throughout the world.

In little more than a decade, the Russian oil industry has been reborn. This chapter describes the remarkable changes that have already taken place in the Russian oil industry in the last decade and explores the challenges that lie ahead in the next phase of their evolution as privately-owned, dynamic, and entrepreneurial companies.

On the Eve of the End: Troubles in the Oil Sector in the 1980s

For the last decade of the Soviet era, the oil sector faced mounting troubles. Twice during the 1980s oil production slipped, only to resume growing again following emergency increases in funding and intense political pressure for fast results. It was evident to Russian oilmen even before the collapse of the Soviet system that a major crisis was at hand.

There were two main problems. The first was the pressure of annual targets, which the Communist Party leaders and the central planners ratcheted steadily upward. The official goals could be met only by throwing quality out the window and driving for maximum near-term production. All too often, wells were badly completed, pipes were poorly laid, associated gas was flared. To maximize early recovery, water injection was used from the start of production, lessening total recovery and shortening the life of the field. When the end came, it came with a rush. Thus the supergiant Samotlor, which peaked at over 185 million tons (mt) a year (or 3.7 million barrels per day [mbd]) in the mid-1980s, slid sharply in the second half of the decade to less than one sixth of its peak by the early 1990s.

The second problem was that the Soviet oil industry was falling behind global trends in technology. In the 1980s the world oil industry began a far-reaching technological revolution. Applications of computer technology brought dramatic cost savings and expanded capabilities, particularly in offshore exploration and production. But Soviet oilmen were largely cut off from these developments (even though, ironically, several techniques had initially been pioneered inside the Soviet Union, such as hydrofracturing). Even in areas where Soviet research and development excelled, such as materials science, theoretical advances failed to migrate to the oil service sector, and Soviet equipment, ranging from muds and cements to drill bits and pumps, remained inferior.

Yet, the declining Soviet economy in its last two decades depended more than ever on hydrocarbons. The Soviet economy got a badly needed shot in the arm from the two oil shocks of 1973 and 1980, and the Soviet leadership came to depend on steady injections of hard currency from oil exports to the West. Oil was also a political stabilizer: Soviet oil exports to Eastern Europe helped to sustain the Soviet bloc, as indeed did deliveries of energy from Russia to the non-Russian republics of the Soviet Union. Low energy prices at home masked the growing inefficiency of industry and disguised the fact that the Soviet economy had largely stopped growing by the early 1980s. Only the advent of large natural gas supplies, which grew strongly from the mid-1970s to the end of the 1980s, relieved the enormous pressure on the oil industry and the Soviet economy as a whole.

The Impact of the Soviet Breakup, 1991-95: Declining Production and Declining Consumption

Mikhail Gorbachev's *perestroika* was hailed in the West as a breath of fresh air, but a more short-sighted, ill-conceived economic policy would be hard to imagine. By removing at one go all the essential controls of the command economy – chiefly the state monopoly over foreign trade and central banking, the compulsory plan targets for enterprises, and the coordinating role of the Communist Party apparatus – Gorbachev knocked the props out from under the system of central planning. In less than three years, essentially between 1987 and 1990, *perestroika* shattered the Soviet economy and destroyed the Soviet system.

The impact of *perestroika* on the Soviet oil industry was especially devastating. The removal of the foreign-trade monopoly and the lifting of restrictions on hard-currency accounts abruptly enabled a host of new players to acquire and export oil on their own. The weakened planning system could no longer coordinate the movements of personnel and supplies; and since exploration, production, and refining all belonged to separate ministries – as indeed did the oil tool sector, air transportation, and electricity – the entire circulatory system of the industry stopped. And as the Party apparatus ceased to function and the oil ministry lost its grip over the oilfields, the local oil divisions began to disintegrate, and the entire industry threatened to explode into its smallest parts, the production and drilling units. By 1991 all central authority was gone, and the country was locked into a deadly and desperate battle of each against all, for power, property, and rents.

In the immediate aftermath of the Soviet collapse, the pattern of oil production and use changed radically. Oil exports to Eastern Europe, which had been nearly half of all Soviet oil exports in the 1980s, practically disappeared overnight. In the initial post-Soviet years (1990–92), deliveries to the non-Russian Former Soviet Union (FSU) remained temporarily strong, while exports to the West collapsed. But by 1994 exports to the West recovered and began a steady growth, while oil exports to the FSU faded away. Overall, Russian oil production plummeted from 516.2 mt (or 10.3 mbd) in 1990 to a low of 301.2 mt (6.02 mbd) in 1996, while domestic consumption fell by well over half, from 250.6 mt (5.01 mbd) in 1990 to 113.3 mt (2.3 mbd) in 1998.

One serious problem for the Russian economy is the lingering legacy of the Soviet system. Ten years after its collapse, the Soviet Union lives on – at least in the sense that the structures built during the Soviet era will continue to affect the Russian economy, and the energy sector in particular, for many years to come.

The energy system built in Soviet times was adapted to the needs of a different country and a different time, yet it remains largely in place today. The layout of pipelines and power lines, the location of power plants and refineries, still mirror the needs of a centrally planned economy whose fifteen union-republics were closely integrated. After the breakup of the Soviet Union, the oil industry had to adapt to the fact that major facilities were now located in foreign countries – for example, the export terminals at Odessa and Ventspils; the Western end of the Druzhba pipeline system and a portion of the pipeline to Novorossiisk; and key refineries, notably Mazheikiu, Lisichansk, and many others. The gas and power sectors were similarly affected.

Likewise, the kinds of energy produced by the Soviet system were more appropriate to the needs of an economy heavily dominated by manufacturing (much of it military), than to the emerging consumer and service economy of Russia today. The oil industry, in particular, inherited a refinery system that still produces too many heavy products (fuel oil, in particular) and too few light ones. Even at the light end of the barrel, there is too much low-octane gasoline and not enough high-test, despite the fact that there are more and more passenger cars on Russian roads and fewer gasoline-fueled trucks and buses.

The Soviet economy was addicted to cheap energy, which of course it consumed wastefully. Technologies and designs were chosen without regard to the real costs of energy. A decade after the end of the Soviet era, the pattern of Russian energy consumption remains stubbornly Soviet-like, locked in by those earlier choices. Most of Russian industry cannot yet afford to invest in up-to-date, energy-efficient plant. The result is a vicious circle that holds back the entire economy: energy prices are kept low so as not to destabilize the economy; but low energy prices perpetuate the inefficiencies that make the low prices necessary in the first place. The oil industry has made better progress than the gas and power sectors in escaping from this trap, but there is still a long way to go, particularly with the impact of crude export restrictions on domestic product prices.

These three aspects of the Soviet legacy – layout, product mix, and price structure

– constrain the oil industry's operations and raise constant political issues, but they reflect the inescapable fact that there is a great deal of inertia to any country's capital stock. Only over time, as the Russian economy evolves away from its Soviet past, will new incentives and new investment gradually yield a more efficient structure.

The Rise of a New Russian Industry

From Isolation to Integration: Five Chapters in the Evolution of a Private Russian Oil Industry, 1991-2001

The Russian oil industry has gone through enormous changes in its brief ten-year history. It has, arguably, already evolved further from its Soviet origins than any other branch of Russian industry. But the story is far from over: the oil industry's evolution in the 1990s has set the stage for even more fundamental transformations in the decade ahead.

In the Soviet era the oil industry was divided horizontally: six different ministries were responsible for exploration, development, refining, distribution, construction, and exports, respectively. Oil producers and refiners could spend their entire careers without ever meeting one another, and neither had any contact with exporters. Exploration was divided between the Ministry of Geology and the Ministry of Oil, which typically behaved more as rivals than as partners. The result was a cumbersome and inefficient industry.

There had long been calls for doing away with such an unwieldy structure and replacing it with vertically integrated units instead. When the Soviet Union broke up in 1991, that is precisely what happened. Over the course of a decade the oil industry went from a horizontal structure to a vertical one. Today Russia's largest oil companies are all vertically integrated corporations (see Figure 1).

But this transformation occurred less through a concerted plan than through a ten-year war, as a wide variety of players, industry veterans and newcomers to the oil patch, did battle against one another for control of the richest prize in Russia. Over the decade of the 1990s the story went through five principal chapters (see Figure 2).

Chapter One: 1991–93, the Oil Generals Take the Lead

The reformers in the new Russian government initially favored creating vertically integrated oil companies under the leadership of the upstream "oil generals." They parceled out the oil industry accordingly, allocating to each of the new companies

Figure 1
The Russian Oil Industry: From Horizontal Monopolies to Vertical Integration Companies

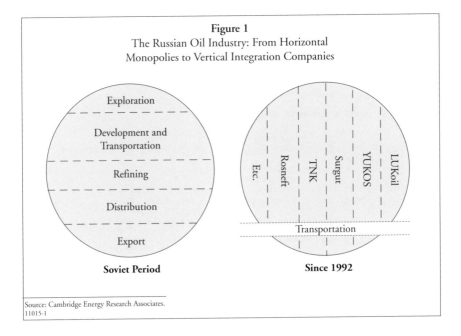

Exploration

Development and Transportation

Refining

Distribution

Export

Soviet Period

Etc. | Rosneft | TNK | Surgut | YUKOS | LUKoil

Transportation

Since 1992

Source: Cambridge Energy Research Associates.
11015-1

Figure 2
Five Generations of Russian Oil Privatization

Generation 1: 1991-1993

Creation of integrated companies based on upstream "oil generals"

Only LUKoil and Surgut actually achieve integration

Generation 2: 1993-1995

New players enter the Russian oil patch: bankers, politicians, traders, Mafiosi

Most oil generals lose control

Resneft carved up to form TNK Sibneft, Slavneft, and Sidanco

Generation 3: 1995-1996

Shares for Loans Deals

Bankers take over state-owened stakes

YUKOS, Sidanco, and Sibneft change hands

Generation 4: 1997-1999

Renewed struggle over control

Wave of bankruptcy suits

Devaluation helps bottom line

Generation 5: 2000-2001

High oil prices and profits

Battle for property settles down

Companies diversify

Investment increases

Source: Cambridge Energy Research Associates.
10715-10

its own upstream producing units, refineries, and market areas. LUKoil was the first to be created in this way, from three upstream "production associations" (as they were called in Soviet times) in West Siberia,[2] two refineries, and a dedicated market region in central Russia. LUKoil was soon followed by two other new creations, Surgutneftegaz and YUKOS.

Chapter Two: 1993–95, Newcomers Enter the Oil Patch

The early reformers soon left the government, and the initial vision of integrated companies led by upstream generals weakened as a host of new players bid for a piece of the industry. Regional governors, big-city mayors, geologists, refiners, traders, and many others besides jumped into the oil patch and attempted to create oil companies of their own. In some instances, local production units broke away and formed small independents. The new integrated companies soon discovered that inheriting assets was one thing; actually controlling them was quite another.

Nevertheless, a few more vertically integrated companies were created during this period, mostly carved out from the state-owned Rosneft, which had inherited the residual assets of the Soviet oil ministry. Sibneft, Slavneft, Sidanco, Onaco, and VNK were all established at this time.

However, these later creations had a more difficult time establishing themselves than the first generation of 1991–93. Several of them have since been absorbed into other companies, and there may be further changes ahead. Thus, Sidanco, created in 1994, was initially scripted (as its name indicates) to be the Siberian and Far Eastern Oil Company, with its crude production based in West Siberia, its refineries and distribution systems scattered throughout East Siberia and the Russian Far East, and its export system focused on the Asian market. Little remains of this initial blueprint today.

Chapter Three: 1995–96, the "Shares-for-Loans" Deals

In 1995 the Russian government, desperately in need of money, made an agreement with the leaders of the increasingly powerful private holding groups to assign the state's remaining shares in the largest oil companies in trust to the holding groups, in exchange for substantial loans. When the state proved unable to repay the loans, the shares became the holding groups' property. Ownership of YUKOS, Sidanco, and Sibneft changed hands in this way. This had a very important consequence, which has turned out to be critical to the subsequent evolution of these companies: a new generation of entrepreneurial leaders, who had built powerful companies in the new financial sector, displaced the traditional oil generals as leaders of their newly acquired companies.

TNK had a different history. It was created in 1995 by the Russian government as a state-owned holding company. The two major upstream components of TNK were Nizhnevartovskneftegaz (NNG), which holds the license to most of the supergiant Samotlor field, and Tyumenneftegaz (TNG), a geological exploration group with licenses in the south of Tyumen Province. In addition, TNK included a refinery at Ryazan' in central Russia and five marketing companies. In 1997 TNK was privatized. Later that year the Novy Group, a group of private investors, acquired forty percent of TNK equity from the Russian government in an investment tender. Following additional purchases, the Novy Group now owns ninety-seven percent of TNK.

Chapter Four: 1997–99, the Great Crash and Its Aftermath

A turning point for the oil industry came in 1997–99. On the one hand, the decline of world oil prices and the real appreciation of the ruble in 1997 and early 1998, combined with growing fiscal pressure from the government, squeezed the companies' margins severely. To maintain their short-term cash flows and lessen their taxes, many companies resorted to transfer pricing. This proved to be a risky policy, because it had the effect of driving their subsidiaries into debt. In 1997, the government passed a new bankruptcy law that enabled creditors to use outstanding debt as a powerful lever for hostile takeovers. This led to a fresh round of battles for control.

On the other hand, the aftermath of the crash soon provided the oil industry with unprecedented opportunities. The massive devaluation of the ruble that followed the crash, combined with the strong increase in world oil prices that began in mid-1999, greatly improved the oil industry's cash flow, setting the stage for the chapter the Russian companies are in today.

But the most important consequence of the crash of 1998 was that the entire Russian political and corporate elite was forced to take stock and to confront the fact that the freewheeling atmosphere of the 1990s had only hurt themselves and Russia. The salutary result (as discussed in the next section) has been a much greater degree of consensus and a lower level of conflict, both within the Russian business elite and between the private sector and the government.

Chapter Five: 2000–01, Political and Corporate Stabilization

The election of a new president, the resumption of fiscal and legal reforms, a sound monetary policy, and a newly cautious and more conservative political atmosphere – all combined with continued high oil prices – have created an unprecedented favorable atmosphere for the stable development of the oil industry. The decade-long battle for control has largely subsided (although less so in some neighboring industrial sectors), and the corporate structure of the industry has stabilized. As a result, in 2000, for the first time since the Soviet era, oil investment increased sharply and production began to rise.

A prime symbol of this more stable atmosphere is the final settlement of a long battle for control of Sidanco. In August 2001 Interros sold its holding in Sidanco, forty-four percent of the company's stock for $650 million to TNK, which also acquired a forty percent stake held by another group of investors. TNK now owns eighty-four percent of Sidanco. BP, which owns 10 percent of Sidanco, will manage Sidanco for three years.

Summing Up the First Decade: Achievements and Shortcomings

Thus, the Russian oil industry has come a long way in the last decade. The new Russian companies bear little resemblance to their Soviet ancestors, either in structure or in behavior. Despite the difficult challenges of the 1990s, they can point to remarkable achievements.

Genuinely Integrated Companies

After a decade of difficult struggle, the leading Russian oil companies have largely achieved genuine financial and management control over their subsidiaries. The key step came at the end of the 1990s, when many of the parent holding companies swapped shares with their subsidiaries, thus consolidating their ownership. (Some companies have not yet done this, such as Slavneft, but are likely to do so once the remaining state stake has been privatized.) This is of course a necessary condition for progress in establishing modern management systems.

Leaner, More Efficient Structure

The Russian companies initially inherited from Soviet days a heavy baggage of top-heavy management, excess personnel, and unrelated businesses. Soviet ministries tried to provide everything they needed for themselves, including exploration and oilfield services, but also catering and food supply, and even local community infrastructure (so-called *sotsialka*) such as schools, housing, hospitals, and roads. Over the last decade the Russian companies have systematically pared away excess personnel and have learned to divest and outsource, while concentrating their management and financial resources on their core businesses. Most oilfield services today, such as drilling, are procured by competitive tender from private contractors.

Changing Management Cultures

The new Russian oil companies have already moved a long way from the corporate culture of the Soviet-era ministries and their production associations. Internally, Soviet institutions were hierarchical bureaucracies, in which promotion was based more on personal loyalties and protection networks than on performance. Distrust was pervasive, information was a power resource to be hoarded rather than shared, and avoiding responsibility was generally more important than showing initiative. This is beginning to change, as the Russian oil companies develop new incentives and a common language of performance and accountability, encouraging employees at all levels to use information to evaluate reality rather than hide facts and shift blame. Training systems are teaching new skills and attitudes.

Improving Corporate Governance

The best Russian companies have learned the value of good corporate governance. More and more Russian managers, especially since the crash of 1998, have understood that business reputation is an asset that pays concrete dividends. Good corporate governance increases the value of a company's stock, decreases the cost of capital, and attracts the best business partners. In the oil sector in particular, as ownership has stabilized over the last three years, standards of corporate governance have risen sharply.

<u>Substantial Market Autonomy</u>

In contrast to domestic electricity and gas prices, which remain closely controlled by the state, oil prices inside Russia today are largely set by negotiations between buyers and sellers. Crude prices were liberalized in January 1995 and product prices followed suit in March 1995.[3] Local authorities initially tried to set upper bounds to retail prices of key products, but they soon learned that they could not enforce price controls without causing massive disruptions. Similarly, attempts by state authorities to mandate allocations of crude and products to specific regions or institutions have proven largely ineffective. In short, in the space of a decade the oil industry has largely succeeded in creating a genuine internal market for its products.

Despite these substantial achievements, the Russian oil companies also share a number of shortcomings. The most serious and fundamental one is that they still largely depend on "Soviet oil," i.e., production from fields and wells that were developed in Soviet times. No Russian company has yet taken the plunge and begun investing really large amounts of capital in new provinces and fields. In 2000, although 43 new fields began production, they yielded only 0.55 mt (4.01 mb) of oil. Out of 3,718 new wells drilled in 2000, only 147 were in new fields. The total output of "new oil" (defined as oil from wells less than five years old) was only about 16 mt (117 mb) in 2000, about 5 percent of Russian total production. These figures testify to the very small share of effort going into new fields.

The second common shortcoming is that in most Russian oil companies strategic planning is still embryonic. Throughout most of the 1990s, most Russian oilmen were preoccupied with survival and could rarely afford the luxury of thinking more than a few months ahead. This was perhaps inevitable, given the unsettled political and economic conditions of the time. It is only in the last few years that leaders and strategists in the oil companies have been able to lengthen their horizons and begin to develop longer-range business plans.

A third weakness is an unresolved tension between owners and managers. In most mature Western companies, ownership is clearly separated from management, and the companies are run by professional managers while owners stay in the background. In most Russian companies, in contrast, owners typically play a direct hands-on role, both in defining the broad strategies of their companies and in making technical decisions. To a degree this is a natural phenomenon. The evolution of the Russian companies to date matches a pattern familiar from business history elsewhere: during their early phase new companies are managed by the founder-entrepreneur; while in a subsequent phase owners commonly turn the reins over to professional managers whose chief mission is to maximize shareholder value. We can assume that this will happen more broadly in Russia as well, and is indeed already happening in some companies.

Challenges for the Russian Oil Majors Today: Stability, Profitability, Valuation, Investment

Two major challenges face the Russian oil companies in their second decade. The first is investment; the second is valuation and diversification.

Investment

Oilfield investment declined sharply throughout the 1990s. By 1998 investment (in real terms) was only twenty-four percent of the 1990 level. Drilling dropped even more precipitously than investment, from 36.2 million meters in 1990 to 5.1 million

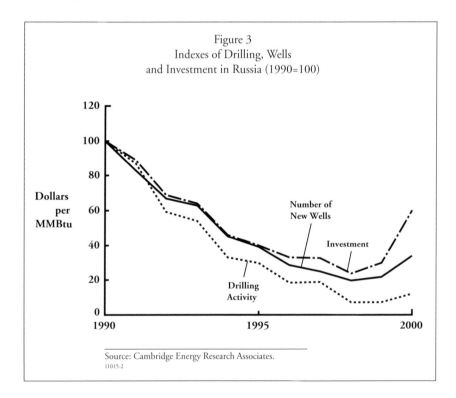

Figure 3
Indexes of Drilling, Wells
and Investment in Russia (1990=100)

Source: Cambridge Energy Research Associates.
11015-2

GUSTAFSON, KUKES, AND RODZIANKO

meters in 1998. It was only in 2000 that investment turned around decisively. New wells, exploration drilling, and development drilling all increased sharply, and there is every sign that the upward trend has continued strongly in 2001 (see Figure 3).

Nevertheless, as noted earlier, little of the capital going into the Russian upstream is being devoted to new fields. To explore and develop the next generation of oil fields and provinces will require much more capital than the $7 billion in upstream investment in 2001. The World Bank, for example, estimates that $11-12 billion a year will be needed to build a new base for the future, of which the bulk must go to the upstream.

Clearly, such sums are beyond the current means of the Russian oil companies. Even through the high oil prices of the last three years have improved their cash flows and made some of them cash-rich, they can hardly base their long-term strategies on the expectation that world prices will stay at higher than average levels indefinitely. With the long-term Brent price being around eighteen billion dollars per barrel, there should be a corresponding impact on oil companies' earnings.

Where will the necessary capital come from? At present, foreign investment is the only plausible answer. However, through 2000 total foreign direct investment (FDI) in the Russian oil industry was four billion dollars, part of which came from offshore Russian capital. Clearly, stimulating foreign investment on a larger scale will require fundamental improvements in the investment climate in Russia, notably more secure property rights, a more predictable tax system, an end to remaining export controls, and pricing parity between the domestic and export markets. Fortunately, there is good news on all of these fronts, as the current Russian government deploys the latest round of market reforms. However, it is also clear that there remains some distance to go.

In the future, more capital will become available from Russian sources, both internal and offshore. Russian capital markets are evolving quickly. Corporate bonds are becoming more common, maturities are lengthening, and liquidity is improving. As Russia moves toward a modern pension system, the capital mobilized by private savings will build up rapidly.

Valuation and Diversification

The Russian oil companies are arguably substantially undervalued by capital markets. This is due to a number of perceptions, some of which are connected to the Russian companies themselves, and others to broader features of the Russian market:

- *Liabilities of Russian companies as perceived by markets.* These include Russian accounting standards, Russian reserves, problems in valuing assets, nontransparent cash flows, unstable ownership, poor corporate governance, etc. Many of these issues are no longer serious concerns, but remain lodged in the minds of investors.
- *Perceived deficiencies of Russian equity markets.* There is a perceived lack of liquidity, poor regulation, embryonic sell-side institutions, vulnerability to global "emerging market" trends, and an overall "Russia risk." Again, these issues are improving but attitudes and impressions will take time to change.

It is not only Russian companies that are undervalued, but also Russian reserves. If one looks at recent acquisitions and the prices paid for them, the implied valuation of Russian reserves ranges from thirty cents to one dollar a barrel. Over time, as both Russia and the Russian oil industry have stabilized, the implied valuations of Russian reserves have tended to rise. Thus TNK's acquisition of eighty-five percent of Onaco in September 2000 set a record, with an implied valuation of $1.50 a barrel. Nevertheless, Russian reserves are still substantially undervalued. It is striking that recent acquisitions of reserves in Sakhalin, which presumably reflect "Western risk" rather than "Russian risk," have ranged between three and four dollars a barrel.

This has negative consequences for the Russian oil companies. In particular, it prevents them from diversifying into international markets. Russian companies cannot pay for acquisitions with equity or asset swaps, as Western companies typically do, without giving away much of the "real" value of their barrels. Thus they are largely limited to paying cash, which limits the scale of acquisitions they can make. In addition, the undervaluation of their assets places the Russian companies in an unfavorable position in negotiating possible joint projects or partnerships with Western companies inside Russia.

The fundamental issue behind the low valuations of Russian companies and reserves is whether "Russia risk" is still as serious as the discounts suggest, or whether Western markets are simply lagging behind the evolving reality in Russia. This is of course a legitimate question, which has to do both with the basic health of the Russian industry and the quality of government policies. The answer depends very much, in particular, on how the two relate to one another.

The Russian State: Partner or Antagonist for the Oil and Gas Industry?

Only ten years ago, the Russian energy sector was an integral part of the Soviet state. Today, a decade after the blow-up of the Soviet system, the energy sector's position vis-à-vis the Russian state could be compared to the aftermath of a nova: some bits ended up in close orbits, while others were blown farther away. The new system is still in the process of stabilizing. Yet, all its new parts continue, in one way or another, to revolve around one another.

Thus, the power sector remains state property, while the gas industry is only partially privatized. Both are acutely dependent on state policies. The oil industry has

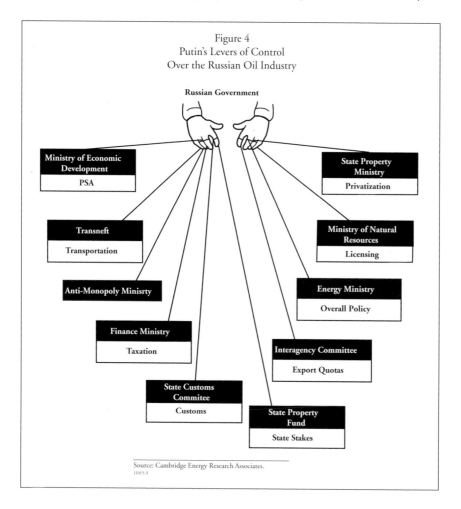

Figure 4
Putin's Levers of Control
Over the Russian Oil Industry

Source: Cambridge Energy Research Associates.
11015-3

achieved the greatest independence, and yet even it continues to be tied to the state in complex and shifting ways. The state retains a wide range of instruments through which it can exercise control over the oil industry, although it does not always use them (see Figure 4).

The Russian state too has evolved over the last ten years, just as the energy sector has. But it is fair to say that it is still searching for its mission. It is no longer the sovereign owner and hands-on manager of the economy, as it was in Soviet times. Its role now is more like that of Western governments – the referee of the marketplace and the provider of last resort. But the Russian government remains ambivalent over just how to regulate the new market economy, with its complex mix of public and private property. This shows up vividly in the state's relations with the oil sector.

There are currently three main issues between the new post-Soviet oil industry and the Russian state: the stability of ownership, the division of the rent and the design of government take, and the autonomy of the sector.

Stability of Ownership

Given the tumultuous process by which the oil industry was privatized in the 1990s, the possibility of a challenge to the new owners by the government could not be ruled out. In his annual address to the Duma in April 2001, President Vladimir Putin stated clearly that he intends no sweeping review of the results of privatization. Several recent government reviews of past privatizations have reaffirmed their validity.

Yet, this does not entirely settle the matter: state actions continue to have a major impact on the stability of ownership in the oil sector, in two main ways. First, the state remains a significant stakeholder in several oil companies, and in a handful of cases, it is still the majority owner. Rosneft is the most important example, because it is still a full-fledged state oil company. At various times the government has considered giving Rosneft much greater importance as the official state company, for example as its agent in production-sharing contracts. Clearly, that would change the rules of the game for all of the private oil companies by creating a favored competitor or mandatory partner/operator in new projects. But just how the state intends to treat Rosneft is still unsettled, as is the broader issue of the state's management (or disposal) of its stake across the board.

Second, state policies affect the stability of ownership in the oil sector in a variety of indirect ways. The most important is bankruptcy law. In 1997 the government

GUSTAFSON, KUKES, AND RODZIANKO

passed a new bankruptcy law that heavily favors creditors. This law has since become a popular weapon for hostile takeovers – some 8,000 in 2000 alone, including a number of widely publicized cases in the oil sector. There have been mounting calls for a reform of the bankruptcy law, including a decision of the Constitutional Court in 2001 declaring key parts of the law unconstitutional. However, at this writing the threat of a hostile takeover emanating from a bankruptcy action remains a destabilizing factor in the oil industry.

Fiscal Policy: The Division of the Rent and the Design of Government Take

Oil and gas between them provide forty percent of the state's revenues from a wide variety of levies and taxes. Thus, the monetary and fiscal stability of the country depends crucially on the hydrocarbons sector. But designing a suitable tax system for the oil industry has been complicated by three specifically Russian factors:

- *The government's ambivalence toward the natural resource sector.* Russia's natural endowment in raw materials is the prime source of the country's wealth. Yet Russians have mixed feelings about this bounty, aware that Russia's role in the international economy today is that of commodity producer. The state considers one of its central missions to encourage the "real economy" – defined as high-tech and manufacturing – by transferring resources from the extractive sector.
- *The rent from Soviet oil versus the need for new investment.* So long as the bulk of Russian oil production consisted of Soviet oil developed prior to 1991, there was at least a case that most of the rent logically belonged to the country and should be captured by the state. But as it becomes increasingly urgent to invest in the next generation of oil, there is inevitably a debate over the division of rents. The debate centers on two points: How much rent is the industry currently throwing off? And how much is needed for new investment? On both of these issues, the industry and the state have not yet reached a common language.
- *The limited capacities of the Russian tax-collection system.* Tax reform has been one of the success stories of the Putin administration so far. The main elements of the Tax Code have been quickly voted into law. As a result, the Russian tax system on paper conforms in all essentials to OECD standards and it boasts some of the lowest tax rates anywhere.

The Autonomy of the Oil Sector Vis-à-Vis the State

The essential difference between a privately owned industry and a state-owned one lies in the word "autonomy." A private owner must have the autonomy to make the decisions that will make his business fructify. That means he must have the independent power to decide what investments to make, what technologies to use, which markets to develop, and how many people to employ. Private ownership that is deprived of autonomy over these decisions loses its comparative advantage over state ownership as a means of creating wealth for the economy.

In Russia the autonomy of the oil companies is still highly constrained. Under Russian law, the state is the sovereign owner of the mineral resources in the ground. As the owner, the state sets the conditions for awarding and managing licenses under which resources will be identified and developed.

The issue is, where is the boundary between reasonable state regulation and unreasonable interference? The answer is neither clear nor predictable. Under current licensing rules (as well as production-sharing legislation) the state claims powers of oversight over services and equipment procurement, industry practices, employment, social welfare, and the distribution of crude and products, as well as many other matters besides. Indeed, the range of state regulation in the oil industry is an excellent example of the excessive interference that President Putin condemned as a major hindrance to the development of the economy in his April 2001 speech to the Duma.

The same problem can be seen in the state's roles in transportation and export policy. The state is currently using its ownership of Transneft to enforce strict controls on the share of crude oil that can be exported in order to support OPEC and other non-OPEC producers in their quest for price stability. The result is that crude is forced by administrative means into the domestic market, lowering prices and destroying value. Currently, domestic crude oil prices are around twenty percent of the world price, while gas prices are around fifteen percent of international prices. While the low domestic oil price will be eliminated when crude export restrictions are lifted, the gas sector is a more intractable problem. The state has in the past justified its policy on gas tariffs in the name of defending a fragile domestic economy and forestalling inflation. But the result is a continued subsidy of domestic consumers, who thus have no incentive to use energy more efficiently. As in Soviet times, the result is excessive consumption.

The Road Ahead: Challenges and Opportunities for the Russian Oil Companies

Russian Oil and Gas Reserves and Production: The Outlook to 2005

<u>Reserves and the Future of Russian Crude Production</u>

Russia has a strong tradition in geological expertise. However, oil exploration and reserves estimation were distorted in Soviet times by political pressures and also by a traditional approach that focused on geological potential alone. In the 1990s the Russian oil companies have revised their reserve estimates, and several have had their reserves audited by reputable Western specialists. As a result, today's company estimates of proven reserves are both more reliable and more closely based on economic potential, rather than on geological potential alone. This process of reestimation is not yet complete, since to date only six Russian companies have had their proven reserves reviewed by Western auditors. As a rule of thumb, Western auditors have accepted about seventy percent of Russian "proven" reserves as meeting Western definitions. This means that the Russia-wide total of 130 billion barrels (or 17.8 billion tons) currently classified as "proven" by the Russian Ministry of Natural Resources would translate to ninety-one billion barrels (or 12.5 billion tons) of "proven" reserves by the Western yardstick.[4] This is substantially larger than the conservative figure of 48.6 billion barrels (or 6.7 billion tons) currently given by an authoritative source, BP's *Statistical Review of World Energy 2001*. BP's estimate includes only the Western audits that have been performed to date.

Roughly three quarters of Russia's proven reserves are located in West Siberia, mostly in small and deep fields with low permeability. As exploration goes forward, the center of gravity of explored Russian reserves will move to the periphery of the country, to the greenfield provinces of Timan-Pechora, East Siberia, Sakhalin, and the North Caucasus and Barents offshore. These regions may add another forty to fifty billion barrels (or 5.5 to 6.8 billion tons) of recoverable reserves.

This migration to the periphery will have two opposing consequences: higher unit costs and lower transportation costs. Most of Russia's greenfield sites are in remote places with difficult climatic or geological conditions; they will require extensive investment in infrastructure and advanced technology. On the other hand, most of tomorrow's prospects will have shorter transportation distances to market via open oceans and waterways; thus tomorrow's Russian oil will increasingly bypass the existing pipeline system.

In sum, Russia still has abundant oil reserves. Although nowhere close to the same scale as Saudi Arabia's, Russia's proven reserves (when fully reestimated to Western definitions) should represent nearly nine percent of the world total, putting Russia in roughly fifth place worldwide, in the same class as Iran and not far behind Kuwait and the UAE. In addition, Russia's unexplored potential is still substantial.

Russian Crude Production: Stabilization and Growth

After stabilizing in 1995–99 at just over six mbd (or about 300 million tons a year), Russian crude and condensate production grew six percent in 2000 and by 7.7 percent in 2001 (see Table 1).

Table 1: Crude and Condensate Production, 1990–2001
(millions of tons nat.)
Source: CERA, TNK

Year	Output
1990	516.2
1991	461.1
1992	395.8
1993	343.8
1994	315.7
1995	306.7
1996	301.2
1997	305.6
1998	303.2
1999	305.0
2000	323.2
2001	348.1

Nearly all of the growth in production in 2000 came from "old" fields, i.e., fields under development since Soviet times. Increases in infill drilling and completion of new wells, combined with well workovers and the use of enhanced recovery techniques, accounted for most of the additions to output (see Figure 5).

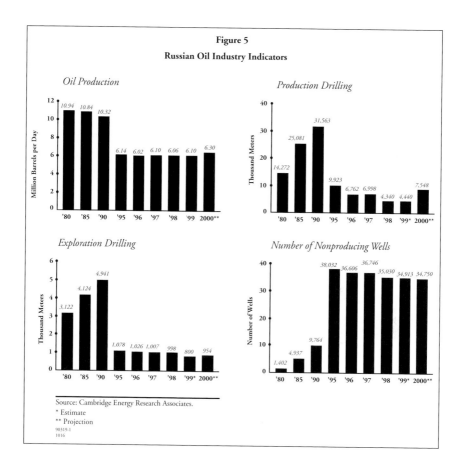

Figure 5
Russian Oil Industry Indicators

Source: Cambridge Energy Research Associates.
* Estimate
** Projection
90319-1
1016

These positive developments over the past two years indicate that stepped-up investment, systematic cost-cutting, and the application of new technologies can still wring increases in output from established fields at acceptable costs. Even though the flow rates from new wells are low (averaging ten tons, or about seventy-three barrels, per day in West Siberia), lifting costs are also very low, thanks in part to the lingering effects of the ruble devaluation of 1998, but also to the Russian companies' success in cutting costs. TNK's lifting costs are about $3.60 per barrel (or about $26.30 per ton) today, and are expected to remain below five dollars until the end of 2002.

The future of the industry, however, ultimately rests with "new" oil from new fields and provinces. The good news since 2000 is that exploration drilling has grown strongly for the first time since the Soviet era, reaching 1.01 million meters in 2000, up 27.8 percent over 1999, and 1.15 million meters in 2001. In addition, in 2000, forty-three new fields began production, and although their contribution was modest that year (205,000 barrels per day [bd], or 10.25 mt), so-called new fields (i.e., fields in production less than five years) now produce five percent of total Russian crude, and their share can be expected to grow steadily.

Continued growth in crude output depends above all on growth in investment. In 2000 and 2001, Russian oil companies invested heavily upstream for the first time since 1996–97. For the first time since the Soviet era, they are shifting toward investing in developing production instead of acquiring existing assets (although some companies, such as TNK, are succeeding in doing both).

The Coming Market Challenge: GDP Growth, Domestic Oil Demand, Export and Transportation Outlook

Forecasting gross domestic product (GDP) growth is always a dangerous enterprise in any country, but especially so with Russia. First, so large a share of Russian GDP is associated with commodities exports and is therefore acutely dependent on global trends. Second, the growth of the domestic economy is hostage to unpredictable government policies, particularly as these affect capital flows, investment, and productivity growth.

Not surprisingly, therefore, the range of forecasts is wide. The International Monetary Fund's July 2001 staff report for Russia projected GDP growth gradually rising from four percent in 2001 to five percent in 2005 and six percent thereafter. Estimates by private sector analysts were broadly in the same range. The outturn of five percent proved better than expected.

The real question for the oil industry is domestic energy demand, and particularly demand for refined products. Product consumption dropped sharply from 1990 through 1998, from 250.6 mt (or five mbd) in 1990 to 113.3 mt (or 2.3 mbd) in 1998. The decline bottomed out at the end of the 1990s, but the recovery of demand in the decade ahead is likely to be slow. The government's official Energy Strategy 2000 projects annual growth of less than one percent for all primary energy sources (see Table 2).

Table 2: Russian Energy Strategy 2000: Energy Demand to 2010
Source: RF Ministry of Energy, Russian Energy Strategy 2000.

	1990	1995	2000	2005	2005
Motor Fuels (million tons nat.)	114	68	61	68	75
Total Consumption of Primary Fuels (million tons coal equivalent)	1257	930	898	955	1000
As a percentage of 1990	100	74	71.4	76	80
Energy Intensity of GDP (tons of coal equivalent per $1,000)	1.27	1.43	1.44	1.21	1.03

The combination of the strong growth of crude oil output and the slow growth of energy demand will create a surplus of crude and a glut of certain types of refined products: gasoline and motor fuels; diesel; and residual fuel. Demand will grow strongly for high-octane gasoline, offset by continuing decline of demand for lower-grade gasolines. Overall, however, gasoline supplies will be in balance with demand. Distillate demand will grow fifty percent between 2000 and 2010, as trucking, agriculture, and industry all develop strongly. Nevertheless, there will be some surplus in this area. There is a likely to be a serious oversupply of fuel oil in the decade ahead. Russian fuel oil has traditionally sold at a premium as an uncracked feedstock, but the market will be problematic in the years ahead.

The clear course for Russian producers is to continue boosting crude production and to maximize exports. The result, however, will be a rush on available export pipelines and terminals. Faced with the prospect of increasingly severe transportation bottlenecks along export routes, Russian oil companies have several possible responses, first, in Russia itself:

- *Support expansion of Russia's export pipeline capacity.* Baltic Pipeline System (BPS), Ukrainian bypass, connections to Caspian Pipeline Consortium (CPC); etc;
- *Build company-owned pipelines and terminals.* LUKoil's Varandey terminal;
- *Support increased terminal capacity.* Novorossiisk, Primorsk, etc;
- *Support increased efficiency and value in the Transneft system.* Quality banking, drag-reducing agents, long-term contracts, etc.

New Opportunities: Expansion Into Central Europe

As Russian companies search for new investment opportunities, they have been increasingly drawn to Eastern Europe. LUKoil was the first Russian company to take a position in Eastern Europe, buying refineries in Romania and Bulgaria and retail gasoline stations in the Czech Republic, Poland, Yugoslavia, and Croatia. In addition, LUKoil has expanded into the Western republics of the FSU, acquiring a refinery and a petrochemical plant in Ukraine as well as retail stations throughout the area.

So far no other Russian company has gone quite so far as LUKoil into Eastern Europe, although several have shown growing interest, such as YUKOS's proposed participation in reversing the Adria pipeline. For the time being, most of the other Russian companies have focused on the Western FSU instead. Thus TNK has acquired a controlling stake in the Lisichansk refinery in Ukraine, while YUKOS plans to take a position in the Mazheikiu refinery.

Eastern Europe has several attractive features that draw the interest of the Russian oil companies. First, the area has long been familiar to the Russian oil industry, since Eastern Europe was tied to Russia through the CMEA and for two decades accounted for more than half of Soviet oil exports. Second, for Russian companies intent on building integrated companies, Eastern Europe's geographic proximity to Russia is an obvious asset. Third, over the last decade the East European economies have broadly fared better than the FSU economies, and the region's higher growth rates and standards of living promise growing demand for oil products. Last, and most important, the prospect of East European accession to the European Union creates a driver for internal reform and marketization that benefits all investors. In addition, as Eastern Europe joins the European Union, it gives Russian companies a forward base from which to compete in the single European market.

In sum, Eastern Europe looks attractively close, familiar, and prospective. For Russian companies seeking investment opportunities outside Russia yet still lacking experience in remote foreign locations, Eastern Europe is arguably the ideal region in which to gain exposure and acquire experience.

But Eastern Europe also has significant drawbacks, and consequently there is controversy over just how attractive the region really is for the Russian companies.

Is Vertical Integration Necessarily the Answer?

Until recently, Western oil companies had largely abandoned the dominant business model of the 1960s, in which upstream companies that were long on crude routinely owned extensive refining and marketing assets. But faced with intense competition, Western oil companies are now discovering new virtues in "reintegration" between upstream and downstream. However, integration is not by itself a magic answer. Two conditions must be satisfied. First, there must be reasonable geographic proximity (or some other strong basis for complementarity) between the upstream and downstream components. Second, both the upstream and downstream must be competitive on their own. For the Russian oil companies, Eastern Europe meets the first criterion (thanks to the established Transneft pipeline system), but not necessarily the second.

Slow Growth, Bureaucratic Obstacles, Resistance

Eastern Europe is a less than ideal market because so far economic growth has been slow and consumption of refined products has been stagnant. Moreover, East European governments and companies in the northern half of Eastern Europe are unenthusiastic about being taken over by outside interests, and may seek to defend national champions against takeover. Consequently, it remains to be seen how successful the penetration of Russian companies into Eastern Europe will ultimately prove.

New Opportunities (II): The Oil Companies Move into Natural Gas

The impending restructuring of the Russian gas industry is about to open up new opportunities for the oil companies to produce and market natural gas. The reform plan proposed by the Russian government in the summer of 2001 promises to end Gazprom's monopoly control of the gas industry, creating in its place a state-owned transportation company that will guarantee open access to gas producers. This opens the door wide to oil companies to enter the gas business. A more detailed restructuring concept may become available later in 2002 once Minster Gref has completed his review of the options.

Hitherto, the oil companies mostly produced associated gas and only minimal amounts of natural gas (25.7 billion cubic meters [Bcm] and 5.3 Bcm, respectively, in 2000). Their options for marketing gas were unattractive, so long as Gazprom controlled both the pipeline system and the sole processor of associated gas, Sibur.

- *Natural gas excluded.* Although in theory Russian law provided for "independent" gas producers and granted them third-party access to the pipeline system, in practice Gazprom limited access to companies with which it had friendly ties.

- *Associated gas constrained.* Most associated gas is sold at a low, state-regulated price to a Gazprom-controlled subsidiary, Sibur, for reprocessing. Sibur strips out the liquids and delivers the dry gas into the Gazprom pipeline system; thus the oil companies lose the value of both. Some gas is sold at a low price to power plants. The remainder is flared or reinjected. While the position of Sibur is now uncertain, oil companies are still likely to face problems in the short term in gaining a fair price for their gas.

Once they gain access to the gas pipeline system, the Russian oil companies, as independent producers, will be able to sell gas directly to final consumers at unregulated prices. This is potentially a very profitable business. In recent years, as gas demand has grown and Gazprom's production has declined, certain categories of consumers have been willing to pay premium prices for gas. As time goes on, domestic gas prices are certain to rise further.

In addition, the Russian oil companies have been positioning themselves to develop gas fields in Eastern Siberia and Sakhalin, to supply the growing gas markets of China, Japan, and South Korea. Since the eastern half of the country was never part of Gazprom's system, the oil companies enjoyed greater freedom of action from the beginning. However, developing this attractive opportunity will require major investment in new infrastructure and pipelines, most likely in collaboration with Western partners.

What Russian Roles for Western Partners? What International Roles for Russian Companies?

In 1991 two worlds of oil that had been separated for decades by the Iron Curtain suddenly found themselves face to face. The Soviet oil industry had grown up almost entirely independently of its Western counterpart. It had its own traditions, its own habits, and its own language. Two alien civilizations were meeting for the first time. Not surprisingly, the result in all too many cases was illusion and misunderstanding, followed by disappointment and bitterness on both sides. It has taken a decade for the Western and Russian oil industries to overcome their initial mistakes and begin to develop a shared view of what collaboration can achieve.

GUSTAFSON, KUKES, AND RODZIANKO

What can Western oil companies bring to Russia? The Russian oil industry in 1991 was like a patient suffering simultaneously from a severe chronic illness compounded by an acute infection. It labored both under the damage inflicted over the years by the Soviet system, plus the crisis caused by its sudden breakup and the aftermath. But the patient also had a strong constitution. It was well adapted to the unique Russian climate and geology and to the available manpower and infrastructure.

Western oil companies had never before encountered a mature oil industry that had grown up entirely on its own resources and its own technologies, and they made the initial mistake of greatly underestimating the skills and experience of their Russian counterparts. Their first response was to fly in Western equipment and manpower and to push the Russians aside. Needless to say, the unforgiving winters and complex reservoirs of West Siberia soon taught them differently. Joint ventures managed in this way yielded mainly high costs and hurt feelings.

The Russian oilmen had illusions of their own. Knowing little about the West, they could not tell the difference between reputable companies and fly-by-night operators. They were baffled by the armies of lawyers and bankers that the Western visitors brought with them, and they did not initially grasp that the real decisions were made by remote boards in far-off places. Above all, they could not accept the Westerners' insistence on control.

A decade later, both sides have learned a great deal about one another, and certain broad principles of collaboration have emerged that are increasingly recognized by both sides:

- *Blended technologies and teams work best.* The key to success is to use the skills ands technologies that work best for each site, using mostly Russian personnel and mixtures of Russian and Western equipment. Service companies have understood this best and have developed mixed teams that work effectively under Russian conditions.

- *Management is more important than capital or technology.* Russian companies soon learned that they could "contract out" for equipment and services, just as Western companies do, and that they can obtain financing through the same banks. The hidden ingredient, they have discovered, is management, which blends these elements into profitable operations.

- *Collaboration must go both ways – into Russia and outside.* Russian companies are increasingly aware that they must expand their operations outside Russia, both to diversify their operations and to acquire the international skills and experience they need. Two-way collaboration, in turn, creates the shared interest that can bind a Western and a Russian company into a solid partnership.

Putting these principles to work on a broad scale, however, will take more time and mutual learning. Take for example the case of greenfield sites in remote locations, such as Sakhalin or the Arctic Ocean. These are places where advanced Western technology and experience come into their own. Yet the Western companies must not repeat the mistake of attempting to work solely with their own people and equipment. The Russian side will insist on a reasonable share of domestic sourcing. Transfer of technology and skills is the name of the game, without which partnership will fail.

Russian Energy in the Former Soviet Union

Oil and Gas Transportation: The FSU is Still a Single Space

In many respects, the FSU is still a single space. Russia, Ukraine, and North Kazakhstan are still part of the same energy grid. There is still a unified gas pipeline system. And the oil pipeline system is still essentially the same one that served the Soviet Union. This has several consequences. First, transportation events within this space remain very much connected. If export capacity increases at one end of the system (such as the construction of the Baltic Pipeline System and the expansion of terminal capacities into the Baltic), it automatically has repercussions for flows at the other end (such as Russian oil flows into the Black Sea and the number of tankers passing through the Bosphorus). For planners and strategists, it is essential to keep the map of the whole FSU firmly in mind. The FSU as a whole remains the relevant playing field.

A decade after the breakup of the Soviet Union, Western companies are rediscovering that the FSU – and the Russian transportation system that lies at its core – remain the most economic transit route for oil and gas on their way to export markets in Europe. The key word here is economics. For all the geopolitical debates about pipelines to the Mediterranean via Turkey and the Persian Gulf via Iran, it remains a fact that adapting an existing system is far cheaper than building a new one.

Opportunities for Russian Companies in Kazakhstan and the Caspian

Russian companies have been active players in the Caspian throughout the 1990s. In the first half of the decade, when the interest of international companies focused primarily on the south Caspian, the Russian company LUKoil took an equity position in the Azerbaijan International Oil Consortium (AIOC), which is developing three major offshore fields along the Apsheron Trend off Baku.

Over the course of the decade, however, a succession of dry holes in the south Caspian has led to the view that most of the South will turn out to be primarily gas-prone. In contrast, the northern half of the Caspian is turning out to be far more oil-rich than previously suspected. This has shifted the perceived "center of gravity" of Caspian oil back to the North, to the Kazakhstani and Russian sectors.

This shift opens up new opportunities for Russian companies. In the Russian sector, LUKoil has made a significant discovery in the Severnoe block, at the Khvalynskoe field, located 350 kilometers south of Astrakhan. According to preliminary estimates, the field may contain 300 mt (2.2 billion barrels) of recoverable light crude. In addition, the Caspian Oil Company, made up of a consortium of Russian companies, has begun exploration in the Russian sector.

The fact that Russian companies are key players in exploring and producing the energy resources of the Caspian Sea puts a very different face on the debate of the 1990s over the geopolitics of the region. Far from "losing influence" in the Caspian, Russia has an indispensable role to play. The key issues will be infrastructure and transportation. Since Russian oil production is likely to rise faster than domestic consumption in the decade ahead, export pipeline capacity will be at a premium, particularly to accommodate the growing volumes from the Caspian. Both the Russian state and Russian private companies are already major shareholders in the Caspian Pipeline Consortium, the first private oil pipeline to cross Russian soil. In addition, Russian companies are showing increasing interest in participating in the proposed Baku-Ceyhan project. Transneft is discussing with Kazakhstani officials the possibility of participating in an export route to Iran. In short, the years ahead are likely to see Russian companies participating actively in creating a diversified transportation system for Caspian oil. It is a win-win situation for all the players.

At this moment the pace of exploration and production is constrained by the difficulty of moving major equipment, particularly offshore rigs, into the Caspian area. It is clear that the growing demand for equipment and services will stimulate the development of new service centers, just as it did at Aberdeen in the North Sea.

In the Caspian there likely will be several such centers, but it is already clear that one of them will be the Russian port city of Astrakhan, and other Russian cities on the Volga will play supporting roles as well. In sum, Russian players will be at the center of every aspect of Caspian oil and gas in years to come.

The Ukrainian Conundrum: Bypass or Partnership?

Ukraine represents a special challenge for Russia, because it is both a problem and an opportunity. Both arise from Ukraine's unique combination of need and leverage. On the one hand, Ukraine depends on outside sources (chiefly Russia and Turkmenistan) for nearly eighty percent of its gas consumption and sixty percent of its oil consumption. As Ukraine's domestic energy consumption turns around, its net energy imports are likely to increase by a further seventy percent between 2000 and 2020, mostly in the form of natural gas.

At the same time Ukraine's strategic location gives it control over key export flows. In 2000 Ukraine transited over sixty-three mt (or 1.26 mbd) of crude oil, via three main channels: the southern branch of the Druzhba pipeline, the main pipelines from West Siberia to the Black Sea, and the oil terminal at Odessa. Ukraine's role in gas transit is even more crucial: Ukraine is the main artery for Russian gas exports to Europe, transiting over 123 Bcm in 2000. Ukraine earns very large revenues for its transit services: over $270 million per year for oil and close to $1.5 billion for gas, in the form of thirty Bcm of gas.

Russia has long objected that Ukraine's transit fees are excessively high. (For example, along the route to Novorossiisk, Ukraine charges a tariff of $2.35 per ton for a stretch of only 364 kilometers, roughly 2.5 times the Russian tariff). In recent years Gazprom and Transneft have taken active steps to reduce their dependence on Ukrainian transit. Gazprom has already built a first bypass pipeline through Belarus and Poland, and is building a second one under the Black Sea to Turkey. Transneft has built a bypass along the route to Novorossiisk (the 254 kilometer Sukhodolnaya-Rodionovskaya pipeline).

Yet, Ukraine can and does use its geographic leverage to counter Russian moves. For years it has pilfered Russian gas passing through Ukraine to Europe; in recent years such disappearing volumes have amounted to over ten Bcm per year. In addition, Ukraine routinely fails to pay for gas contracted for its own use. There have been constant disputes over the last decade, which a series of high-level accords has not resolved.

Similarly, on the oil front, Ukraine threatens to use its leverage to retaliate for any loss of transit revenue as a result of the Novorossiisk bypass. It can effectively block Russia's plans to reverse the Adria pipeline by demanding higher tariffs. More ominously, Ukraine has invested its tariff revenues in new pipeline from Odessa to Brody, which could displace Russia's access to Central Europe via the southern Druzhba, although the absence of a quality bank in the Druzhba line has meant that Caspian producers currently see no interest in using the line. Russian oil companies investing in Central Europe's downstream can effectively be held hostage by Ukraine's high tariffs.

Amid all these problems, however, there is also opportunity. Although Ukrainian oil consumption is modest and throughput in Ukrainian refineries has declined sharply from sixty mt per year (or 1.2 mbd) in the late 1980s to just over nine mt (or 180,000 bd) in 2000, there is likely to be growing demand in coming years for refined products throughout the southern region, including south Russia, particularly as agriculture rebounds. To develop this potential market TNK has acquired the Lisichansk refinery and is supplying it with steadily growing volumes, reaching as much as 4.5 mt (or 90,000 bd) in 2001. Several other Russian companies have also acquired positions in Ukrainian refineries, taking advantage of the recent willingness of Ukrainian authorities to allow privatization and takeover by outside companies. Conceivably the same thing will happen eventually with the Ukrainian pipeline system, as the Ukrainians are forced to face the huge expense of maintaining and upgrading the system.

Energy Across Eurasia: Challenges for the Future

Despite some nostalgia here and there, there is no serious question of recreating the Soviet Union as a political entity. Yet, the territory of the FSU remains in several respects a single market, particularly in energy. And while Russian companies, to win market share in today's new Eurasia, will have to compete vigorously in an open business environment, they enjoy a number of significant advantages. Chief among these are language, experience, geography, infrastructure, and political ties. Russian remains the dominant language of business and international communication throughout most of the FSU, and will likely do so for decades to come, despite the strong rise of English. Furthermore, despite the end of central planning and the transition to market economies, all of the former Soviet republics share a common background, common understandings, and a common informal culture which arise from the Soviet past. Old school ties and shared early careers are still common.

Moreover, the shortest distance between two points in the FSU often passes through Russia. For example, Russia clearly offers the cheapest transportation routes from the Caspian and Central Asia to European oil and gas markets. As companies plan where their oil and gas "want to flow," Russia's central location remains a key asset. Power grids and oil and gas transportation systems still connect the republics of FSU to one another in a dense network. All other things being equal, because of the infrastructure it still makes business sense to refine Russian crude in Ukraine or Kazakhstan, to supply West Siberian gas to the Baltic Republics, or to supply electricity to Russia, Ukraine, and Kazakhstan through the same power grid.

Finally, even in market economies, energy remains in substantial measure a political commodity. Russia's friendly ties with the former Soviet republics, which are growing stronger again as the shock of the Soviet breakup recedes into the past, lower political risk for Russian companies working in the FSU.

The persistence of these strong assets has several implications for the Russian oil companies, and indirectly for Western ones as well. As they evolve into efficient global competitors, the Russian companies are increasingly well positioned to do good business in the FSU. This makes them potentially attractive partners for Western companies interested in working in the non-Russian republics. Russian companies can not only help Western companies to win market positions in the non-Russian republics, but also help open the way to transit through Russia or to reach attractive market opportunities in Russia as they develop.

NOTES TO CHAPTER 6

[1] This chapter reflects the state of the Russian oil industry in late 2001 and early 2002. The primary author of the chapter is Thane Gustafson with support from Paul Rodzianko. Simon Kukes, then-President of the Tyumen Oil Company, presented this chapter as a paper at the Seventh Liechtenstein Colloquium on European and International Affairs, "The Future of the Russian State," 15 March 2002, and Paul Rodzianko presented it before the Asia Society on 8 April 2002.

[2] The three upstream production associations were Langepas, Urai, and Kogalym – hence the initials LUK which became the basis for the company's name.

[3] This is a separate issue from the reasons why Russian domestic oil prices are so much lower than the world level. That question is addressed in below.

[4] Official Russian oil reserve estimates are still considered "state secrets," and consequently authoritative estimates of the national total are not publicly available. However, in recent years unofficial estimates have been circulated by the Ministry of Natural Resources and the Ministry of Energy. In addition, individual Russian companies are publishing increasingly detailed reserve numbers, which are available on the companies' websites.

GUSTAFSON, KUKES, AND RODZIANKO

CONTESTED CURRENCY
Russia's Ruble in Domestic and International Politics
RAWI ABDELAL[1]

Abstract

The 1990s were a difficult decade for the ruble, the Soviet currency that in 1991 became the common currency for all fifteen post-Soviet states, and by 1995 had become Russia's currency alone. Within Russia the ruble was systematically rejected by firms and citizens in favor of complicated barter arrangements, leaving many important sectors of the Russian economy essentially demonetized. Several of Russia's provinces issued their own currencies, and many financial institutions and firms issued monetary surrogates, undermining the Russian state's monopoly on the definition of money. The ruble experienced prolonged bouts of severe inflation, its most recent period of stability ended by the financial crisis of August 1998. The Central Bank of Russia (CBR) in July 1993 announced, without warning, that all ruble notes printed between 1961 and 1992 would no longer be legal tender, leading to a crisis of Russians' confidence in their monetary system. The behavior of the second director of the CBR, Viktor Gerashchenko, led the Harvard economist Jeffrey Sachs to call him, famously, "the world's worst central banker." The ruble fared little better outside Russia. The currency was subject to severe exchange-rate instability, and to repeated speculative attacks. Several post-Soviet governments rejected the "occupation ruble" in early 1992 and introduced their own national currencies.

Although the International Monetary Fund (IMF) counseled post-Soviet governments to maintain their monetary union, the so-called ruble zone, the monetary relations among them were both chaotic and discordant until the union finally fell apart in the autumn of 1993. The experience of the ruble during the first post-Soviet decade illuminates three of the most important issues in the politics of Russia and the former Soviet Union. First, money was a critical nexus between economic reform and state building within Russia. Second, Russia's internal debates about the ruble zone mirrored broader debates about Russian national and state identities, particularly as they related to the rest of the post-Soviet Eurasia. Third, the decline and fall of the ruble zone reveals a great deal about how the other fourteen successor states, and the societies living within them, viewed their relations with Russia and among themselves. Analysis of the ruble thus offers insights into the nature of political and economic institutions, as well as social identities, in Russia and the other fourteen post-Soviet states.

In this article I address all three of these issues. I observe, first, that Russia's demonetization reflected the broader failure of Russian state institutions. In the next section, on Russia's policies toward the ruble zone, I suggest that Russia's ambivalence toward the monetary union reflected contrasting interpretations of Russian national and state identity: political elites within Russia could not agree whether Russia was a "Western" or "Eurasian" power, and whether its priority should be economic reform within or political influence outside Russia. Ultimately, Russia was forced to abandon the ruble zone because it could not afford such expensive influence.

Finally, in the third section, I show that the other post-Soviet governments themselves had contrasting interpretations of the ruble zone. Some, such as Lithuania, viewed the ruble zone as an instrument of Russian imperialism, while others, such as Belarus, operated as though the ruble zone was a mere convenience. These interpretations were derived from the identities of post-Soviet societies, and their national identities in particular. The content and contestation of the national identities of post-Soviet societies, I conclude, led to their contrasting policies toward the ruble zone. Their national identities also, therefore, influenced their perspective on the independent currencies all of them had introduced by 1995. For some post-Soviet states an independent currency was a source of pride and autonomy, as well as a symbol of sovereignty. But for others an independent currency was seen almost as a liability that hampered their efforts to reintegrate the post-Soviet economic space.

* * *

Money, Capitalism, and the State in Russia

The conventional wisdom about Russia's transition from state socialism to capitalism is that the Russian government did not go far enough in its efforts to reform the economy. This view is at best incomplete. An alternate view has emerged among a number of political scientists, namely, that the central problem of Russia's attempt to create capitalism was the weakness of its state institutions. In this way of thinking about the problem, some of Russia's reformers, as well as the Western economists advising them, had mistakenly assumed that institutions would be generated spontaneously by the process of reform. Indeed, the reformers' efforts to tear down the institutions of the Soviet state without building new institutions for

ABDELAL

the Russian state emerging in their stead was perhaps their single most consequential decision of the early 1990s. Regardless of whether or not Russia's reformers, by taking a different approach to reform, could have built new state institutions quickly enough to accommodate the profound economic changes underway, by the middle of the 1990s the Russian state clearly was unable to perform the most basic tasks of the modern state – to collect taxes, enforce laws and contracts, pay the salaries of bureaucrats and the military, provide social services, create infrastructure, project authority across the entire territory, and maintain a monopoly on the legitimate use of force.[2] Modern states have almost always attempted to maintain a monopoly on the definition of money within their territories, and the vast majority have assumed the sole responsibility of issuing currency as well.[3]

The Russian state lost its monopoly on the definition of money within its territory during the early 1990s. After the government freed most prices on 2 January 1992, barter, which had been common in the Soviet economic system, declined. Only two years later, however, barter reemerged as a central feature of the new Russian economic system. Remarkably, the forms of barter had changed; Russia's emerging problem with barter was uniquely post-Soviet.

While Soviet-era barter networks had emerged to deal with shortages of goods, the post-Soviet barter networks arose apparently in reaction to shortages of cash. And the demonetization of the Russian economy was unmistakable. In January 1992 less than ten percent of industrial sales were completed by barter. But in January 1999 almost fifty percent of industrial sales involved barter, with some estimates ranging as high as seventy percent.[4] Professional intermediaries began to organize the barter trade. Even more problematic, from the perspective of Russian federal authority, was the emergence of monetary surrogates, which existed primarily as local currencies. Political scientist David Woodruff astutely analyzes Russia's problem of monetary consolidation, which he defines as "state building in the monetary realm – the process whereby a state acquires a monopoly over the means of payment that is used across the territory it rules."[5]

The rise of barter in Russia was in large part a consequence of the center-regional conflicts that plagued the Russian federal system.[6] A complicated chain of events led to Russian firms' and local governments' departure from the ruble. In the middle of 1993 monetary policy changed substantially: the CBR attempted to tighten its control over the money supply within Russia and the entire post-Soviet region as well (of which more later). The moment of the CBR's most generous extension of credit to the country's ailing firms was ending, as was its very institutional authority to ensure its credit ended up in the appropriate accounts. In addition, when direct subsidies from the state to firms were cut, the demand for most industrial products collapsed. Partly as a result of these factors, many firms had accrued debts to suppliers, especially energy and transport suppliers, which they could not afford. Firms, most decisively in the energy and transport sectors, began to accept in-kind payments for debts. They were forced to make estimates of the worth – in rubles – of these transactions.

Of course, these firms' transactions created tax obligations, also denominated in rubles. Local governments began to accept in-kind payments for taxes as well. They were forced to do so in part because these firms provided infrastructure and social services, in addition to employment, for the regions in which they were located. Legacies of Soviet industrial planning, these firms were integral to their local economies, much more than mere producers of goods and consumers of energy and transport services. Most could not simply go out of business. In addition, a number of commercial banks and firms, particularly influential fuel and power companies, began to deal with what they considered to be a serious shortage of cash rubles by issuing their own pseudo-currencies, including promissory notes called *vekselia*. Some regional governments, such as Tatarstan's, issued their own money substitutes as well.

Once this practice was institutionalized at the regional level within Russia it was almost inevitable that the federal government would have to deal with it one way or another. Eventually, in late 1994, the federal government began to accept in-kind tax payments as well. In 1996 this new federal practice reached its height when more than one-quarter of the government's revenue was "non-cash."[7] The federal government encountered considerable difficulty weaning itself off of in-kind tax payments during the latter half of the decade.

Thus, according to Woodruff, "it was Russian provincial governments that challenged the central state's exclusive claim to monetary sovereignty."[8] That is, monetary innovation in the regions undermined the Russian state's authority over what citizens and firms considered money. Not only was the state's power thereby undermined, but these troubles of the ruble encouraged disintegrative trends in the Russian economy. Economic policy making in general, including monetary policy, was in turn made enormously difficult, since the Russian economy never became a single monetary space. This struggle between the center and the regions appeared in other areas of the economy as well, more visibly in the federal government's authority and ability to collect taxes.[9]

At the end of the 1990s it had become clear that the challenge to rebuild the authority of the Russian state was daunting, to say the least. The Russian state lacked autonomy (the independence of state institutions from societal pressure), capacity (the ability and effectiveness of the state to perform its basic political and economic functions), and legitimacy (society's belief in the state and consent about its social purpose). Russia's trouble with the ruble was one of the most visible symptoms of state weakness. Demonetization and the other negative consequences of declining state capacity were, unfortunately, mutually reinforcing.

Russia and the Ruble Zone

The ruble zone – the monetary union shared by all fifteen post-Soviet states in 1991 – collapsed in fits and starts during 1992 and 1993, finally disappearing in May 1995. The monetary union disintegrated for two primary reasons.[10] First, several post-Soviet governments considered their membership in the ruble zone illegitimate, a limitation on their newly acquired sovereignty. So, in the middle of 1992, these autonomy-minded governments exited the ruble zone and introduced independent currencies. Still, nine post-Soviet states remained as late as July 1993, when Russia destroyed the monetary union. The governments of many of these states indicated that they were quite content with their membership of the zone. Clearly the monetary union could have, in one form or another, lasted for a while.

Thus, the second reason the monetary union disintegrated was Russian policy itself, and in particular its reversal between the end of 1991 and the middle of 1993. Russia initially sought to hold the monetary union together. This policy reflected the Russian government's intention to maintain influence in the near abroad, influence for which Russian policy makers were prepared to pay. The Russian government linked its trade in energy to the region's monetary politics. After the collapse of Soviet institutions, Russia continued to subsidize production in the other successor states with hugely discounted energy and raw materials, by some estimates at sixty to seventy percent below world prices. Russia offered this deal only to ruble-zone members, however, a fact that created incentives for nearly all post-Soviet states to remain in the union. Russia's policy was the classic monetary diplomacy of great powers, which have often sought to cultivate what political scientist Jonathan Kirshner calls the "monetary dependence" of less powerful states for the sake of increased influence.[11]

Ruble-zone membership turned out to be materially beneficial to the non-Russian members also for reasons having to do with its institutional design, a fact that created another problem for Russian policy makers. The problem turned out to be straightforward: a single currency shared by fifteen independent monetary authorities.[12] The CBR controlled the printing presses, so it alone could create cash (*nalichnye*) rubles. Before 1991 the Soviet state bank, Gosbank, had local branches in all of the republics. After the dissolution of the Soviet state, those local branches of Gosbank became the central banks of the newly independent states and could create non-cash (*beznalichnye*) rubles by emitting credit. This institutional structure not only led to a competition for seigniorage among post-Soviet states, problem enough for a monetary union; the non-Russian successor states also found that they could finance their trade deficits with Russia by issuing credit to local commercial banks, which could extend it to local importers, with the resulting ruble credit balances ending up in the accounts of the CBR. Because Russia had a trade surplus with all the other post-Soviet states in 1992, these fourteen financed their deficits with rubles they created themselves. The result was a transfer of real resources from Russia, in addition to the implicit subsidies Russia already offered the successor states with its energy and raw materials discounts.[13]

Another problem was the lack of a single Russian policy toward the monetary union. The executive branch of the government and the CBR expressed contrasting views and undertook divergent policies on the ruble zone, operating frequently at cross-purposes. President Boris Yeltsin and his economic team, as the political scientist Juliet Johnson shows, "increasingly began to regard the ruble zone as an economic liability, as it became clear that most other ruble-zone members preferred to reform their economies at a relatively slower pace." Meanwhile, the CBR under Gerashchenko sought to maintain the ruble zone under its own authority.[14]

The first Russian attempt to restrain the largesse of the other ruble-zone states came in the summer of 1992. On 21 June 1992, President Yeltsin warned ruble-zone members that they would have to accept CBR control over their credit emissions and issued a decree that the Soviet-era ruble was now Russian.[15] Still, Gerashchenko's CBR regularly exceeded the limits the Yeltsin government tried to impose on the credits extended directly from Russia to the other states.[16]

A little later, on 1 July 1992, the CBR began keeping separate ruble accounts for each state.[17] This meant that, although the central banks of the other states could still create credit, the CBR would begin to keep track, bilaterally, of which banks issued how much and where it ended up. The *beznalichnye* rubles were no longer all alike: Belarusian credit, for example, was distinct from Ukrainian credit, and clearly distinct from CBR credit. In August 1992 the Russian government announced that other post-Soviet states could now trade directly with Russian exporters through commercial banks rather than through their respective central banks. Importers of Russian goods now needed credit issued by the CBR. Credit created by the other central banks became useful only within the state whose bank created it. Each state had its own version of the ruble circulating in banks, though all shared the same ruble circulating as cash. Finally, in April and May 1993, the CBR suspended other ruble-zone members' power to create credit.[18]

During the first half of 1993, as the Russian government and CBR were attempting to rationalize the credit emission of the other central banks in the ruble zone, the CBR was also issuing new ruble notes. These new notes were distinctively Russian rubles, in contrast to the Soviet rubles, with their picture of Lenin and fifteen languages of the constituent republics, that had been circulating until then. The CBR kept nearly all of these Russian rubles within Russian territory, continuing to send the old notes to the other ruble-zone members. On 24 July 1993, the CBR announced that all rubles printed before 1993 would no longer be legal tender in Russia as of 26 July, and that they could be exchanged at a set rate within Russia.[19]

It is not yet clear whether President Yeltsin or Prime Minister Viktor Chernomyrdin approved Gerashchenko's move in advance, but Finance Minister Boris Fedorov was apparently caught unaware.[20] Fedorov complained publicly and bitterly about the currency exchange, calling it "stupid, scandalous, and senseless."[21] The fact that the president's and prime minister's offices immediately issued separate statements with revisions both to the timetable and to the limits on the currency exchange, as well as different logics for the move, suggests that the CBR had not fully coordinated its actions with other institutions within the Russian state.[22] The parliament was caught completely unprepared and complained about the move.[23] Perhaps most surprised were the other ruble-zone members themselves, since Russia had agreed to inform them before adopting any currency reforms. In any case, the purpose of the currency reform was the subject of much debate within Russia and abroad. Fedorov, for example, assumed that Gerashchenko had sought to undermine popular support for the reform process and demanded his resignation.[24]

In retrospect it seems that the CBR's primary reason for the currency reform was to settle the issue of authority within the ruble zone once and for all.[25] "Russia appears to have achieved the main objective of its currency reform," the *Financial Times'* John Lloyd reported, Gerashchenko "said yesterday that the forced exchange of pre-1993 rubles had compelled former Soviet republics still using the Russian currency to opt in or out of the ruble zone."[26] Gerashchenko continued to explain the currency reform as a policy directed toward ruble-zone members that had not either accepted CBR authority or introduced their own currencies.[27]

In addition, the Russian government's and CBR's view of the function of the ruble had been changing in the months leading up to the July 1993 decision. In 1992, the CBR under Gerashchenko, the directors of industrial firms, and some members of the Russian government argued that monetary policy should be used to maintain the links among firms. A prominent view held that some of the country's economic problems stemmed from the fragmenting of links among Russia's, and the post-Soviet region's, otherwise productive firms. Eventually the CBR recognized its limited ability to maintain the production links among firms by providing money. When the ruble's role in Russia's economy came increasingly to be seen in more conventional – and capitalist – terms, maintenance of the links among Russian and other states' firms also lost importance as a goal of the CBR's policy. Thus, the diminishing influence of what Woodruff calls the "national productivist project" undermined one logic the CBR might have used to support the ruble zone.[28]

After several weeks of monetary chaos, during which four former republics announced their plans to issue independent currencies immediately, Gerashchenko and the Russian government offered the five post-Soviet states still using the old Soviet ruble a reconstituted monetary union. This *rublevaia zona novogo tipa,* the "ruble zone of a new type," was to be orderly and centralized. In exchange for the material benefits of a currency union with Russia, governments that joined the new-type ruble zone agreed to let the CBR make monetary policy for them all.[29]

The terms the government demanded of prospective members of the new-type ruble zone called Russia's commitment to monetary union into question, however. The new cash rubles would indeed be given to ruble-zone members, but as state credit; the central banks of member states would be obliged to pay interest to the CBR as if the ruble notes were a loan. Russia also insisted that ruble-zone members deposit at the CBR hard currency or gold worth fifty percent of the value of the ruble "loan." Prospective members considered the rate of exchange from old rubles to new to be, at three for one, confiscatory. And members of the new-type ruble zone were required not to introduce an independent currency for a period of five years.[30]

Almost all of the prospective members of the reconstituted monetary union interpreted these conditions as "impossible," not least because they simply did not have hard currency or gold worth fifty percent of the value of the ruble notes. Even if they had they would have had difficultly affording imports with so much of their foreign exchange deposited at the CBR. The prospective members complained that Russia had intentionally destroyed the ruble zone and any chance for its resurrection.

Except for Tajikistan, mired in its civil war, they all introduced independent currencies, protesting that they had been forced to do so. It is still not clear whether the Russian government and CBR really expected the prospective members of the new-type ruble zone to accede to their demanding conditions or, for that matter, which of them designed the conditions in the first place. Whatever the case, one incontrovertible conclusion is that the debate within the various institutions of the Russian state, including the executive branch and central bank, was by autumn 1993 settled in favor of those who did not want to continue to pay such a high price for the influence given by the ruble zone.[31]

Thus, the evolution of Russia's relationship to the ruble zone was closely related to two important debates within Russian society and government, the first of which directly implicated the ruble zone. Members of the political elite differed sharply on the ruble zone, particularly as it related to Russia's attempts to transform its own economic institutions. Clearly Yeltsin and Gerashchenko did not always agree on monetary relations with other post-Soviet states, but neither man's motivations seemed clear. The debate was perhaps epitomized best by the disagreements between Yegor Gaidar and Boris Fedorov, on one side, and Viktor Chernomyrdin, on the other. Gaidar and Fedorov, liberal reformers, argued that the ruble zone complicated Russia's economic reform and stabilization, and that Russia should shed the economic burdens of empire to concentrate on the creation of capitalist economic institutions. In contrast, Chernomyrdin sought to hold the ruble zone together in order to institutionalize Russian regional hegemony and its influence in the near abroad.

This debate over the ruble zone was necessarily linked to a broader foreign policy debate within Russia over its status in relation to the other post-Soviet states. At issue was the meaning of both the Russian nation and the Russian state. The theoretical distinction between national and state identities is important in general, and crucial for understanding the conceptual challenges facing the Russian political elite after the collapse of the Soviet Union. National identities are informed by domestic societies, whose identities refer to the population of a state rather than to the state itself. State identities are informed by international norms, which specify how certain categories of states (for example, civilized states, European states, welfare states) are both regulated and constituted by the practical content of international society. The political scientist Peter Katzenstein summarizes the position thus: "State identities are primarily external; they describe the actions of governments in a society of states. National identities are primarily internal; they describe the processes by which mass publics acquire, modify, and forget their collective identities."[32]

For Russia, as for the other fourteen post-Soviet states, debates about the content of societal – and especially national – identities were consequential for their international relations. National identities vary – from society to society and over time – in two primary ways: in their content and contestation. The content of a national identity includes definitions of membership in the nation, the fundamental purposes of statehood, and the states that threaten those purposes. A national identity's content is inherently directional, not least because nations are often imagined to have a most significant "other," against which they are defined. Because nationalist movements arise in interaction with (and in opposition to) other nationalisms and states in the international system, the formative contexts of nationalisms influence their goals. The other variable, contestation, is closely related, because societies collectively interpret their national identities.

Every society has nationalists, who seek to define the content of their society's collective identity. Not everyone in society, however, always agrees with how the nationalists seek to construct their identity. Nationalists can only offer proposals for the content of societal identity; they cannot dictate the content. Specific interpretations of the goals of the nation are sometimes widely shared in a society, and sometimes are less widely shared. The further apart the contending interpretations of national identity, the more that identity is fragmented into conflicting and potentially inconsistent understandings of what the goals of the nation should be.[33]

Within Russia, debates about the meaning and purpose of the nation implicated both history and foreign policy. The process of contestation was clear, as the Soviet Union was unraveling in the late 1980s, and continued throughout the decade. At the center of these debates was how Russia would deal with what many inside and outside the country considered to be the end of its empire. Should Russia attempt to maintain its influence, formal or otherwise, in the former Soviet Union, or should it concentrate on its domestic troubles? The debate was complicated by the fact that "Russia," as the territorial state it was in the 1990s, never existed before 1991. Prior to 1917, "Russia" was Tsarist Russia, an empire ruled by the Romanov dynasty. That empire covered most of the territory that, after the Russian Revolution, became part of the Soviet Union. The "Russia" that existed in Soviet times was one of fifteen constituent Soviet republics. And according to some observers, most clearly in Soviet republics that did not accept Soviet authority, the Soviet Union was itself a kind of renewed Russian empire.[34]

One of the main problems facing Russia, then, was to define itself as a nation-state for the first time, after a history of being at the center of the tsarist empire and the Soviet Union.[35] Russia's debates about its national and state identities have been dissected in a variety of ways. In 1989 historian Roman Szporluk distinguished between "empire-savers" and "nation-builders."[36] Political scientists have offered more complex divisions.[37] Karen Dawisha and Bruce Parrott explicated five categories of Russian foreign policy attitudes: Westernist; Eurasianist; Great Power; Isolationist, or Slavophile; and Extreme Nationalist.[38] Astrid Tuminez, in her analysis of Russian nationalism, identifies four distinct traditions: statist nationalism; liberal nationalism; Westernizing democracy; and national patriotism.[39] And, most recently and specifically on this relationship, Ted Hopf distinguishes four conceptualizations in the debate about Russian identity: New Western Russian; New Soviet Russian; Liberal Essentialist; and Liberal Relativist.[40]

It is beyond the scope of this chapter to review these distinctions, but clearly there is little agreement within Russia about the purposes and scope of its nation, or about what kind of state post-Soviet Russia ought to become. A defining issue in these debates was the appropriate relationship between Russia and the other former Soviet republics. The rise and fall of approaches to that issue within the government influenced how the Russian government understood its role in the near abroad, both directly – by offering specific interpretations of and motivations for Russian influence in the region – and indirectly, because the very lack of agreement prevented Russia from undertaking a consistent foreign policy over the course of the decade. The lack of a coherent approach to the ruble zone was symptomatic of a lack of agreement on how and whether to pursue Russian regional hegemony.

Other Post-Soviet States and the Ruble Zone

In the previous section I argued that Russia itself destroyed the ruble zone in the summer and autumn of 1993. But Russia's experience cannot be the entire story of the decline and fall of the ruble zone; the other post-Soviet states influenced how and when the monetary union disintegrated. Before Russia's policies toward the ruble zone changed in 1993, five post-Soviet states – Estonia, Latvia, Lithuania, Ukraine, and Kyrgyzstan – had already left. The rest reacted differently to the 1993 currency reform. Four – Azerbaijan, Georgia, Moldova, and Turkmenistan – reacted to Russia's destruction of the ruble zone by rejecting the possibility of currency union, while the other five – Armenia, Belarus, Kazakhstan, Tajikistan, and Uzbekistan – attempted to reconstitute it with the new-type ruble zone. Thus, the post-Soviet monetary union collapsed during three distinct moments. This raises another compelling question regarding the ruble: what accounts for the variety of post-Soviet governments' policies toward the ruble zone? Why did some post-Soviet governments leave the ruble zone immediately, while others intended to delay introducing an independent currency indefinitely?

The First Wave: Summer and Autumn 1992 and Spring 1993

There was never any chance that Estonia, Latvia, and Lithuania would remain in the ruble zone. The political elites in the three Baltic states had been planning to introduce independent currencies since the late 1980s. In 1989 all three adopted plans for increased economic autonomy, plans that outlined their intentions to create their own currencies.[41] With the collapse of the Soviet Union in 1991, the governments of all three states made more concrete plans to leave the ruble zone. The IMF's ominous warning – that departing from the ruble zone was tantamount to "economic suicide" – mattered little to the newly independent states. Nor were they dissuaded by the IMF's threat that any post-Soviet state introducing a new currency would not be entitled to IMF financing.[42] Highly dependent on energy and raw materials imports from Russia, and, therefore, three of the largest beneficiaries of ruble-zone membership, Estonia, Latvia, and Lithuania "were expected to experience very large immediate income losses" as a result of their monetary choices.[43] The Baltic states had a great deal to lose, in material terms, by their policies of monetary autonomy. The prospect of economic sacrifice for a national goal added drama to what might have appeared to be a technical decision.

The decision was anything but technical in Estonia, the first state to leave the ruble zone in June 1992 when it introduced the kroon.[44] On 22 June at the Viljandi "Ugala" Theater in Tallinn, Estonians held the Kroon Ball to honor the symbol of their monetary sovereignty. Stories of Estonians buying new wallets for their new kroons circulated.[45] Latvia quickly followed Estonia's move. After having introduced a parallel currency, the Latvian ruble, the government withdrew Russian rubles from circulation and established an independent monetary authority by the end of July 1992.[46] And Lithuania issued the talonas as a provisional currency in October 1992, simultaneously withdrawing rubles from circulation.[47] The primary difference among the Baltic states' monetary strategies was their choice of external nominal anchors. The Estonians pegged the kroon to the German mark; the Lithuanians pegged the litas to the U.S. dollar; and the Latvians let their lat float. Otherwise, these three governments were similarly motivated to reject the "occupation ruble," a symbol, they suggested, of Russian imperialism.[48]

Ukraine was next to leave the ruble zone, in November 1992. But the Ukrainian government appeared less decisive than the Baltic governments had been. Originally Ukraine had made ambitious plans in the spring of 1992 to introduce an independent currency and reorient the economy away from Russia and toward the West. As early as March 1992 President Leonid Kravchuk had outlined a plan to achieve economic autonomy from Russia.[49] Politicians lacked consensus on the move, however, and powerful economic actors vigorously opposed the plan. In the end Kravchuk's radical autonomy plan was tempered, and the new currency was postponed.[50] Ukraine's temporary currency, the karbovanets, lasted from November 1992 until September 1996, when the hryvnia was introduced.

Kyrgyzstan introduced its som in May 1993, but not as part of an attempt to achieve greater economic autonomy from Russia. Rather, the IMF convinced President Askar Akaev to introduce a new currency as part of an economic reform package.[51] Obviously the IMF had dramatically changed its approach to the ruble zone, and by the middle of 1993 was urging independent currencies on all post-Soviet states.[52] The IMF's policy reversal undermined its credibility among post-Soviet governments, and it was able to convince only Kyrgyzstan to follow its new lead.

The Second Wave: Summer 1993

Russia's surprise currency reform in July 1993, described above, forced the remaining nine ruble-zone members to choose their monetary futures more decisively. Azerbaijan, Georgia, Moldova, and Turkmenistan reacted to Russia's decision by moving to introduce independent currencies.[53]

Azerbaijan, like Ukraine, had planned to introduce an independent currency much earlier but was delayed by internal political disagreements about the decision. In June 1992, after Abulfaz Elcibey, head of the Azerbaijani Popular Front, was elected president, the Azerbaijani government withdrew from the Commonwealth of Independent States (CIS) and proposed ambitious plans for economic autonomy, including, of course, a new currency. In August 1992, Azerbaijan introduced the manat as a supplemental currency and planned to abandon the ruble completely in June 1993. However, when, a few days before the currency changeover was to take place, rebels overthrew Elcibey's government and returned the former Communist boss Heidar Aliev to power, Azerbaijan delayed the move until after Russia forced a decision. Aliev's return to power signaled a broader rapprochement with Russia, as

Azerbaijan also reentered the CIS.[54] Similarly, Georgian and Moldovan nationalists had intended to introduce independent currencies and leave the ruble zone in early 1992, only to have their plans delayed by a lack of domestic political consensus and their eventual fall from power as well. The Georgian menati and Moldovan leu were introduced in August and November 1993.[55]

For Turkmenistan the monetary disorder unleashed by Russia in July 1993 was a crucial moment, helping to convince the government that Russia was essentially an unreliable economic partner. Turkmenistan reacted by announcing that it would leave the ruble zone as quickly as possible and would not consider monetary reintegration. The manat was introduced, finally, in November 1993.[56]

The Third Wave: Autumn 1993

Armenia, Belarus, Kazakhstan, Tajikistan, and Uzbekistan reacted to the July currency reform by insisting that they would remain in the ruble zone.[57] In practice this meant that these five states continued to use the old, pre-1993 ruble notes that were no longer legal tender even in Russia. They could not print more of the Soviet rubles, though several had issued currency supplements to provide enough liquidity for their economies to function. Still, the governments of these states hoped that Russia would offer a way to reconstitute the monetary union.

These hopes were ostensibly and momentarily realized in August and September 1993 when they, along with Russia, agreed to create the abovementioned "new-type" ruble zone. When it became clear that Russia's conditions for membership in the new monetary union were unacceptable, primarily because these states could not afford the hard-currency deposit, Armenia, Belarus, Kazakhstan and Uzbekistan introduced independent currencies in November 1993, complaining bitterly all the way out of the ruble zone. As President Nursultan Nazarbaev of Kazakhstan explained to his parliament, "We made all possible concessions, but now Moscow has asked us to do the impossible – hand over billions of dollars."[58] Russia had, by their assessments, forced these governments to introduce independent currencies. Only Tajikistan, in the chaos of its civil war, continued to use the ruble until May 1995, by which point Russia had distributed the new ruble notes to the war-torn country for "humanitarian" reasons.[59] And although Belarus continued to negotiate its return to the Russian ruble throughout 1993 and 1994, even agreeing in principle to monetary union with Russia periodically between 1996 and 1999, by the end of the first post-Soviet decade only Russia continued to use what was now a distinctively Russian ruble.[60]

National Identities of Post-Soviet Societies

Debates within post-Soviet societies about their national identities influenced their governments' interpretations of and policies toward the ruble, and these varied quite dramatically.[61] After 1991, nationalist movements in each post-Soviet state offered proposals for the content of their societies' national identity. Among post-Soviet states, levels of nationalist mobilization were uneven, as was the success of nationalist political parties in winning popular support for and implementing their agendas.[62]

As domestic political alignments within post-Soviet states emerged in the 1990s, the former Communists' reactions to the nationalists were the most consequential – and revealing – politically. During the first post-Soviet decade, the defining political difference among the fourteen non-Russian states was the relationship between the formerly Communist elites and the nationalists in each – whether the former Communists marginalized the nationalists, co-opted them, or tried to become like them. These different relationships indicated the degree of consensus among them about the purposes of nationhood and statehood after Soviet rule.

These politics of national identity influenced the economic strategies chosen by post-Soviet governments, and for almost all of them monetary choices were part of broader strategic objectives. Almost all nationalist movements and parties throughout the former Soviet Union advocated the creation of a national currency for their newly independent states. Currencies, they tended to argue, would insulate their economies from Russia's, ensure autonomy from the CBR, and serve as a powerful symbol of statehood. Nationalists also asserted that autonomy from Russia was worth any costs and that appropriate rewards would accrue to future generations of the nation.

Many disagreed with the nationalists' views of monetary autonomy and sacrifice. Other groups, notably the powerful industrialists and other organized business interests, in every state opposed the introduction of an independent currency and departure from the ruble zone. Monetary union served their interests well, certainly better than the uncertain benefits of a new currency that separated them from their historical production links and, perhaps even worse, ensured that they would face world prices for imports of energy and raw materials. These two basic views of the ruble zone were incompatible. Post-Soviet societies and politicians were forced to choose; they could side either with the nationalists and leave the monetary union, or with the industrialists and accept the authority of the CBR.

Post-Soviet societies can be divided into roughly three groups according to how they resolved these internal debates, which is a preliminary indicator of the content and contestation of their national identities. First, there are those societies with national identities whose content, proposed by nationalist movements and parties, was widely shared. In Estonia, Latvia, and Lithuania, nationalists came to power and influenced public debates about economic strategy so that the entire political spectrum, including most former Communists, embraced the nationalist agenda of economic reorientation from Russia. In Armenia, where national identity was also coherently and widely shared, the nationalist agenda also became ascendant, but it was unique among post-Soviet nationalist movements in its generous interpretation of Russia as a historical ally against Muslim neighbors.[63]

Then, there were those societies in which the nationalists' proposals for the content of their national identities was heavily contested, with significant *regional* variation in mass public interpretations of their collective identities. Azerbaijan, Georgia, Moldova, and Ukraine fall into this category, and they demonstrate how the preferences of the first post-Soviet governments were insufficient to achieve their goals. This was true, first, because of a failure of public resolve, since the goals of the governments were not as widely shared as in other societies – for example, in the Baltic region. Also, especially in the case of Azerbaijan, Georgia, and Moldova, internal state weakness and contestation of state purpose within the society allowed Russia to influence their domestic politics and affect military and economic outcomes. It was not that the governments of these four states preferred their ambivalent monetary strategies: rather, their erratic strategies and relatively late decisions to leave the ruble zone were product of the interaction among varying government preferences, the ambivalence of their societies' collective identities, and the limited capabilities of their states to resist Russian influence.

Finally, there were those societies whose collective interpretation of their national identities was either ambiguous, incoherent, fragmented, or highly contested: Belarus, Kazakhstan, Kyrgyzstan, Tajikistan, Turkmenistan, and Uzbekistan. In these states, anti-Soviet, anti-Russian, and anti-CIS agendas proposed by nationalist groups were largely rejected by most other actors, and by former Communists most aggressively. In 1992 and 1993 their governments did not interpret monetary dependence on Russia as a threat to state security or economic autonomy. They accepted ruble-zone membership because their leaders believed that it was at least a partial solution to the difficult economic situation they faced, despite the obvious limitations on their monetary sovereignty. The currencies that Russia eventually forced them to adopt after 1993 did little to rally their societies around a renewed, shared vision of the purposes of their nations and states.

ABDELAL

Conclusions

The story of the Russian ruble in the 1990s implicated the nationhood and statehood of the fifteen former Soviet republics. Within Russia, barter, demonetization and the rise of surrogate monies reflected one aspect of the weakness of state institutions. Russia's trouble with the ruble epitomized the challenges of state building and institution creation facing political leaders, and related to some of the other most visible economic problems of the decade, including the government's persistent fiscal woes and disintegrative trends in the regions. The ruble revealed the incompleteness of Russia's post-Soviet sovereignty.

In addition to what the ruble indicated about the state as such, Russia's ambivalent policies toward the ruble zone resulted from ambivalence about the specific role of the Russian state – in short, its identity – in international relations, as well as contending interpretations of the social purposes ascribed to Russian nationhood. Debates within Russia about how to define a historically unique Russian nation-state, particularly in relation to the near abroad, influenced the government's and CBR's approaches to the monetary union that all post-Soviet states inherited. Central to these debates was the decision – implicit in the debate about whether to focus on domestic reform and abandon the ruble zone or subsidize its continued existence – to cultivate economic influence in the other Soviet successor states. It became increasingly necessary, in the face of declining resources, to clarify and justify the underlying reasons for constructing Russia as a "Eurasian" great power.

Finally, the ruble's place in the region revealed a great deal about the political and economic relations between Russia and the other fourteen former Soviet republics. The monetary arrangements of post-Soviet Eurasia were characterized by a complex mixture of disintegration, proposals for reintegration, and ultimately the proliferation of fifteen new currencies – some of which were cherished by the societies that chose them as markers of their sovereignty and enhancements of their autonomy, and others of which were treated with skepticism by the societies on which they were forced. At the center of it all was the ruble, which post-Soviet governments interpreted in contrasting ways. Some considered the ruble a symbol of Russian imperialism, while others saw it as a useful mechanism for economic reintegration with Russia and the rest of the post-Soviet region. The national identities of post-Soviet societies decisively influenced their governments' interpretations of the ruble and preferences for the economic future of the region.

Those national identities also influenced the identities they tried to choose for their new states. The international community considered them all merely "post-Soviet," but some of them insisted they were "European." In a number of Soviet republics, nationalist movements in the 1980s had been not only anti-Soviet and anti-Russian, they had been pro-European as well. This was especially true in the Western borderlands, as nationalists in Belarus, Estonia, Georgia, Latvia, Lithuania, Moldova, and Ukraine insisted that their cultures were inherently European and that their states should "return to Europe."

For many of these nationalists, an orientation away from "Eurasia" and toward "Europe" were equivalent. In Lithuania, for example, a member of the Lithuanian parliament, the Seimas, explained to the historian Timothy Garten Ash that "Europe is . . . not-Russia."[64] Drawing a mental map of Europe that excluded Russia involved some creativity, however, because Lithuanians, like their neighbors, tended to commemorate their state's location in the "center" of Europe, not its "east." Just north of Vilnius is the Europas Parkas, "Open-Air Museum of the Center of Europe." Founded in 1991, the Europe Park is located at the geographical center of Europe, at least as it was determined by the French National Geographic Society in 1989. Of course, the Europe Park can only be at Europe's center if its eastern boundary is the Ural Mountains in Russia. Despite the inconsistency, both meanings of Europe – Russia's exclusion and Lithuania's centrality – were important to Lithuanian national identity in the 1990s, because they suggested that the nation lived in a "European" state. And Lithuania, along with Latvia and Estonia, sought to enter the EU and join Europe's monetary union. They may, in the medium term, succeed in acquiring the European currency, but if so they will likely be the only three of the fifteen to have exchanged the Soviet ruble for the euro in the space of a generation.

NOTES TO CHAPTER 7

[1] I am grateful to Matthew Evangelista, Ted Hopf, Yoshiko Herrera, and David Woodruff for insightful and helpful suggestions. The research for this paper was supported by the Division of Research, Harvard Business School. This chapter was previously published in *Journal of Communist Studies and Transition Politics* 19 (2003): 55-76. See http://www.tandf.co.uk.
[2] For two popular and perceptive overviews of the issue, see Chrystia Freeland, *Sale of the Century: Russia's Wild Ride from Communism to Capitalism* (New York: Crown Business, 2000); and Thomas L. Friedman, "BizCzarism," *New York Times*, 18 April 2000. For an introduction to the political science literature on the Russian state and its relation to the Russian economy, see Thane Gustafson, *Capitalism Russian-Style* (Cambridge: Cambridge University Press, 1999); Yoshiko Herrera, "Russian Economic Reform, 1991-98," in Robert Moser and Zoltan Barany, eds., *Challenges of Russian Democratization* (Cambridge: Cambridge University Press, 2001); Stephen Holmes, "What Russia Teaches Us Now: How Weak States Threaten Freedom," *American Prospect* 8, no. 33 (1997): 30-39; Michael McFaul, "State Power, Institutional Change, and the Politics of

Privatization in Russia," *World Politics* 47, no. 2 (1995): 210-243; Gordon B. Smith, ed., *State Building in Russia: The Yeltsin Legacy and the Challenge for the Future* (Armonk: M. E. Sharpe, 1999); and Valerie Sperling, ed., *Building the Russian State: Institutional Crisis and the Quest for Democratic Governance* (Boulder: Westview, 2000). Economist Joseph Stiglitz also shares this institutionalist interpretation; see his "Whither Reform? Ten Years of the Transition," presented at the Annual Bank Conference on Development Economics (ABCDE), World Bank, 28-30 April 1999.

[3] See, for example, Max Weber, *Economy and Society*; Guenther Roth and Claus Wittich, eds., two volumes (1922; reprint Berkeley: University of California Press, 1978), vol. 1, 166-168; and Karl Polanyi, *The Great Transformation: The Political and Economic Origins of Our Time* (1944; reprint Boston: Beacon Press, 1957.)

[4] See, for example, International Monetary Fund, *IMF Country Staff Report: Russian Federation*, no. 99/100 (1999): 141. For a recent review of demonetization, see OECD, *OECD Economic Surveys, 1999-2000: Russian Federation, 1999-2000* (Paris: OECD, 2000), 83-112.

[5] David Woodruff, *Money Unmade: Barter and the Fate of Russian Capitalism* (Ithaca: Cornell University Press, 1999), 3. Also see Woodruff, "Barter of the Bankrupt: The Politics of Demonetization in Russia's Federal State," in Michael Burawoy and Katherine Verdery, eds., *Uncertain Transition* (Lanham: Rowman and Littlefield, 1999); and Woodruff, "Rules for Followers: Institutional Theory and the New Politics of Economic Backwardness in Russia," *Politics & Society* 28, no. 4 (2000): 437-482.

[6] Woodruff, *Money Unmade*, Chapter 1, especially 4-5, 18-19. For alternate interpretations that emphasize the value destruction of Russian enterprises and the efforts made by firms to avoid taxes, see, among others, Clifford G. Gaddy and Barry W. Ickes, "Russia's Virtual Economy," *Foreign Affairs* 77, no. 5 (1998): 53-67; and Kathryn Hendley, Barry W. Ickes, Peter Murrell, and Randi Ryterman, "Observations in the Use of Law by Russian Enterprises," *Post-Soviet Affairs* 13, no. 1 (1997): 19-41; and Hendley, "How Russian Enterprises Cope with Payments Problems," *Post-Soviet Affairs*, 15, no. 3(1999): 201-234.

[7] IMF, *IMF Staff Country Report: Russian Federation*, no. 00/150 (2000): 80.

[8] Woodruff, *Money Unmade*, 18.

[9] See, for example, Daniel S. Treisman, "Russia's Taxing Problem," *Foreign Policy*, no. 112 (1998): 55-67; and Gustafson, *Capitalism Russian-Style*, 196-198. For a review, see also OECD, *OECD Economic Surveys, 1999-2000: Russian Federation*, 113-146. The literature on center-regional relations in post-Soviet Russia is now quite large. For recent, sophisticated analyses, see Yoshiko Herrera, *Imagined Economies: Regionalism in the Russian Federation*, unpublished manuscript, Harvard University, 2001; Stephen Solnick, "Is the Center Too Weak or Too Strong in the Russian Federation?" in Sperling, ed., *Building the Russian State*; Kathryn Stoner-Weiss, *Local Heroes: The Political Economy of Russian Regional Governance* (Princeton: Princeton University Press, 1997); and Daniel S. Treisman, *After the Deluge: Regional Crises and Political Consolidation in Russia* (Ann Arbor: University of Michigan Press, 1999).

[10] I have written elsewhere on the politics of the ruble zone. For a more detailed account, see Rawi Abdelal, *National Purpose in the World Economy: Post-Soviet States in Comparative Perspective* (Ithaca: Cornell University Press, 2001), Chapter 3; and Abdelal, "National Strategy and National Money: Politics and the End of the Ruble Zone, 1991-94," in Jonathan Kirshner, ed., *Monetary Orders* (Ithaca: Cornell University Press, 2002).

[11] See Jonathan Kirshner, *Currency and Coercion: The Political Economy of International Monetary Power* (Princeton: Princeton University Press, 1995), Chapter 4.

[12] Jeffrey Sachs and David Lipton, "Remaining Steps to a Market-Based Monetary System in Russia," in Anders Åslund and Richard Layard, eds., *Changing the Economic System in Russia* (London: Pinter, 1993); Carsten Hefeker, *Interest Groups and Monetary Integration* (Boulder: Westview, 1997), Chapter 7; Marek Dabrowski, "From the Soviet Ruble to National Rubles and Independent Currencies: The Evolution of the Ruble Area in 1991-93," in Bruno Dallago and Giovanni Pegoretti, eds., *Integration and Disintegration in European Economies* (Brookfield and Aldershot: Dartmouth, 1995); and King Banaian and Eugene Zhukov, "The Collapse of the Ruble

Zone, 1991-93," in Thomas D. Willett, Richard C. K. Burdekin, Richard J. Sweeney, and Clas Wihlborg, eds., *Establishing Monetary Stability in Emerging Market Economies*, (Boulder: Westview, 1995).

[13] See Benjamin J. Cohen, *The Geography of Money* (Ithaca: Cornell University Press, 1998), 78-80; and Patrick J. Conway, *Currency Proliferation: The Monetary Legacy of the Soviet Union*, Princeton Essays in International Finance, no. 197 (1995).

[14] Juliet Johnson, *A Fistful of Rubles: The Rise and Fall of the Russian Banking System* (Ithaca: Cornell University Press, 2000), 89.

[15] "O merakh po zashchite denezhnoi sistemy Rossii" (On Measures for the Defense of the Monetary System of Russia), Presidential Decree no. 636 (21 June 1992).

[16] Johnson, *Fistful of Rubles*, 89.

[17] John Lloyd and Dmitri Volkov, "Russia Cracks the Whip Over the Ruble Zone," *Financial Times* 31 July 1992; and Anders Åslund, *How Russia Became a Market Economy* (Washington, D.C.: Brookings Institution, 1995), 125.

[18] See, for example, "The Ruble Zone: Behind the Façade," *The Economist*, 19 September 1992; and "The Ruble: Twilight Zone," *The Economist*, 22 May 1993.

[19] "Soobshchenie Tsentral'nogo banka Rossiiskoi Federatsii" (Announcement by the Central Bank of the Russian Federation), *Rossiiskaia gazeta*, 27 July 1993.

[20] In his memoirs Boris Yeltsin claims that he knew about the currency exchange in advance. See his *Struggle for Russia* (New York: Belka Publications Corporation, Times Books, 1994), 218-222. Of course, some sort of currency exchange had been considered for some time, so one might speculate that Fedorov strategically overstated his objections to Gerashchenko's move.

[21] Vera Kuznetsova, "'Gluppo, i skandal'no, i bessmyslenno'" ('Stupid, Scandalous, and Senseless'), *Nezavisimaia gazeta*, 30 July 1993.

[22] See "Zaiavlenie Pravitel'stva Rossiiskoi Federatsii" (Statement by the Government of the Russian Federation); and "Ukaz Prezidenta" (President's Decree), both in *Rossiiskaia gazeta*, 27 July 1993.

[23] "Zaiavlenie Predsedatelia Verkhovnovo Soveta Rossiiskoi Federatsii" (Statement by the Chairman of the Supreme Soviet of the Russian Federation), *Rossiiskaia gazeta*, 27 July 1993.

[24] John Lloyd, "Ruble Reform Splits Cabinet: Finance Chief Wants Central Bank Measure Overturned," *Financial Times*, 28 July 1993.

[25] See especially Mikhail Deliagin, "Rubl' byl v SNG valiutoi" (The Ruble Was the Currency of the CIS), *Nezavisimaia gazeta*, 5 August 1993.

[26] John Lloyd, "Currency Change Puts Pressure on Republics," *Financial Times*, 28 July 1993.

[27] Boris Krotkov, "Viktor Gerashchenko: Credity blizhnemu zarubezh'iu daiutsia tol'ko na osnove mezhpravitel'stvennykh dogovorennostei" (Viktor Gerashchenko: Credits to the Near Abroad Are Given Only On the Basis of Intergovernmental Agreements), *Delovoi mir*, 30 September 1993.

[28] On this "productivist" logic in Russian monetary policy, see Woodruff, *Money Unmade*, Chapter 3.

[29] The agreement, negotiated for little more than a month, was "Soglashenie o prakticheskikh merakh po sozdaniiu rublevoi zony novogo tipa" (Agreement on Practical Measures for the Creation of a Ruble Zone of a New Type), Moscow, 7 September 1993.

[30] Irina Demchenko, "Gosudarstvam rublevoi zony pridetsia prislushivat'sia k Rossii" (Governments of the Ruble Zone Will Have to Heed Russia), *Izvestiia*, 8 September 1993; Viktor Kiianitsa, "Proshchanie s rublem" (Bidding the Ruble Farewell), *Moskovskie novosti*, 21 November 1993; and Yuri Petrov, "Natsional'nye valiuty" (National Currencies), *Delovoi mir*, 13 December 1993. Also see Gregory L. White, "Russian Talks over Ruble Zone Hit Roadblock," *Wall Street Journal Europe*, 2 November 1993; Geoff Winestock and Sander Thoenes, "Russia: Ruble Zone Fails After Two Months," *Inter Press*, 3 November 1993; and Wendy Sloane, "Two Former Republics Drop Soviet-Era Ruble; Moscow's Conditions for Joining Ruble Zone Called Too Stringent," *Christian*

Science Monitor, 17 November 1993.

[31] For an insightful argument that Russia's fiscal constraints have systematically prevented it from reasserting its influence in post-Soviet Eurasia, see Henry Hale, "Russia's Fiscal Veto on CIS Integration," Program on New Approaches to Russian Security Policy Memo no. 15 (1997).

[32] Peter J. Katzenstein, "United Germany in an Integrating Europe," in Katzenstein, ed., *Tamed Power: Germany in Europe* (Ithaca: Cornell University Press, 1997), 20.

[33] For further elaboration of these ideas, see Abdelal, *National Purpose*, Chapter 2.

[34] Empires, as Mark Beissinger shows, are intersubjective constructs, not objectively defined political units. See especially his "The Persisting Ambiguity of Empire," *Post-Soviet Affairs* 11, no. 2 (1995): 149-184; and Ronald Grigor Suny, "Ambiguous Categories: States, Empires, and Nations," *Post-Soviet Affairs* 11, no. 2 (1995): 185-196. For an insightful comparison of the Russian Empire and Soviet Union along these lines, see Dominic Lieven, "The Russian Empire and the Soviet Union as Imperial Polities," *Journal of Contemporary History* 30, no. 4 (1995): 607-636. On the collapse of the Soviet Union as a moment of imperial disintegration, see Rogers Brubaker, "Nationalizing States in the Old 'New Europe' – and the New," *Ethnic and Racial Studies* 19, no. 2 (1996): 411-437; Karen Barkey and Mark von Hagen, eds., *After Empire: Multiethnic Societies and Nation Building* (Boulder: Westview, 1997); Karen Dawisha and Bruce Parrott, eds., *The End of Empire? The Transformation of the USSR in Comparative Perspective* (Armonk: M. E. Sharpe, 1997); Alexander Motyl, *Revolutions, Nations, and Empires* (New York: Columbia University Press, 1999). For a comparison of the political economy of post-Soviet Eurasia with other post-imperial regions in the twentieth century, see Abdelal, *National Purpose*, Chapter 7.

[35] This theme has been thoughtfully explored by Alain Besançon, "Nationalism and Bolshevism in the USSR," in Robert Conquest, ed., *The Last Empire: Nationality and the Soviet Future* (Stanford: Hoover Institution Press, 1986); John Dunlop, "Russia: Confronting the Loss of an Empire," in Ian Bremmer and Ray Taras, eds., *Nations and Politics in the Soviet Successor States* (Cambridge: Cambridge University Press, 1993); Dunlop, "Russia: In Search of an Identity?" in Ian Bremmer and Ray Taras, eds., *New States, New Politics: Building the Post-Soviet Nations*; and Geoffrey Hosking, *Russia: People and Empire* (Cambridge: Harvard University Press, 1997).

[36] Roman Szporluk, "Dilemmas of Russian Nationalism," *Problems of Communism* 38, no. 4 (1989): 15-35. See also Szporluk, "After Empire: What?" *Daedalus*, 123, no. 3 (1994): 21-40.

[37] In addition to those reviewed here, see also the reviews in Celeste A. Wallander, "Ideas, Interests, and Institutions in Russian Foreign Policy," in Wallander, ed., *The Sources of Russian Foreign Policy After the Cold War* (Boulder: Westview, 1996); Jeffrey Checkel, "Structure, Institutions, and Process: Russia's Changing Foreign Policy," and Jonathan Valdez, "The Near Abroad, the West, and National Identity in Russian Foreign Policy," both in Adeed Dawisha and Karen Dawisha, ed., *The Making of Foreign Policy in Russia and the New States of Eurasia* (Armonk: M. E. Sharpe, 1995).

[38] Karen Dawisha and Bruce Parrott, *Russia and the New States of Eurasia* (Cambridge: Cambridge University Press, 1994), 198-207.

[39] Astrid S. Tuminez, "Russian Nationalism and the National Interest in Russian Foreign Policy," in Wallander, ed., *Sources of Russian Foreign Policy*. See also her *Russian Nationalism Since 1856* (Lanham: Rowman and Littlefield, 2000).

[40] Ted Hopf, *Social Origins of International Politics: Identities and Foreign Policies, Moscow, 1955 and 1999* (Ithaca: Cornell University Press, 2002), Chapters 4-5.

[41] See Kalev Kukk, "Five Years in the Monetary Development of the Baltic States: Differences and Similarities," *Bank of Estonia Bulletin*, no. 5 (1997). Also see Seija Lainela and Pekka Sutela, "Escaping from the Ruble: Estonia and Latvia Compared," in Dallago and Pegoretti., ed., *Integration and Disintegration in European Economies*.

[42] See Brigitte Granville, "Farewell, Ruble Zone," in Anders Åslund, ed., *Russian Economic Reform at Risk*, (London and New York: Pinter, 1995).

[43] Linda S. Goldberg, Barry W. Ickes, and Randi Ryterman, "Departures from the Ruble Zone: Implications of Adopting Independent Currencies," *World Economy* 17, no. 3 (1994): 293-322, 318-319. Also see David G. Tarr, "The Terms-of-Trade Effects of Moving to World Prices on the

Countries of the Former Soviet Union," *Journal of Comparative Economics* 18, no. 1 (1994): 1-24.

[44] See Leonid Levitskii, "Estonia proshchaetsia s rublem" (Estonia Bids Farewell to the Ruble), *Izvestiia*, 22 June 1992; and Ardo Hansson and Jeffrey Sachs, "Crowning the Estonian Kroon," *Transition* no. 9 (1992): 1-2. Also see Philippe Legrain, "Estonia Proudly Wears Its Kroon of Thorns: The First Ex-Soviet Republic to Dump the Ruble and Beat Inflation – But at a Price," *Financial Times*, 23 June 1993; Daniel Michaels, "Focus on Estonia – Baltic Success: Estonia Defies Advice in Creating Currency That Boosts Economy," *Wall Street Journal Europe*, 30 August 1993.

[45] See Philippe Legrain, "Real Money," "Last Days of the Ruble In Estonia," and "Estonians Wait and Then Celebrate the New Money's Coming," all in *Baltic Independent*, 26 June 1992; and "The Ruble: Helter Skelter," *The Economist*, 27 June 1992.

[46] Philippe Legrain, "Kroon Prompts Latvian Move," *Baltic Independent*, 10 July 1992. The Latvian lat was not officially introduced until 1993; see "Latvia Finally Ditches Temporary Money," *Baltic Independent*, 22 October 1993.

[47] In June 1993 the litas, the permanent currency, was introduced. See Iurii Stroganov, "Litva vvodit svoiu valiutu" (Lithuania Will Introduce Its Own Currency), *Rossiiskaia gazeta*, 24 June 1993; Andrius Uzkalnis and Peter Morris, "Litas to Replace the Talonas," *Baltic Independent*, 25 June 1993; and Abdelal, *National Purpose*, Chapter 4.

[48] See "Kroons, Lats, Litas," *The Economist*, 3 July 1993.

[49] The plan was reprinted in "Kravchuk's Report Had the Effect of an Exploding Bomb," *Komsomol'skaia pravda*, 26 March 1992, in *Current Digest of the Post-Soviet Press* 44, no. 12 (1992): 15-16.

[50] See Paul D'Anieri, "Dilemmas of Interdependence: Autonomy, Prosperity, and Sovereignty in Ukraine's Russia Policy," *Problems of Post-Communism* 44, no. 1 (1997): 16-26; and Abdelal, *National Purpose*, Chapter 5.

[51] Eugene Huskey, "Kyrgyzstan Leaves the Ruble Zone," *RFE/RL Research Report*, 2, no. 35 (1993): 38-43; and Claudia Rosett, "Kyrgyzstan Is Out From Under the Ruble Zone," *Wall Street Journal*, 18 May 1993.

[52] Conway, *Currency Proliferation*, 40.

[53] See, for example, "How the Republics View the Ruble Purge," *Associated Press*, 26 July 1993.

[54] See Tadeusz Swietochowski, *Russia and Azerbaijan: A Borderland in Transition* (New York: Columbia University Press, 1995), 221-227.

[55] See Conway, *Currency Proliferation*, 50-54; "Moldova to Issue New Currency," *Wall Street Journal*, 24 January 1992; "Moldova Sets Currency," *New York Times*, 25 November 1993.

[56] "New Currency for Turkmenistan," *Financial Times*, 20 August 1993; "Turkmenistan Sets New Currency," *Wall Street Journal*, 20 August 1993.

[57] John Lloyd, "Some Rubles Are More Equal than Others," *Financial Times*, 28 July 1993.

[58] Quoted in Steve Levine, Gillian Tett, and John Lloyd, "Turkmenistan Leads New Ruble Refugees," *Financial Times*, 2 November 1993.

[59] "Tajik Ruble Substitute for Russian Ruble," *New York Times*, 15 May 1995.

[60] For more on Belarus's foreign economic policy, see Abdelal, *National Purpose*, Chapter 6.

[61] This explanation for the politics of the ruble zone departs significantly from existing scholarship. Elsewhere I show that neither the theory of optimum currency areas, nor the institutional design of the monetary union, nor the differential material incentives resulting from post-Soviet energy trade can adequately account for the timing and motivation of the three moments of the ruble zone's collapse. See Abdelal, "National Strategy and National Money."

[62] The literature on Soviet and post-Soviet nationalisms is quite rich. See especially Ronald Grigor Suny, *Revenge of the Past: Nationalism, Revolution, and the Collapse of the Soviet Union* (Stanford: Stanford University Press, 1993); Suny, *The Soviet Experiment: Russia, the USSR, and the Successor States* (New York: Oxford University Press, 1998); and Suny, "Provisional Stabilities: The Politics of Identities in Post-Soviet Eurasia," *International Security* 24, no. 3 (1999-2000): 139-178.

⁶³ See, for example, Nora Dudwick, "Armenia: Paradise Lost?" in Bremmer and Taras, eds., *New States, New Politics.*

⁶⁴ Timothy Garton Ash, "Journey to the Post-Communist East," *New York Review of Books,* 23 June 1994.

PUTIN AND MILITARY REFORM
DALE R. HERSPRING[1]

Abstract

Vladimir Putin was faced with a military that was in a mess when he took over. Morale was at rock bottom, junior officers were leaving in droves, equipment and weapons were failing, soldiers were deserting, the draft was a joke, crime was on the rise, planes were crashing, and most important, Chechnya remained a major distraction. Putting the Russian military back together is a formidable task indeed.

Despite Putin's efforts, many of the problems noted above remain; indeed some have worsened. But it is worth noting that for the first time since the break-up of the USSR, a Russian leader is making a serious effort to deal with the problem. How successful he – and his successor – will be only time will tell.

* * *

Putin has become serious about military reform. The process is far from complete and could still be derailed if he or his successor does not continue to push it, but he has laid the foundation and in five to six years we should begin to see a far different military, from the forces that Yeltsin's policies decimated. While change is taking place, it will continue to be incremental. Indeed, as Lilia Shevtsova pointed out in her book on Putin, whereas Boris Yeltsin was a revolutionary, a man who destroyed the preexisting communist political system, Vladimir Putin is a bureaucrat, a man who considers his primary task to bring stability to Russia.[2]

Before continuing, something about Putin, the politician: five factors characterize Putin's approach to politics.[3] First, as noted above, Putin is a bureaucrat. Putin believes that the leader at the top should be able to set the system's parameters; once having done so, he would prefer to leave policy implementation to the bureaucrats, but he recognizes that the bureaucracies often work to subvert a political leader's wishes. This is especially true of the military that tends to be very conservative and sometimes lives in the past. Generals and admirals often like doing things "the old way." Forcing a bureaucracy to change is a slow, frustrating process, but Putin believes that such organizational structures can only be changed by continually pushing them, by gradually changing the structure, attitudes, and personnel in the bureaucratic system. Given its highly bureaucratized nature, Putin fully understands that it cannot be turned upside down as the Bolsheviks did the Tsarist army during the civil war. He has to work with what is available. This is why those observers (including this writer) who expected Putin and his hand-picked defense minister, Sergey Ivanov, to take the kind of "bold" decisions necessary to make military reform a reality in a relatively short period of time were mistaken. Bold decisions are not part of Putin's leadership style.[4]

Putin's second characteristic is respect for Russian political culture. While he may be seen as a "Westernizer" of the Peter the Great type by many in the West, he believes that it would be wrong to force the Russian military (or any other part of Russian society) to mimic the West. He wants to move the Russian military closer to the kind of system found in the West, but he is smart enough to know that in the end, it will continue to have its Russian idiosyncracies.

The third factor that characterizes Putin's leadership style is his non-ideological approach to dealing with policies. When he was a KGB officer, his primary goal was to find a way to solve problems. If a liberal idea would "work," fine; he would accept that. If a conservative approach worked better, he was ready to accept that approach as well. The result: he is pragmatic, and flexible when it comes to policy issues.

Fourth, Putin is *not* a long-term planner. He lives in the here and now, just as he did in the KGB. This helps explain why he did not come up with a well thought-out long-term plan to reform the military (or any other part of the Russian polity) – other than to push the at times vague concept of military professionalism. He does not conceptualize problems or answers; rather, he takes whatever the situation will permit – and that includes retreating on occasions, but always pushing for a professional military.

Finally, and much to the frustration of many Western observers and policymakers, Putin is cautious when it comes to making changes. His decision-making approach tends to be incremental. He knows he does not have enough power to make all the changes that Russia desperately needs at once. The country is in too bad shape for that approach. Nevertheless, he also knows that if Russia is to survive, it must change. The state must be rebuilt if it hopes to handle the country's problems in an efficient manner. It is also worth noting that Putin will take advantage of events – as he did with the 11 September 2001, terrorist attacks against the United States – to get the military to do what he wants, but in the end, he is the opposite of a Khrushchev with his "hair-brained" schemes. Putin is more the tortoise than the hare (and we all know that in the end, it was the tortoise that won the race). He takes one small step at a time, always pushing the system to change, but backing off if bureaucratic resistance gets too strong.

Before going into the kind of changes Putin has been making in the military, let us turn to the situation the Russian military found itself in when Putin took over as Russia's president.

Problems in the Russian Military

One could easily write a book just on the problems in the Russian armed forces under Yeltsin. This chapter does not go into this topic in great detail.[5] Nevertheless, it would be helpful for the reader to understand just how serious the situation was. For example, "Russian defense spending declined from 142 billion dollars in 1992 to four billion in 1999, a ninety-eight percent decrease."[6] Moscow was fighting in Chechnya for the second time in less than ten years and pay was so bad that officers committed suicide in order to ensure that their families received their pensions – on time – in contrast to "the delays faced by those on active duty."[7] In addition to salary problems, there was housing. In 1999, there were 92,400 homeless officers; by January 2000 that number had increased to 93,000.[8] It should not come as a surprise that in 1998 alone, 20,000 officers under the age of thirty resigned.[9] Why would anyone want to be an officer under those conditions?

Then there was the draft. In 1997, 2,200,000 Russian men were subject to call-up. Of that number 1,500,000 had deferments, 225,000 had medical problems, 71,000 were in jail, thereby leaving 437,000 available for service. Fifty thousand evaded military service and 12,000 went AWOL.[10] And the quality of recruits was continuing to decline. In 1999 it was announced that in comparison with 1992, the syphilis rate had increased one thousand percent. Alcoholism, drug abuse and solvent abuse increased one hundred percent and pleurisy related to tuberculosis had increased fifty percent among men of draft age.[11] Furthermore, in 1998 it was reported that forty percent had not attended school or held a job two years prior to reporting. "One in twenty had a police record."[12] In 1999 a new problem came to the fore – 57.6 percent had a limitation on where they could serve for health reasons.[13] What this meant was that 56 percent of those actually drafted could not be sent to elite units like the Naval Infantry, airborne units, the submarine service, or some special infantry units.

Once the young man joined the Army, he faced the problem of *dedovshchina*, the harassment of junior recruits by more senior ones, a process that could involve everything from beatings, to the theft of the individual's property, to rape, and even to murders on occasion. In the first nine months of 1997 more than 1,400 servicemen were abused by being brutally hazed.[14] In May 1998 "a young soldier was buried in the southern city of Budennovsk. He was beaten to death because he refused to mend an older conscript's soccer shoe. . . . Then during the first eleven months of 1998, 57 soldiers died, and 2,735 were injured from hazing."[15] "In the first eleven months of 1999 300 soldiers committed suicide – many because of their inability to put up with hazing."[16] Brutality was not limited to recruit on recruit. There was also a serious problem with inebriated officers who would beat recruits.

This brings us to the issue of contract soldiers; after all, they were supposed to take care of the problem. Unfortunately, the situation did not improve. In January and February of 1997, for example, while 2,755 men were accepted as *kontraktniki* (or professionals), 5,942 quit.[17] Furthermore, while the Kremlin could boast of having 230,000 *kontraktnikis* on active duty, of this number, 115,000 were women – primarily the spouses of military officers who were trying to make ends meet and they were almost always in staff positions.[18] To make matters worse, there were problems with the quality of male recruits. General Lieutenant Vladislav Putilin, discussed the problem when noted that given the dangerous service, and low pay faced by many contract soldiers, a person who volunteered for such service, "would either be one of the long-term unemployed or someone who has already poisoned his mind with alcohol."[19]

Crime and corruption were also problems. By the end of 1997, twenty-one Russian generals were under investigation for corruption.[20] In May 1999, Russian law enforcement officials discovered several criminal schemes that were just the tip of an iceberg. "Russian intelligence officers seized large amounts of weapons and explosives that soldiers from the Russian Navy's Pacific Fleet were trying to sell on the black market."[21] Then during the first eleven months of 1998 crimes in the military rose from ten thousand in 1997 to 10,500.[22] Discipline appeared to be collapsing. In 1997, for example,

"The Chief Prosecutor noted that fifty soldiers were shot that year by their fellow servicemen. And these were only the number of soldiers who were on guard duty. It did not include soldiers shot while not on guard duty. Then in May, 1998, four soldiers in the Far Eastern Military District shot and killed their commanding officer. Even more alarming has been the spate of shootings at nuclear weapons facilities. The situation became so serious that on 20 October 1998, President Yeltsin ordered an inspection of troops at a nuclear weapons production facility."[23]

Partly as a result of the personnel problems noted above, combat readiness also suffered. In 1997 Marshal Sergeyev, the Defense Minister noted that "not a single unit was combat ready except for the nuclear forces and some paratroopers."[24] The military's financial situation became so bad that almost all government meteorological stations stopped passing critical weather information to the military, and Premier Chernomyrdin had to sign an order forcing power stations to keep supplying military installations with power even if they had not paid their electrical bills.

In 1998 Sergeyev reported that "53 percent of aircraft and 40 percent of the anti-aircraft systems, helicopters, armored equipment and artillery were in need of repair."[25] The Navy was in even worse condition. More than seventy percent of its ships were in need of major overhauls.[26] The bottom line was that in 1998, the Kremlin had a military "incapable of conducting strategic operations or speedily carrying out a major redeployment of troops."[27] Duma Security Chairman Viktor Ilyukhin went so far as to say that Russia's armed forces could no longer serve as a guarantor of Russian security.[28] A few months later, Sergeyev painted an even bleaker picture. About one-third of the armed forces' military hardware is not combat-ready and that some sixty percent of the country's strategic missile systems have been in service for twice their service life. Some seventy percent of the ships in Russia's navy require repair, he continued, while in the air force about two-thirds of all aircraft are incapable of flying. This year, Sergeyev said, the armed forces had not received a single nuclear submarine, tank, combat plane, helicopter, or piece of artillery.[29]

Given the mess it was in, it is a miracle that the Russian military did as well as it did during the Second Chechen War. Indeed, one could argue that it was only because of the use of massive force that the army was able to conquer most of the country, including its major cities, but not the mountains.

Putin and Structural Changes

In order to ensure that the military could not be used against him politically, Yeltsin intentionally created a situation in which military authority was split between the minister of defense and the chief of the general staff. Technically, the minister of defense was superior, the chief could go directly to the president if he saw fit. Furthermore, the chief had operational responsibility over Russian forces. In practice this meant that while the minister of defense could order the Chief of the General Staff to do something, it was up to the latter to implement the minister's directive

– and in the process he could modify or changed the order so that the minister's order was effectively neutralized if not ignored.

The above situation was made even worse because the Minister of Defense Marshal Sergeyev and the Chief of the General Staff, General Anatoly Kvashnin did not get along. Sergeyev was the from the Strategic Rocket Forces (SRF) and believed that given its limited resources, Moscow should pay primary attention (including the allocation of funds) to the SRF. Kvashnin, on the other hand, was an infantry officer who believed that nuclear weapons were useful only to deter other nuclear forces. If nothing else, the wars in Chechnya demonstrated clearly Moscow's need for modern conventional forces. As a result, the two men were constantly at each other's throats.

Putin could have resolved the problem by promptly firing one or both of these individuals. However, given his gradualistic approach for dealing with such problems, he did nothing at first. There was a debate of a new military doctrine which Putin signed in April 2000. Kvashnin emerged in a stronger position, but Putin extended Sergeyev's tour of duty as defense minister for another year – until 10 May 2001. Putin's primary concern was to avoid instability in the high command at a time when he was new to the office of president.

Meanwhile, the battle between Sergeyev and Kvashnin continued. On 12 July 2000 there was a meeting of senior officers. Kvashnin took the opportunity to call for disbanding the SRF. For example, he called for cutting the existing nineteen ICBM divisions to only two. In addition, he tried to cut the number of ICBMs from 756 to only 150 by 2003, to cut production of the Topol-M (SS-27) long range missile, and to downgrade the SRF to a command. The SRF's share of the budget would be cut from eighteen to fifteen percent, with the money saved being given to the Ground Forces.[30]

Sergeyev responded publicly in an interview where he called Kvashnin's plan "criminal stupidity and an attack on Russia's national interests." Putin jumped in the fray the next day by ordering his generals "to silence their debate and come up with realistic policy proposals."[31] Shortly thereafter, a number of Sergeyev's key supporters were removed from the Defense Ministry. However, the battle between the two senior officers continued. At a meeting in August he made it clear that he was tired of the bureaucratic infighting. "I have been rather tolerant of the debates in the defense ministry and society as a whole . . . now is the time to bring the matter to its rightful conclusion."[32]

The plan adopted at a key meeting held on 11 August favored Kvashnin. Kvashnin noted that the plan adopted at the meeting called for the "harmonious development of all services of the Armed Services."[33] Since most resources had been going to the SRF, the term "harmonious development," was a code word, indicating that the ground forces would be treated more equally. In addition, the meeting decided to reverse Sergeyev's 1997 decision to disband the Ground Forces as a separate service and it downgraded the SRF to command. Alexander Gol'ts remarked that this was really not a plan at all; rather, it "simply strengthened the victory . . . of the 'combat arms generals' over the 'missile' generals."[34]

Putin continued to make it clear that while he accepted the fact that strategic weapons were important, he thought it was time to devote increased attention to conventional forces. As he put it in a meeting with the high command in November 2000,

"The Army and the Navy must be ready in all strategic directions to neutralize and repulse any army conflict and aggression. And one important task – the creation and stationing of groups of permanent readiness units in the South-Western and Central Asian strategic directions. Here the state of the general purpose forces is of primary importance. Such forces must have the latest technology."[35]

This was again raised at a meeting of the Security Council on 9 November 2000. The findings of the commissions Putin had set up earlier that year formed the basis for discussion on the future of the Russian Army up to the year 2010. The key issues concerned topics such as improving management, raising combat readiness, improving the defense industrial complex, upgrading the status of servicemen, increasing financial assistance to the military, and improving command and control.[36] It was clear that Putin's primary concern was to improve the Army's conventional capabilities. The plan adopted by the meeting foresaw a two-stage process. The first covered 2001 to 2005. This would focus attention on personnel. 470,000 military personnel and 130,000 civilians would be eliminated. By 2005 the total size of the Kremlin's security services (including the military) would be reduced by 19.7 percent. He confirmed that the Army would be cut by 365,000 while Sergeyev's beloved SRF would lose sixty thousand personnel by 2005.[37]

The second phase focused on providing the military with the kind of logistical support it needed. Greater emphasis would be placed on personnel issues such as improving infrastructure and salaries. On 15 January 2001, Putin approved this plan.

The key point in comparing Putin's approach with the various reform plans put forth during Yeltsin's tenure was that Putin's plan read more like a generalized approach for dealing with a variety of problems. There was no grand, glitzy master plan. Instead, like the bureaucratic problem solver he is, Putin focused on specific issues and attempted to deal with them systematically.

Recognizing the need to do something to stop the bickering between Sergeyev and Kvashnin, on 28 March 2001 the Kremlin announced that Sergeyev had stepped down as defense minister to become a presidential advisor.[38] He was replaced by Sergei Ivanov, up to that time head of the Security Council and one of Putin's closest confidants. The two had served together in the KGB and Putin decided that Ivanov, a former general, and a man who had been intimately involved in the Security Council's efforts to come up with a meaningful reform plan, understood the military and was the one to bring order into the armed forces. His task would not be an easy one, although as head of the Security Council, he had helped draft the plan Putin signed in January. Putin also took the unprecedented step of appointing a woman, and a civilian, Lyubov Kudelina, to become a deputy minister of defense. She came from the Finance Ministry and was given the task of making sense out of the financial chaos in the defense ministry.

When Ivanov was first appointed, there was hope that he would quickly take charge and reform the armed forces. It was believed that his close ties to Putin would enable him to make major changes as one analyst pointed out,

"Ivanov can made the decision and make things happen. He can implement the reforms the military badly needs and actually create a smaller, more capable professional army. Ivanov, fully supported by the Kremlin, can bypass Russia's corrupt and ineffective bureaucracy. He can suppress dissent among the generals."[39]

Unfortunately, such comments were overly optimistic. Ivanov faced a number of difficulties. First, he was an outsider – from the KGB. In addition, he was up against a general – the Chief of the General Staff – who tended to ignore the defense minister and do as he wished. Besides, Kvashnin had just won a major bureaucratic victory – the ouster of Sergeyev – and it would not be easy to convince him to play second fiddle to Ivanov. The one thing that was clear, given his close ties to Putin, was that Ivanov would follow an evolutionary approach to military reform. He emphasized this point by making it clear that he had no intention of being a "revolutionary," when it came to stabilizing and modernizing the military.[40] He understood how desperate and difficult the situation was in the armed forces, but he also knew that Putin would never support a policy aimed a solving the military's problems over night. Changes would be gradual. They would focus on streamlining and reorganizing the army.

Ivanov's task was to implement these changes; changes that Putin had approved, and the latter made it clear that Ivanov would be key to any reform process. As Putin put it, "He was the head of the group which worked out the main parameters of reform."[41] Furthermore, if there was any doubt about Ivanov's seriousness about implementing the Putin plan, he removed it in May when he observed, "Today, the discussions are over. . . .The armed forces reform plans have been approved by the president, it's time to implement the approved decisions."[42]

Meanwhile, on 24 March 2001 Putin had signed *ukaz* 337, "On Supporting the Plan for Conversion and Development of the RF Armed Forces and Improving Their Structure." As a result, the SRF was broken into two commands (*rodi*), the Strategic Missile Troops and the Space Troops. Finally the *ukaz* set the size of the Russian military at one million as of 1 January 2006.[43]

Personnel Problems

Putin was well aware of the horrible conditions the average soldier or sailor lived in. On 11 May 2001, a commission Putin had created presented him with proposals for dealing with social problems faced by military personnel. Based on this report, Putin placed a priority on reforming the pay and allowances systems as well as improving housing and medical services. Then on 17 October, Putin chaired a session of the Security Council that focused on the military-industrial complex. It led to increased attention on the need to reform the military-industrial complex from the old Soviet model to a new, more competitive one. In addition, Putin announced that the military would be getting more money. "Deputy Minister Aleksei Kudrin, who was present at the meeting said that an additional 4 billion rubles would be found for the army this year, and that funding for military procurement would be upped by some 27 billion in the year 2002."[44] Then on 27 November 2001, Putin chaired a Security Council meeting that focused on the question of mobilization readiness. Putin was also instrumental in ensuring that another 34.6 billion rubles were allocated for pay and allowances and he worked on repaying the ministry of defense's outstanding debts – inherited from the Yelstin era.[45]

Given his proclivity to work within the bureaucracy, it is not surprising that Putin waited for the military to provide him with a proposal for changing its form of technical support – a plan that was delivered on 1 November. He received other suggestions as well. He approved them on 16 November. This was also when he ordered the high command to "come up with a reform plan that would see through a transition to a fully professional military by 2010."[46] With that in mind, the generals proposed an experiment with one or two units in order "to determine more precisely the nature and scope of measures and the outlays necessary for converting them to the contract method of manning with servicemen."[47]

By January of 2002, the high command could report that there were 157,000 professionals (or *kontraktniki* – those serving on contract) in the military. Unfortunately, from the military's standpoint, forty percent of them were still women – officers' wives and daughters. While one could understand the continued need for officers' families to find employment given their husband and fathers' low salaries, and while many officers considered the women more reliable because of the lower level of alcoholism, the high percentage of women represented a problem for the military. "As a rule, the men are sent to Chechnya, Tajikistan, and other hot spots, while contract servicemen are paid more than an average of 1,500 rubles a month."[48] These women were getting the pay of a *kontraktniki* without having to serve in "hot spots."

Putin's renewed interest in professionalizing the military began with an experiment in an airborne regiment stationed at Pskov, an undertaking opposed by many senior officers who remained convinced that Russia must rely first and foremost on conscripts. Professionals were too expensive and besides, many of the generals enjoyed having conscripts to help them with the construction of their dachas or to rent out to civilian firms and farms. The experiment began on 1 September 2002. It was to last a year and then the government would evaluate it. The contracts these soldiers signed made it clear that the *kontraktniki* were expected to serve in difficult/dangerous combat areas such as Chechnya. In addition, the individual had a right to housing – something new for enlisted personnel in the Russian Army. In order to make the experiment a success, not only would salaries be raised, but infrastructure would also be improved. If there was one thing that was clear from past experience with *kontraktnikis* it was that they would not join or stay in the military if they were expected to live in the same kind of barracks as conscripts. As General Nikolai Nikolayev, the Chairman of the Defense Committee of the Duma noted, "You cannot drive contract servicemen into dilapidated barracks."[49] In addition, they expected things like schools, stores, and social services for themselves and their families, and each *kontraktniki* was promised individual quarters.

In the meantime, there continued to be problems with the quality of those who signed up to be professionals. One writer referred to Pskov as "a criminal zone with marauding drunken kontraktniki."[50] Putin personally expressed dissatisfaction with discipline in the unit. "Last year there were 41 deaths in this part of the Armed Forces, and in the first half of this year, there have already been 32 deaths among the paratroopers due to various accidents."[51] Clearly, something had to be done.

Putin was not happy with the generals and their efforts to sabotage the experiment. After all, according to the plan the generals drew up, the transition to an army consisting of fifty to sixty percent *kontraktniki* was divided into three stages – the second one would end after he left office in 2008. It was clear what the generals were doing – they planned to wait him out. Meanwhile, it took sixteen months to fully man the 76th with *kontraktnikis*.

While the Putin administration recognized that while there had been problems with the Pskov unit – and others as well – it was convinced that *kontraktnikis* were the army's future. It planned to place them in what Moscow called permanent readiness units. The idea was that after 2008, there would be approximately 144,00 volunteers serving in such units, while conscripts would only serve for one year and then serve in the reserve. However, there was one major problem – money. The pay for *kontraktnikis* would have to be raised, and the army would have to do a better job in coming up with creature comforts.

Despite numerous problems like those cited above, the Putin administration has had some successes. In 2005 Ivanov announced that close to sixteen thousand individuals had been selected to be privates and sergeants during 2004 which enabled the government to complete the manning of the 42nd Motorized Division in Chechnya. It was also able to build housing for it.[52] The 2006 budget directly addressed the issue of creature comforts. "Funds allocated to the special federal program 'Transition to the All-Volunteer Force in 2004-2007' will amount to 22.3 billion Russian rubles ($789 million) next year, which is 15% more than the 2005 budget (19.7 billion rubles - $697 million) and two-fold as much as the 2004 budget of 9.6 billion rubles ($340 million)."[53]

How successful this program will be in recruiting the kind and numbers of professionals the Kremlin wants is open to question. Problems with the quality of *kontraktniki* remain. However, as the foregoing demonstrates, the Putin administration is committed to dealing with them to the degree that the budget will permit.

Dealing with High Level Intrigue

By the end of 2003, it was clear that conflict between Kvashnin and Ivanov was out of hand. As he had with Sergeyev, the latter continually ignored the former when implementing his orders. It made little difference what Ivanov ordered – it was implemented according to Kvashnin's wishes. In January 2004 with Putin's support, Ivanov suggested that the General Staff needed to be overhauled. In particular, he argued that the General Staff should stop its involvement in operational matters.[54]

Then on 14 June, the Duma changed Article 13 of the "Law on Defense" to mention only the Defense Ministry. "Oversight for the Armed Forces of the Russian Federation is carried out by the defense minister via the Defense Ministry."[55] Furthermore, Article 15, that had listed the main functions of the General Staff, was declared null and void. In essence, this meant that the Chief of the General Staff now worked for the Defense Minister.

Furthermore, it was ruled that in the future, the General Staff would stay out of operational matters. As Ivanov put it, "in the view of the supreme command [Putin], it is important that the General Staff focus more on future wars and the prospective development of the armed forces, and not be involved in routine affairs."[56] Putin then fired Kvashnin after seven years on the job using raids against military posts and villages in Ingushetia, as a pretext.

Putin had made his decision. The Chief of the General Staff lost his right to appeal directly to the commander-in-chief. In the future, Ivanov would be responsible for actions taken by all the services. He now had the authority and the responsibility to make decisions, a point Ivanov emphasized. "There is one immutable constant in military organization: the principle of one-man command and one-man control. Armed forces remain what they are only for as long as this principle prevails and a rigid vertical command structure is ensured."[57]

Weapons and the Budget

As pointed out above, the Russian military was in desperate straits both in terms of its weapons and budget when Putin took over. However, Putin immediately began by reversing Yeltsin's starvation budgets. It is important to recognize, however, that he has not gone as far as the generals and admirals would have liked. The generals argued that 3.5 percent of GNP should be allocated to the military accordance with a 1998 presidential decree by Yeltsin. However, Putin was not in a position to go that far as Table 1 demonstrates.

The infusion of money under Putin went a long way toward stabilizing the situation, although as Ivanov (at that point still head of the Security Council) observed, it was not enough to get the armed forces out of their crisis.[60] Past budgetary

Table 1: Defense Budget as a Percentage of GNP, 1999 - 2006[58]

1999	2000	2001	2001	2003	2004	2005	2006[59]
2.34	2.63	2.66	2.60	2.65	2.69	2.8	2.74

restrictions meant that almost nothing had been spent on weapons purchases or research and development since before the collapse of the USSR. Besides, inflation was a constant problem. No matter how much money Putin found for the military, the armed forces were in such a mess that it was insufficient over the short run.

To deal with the weapons problem, in January 2002 the Putin administration adopted the "State Program for Armaments for the Period up to 2010" that increased spending on arms and research. "Klebanov said the procurement plan tops last year's expenditure by nearly 40 percent . . . The 40 percent figure corresponds to remarks made last year by Finance Minister Alexei Kurdin, who said that the 2002 procurement budget would likely increase by 27 to 79 billion rubles ($850 million to $2.5 billion)."[61]

Reequipping and modernizing the Russian Army would remain a long-term process in spite of Putin's efforts. For example, Klebanov, the Minister of Science, Industry and Technology, stated that "in-depth modernization of combat aircraft, ships, nonstrategic missiles, precision weapons systems, and other military hardware on the existing basis will make it possible to carry out work also in the sphere of (long-term) research and development."[62] This meant that it would be a long time – 2010, according to the commander of ground troops, before new weapons and equipment would be available.[63] In the meantime, what money was available for weapons and equipment would be used to modernize already existing systems. And there was a tremendous need for modernization. For example, General Lieutenant Sergey Solntsev, who was in charge of flight safety for Russian forces, commented in 2002 that over half of Russia's airbases were in need of complete refurbishment, while another report on the Air Force commented that,

> "The share of up-to-date aircraft of the fourth generation amounts to less than 45 percent of the aircraft fleet. The share of operational aircraft in general has fallen to 60 percent. Only a little over 30 per cent of airfields are ready for operation. The personnel's annual flying hours do not exceed 20 to 25 percent of the required number."[64]

In 2002 the long and exceedingly slow process of rebuilding began. The Air Force was scheduled to received twenty modernized Su-27 general-purpose planes in

2003 while it had obtained twelve modernized planes in 2002.[65] It was clear that the Putin administration was trying to turn things around.

2003 brought more of the same. In March the Deputy Commander of the Air Force, Yuri Grishin complained that the Air Force would "have to fly planes that are 20 to 40 years old."[66] Another source echoed his concern by noting that "Some 80% of Russia's military-industrial complex is obsolete . . . the average years of service for the machinery of the complex is 30, as compared with 7-8 years in the developed nations of Europe."[67]

In 2004 some new weapons began to appear, albeit in extremely small numbers. For example, in July it was announced that the Army had obtained fourteen T-90S tanks, and it hoped to get another twenty to thirty tanks in 2005.[68] The 2006 draft budget included 225 billion rubles for acquisition. This is a growth of one billion rubles over the proceeding year. This will permit the military to acquire seven Topol-M missiles and seventeen tanks while seventeen Su-fighters will be modernized.[69] At the same time, the Army's main strike helicopter, the Mi28N will begin to enter service.[70] The point is not that the military is being modernized, this is a drop in the barrel when it comes to bringing the armed forces up to world standards. What is notable, however, is that rather than wait until 2010 – as previously suggested – the Putin administration has begun to bring new systems on line, albeit in limited quantities.

In addition to hiring Kudelina to oversee the budget, the Putin administration took a number of structural actions in an effort to improve efficiency in purchasing weapons and equipment. To begin with, a single purchasing agent system was set up. According to Ivanov, when he took over as defense minister there were fifty-two entities inside the defense ministry that had the power to purchase military equipment and weapons and to order research and development. The number was first cut to twenty and then to only one.[71]

Putin's plan was to systematically rebuild the country's military in ten years. Will he be successful? It is impossible to say. Much will depend on how the economy does and how persistent Putin is in pushing his modernization plans. There was no question that the country was capable of producing high quality weapons as the willingness of the Chinese to outfit their military by purchasing almost exclusively Russian weapons demonstrated.

Raising Pay and Getting Housing

As the reader is aware from the proceeding sections, pay and housing were very serious problems. Pay actually worsened during the first part of Putin's time in office. Pay was increased somewhat, but inflation combined with the government's introduction of a new plan aimed at helping local communities with the cost involved in maintaining its transportation services wiped out whatever gains the officer corps had made. The idea of the plan, in a nutshell, was to replace the free transportation that had long been available to military personnel with a cash allowance.[72] To suggest that the matter was poorly handled would be an understatement. Officers who lived in large cities quickly learned that their allowance fell far short of what was needed to get to and from work. Adjustments were made but complaints concerning pay continued. From 2003 until the beginning of 2006 there were no salary increases, despite promises that it would be indexed to cover inflation.

Then, in a meeting with senior officers in November 2005, Putin announced a major change. Recognizing the legitimacy of complaints on the part of officers concerning their pay, Putin stated that beginning 1 January, salaries would be increased by fifteen percent and that over the next three years they would be increased by sixty-seven percent.[73] The problem, however, is serious. In November 2005 Ivanov announced that "over 12,000 officers have retired early from the armed forces."[74] The salary increase is a beginning, but it is difficult to say if it will reverse this trend and convince officers to remain in the armed forces. However, it does indicate that the administration not only recognizes the problem but is attempting – at long last – to fix it.

Turning to housing, the Putin administration came up with a novel way of dealing with it. At the end of 2002 Ivanov announced that the government would be "radically transforming the system of providing housing to servicemen."[75] Military personnel were divided into three categories. The first included those who had been discharged and who must be provided with housing because the state had promised to provide it. The second dealt with those who joined the military after 1998. They must also be provided with housing by the military. The third group dealt with those who joined after 2003. This group will be covered by a new plan – a savings system. According to this plan, service members and the military will contribute to a personal account that a service member can drawn on to purchase an apartment. This does not mean that the housing problem is solved. But it does indicate that the Russian military is attempting to rationalize the problem – for the first time in its thirteen year existence.

Crime, Corruption, and Dedovshchina

In spite of considerable efforts, Putin has not been able to make major inroads in these critical areas. All three remain serious problems. To quote just one source with regard to crime,

"No one has ever been able to put a figure on the scale of theft in the Russian armed forces overall. Rations are sold while soldiers go hungry. Arms and ammunition disappear, perhaps to hunters, gangsters or terrorists, but no one knows. Fuel, spare parts and vehicles can be bought: recently in Mulino, home of a permanent-readiness motor rifle regiment, tanks ran out of fuel on the ranges because it was being sold by the tanker-loader to local businesses. A motor rifle regimental commander sold all his unit's lorries, becoming briefly, a millionaire."[76]

The situation with *dedovshchina* was even worse than it had been under Yeltsin. Why? For several reasons. To begin with there were twenty-five reasons for deferments. This meant that the majority of young men could not be drafted. And then to make the situation worse,

"20 percent of the draftees have primary education, and only 1.8 percent higher education. Every fourth conscript has grown up in a family without a father and 1 percent are orphans. Forty-three percent had studied and 37 percent had worked before service. Eleven percent frankly confessed to alcohol addiction being their worse habit. Up to 4 percent of respondents used drugs and 11 percent already had police records for various reasons."[77]

Given the poor quality of draftees, wide-spread crime and theft and the continuing lack of NCOs, it was not surprising that "barrack room fagging and bullying is endemic."[78] The high command reacted by posting morale officers to units – but to little avail. "'The older soldiers educate young troops,' says the young lieutenant, who identifies himself only as Dmitry. 'This is the way the army is built. We mustn't break established rules'." Then to give an idea of how he understands the concept of discipline, he produced a "72-centimeter, hard-nosed baton he uses to punish unruly soldiers. He refers to it as an 'educator'."[79]

What to do? The Putin administration was only too aware of these problems and set about to deal with them. First, the high command believed that the decision to cut the length of conscription to one year beginning in 2008 would break up the *dedovshchina* process. If recruits served only for one year beginning 2008 it would break up the *dedovshchina* process. If recruits served for one year vice two, it would mean that there would only be two age groups serving at any one time. The second group would not have been in the military long enough to pick up the habits of the *deds*.

Ivanov also launched a number of campaigns in an effort to increase both the number and quality of recruits. First, the Army fought hard against the idea of alternative service – a battle that it lost. However, in losing the battle, the military succeeded in attaching restrictions that made alternative service a very unattractive concept except for those who had a very strong moral commitment to avoiding military service.

Then there was the question of deferments. One of his major venues of attack was the educational system. According to Ivanov, prior to 2005 Russia had 229 universities offering ROTC courses. "There are more military departments in the Russian Federation than there were in the Soviet Union."[80] The problem was that very few of the graduates – who were reserve officers – ever did active duty. To counter what some generals saw as "draft evasion" and to improve the quality of recruits (and thereby further undercut the *dedovshchina* process), Ivanov cut the number of universities that could offer ROTC to between thirty and thirty-five (from 229). Those who elected to take ROTC would receive financial assistance from the Ministry of Defense, but they would also agree to serve at least three years on active duty. Other college graduates would be required to serve for one year as enlisted men upon graduation.

Another action taken by the military to deal with problems such as *dedovshchina* was to consider the use of chaplains. Traditionally, the Imperial Army had used them, but the Soviet military refused to have anything to do with them. On 5 January 2005, Ivanov met with the Patriarch of Moscow to thank him for the Church's spiritual support of the army, while the military's prosecutor general called on the military to make use of the Orthodox Church in the Army's fight against crime. Finally, on 10 June, General Nikolai Pankov, who was in charge of personnel and educational issues in the Army, stated, "We will actively work with all traditional religions."[81]

The question is will the Putin administration's plan work? Will splitting the army into permanent readiness units and one year conscripts help with *dedovshchina*? What about Non-Commission Officers? There are rumors that NCOs from professional units will be used to train conscripts (and live in the barracks) thereby ensuring that *dedovshchina* is stopped. What about closer ties to the Orthodox Church? What about crime and corruption – will the higher salaries convince military personnel to live on their salaries? The idea is that if salaries are improved and if the military prosecutor gives those who are corrupt or commit crimes harsh sentences, then the problem will resolve itself. We will see.

Fighting Terrorism

If there was anything that functioned as a wake-up call for Putin, it was the 11 September 2001 attack on New York and Washington, D.C. It was clear to him that what happened in New York and Washington could have happened in Moscow. Terrorism was no longer limited to the War in Chechnya. Putin was the first foreign leader to call President George Bush after the attacks, and he joined the War on Terrorism. He immediately offered assistance to the United States for its war against the Taliban in Afghanistan – in spite of opposition from the General Staff.

Then on 22 October 2002 Chechen rebels seized a Moscow theater taking eight hundred people hostage. Putin refused to negotiate and instead gave the special services the go-ahead to seize the building. In the process, the special services bungled the operation. 120 hostages died and close to six hundred were injured because a dangerous gas was used.

Putin then informed the security organs (including the military) that its new objective was "to fight terrorism at the global level."[82] A few days later, Ivanov gave an interview in which he declared that "war has been declared on Russia, a war without frontiers, borders, or visible enemies." He reiterated a statement he had made to the effect that Moscow must be in a position to carry out, or finance, such undertakings. He emphasized that "Russia reserves the right to use precision-guided weapons to strike training bases or other objects related to international terrorism."[83]

Increasingly, decision-makers like Ivanov had begun to speak of Russia facing a new kind of threat. The danger of military aggression from the United States or NATO or any other source had significantly declined. As he noted at a meeting of the Academy of Military Sciences in Moscow on 18 January 2003, "After September 11, 2001 and [the 23-26 hostage drama in Moscow], it has become completely clear that the Cold War has been replaced by a new type of war, the war against international terrorism."[84]

On 1-3 September, 2004 the grammar school at Beslan was attacked. This traumatic event had a deep impact not only on Putin, Moscow, the military, and Russia, but the rest of the world as well. 339 people were killed, most of them children. Putin responded immediately. First, he initiated a major overhaul of Moscow's centralized political structure by announcing that governors of the country's eighty-nine regions would no longer be elected by popular vote, but that he would appoint them to approval by the local legislature. As he had in the past, Putin decided that the best way to deal with what he perceived to be local incompetence was to centralize matters – to transfer authority to Moscow. He also moved to gain greater control over elections to the Duma, the lower house of parliament.

In February 2005 the Duma changed the law "On Defense" to permit the Army to take part in counter-terrorism actions involving the use of military force. The action was taken at Putin's request in an effort to clarify the procedure for using the military in situations such as Beslan as well as the use of armed forces outside of Russia's boundaries.

Combat Readiness

In spite of Putin's and Ivanov's efforts to stabilize the situation inside the military, the Army continues to face problems with combat readiness. On the plus side, training was improved. For example, pilot's flying time has reportedly increased. "While three or four years ago, pilots spent 20 to 22 hours in the air a month due to the shortage of funds to buy fuel, now they fly 50-70 and in some units 100 hours."[85]

The bottom line is that the frequency of training exercises has increased significantly. For example, in August 2005 Russian forces engaged in four exercises beginning the same day.[86]

Furthermore, it was announced that sixty battalion level tactical exercises were carried out in September, and the first logistical exercise was carried out in six years.[87] While Russia may lag behind the rest of the world when it comes to exercises, this marks a major step forward in comparison with what took place under Yeltsin.

Conclusion

Putin has been very different from his predecessor. His goal was to stabilize the system while at the same time working to rebuild it, and that included the armed forces. He has been a much more decisive leader than Yeltsin and he has shown his interest in the military and rebuilding it.

A number of generals disagreed with Puin – for example, Sergeyev and Kvashnin – on the direction he was taking in rebuilding the military. In spite of that, however, they appreciated the fact that he was taking the armed forces seriously. They had a strong arm at the helm in the form of a man who was deeply committed to bringing about change in the military.

Putin has not by any means solved all of the military's problems. Indeed, the military continues to be faced with so many problems that there are serious questions about the eventual outcome of his reform. However, the important point from the generals' standpoint is that he has dealt with the military in a serious fashion. He and Ivanov made mistakes – for example the way the plan to replace free travel on public transport was replaced by money to cover their transportation costs. He has also not been able to give them as much money as they would have liked for arms, salaries, and training. He also did little to deal with problems like crime, corruption and *dedovshchina* apparently believing that time, the structural change to be introduced in 2008, and a more affluent Russia would help resolve them. But like the tortoise he is, he has gradually began to reform and restructure the armed forces.

NOTES TO CHAPTER 8

[1] This chapter is reprinted by permission of Rowman and Littlefield Publishers, Inc., from Dale R. Herspring, ed., *Putin's Russia: Past Imperfect, Future Uncertain* (third ed.).

[2] Lilia Shevtsova, *Putin's Russia* (Washington, D.C.: Carnegie Endowment for International Peace, 2003), especially chapter 3. See also, Richard Sakwa, *Putin's Russia,* (London: Routledge, 2004).

[3] Dale R. Herspring, ed., *Putin's Russia: Past Imperfect, Future Uncertain* (Boulder: Rowman and Littlefield, 2002), 259–262.

[4] See for example, Stephen Blank, "This Time We Really Mean It: Russian Military Reform," *Russia and Eurasian Review* 2, no. 1 (7 January 2003); Roger N. McDermott, "Putin's Military Priorities: Modernization of the Armed Forces," *Insight* 3, no. 1 (2003); Dale R. Herspring, "De-Professionalizing the Russian Armed Forces" (London: Palgrave, 2002), 197–210; Herspring, "Putin and the Armed Forces," in Herspring, ed., *Putin's Russia,* 155–175; Peter Rutland, "Military Reform Marks Time," in Peter Rutland, "Russia in 2002: Waiting and Wondering" for *Transitions Online* (www.fol.cz).

[5] See this writer's *The Russian High Command and Presidential Authority: From Gorbachev to Putin* (Lawrence: University Press of Kansas, 2006) as well as Zoltan Barany, "Politics and the Russian Armed Forces," in Zoltan Barany and Robert G. Moser, *Russian Politics: Challenges of Democratization* (Cambridge: Cambridge University Press, 2001), 175–214; Herspring, "De-Professionalizing the Russian Armed Forces."

[6] Brian D. Taylor, *Politics and the Russian Army: Civil-Military Relations, 1689-2000,* (Cambridge: Cambridge University Press, 2003), 308.

[7] "Armed Forces Crime Figures for 1998 Announced," Interfax, 1 December 1999.

[8] Roger N. McDermott," Putin's Military Priorities: The Modernization of the Armed Forces," in Anne C. Aldis and Roger N. McDermott, *Russian Military Reform, 1992-2002,* (London: Frank Cass, 2003), 266.

[9] "Russia Continues to Lose Officers," *The Monitor,* 13 October 1999.

[10] "Moscow Military Urges Deserters to Return," *The Monitor,* 14 May 1998.

[11] "Doctors Find New Draftees Less Fit for Duty," *The Russian Journal,* 8 March 1999, 3.

[12] "The Russian Army, Reeling from the War in Chechnya and Facing Brutality in its Ranks, has Found a New Enemy – Itself," *Transactions,* November 1998.

[13] Michael J. Orr, *Manpower Problems of the Russian Armed Forces,* Conflict Studies Research Centre, D62, February 2002, 4.

[14] "The Russian Army, Reeling from the War in Chechnya and Facing Brutality in its Ranks, has Found a New Enemy – Itself," *Transactions,* November, 1998.

[15] "Russia's Army Faces Battle Within its Ranks," *Christian Science Monitor,* 1 February 1999.

[16] Ibid.

[17] "The Army is Shooting its Own Men," *Izvestiya,* 6 June 1997.

[18] "Defense Ministry to Submit Program on Contract Service by Autumn," *Novosti,* 15 July 1997.

[19] "Army Struggles with Contract Military Service," *The Monitor,* 15 October 1997.

[20] David J. Betz, *Civil-Military Relations in Russia and Eastern Europe* (London, RoutledgeCurzon, 2004), 53.

[21] "Generals, Admirals Convicted of Corruption," *RFE/RL Daily Report,* 6 July 1999.

[22] "Armed Forces Crime Figures for 1998 Announced," *Interfax,* 1 December 1999.

[23] "Yeltsin Orders Probe of Security for Nukes," *Washington Times,* 21 October 1998.

[24] Stephen Blank, "Valuing the Human Factor: The Reform of Russian Military Manpower," *The Journal of Slavic Military Studies* 12, no. 1 (March 1999): 83.

[25] "Defense Chief Describes Army's Woes," *The Monitor,* 9 April 1999.

[26] "Russia Tries to Save Military," *AP,* 2 July 1999.

[27] Walter Parchomenko, "The State of Russia's Armed Forces and Military Reform," *Parameters* (Winter, 1999-2000): 104.

[28] Ilyukhin, Russia's National Security Threatened," *Interfax,* 17 September 1998.

[29] "Russian Army Woes Outlined," *The Monitor,* 14 December 1998.

[30] Nikolai Sokov, "'Denuclearization' of Russia's Defense Policy," *CNS Reports,* Monterey Institute of International Studies, 17 July 2000.

[31] "Hope Glimmers for Reform," *Moscow Times,* 29 March 2001 in Johnson's List, 28 March 2001.

[32] "Development Strategy of the Armed Forces Defined," *Military News Bulletin* no. 8 (August 2000).

[33] Stephen Main, "The Strategic Rocket Force, 1991-2002," in Aldis and McDermott, ff. 114.

[34] Aleksandr Gol'ts, *Armiya Rossii: 11 poteryannykh let* (Moscow: Zakharov, 2004), 80.

[35] "Vystuplenie Prezidenta Rossiyskoi Federatsii V. V. Putina na sborakh rukovodyashchego sostava Voruzhennykh Sil Rossiyskoy Federatsii, 20 noyarbrya 2000 goda." http://president/kremlin.ru/events/102.html.

[36] "Survey of Military Reform in the Russian Federation," *Yadernyy kontrol,* 19 April 2002, in WNC@apollo.fedworld.gov. WNC Military Affairs, 6 September 2002.

[37] "Decisions on the reform of the state's military organization have been adopted," *Military News Bulletin* no. 11 (November 2000).

[38] Main, "The Strategic Rocket Force," 29.

[39] "Russia: Analysts Assess Kremlin Reshuffle," 29 March 2001 in Johnson's List, 29 March 2001.

[40] Ibid.

[41] "High Level Shake-up, Putin Replaces Russia's Defense, Interior and Nuclear Energy Chiefs," *New York Times,* 29 March 2001.

[42] Vladimir Mukhin, "Reshuffle Bring Putin People to the Top," *The Russia Journal,* 4 May 2001.

[43] See Roger N. McDermott, *The Recreation of Russia's Ground Forces High Command: Prepared for Future War?* A103, March 2002, Conflict Studies Research Centre, 2.

[44] "Assessing Putin's Meeting with the Military Command," *The Monitor,* 29 October 2001.

[45] "Survey of Military Reform in the Russian Federation," *Yadernyy kontrol,* 19 April 2002, in WNC@apollo.fedworld.gov. WNC Military Affairs, 6 September 2002.

[46] "More than Half of Russians Unfit to Serve in the Army," *AFP*, 29 November 2001 in Johnson's List, 1 December 2001.

[47] Ibid.

[48] "What is the Price of a Professional?" *Itogi*, 22 January 2002 in Johnson's List, 28 January 2002.

[49] Roger McDermott, "Putin's Military Priorities: The Modernization of the Armed Forces," in Aldis and McDermott, *Russian Military Reform*, 270.

[50] "The Military Reform Card," *Moscow Times*, 22 May 2003.

[51] "Military Reforms: The First Steps," *Mir novostei*, 18 July 2002 in Johnson's List, 18 July 2002.

[52] "Russia to Man 40 Units, Formations with Contract Soldiers in 2005," *ITAR-TASS*, 12 February 2005; "Russian Military to Finish Building Housing for Chechnya Based Units in 2005," *Agentstvo voyennykh novostey*, 28 March 2005, in WNC@apollo.fedworld.gov. WNC Mitlitrary Affairs, 28 March 2005.

[53] "All Volunteer Force Program Funding Expected to Increase by 15%," *Agentstvo voyennykh novostey*, 9 September 2005 in WNC@apollo.fedworld.gov. WNC Military Affairs, 10 September 2005.

[54] "General Staff Should Be the Brain of the Army," *RIA-Novosti*, 8 February 2004 in Johnson's List, 9 February 2004.

[55] "Federal'nyy zakon 'ob oborone'," 24 April 1996 in www.mil.ru/articles3863.shtml contains the old language; "Oversight for the Armed Forces is carried out by the Defense Minister via the Defense Ministry," *Russkii Kurier*, 29 April 2004 in Johnson's List, 30 April 2004.

[56] "As Defense Minister Says General Staff to Focus on Future Wars," *RFE/RL Daily Report*, 20 July 2004.

[57] "General Staff Relieved on Superfluous Functions. While Defense Minister is Handed All the Reins of Control Over the Army," *Rossiyskaya gazeta*, 15 June 2004 in WNC@apollo.fedworld.gov. WNC Military Affairs, 17 June 2004.

[58] Alexi Arbatov, "Military Reform" From Crisis to Stagnation," in Steven E. Miller and Dmitri Trenin, eds., *The Russian Military: Power and Policy*, (Cambridge: MIT Press, 2004), 100. The figure for 2004 is from "Defenceless Defence," *RIA-Novosti*, 26 November 2003 in Johnson's List, 26 November 2003. The 2005 figure is from "Russian State Duma Approves Increase in Defense Budget," *Agentstvo voyennykh novostey*, 23 June 2005 in WNC@apollo.fedworld.gov. WNC Military Affairs, 24 June 2005.

[59] This is an estimate.

[60] "Budgetary Situation Stabilized," *ITAR-TASS*, 17 October 2001 in WNC@apollo.fedworld.gov. WNC Military Affairs, 18 October 2001.

[61] "State Oks $2.5 billion Arms Budget," *Moscow Times*, 18 January 2002 in Johnson's List, 18 January 2002.

[62] "Klebanov Stresses Need for 'Modernization' of Old Army Hardware," *Rossiyskaya gazeta*, 8 August 2002, in WNC@apollo.fedworld.gov. WNC Military Affairs, 9 August 2002.

[63] "Russia's Ground Troops Not to Get New Weapons Soon," *ITAR-TASS*, 26 December 2001 in WNC@apollo.fedworld.gov. WNC Military Affairs, 29 December 2001.

[64] "Russian Military Aviation Said in Crisis," *Interfax*, 18 September 2002 in Johnson's List, 19 September 2002.

[65] "Russian Air Force to Receive 20 Modernized Planes in 2003," *ITAR-TASS*, 16 January 2003.

[66] "Russian Air Force Command Worried About Aging of Aircraft," *ITAR-TASS*, March 26, 2003 in WNC@apollo.fedworld.gov. WNC Military Affairs, 27 March 2003.

[67] "80% of Russia's Defense Industry is Obsolete," *Rosbalt*, 18 August 2003 in Johnson's List, 20 August 2003.

[68] "Russian Army to Acquire 14 T-90S Tanks in 2004," *ITAR-TASS*, 6 July 2004 in WNC@apollo.fedworld.gov. WNC Military Affairs, 10 July 2004.

[69] "Defense Spending is Growing, Armed Deliveries are Sliding," *Nezavisimoy voyennoye obozrenie*, 31 August 2005 in WNC@apollo.fedworld.gov. WNC Military Affairs, 2 September 2005.

[70] "Russian Army to Get New Strike Helicopter from 2006," *ITAR-TASS*, 11 October 2004.

[71] "We Need at Least One Million Military Personnel," *Izvestiya*, 22 February 2005 in Johnson's List, 22 February 2005.

[72] "Russian Government Proposals to Remove Servicemen's Privileges Criticized," *Vremya MN*, 31 May 2003 in WNC@apollo.fedworld.gov. WNC Military Affairs, 1 June 2003.

[73] "Stenograficheskiy otchet o soveshchanii rukovodyashchego sostava Booruzhennykh Sil," 9 noyabrya 2005, president.kremlin.ru/text/appears/2005/11/96885.shtml.

[74] "Russian Defense Minister Concerned by Number of Officers Leaving the Army," *Agentstvo voyennykh novostey*, 2 November 2005 in WNC@apollo.fedworld.gov. WNC Military Affairs, 3 November 2005.

[75] "Russian Defense Minister Welcomes New Housing Program for the Military," *ITAR-TASS*, 2 August 2002, in WNC@apollo.fedworld.gov. WNC Military Affairs, 9 August 2002.

[76] Michael Orr, "Reform and the Russian Ground Forces, 1992-2002," in Aldis and McDermott, *Russian Military Reform*, 137.

[77] "Poll Reveals 11 Percent of Russian Soldiers with Alcoholism," *Interfax*, 6 December 2001 in WNC@apollo.fedworld.gov. WNC Military Affairs, 7 December 2001.

[78] Paul Jenkins, "Red Army Blues," *The World Today*, 3 September 2001.

[79] "As Desertions Continue, Russia's Military Drafts Men with Mental Illnesses and Criminal Records," *AP*, 6 October 2002.

[80] "Russian Defense Minister Says Military Departments in Universities 'Ineffective'," *ITAR-TASS*, 2 February 2005.

[81] "Defense Minister Thanks Patriarch for Spiritual Support of Army," *RFE/RL Daily Report*, 6 January 2005.

[82] "The Russian Military Gets a New Objective," *Novaya gazeta*, 2 November 2002 in Johnson's List, 2 November 2002.

[83] "Defense Minister Says Russia is at War," *The Monitor*, 6 November 2002.

[84] "Ivanov on Terrorist Threat," *RFE/RL Daily Report*, 20 January 2003.

[85] "Russian Air Force Command Worried by Aging of Aircraft," *ITAR-TASS*, 26 March 2003 in WNC@apollo.fedworld.gov. WNC Military Affairs, 29 March 2003.

[86] "Sergey Ivanov Tests His Doctrine – Armed Forces Train to Combat One Major War and Two Local Wars Simultaneously," *Nezavisimaya gazeta*, 21 August 2005 in WNC@apollo.fedworld. gov. WNC Military Affairs, 22 August 2005.

[87] "Russia Plans Over 60 Exercises in September for Armed Forces," *Agentstvo voyennykh novosety*, 19 September 2005 in WNC@apollo.fedworld.gov. WNC Military Affairs, 20 September 2005.

RUSSIA AND EUROPE
Between Ambivalence and Association
CURT GASTEYGER

Abstract

Today's Russia is, its mental ambiguity about its real identity notwithstanding, more "European" than its Communist and Tsarist predecessors have been in the last two centuries. This fact has many psychological, economic and, above all, strategic implications. Russia's second president, Vladimir Putin, is in this respect more pragmatic than his predecessor, Boris Yeltsin. He realizes that his country, while still big, is no longer a valid counterweight to the United States and as such is strictly limited in its strategic options for any foreseeable future. Hence, Putin's interest in an acceptable strategic accommodation with Washington, a political rapprochement with Europe (and its institutional core, the European Union), as well as economic cooperation with both.

Two factors contribute to this reappraisal: first, the painful recognition that Russia's potential for great power status and attractiveness will remain limited for a long time, and, second, that by joining the "war on international terrorism" it may enhance – at least temporarily – the chances for such accommodation.

There are basically three obstacles working against such a strategy:

- The still limited capacity for wide-ranging internal reform, including relations with often restless republics;
- America's growing predilection for unilateralism, encouraged by unmatched superiority in all strategically relevant fields;
- NATO's eastward expansion leaving an undefined place for Russia.

Various developments could possibly affect – either reduce or enhance – Russia's position in Europe and beyond: developments in the "Community of Independent States" (CIS), either by a tendency towards more authoritarian rule or, more likely, a gradual process of political democratization and economic reforms (or "liberalization"). In no country could the latter become more important – both for Russia and for Europe – than in Ukraine. Its "Orange Revolution" in late 2004 could take the country on the way to important reforms at home and a more balanced relationship with Russia on the one hand and the European Union, possibly even NATO, on the other.

* * *

When trying to answer the time-honored question whether Russia is a European, Eurasian, or simply a geographically indefinable power we are reminded of Winston Churchill's definition of Great Britain and its relationship to and with Europe. "My country is," said Churchill with his masterful ambiguity, "*of* Europe but not *in* Europe." Perhaps the reverse is true for Russia: it is "in Europe" (and, heaven knows, has left no doubt about that in the last three hundred years) but, in many respects, it is not "of Europe." That at least is what many Russians feel when looking at the still vast expanses of their country, the leftovers of the Soviet Union, successor to the Tsarist Empire, broken up into fifteen pieces. Indeed, the Russian Federation reaches well into Central and East Asia; it stretches from the Baltic Sea to the Pacific. In short, the double-headed eagle in Russia's coat of arms still looks both East and West.

And yet, on both sides of the recently retrenched Russian border the idea of a "European Russia" remains alive. General de Gaulle had never any doubt that Europe stretched "from the Atlantic to the Urals," President Gorbachev dreamed of a common European house and, most recently, President Putin assured his French guest, Chirac, that Europe stretches indeed from the Atlantic to the Urals.

Such definitions and assertions aside, nobody can deny that the newly constituted Russian Federation is now more "European" than its Communist and Tsarist predecessors have ever been since Peter the Great. After all, the surprisingly peaceful dissolution of the last colonial empire in the world let some fifty million non-Russians into an ambiguous kind of independence, while another sixty-six million live in Ukraine, Belarus, and Moldova. In Russia itself, some nineteen percent of the population are non-Russians. The main point here is that nobody can be absolutely sure whether such a new political-demographic configuration, hardly fifteen years of age, is more or less definitive (always a highly relative term in human history) or is likely to undergo again substantial modification. So, in the final analysis, our view of Russia as a truly European or European-oriented power will be determined not just by the political "pronunciamentos" of erstwhile leaders. Rather, it will be shaped by the vagaries of political, ethnic, and demographic developments. The "homecoming" of Russia as a truly "European power" will therefore remain on the international agenda for some time to come.

Russia's Ambivalence

Both Europe and Russia will have to live with such uncertainty. It is well described by Nikolaj Danilevski. When asked whether Russia belongs to Europe, he gave the ever valid but noncommittal answer, "As it pleases. If it suits Russia, she will be part of it; if it doesn't, she won't – partly and as much as it pleases."[1] Such ambivalence is understandable given its manifold special features. But it can also be seen as an expression of Russia's fear to be seen, in its present state of at least partial weakness, as a second-rate country should it really wish to be fully associated with Europe, let alone with the U.S.-dominated Western world. Under such circumstances, Russia may prefer to play its "Eurasian card." As a Eurasian power it can rightly claim to be the strongest in the region.[2]

Here Russia does not have to face up to unfavorable comparisons. Nobody questions its superiority even though it may be resisted or resented. We are thus left with ambiguity when it comes to defining Russia's policy towards and its role in Europe and European security. It is probably safe to predict that this is likely to remain so except if Russia should join NATO and/or the European Union as a full-fledged member, a prospect that most observers still consider as highly unlikely.

In the light of such uncertainty about Russia's identity and future orientation, a recent opinion poll is, for whatever it is worth, somewhat surprising. The poll taken in early spring of 2001[3] reports that fifty-nine percent of the persons interviewed, when asked whether Russia should seek membership with the European Union, answered in the affirmative. Such a positive if not flattering attitude was particularly pronounced among people with high educational and income levels, as well as with respondents in the eighteen to thirty-five age group. Only nineteen percent opposed Russia's entry into the EU, a large proportion of them being supporters of the Communist Party. One can wonder whether such a rather positive view of the European Union still prevails in the light of the serious turbulences this very EU is going through since its enlargement by ten new members and the rejection of its new constitution by a majority of French and Dutch voters.

On the other hand, forty-six percent of respondents, when asked whether it was more important to develop relations of partnership with the United States or the EU, preferred the latter. Only ten percent opted for the United States, and twenty-eight percent answered that good relations with both were equally important. Whatever the ephemeral value of such polls may be, it would seem that the United States as the only superpower is suffering in Russia a similar fate of dislike or skepticism as it does in many other parts of the world, Western Europe included. The question, therefore, whether Russia is on the way to distancing itself from the United States and moving closer to Europe and its various institutions, seems legitimate. However, it is still the wrong one. To be sure, there are, in addition to the kind of survey just quoted, signs that Putin's Russia sees, for the time being, more advantages and possibilities of developing closer and more institutionalized relations with Europe, however defined. If so, this would signal an important change in Russian foreign policy and strategy since the end of World War II. It could be seen as the resigned, if not definitive closure of a seemingly glorious chapter of Russian-Soviet aspirations to superpower status – a status on a par only with the United States, meaning unmatched power and global reach. After such a farewell to grandeur, Russia would thus have to content itself with the status of a full-fledged part and partner in, and of, predominantly European politics.

Of course, we cannot be sure about such perspective. It would signal a resignation on part of an erstwhile world power, however short-lived this status may have been. Nor indeed can the Russians themselves. Geography and, as its consequence, history speak against such a one-sided option, though even if it now seems clear-cut, possibly desirable, and probably definitive. Russia, even reduced in territorial size, weakened in economic performance, and uncertain about its internal cohesion, is and will remain more than an unquestionably important player in Europe. Its membership with the EU is a dream at best but a nightmare for all the parties concerned, and that for a long time.[4] The brutal fact is that no real consensus exists in Russia on the kind of status and priorities it should seek on the international, let alone global stage.

Still, a number of hard realities in today's Russia will give us some indication of what we can expect from its foreign and security policy in the years to come both in general terms and with regard to its policy towards its immediate neighbors and towards Europe in general. The first and probably most important clue for our understanding of Russia's foreign policy can be found in the now probably generally accepted recognition that "the new situation (i.e., after the break-down of the Soviet Union) is by and large considered to be irreversible."[5] As the authors of this dictum, Baranovsky and Arbatov, put it, the rise of a significant revanchist trend in Russian foreign policy seems impossible.

Some observers, Russians and non-Russians alike, may consider such a rather reassuringly definitive assertion as either too optimistic or premature. They can point out that the present geographic configuration of Russia and its neighborhood could be subject to modification. Furthermore, the deep-seated and deeply hurt Russian nationalism, a mixture of social-religious messianism and unrequited grandeur, can transform today's more sanguine and pragmatic attitude into a potentially more aggressive one if the outside world is perceived to be condescending if not hostile. Others will remind us that Russia is still the second biggest (in terms of sheer numbers even the biggest) nuclear power in the world, practically on par with its former rival, the United States. Paradoxically, huge stocks of aging nuclear weapons can serve as much, if not more, as a bargaining chip as fully operational ones. Finally, nobody contests Russia's unique wealth in terms of human and natural resources and technological skills.

All these are assets of undisputed importance. But most of them belong to what we may call "traditional" elements of state power. In a market-oriented, high-technology environment they are, however, losing some, if not most of their erstwhile relevance. It is in this context that, to use Klaus Knorr's term, it seems appropriate to ask whether Russia lost its "war potential," a "potential" that goes well beyond the capacity of being able to fight a nuclear war. If proof for such a loss of "war potential" by Russia was still needed, it is provided by the disastrous and humiliating performance of its forces in the two Chechen wars. Here the state and morale of the armed forces proper on the one hand and the rapidly changing nature of conflict and conflict management on the other, leave little doubt that Russia has lost a great deal of what used to make up much of its erstwhile power and influence, i.e., its traditional war potential. The problem is that Russia is either not yet prepared to acknowledge this painful truth or continues to see the use of military power in terms that its Western partners consider to be no longer relevant or disproportionate. As a consequence, Russia's security agenda tends to diverge ever more from that of the West. This helps to explain why so far any security dialogue with Moscow is difficult and occasionally counterproductive.

To take this reflection one step further we can quote once more from Baranovski and Arbatov. "Russia," they state, "seems to be incapable of expanding influence without force, i.e., by more superiority or attractiveness of its own system."[6] Indeed, one need not agree with Fukuyama's theory about "the end of history" to conclude that with the hopefully definitive end of totalitarian ideologies and the systems that sustained them, the successor of the Communist Soviet Union has lost about every appeal or attractiveness to third countries or associated political movements. It was with their help that it could gain influence by peaceful means beyond the promotion of some common, and often short-lived, political, strategic, or economic interests. When examining later Russia's policies vis-à-vis Eastern Europe we will find this observation confirmed. Russia lost its appeal, if there ever was one, once its ideological leadership went bankrupt. In this sense we can already now conclude that Russia's future role and influence in Europe, particularly vis-à-vis its immediate neighbors, will largely be determined by the way Russia solves its own internal problems, and thus can become a new pole of attraction.

The one important exception to this Russian "Alleingang" (pursuing a specific policy of its own) is Moscow's declared solidarity in the fight against "terrorism" writ large ever since the devastating tragedies of terrorist attacks first in a Moscow musical theatre in 2002 and then against a school in Beslan in 2005. Russia fully joined the international community in its fight against terrorism. But even here, Russia was, and still is, principally concerned with terrorism "at home" rather than abroad. Its principal and most threatening enemy being Chechnya and, more recently, Dagestan and the embittered fight about the former's future political status. To be sure, here too, Islam and its fundamentalist version play a role but the motivation is clearly more political than religious. Hence, we can detect even here a policy that is specifically more Russian than international.

Russia and the West

In the light of the preceding, at least three specificities of Russia's attitude towards, or relations with, "the West" become fairly clear. First, that Moscow against all odds sticks to its claim of still being a world power, its internal weaknesses and only partly satisfactory economic performance, its ageing and dwindling population and huge disparities in wealth distribution notwithstanding. Second, that Russia, when looking westwards, is now confronted with what we may call "a triple West." There are, first, Russia's immediate neighbors, the three Baltic States that are now all members of the Atlantic Alliance and the European Union. In other words, they are lost likely forever as "potentially recoverable territories." Then there are Belarus and Moldavia whose future political status remains uncertain. And finally, there is the very special case of the Ukraine to which we will return in a moment.

The second group of countries include Russia's or rather the Soviet Union's former allies, i.e. the Czech Republic, Hungary, Poland, Slovakia – all of them now, like the Baltic States, members of NATO and the EU. Romania and Bulgaria, while already members of NATO, are still waiting to join the EU. And finally, still further west, we encounter the former "adversaries" of the Soviet Union plus some non-aligned or neutral countries, most of them also members of the EU.

All of this makes, in Russian eyes at least, for a fairly complex geo-strategic situation, full with uncertainties regarding the future status and allegiance of Russia's immediate or more distant neighbors.[7] Moscow's attempt to regroup the former Soviet republics under the heading and control of the "Commonwealth of Independent States" (CIS) has met with scarce and short-lived success. Ukraine, in particular, has never been a full-fledged member of the CIS. Most of the over eight hundred bi- and multilateral CIS treaties and agreements remain dead letters. In the light of such disappointing experiences, the remarks by President Putin's top security advisor, Sergei Ivanov, are interesting. In a speech in Munich in early February 2001, he announced "a reappraisal of Russian policies in the CIS." Its starting point, he said, "became the conclusion that in the nearest future accelerated development of (the) Community into a full-scale integrated union is impossible." While Russia would not abandon multilateral forms of cooperation or integration within the framework of CIS, such cooperation "may not become an end in itself." In other words, Russia considers the CIS as much of a burden as an advantage. It is looking for other forms of cooperation including ones of a bilateral nature.[8]

Can one conclude from this somber assessment of the CIS that Russia has abandoned the controversial and quite condescending notion of "near abroad" when describing its relationship with the former Soviet republics? The term is certainly much less used nowadays. What remains is the fact that the break-up of the Soviet Union left Russia with two kinds of border. On the one hand, there is Russia's border proper, now stretching from the Leningrad district to the Transcaucasus, from the Baltic States via Belarus and Ukraine to the still-unsettled region of Moldova/ Transnistria. Fifteen years after the demise of the Soviet Union, nobody can be sure whether these borders are definitive. Somewhere, in the back of some Russian minds, the hope may still linger that this border is not final. In the case of Belarus such an assumption may not be totally unjustified. It finds its justification in the various attempts by both sides, Moscow and Minsk, to work towards some form of closer cooperation if not an as yet undefined reintegration.

The upshot of such real or feigned uncertainty is that Russia (and its military) assume that the protection of the Western borders of Ukraine and Belarus constitutes the second security belt. It is in other words perceived to be part and parcel of Russia's own security. Three central considerations come into play in this context. First, as was rightly remarked already in the early years of post-Soviet Russia,[9] the stability of Russia's periphery is not a precondition to its internal stability. Rather the reverse is true. That means that a stable and self-assured Russia is likely to look at its neighbors in a more relaxed and hopefully less condescending way than it had the habit of doing for centuries. Second, the faster and wider the political, economic, social, and legal reforms take hold in the former Soviet republics, the smaller is the chance of their remaining dependent on Russia or in fact becoming vulnerable to Russian pressure, if not take-over. Third, the destiny of Russia's immediate Western neighbors, from the Baltic to Moldova, depends very much on the policies that both NATO and the EU pursue towards them and towards Russia itself. It is this triple and interlinked set of conditions that is likely to determine the future political and security order of Europe as a whole and of Eastern Europe in particular.

The key country in the present context, i.e. Russia's policies and strategies in and towards its "triple West," is undoubtedly Ukraine. Belarus, the other former Soviet republic, is important in our context only in as much as we do not know the degree to which it will be close to, or become still more dependent on Russia. One can speculate about the duration of the Lukashenko regime and the degree of the population's will to remain basically independent. What remains certain is that the country's strategic importance to Russia is a function of the extent and speed of NATO enlargement eastward. Of considerable importance is also the fact that Russia has decided to build, with Western and above all German aid, a second major oil pipeline via the Baltic sea that circumvents both Ukraine and Belarus on the one hand and Poland on the other. One is probably right in suspecting that such a decision is likely to put additional pressure on Ukraine and increase its dependence on Russia. All this may explain the rather flippant remark of a Russian expert. He stated that NATO's military enlargement eastward is being largely compensated by Russia's network of pipelines going westward.[10] Such an assertion testifies in any case to the fact that the debate on new dimensions of security is shifting even more from the military to the non-military, primarily economic-technological field.

The Special Case of Ukraine

As pointed out before, the key country in the debate about the future political order in Central-Eastern Europe in general, and Russia's place and role in it, is Ukraine. Lord Robertson, then the Secretary General of NATO, spelled out the nature and overall objective of his organization's objectives with regard to Ukraine's domestic reforms and foreign policy orientation. He applauded the country's "consistent policy of good relations with all neighbors, including NATO members Poland and Hungary." He praised Ukraine's "participation in the NATO-led peace-support operations in Bosnia and Kosovo," a broad range of activities taking place under the umbrella of the NATO-Ukraine Charter. He mentioned also that the NATO Information and Documentation Center in Kiev is "the first NATO office in a country which was part of the Soviet Union."

After all this and more praise, Lord Robertson added however that the alliance pays "special attention to this important country." And then came the veiled warning that it was essential for Ukraine to pursue the path to get over some "tough political, economic, and defense hurdles" and adhere to the "high democratic standards that are the norm among its partners in Europe."[11]

Lord Robertson's diplomatically expressed reservations about Ukraine's internal situation and ambivalent record with regard to both its political and economic reforms pointed to serious problems the country was then – and after its "orange revolution" in late autumn 2004 – is still faced with. They can be summarized under four headings: external debt, dependence on mainly Russian energy supply, elimination of important and widespread corruption and, last but not least, political reforms and a clearer separation of the executive, the legislative, and judiciary institutions. To be sure, the huge and unexpected street demonstrations in November and December 2004 eventually culminated, after two invalidated elections, in Victor Yushenko's victory as new president of the Ukraine. They became a turning point in Ukraine's so far rather disappointing development after independence. And yet, former Soviet president Gorbatchev's dictum that this orange revolution was the "second fall of the wall" after that in Berlin in November 1989 still seems, however flattering, somewhat premature.

To be sure, the Ukrainian society, not unlike the societies in the former Communist countries of Central-Eastern Europe, had moved faster than their own political regimes. That fact in itself is something the leaders of totalitarian or authoritarian regimes rarely realize and, if they do so eventually, it is too late for them. In Ukraine the much acclaimed "privatization" under former president Kuchma enabled government insiders, and their "outside" friends, to buy state enterprises at bargain prices, tax evasion, and the elimination of competitors.[12]

This was the harsh reality the new president had to deal with. Not surprisingly, the honeymoon he and his team, particularly his high-profile and ambitious Prime Minister, Ms. Timoshenko is over. It is an uphill battle in order to make their country both livable at home and credible abroad. As London's *Economist* phrased it when looking back at the first half year of the Yushenko's presidency, "Revolutions may change governments, but they cannot instantly transform a country.[13] This is not just true for the profiteers of the old regime. It is equally, if not more true for the reversal of the scandalous privatization. Third, it is true for the important minority of Russians living in the highly industrialized Eastern Ukraine which still feels itself much, if not more attached to Russia than to the country they are now citizens of.

This brings us to the future of Ukraine on the European continent. Three options appear to be the most likely ones to offer themselves. First, Ukraine is closely tied to its erstwhile hegemeon, Russia, though entering into some looser forms of association or cooperation with the West, i.e. primarily NATO and/or the EU.

The second is Ukraine's gradual inclusion into, if not full membership with NATO and/or with the European Union, or indeed both of them. Such an association might, however, be compensated by a special relationship with Russia, be it for economic reasons alone – Ukraine's dependence on Russian oil and gas – or also because of its Russian minority's continuing links with Russia. Third, a policy of "going it alone," meaning the adoption of an intermediary position between "the West" and Russia, sanctioned and supported by respective agreements with both sides.

In a fascinating study, Roman Szporluk offers something like a fourth option coming this time from Russia. According to Szporluk, Russia should define its new identity not by ethnic but rather by "civic" and/or territorial standards. In other words, "citizens of Russia must come to see themselves primarily not as ethnic Russians ("russkie") allied with other Russian's outside the borders of today's Russian Federation but as accepting the sovereignty of those borders and the multiethnic population that lives within them."[14]

Such an approach is nowhere more crucial with regard to Russia's attitude towards, and vision of Ukraine and its future relationship with Russia. The latter should in other words, to follow on with this argument, shed its attempts "to ethnize politics and identity" and treat Ukraine as a political entity that generates for its citizens the kind of allegiance and loyalty on which any state or nationhood rests.

As convincing as such a suggestion seems, its acceptance would seem to lie far in the future. Russia is not sure about the nature of its own identity nor indeed about the finality of its borders. Seen from Ukraine such a new "vision" on the part of Russia's perception of itself and its identity might be both welcome and reassuring. But so far there are few, if any indications that such a "conversion" in Moscow is in the offing. As long as this is so, Ukraine will have to live between a marginalized and possibly frustrated Russia and an enlarged EU and NATO.

Coming back to the three options above we recognize that the first two are not necessarily mutually exclusive. It is true that Ukraine declared its formal independence

GASTEYGER

already on 24 August 1990, more than a year before the official dissolution of the Soviet Union. It is also true that Ukraine kept its distance to the "Commonwealth of Independent States" (CIS) and the various attempts by Russia to tie the former Soviet republics as closely as possible to itself. Ukraine also, rather halfheartedly, joined such a heterogeneous group as is GUAM, standing for the first letter of its four members, Georgia, Ukraine, Azerbaijan, and Moldova. None of these and other linkages would seem to be deeply rooted and restraining Ukraine's freedom of choice when entering into new international relationships. Thus, when it comes to defining and formalizing its complex relationship with Russia, Ukraine's best option may be to propose some kind of "cooperative coexistence" or "accommodation."

With these actual or potential restrictions in Ukraine's freedom of choice with regard to its international relationships we can conclude that it will take still some time until, if at all, it can choose freely the "pro-Western option." That may sound somewhat overcautious given the fact that, after Russia, Ukraine is the largest country in Europe and has its fifth largest population (forty-eight million). As such, Ukraine is, and will remain, a long-term asset to whichever side it will eventually turn to or in fact be institutionally associated with. So far, such an outcome remains open for all sides concerned, all declarations of the various parties notwithstanding. Thus, Ukraine is likely to remain more a bridge between "East" and "West" than a constituent part of either.

Russia and the Enlargement of the EU

From what is said above it becomes clear that in a sense the future position of Ukraine will also co-determine the scope and possible limits of the European Union's enlargement and Russia's future position and role in Europe. For the former it will become a test of how many, particularly heavy-weight countries, it can absorb without serious damage to its internal cohesion and external operational capacity. For the latter, it will be the most serious test as to whether it really wants to be seen as a European power or a "Eurasian outsider."

As we can see, Russia's position in Europe becomes ever more a function of the – admittedly increasingly difficult – process of European integration. Ukraine and its future place and role in the process are part of this. In other words, the question here is not just whether Ukraine will or should or can join the European Union. The more fundamental question is whether the EU will remain the pole of almost irresistible attraction to outsiders or become, as a result of its dwindling cohesion and diverging visions of its future, an entity that, while no doubt important, is loosing some of its attractiveness or, by becoming more of a free trade association, weakening its political clout.

Between Equilibrium and Integration

Russia's policy toward and interest in its "triple West" are not only a function and reflection of the legacies of the past and the situation of the present. They are also very much determined and shaped by the developments and objectives of Russia's international environment. Nowhere is this more true than with regard to its former rival and competitor, the United States. Or, more precisely, the latter's determination to expand its political influence and strategic commitment well beyond the perimeter of the Atlantic Alliance. With the admission of Poland, the Czech Republic, and Hungary, a first step of both symbolic significance and strategic implications was made. It was followed, almost in conjunction with the admission on 1 May 2004 of several Central-East European countries to the European Union by a second series of eight more countries on 9 May, namely Bulgaria, Estonia, Lettland, Lithuania, Romania, Slovakia, and Slovenia.

Whether legitimate, inevitable, or unnecessary, the implications of such double enlargement, that of the Alliance itself and that of its principal power, the United States, are important. They are important with regard to the way they change the political landscape of Europe and the way these changes are perceived by the parties concerned.

Such change is probably most important for Russia. Its strategic situation has undergone dramatic modification as a geographic and political retrenchment of historical proportions. It might possibly have mattered somewhat less, had it not been accompanied by a growing expansion of influence on the part of the United States. Indeed, what we have been witnessing ever since the strategic comeback of the United States a few years after World War II is the gradual transformation of an erstwhile almost exclusively maritime power into a full-fledged land power. This process is not just limited to Central-Eastern Europe. As part of the "war against terrorism" after the double attacks in New York and Washington on 11 September 2001, the United States established military bases in Uzbekistan, Tajikistan and Kyrgyzstan, former republics of the Soviet Union and still closely connected with Russia. It is easy to imagine that the latter – and in particular its military establishment – consider such American military presence of unlimited duration as more than unwelcome, if not provocative and disquieting. The only precedent of somewhat similar proportions was Great Britain's erstwhile penetration of the Indian Subcontinent.

To Russia, such territorial expansion of American power represents, after Napoleon and Hitler, the most serious because of the open-ended challenge to its own position as the major land power on the continent, if not the world, that has been the very backbone of its influence and prestige for several centuries. It will therefore be difficult, if not impossible, to persuade Russia's political and military leaders that such penetration and control of the continent by the United States is only for the good of everybody, because it will enhance security for all and promote democracy everywhere.

Not only the Russians but political observers in general must conclude from what can be called "a geopolitical revolution," that with Russia's retrenchment and NATO-American expansion we witness the end of the time-honored system of "balance of power" in Europe. It has simply lost its *raison d'être*. Ever since William III, in 1701, exhorted the Protestant powers to resist France's hegemonic aspirations under Louis XIV, this principle provided the incentive, cleverly used by maritime Britain itself, to fight hegemonic aspirations of any dangerously emerging continental power, be it France, the Habsburg empire, Hitler's "Third Reich," or the Soviet Union. The objective was always the same: to attain a more or less stable equilibrium of power in Europe.[15]

With the arrival of Peter the Great at about the same time as William III, Russia became part of this emerging European system. The disintegration of both the Warsaw Pact and the Soviet Union spelled the demise of this political device. It eliminated well entrenched dividing lines and ended the time-honored zones of influence. Europe became an ever more open, if not open-ended continent, with Russia in retreat and NATO and, more slowly, the EU, in advance. That, in Russian eyes, is far from building a new kind of equilibrium, apt at creating a mutually acceptable, because balanced, framework in which political and security responsibilities can be shared on an equal footing – in other words, a framework within which Russia is given its share of responsibilities and influence to which it still feels entitled.

Now such expectations may seem outdated and Russia's view of itself inflated. In the new area, in which traditional military power recedes ever more behind other forms of power and influence, European security has to be built, in the eyes of NATO and the EU, on institutions like association and integration, and on principles like political democracy and market economy. In other words, irrespective of whether Ukraine, Moldova, and Belarus can and will join NATO – at best a distant prospect

– Europe, so the argument goes, will have to develop new forms of association and cooperation of which Russia can and should be part. Even so, none of these new forms of security building are likely to eliminate the overwhelming presence and influence of the United States. Less friendly observers may be tempted to call this a new (institutionalized) form of hegemony.

Russia's options to counterbalance or neutralize such American preponderance on the continent and beyond are doubly limited. This is true for two reasons: first, because of Russia's own internal, structural, and economic weaknesses, and, second, because, besides full membership with NATO and the EU, the options for wielding decisive and sustained influence are if not non-existent, then certainly highly limited.

It can, of course, be argued that today's Russia is in many ways and on several levels well included, if not integrated, into post-Cold War Europe, certainly more than ever before.[16] Russia is a founding and influential member of the CSCE which has turned, by its own initiative, into OSCE in Budapest in 1994. It has become an often-disputed member of the Council of Europe. Russia participates, though often reluctantly, in NATO's "Partnership for Peace" program and the "Europe-Atlantic Partnership Council" (EAPC), the successor to the over-hastily created North Atlantic Cooperation Council (NACC). The two sides, NATO and Russia, signed on 27 May 1997, the "Founding Act of Mutual Relations, Cooperation and Security" with, as its institutional backbone, a NATO-Russian "Permanent Joint Council."[17]

The EU in turn made a special effort to ensure that Russia not be sidelined by the enlargement process.[18] Among the various steps taken we find a "Partnership and Cooperation Agreement" between the two signed in June 1994 but, because of Chechnya, not ratified until December 1997. The European Council, at its Cologne Summit in June 1999, approved a "Common Strategy on Russia." It foresees four areas of action: consolidation of democracy, the rule of law, and public institutions; integration of Russia into a common European economic and social space; stability and security; and dealing with common challenges on the European continent. This is a vast and ambitious program of cooperation if there ever was one. Its final destination is the European-Russian Strategic Partnership.

We can add to all this and more Russia's active participation in smaller regional institutions.[19] In the South, it is the "Black Sea Cooperation Council," so far, however, of more symbolic than politically substantive value; in the North, it is the "Council of Baltic Sea States" and the "Barents Europe-Arctic Council." Interestingly and significantly, Russia is absent from the various groupings in Central and South

East Europe, except for the so far not overly convincing "Stability Pact."

All these links, institutions, and programs add up to a seemingly strong and resilient network tying Russia into Europe and gradually paving the way towards a new kind of pan-European order of which it is, or will almost be, an integral part. The emphasis here lies, however, on "almost." Those who are (or want to be) optimists, this "almost" signals a passing situation. It implies fluidity more than stagnation, let alone exclusion. In other words, in this view it is a matter of time, not principle, that Russia will eventually become part and parcel of an enlarged NATO/EU-led Europe.

We would argue that, for any foreseeable future, that is ten to fifteen years, such expectation is, at best, wishful thinking, and at worst, insincere or unrealistic. But who knows? In an article in the French newspaper *Le* Monde,[20] and also in other publications, the possibility of Russia being invited to join the Alliance is ventilated. The United States with President Bush has, after a first and surprisingly positive encounter in summer 2001, become again more cautious, if not critical of Russian policy. To be sure, 9/11 has brought the two former rivals together in their fight against terrorism, though reservations on the American side remain as to Moscow's warlike operations in and against rebellious Chechnya. More seriously still is Russia's joining with Germany and France in distancing itsself from America's war in Iraq on the one hand, and repeated, though eventually futile support for Ukraine's former Prime Minister Yanukovich as presidential candidate against the victorious Yushchenko.

Still, Russia remains in the same respects an important interlocutor for the United States, first because of their common interest in controlling and reducing their still huge arsenal of nuclear weapons – some seven thousand on each side – and fissile material; second because of Russia's huge oil and gas reserves that an ever needy United States wants to profit from, and, finally, because of their common or at least partly converging interests in preventing or even solving conflicts in various regions, Central Asia, Afghanistan, the Middle East, and North Korea in particular. But all this remains a far cry from Russia being invited to join NATO.

A sort of counter-argument is given, somewhat provocatively, by a well-known Russian journalist.[21] He argues that, should Russia really be admitted to NATO, this would change radically the latter's very nature. The reason for this is that in such a case, U.S. strategic protection of its European allies would no longer be needed, not just because there would no longer be a potential nuclear armed enemy (Russia), because this former enemy would henceforth provide the kind of strategic protection offered so far by the United States. One can imagine the consequences of such a scenario: the United States leaving Europe and returning to its erstwhile mission as a sea power, Russia in turn advancing if not as a land at least as a nuclear power in charge of Europe's strategic protection, whatever this means in actual political terms.

The Military and the Balkans

No doubt the reality is more complex. Russia's position in and policy towards Europe, in particular towards its "triple West," is far from being clear and predictable. To date, the only European security organization of which Russia is a full participant is the OSCE. And even here Russia's policy has been far from successful and constructive. Russia in fact has, according to various observers, missed a chance to transform this organization into a fully operational and widely accepted pan-European security organization. To be fair, several other important countries, the United States among them, were neither very helpful nor particularly supportive of such a transformation. Still, there existed some potential for improvement and reform.

Today, with some fifty-five participating countries, the OSCE is too big in numbers and too heterogeneous in terms of political outlook and commitment to offer a credible alternative. It remains a useful forum of consultation and, occasionally, delicate but necessary missions nobody else is willing to undertake. But it certainly is not a "security provider." It does not offer a valid framework within which rivaling powers and interests can be properly controlled, possibly assuaged, and hopefully used for the benefit of all parties concerned. If proof for this were needed, it was provided by the last OSCE summit in Istanbul just before the end of the twentieth century. Neither the much labored concept of a "common security" nor the separate agreement with Russia concerning Chechnya has in any way altered, let alone tangibly improved, the overall security situation in Europe in general and in the Balkans in particular.

The two regions just mentioned are relevant in as much as they demonstrate two interrelated problems of particular importance to Russia. The first relates to the role and mission of armed forces, the latter to possibilities and limits of conflict-management in areas of conflict. Even granting that these are highly delicate issues one is tempted to state that Moscow has so far not passed the test in either.

Russia's armed forces are, as officially admitted and generally recognized, in a desolate state. They consider themselves to be the big loser of the Cold War and, as a consequence, the most humiliated element in Russian society. They were ordered to withdraw from what they considered to be the hard-won control of vast parts of Central-Eastern Europe, a security belt of inestimable value, and to give up the position as unquestioned leader of the Warsaw Pact alliance. Such double withdrawal under sometimes humiliating and dire conditions transformed the "Red Army" into a seemingly redundant, socially marginalized part of Russian society. The various attempts to improve this dire condition by way of reforms and readjusting military strategy, have been marred, if not largely discredited by its pitiful operations in Chechnya, not to mention Afghanistan, Georgia, and the Kursk tragedy. Retraction from abroad, humiliation at home and a reduction in size are open wounds. They will heal, if at all, only very painfully and slowly.

Under such trying circumstances, any attempt at serious and lasting military reform is a very demanding undertaking indeed. It is even more so if the ambition remains still alive to stand up against a U.S.-dominated unipolar world and to advocate a multipolar one in which Russia, possibly together with others, insists on being a principal player.[22]

Partly as a consequence of this attitude and partly as a reaction to NATO's enlargement, Russia's military doctrine has shifted since 1992. If in the early years of the newly constituted Russian Federation, the main security threat was seen to come primarily either from the "near abroad," i.e. the former Soviet republics, or indeed from within the Federation itself, this perception shifted toward the classical assumption of a possible attack from the West. This, as recent staff exercises have shown, is no doubt a reaction, however excessive it may appear to Western observers, to NATO enlargement. It found its formal confirmation in the current military doctrine entered into force in April 2000.

When and how this doctrinal change will find its implementation and its reflection in actual hardware on the one side, and a thorough modernization of Russia's armed forces on the other, remains to be seen. It is going to be a difficult and demanding process in any case. The central impulse for its moving ahead comes no doubt from the new strategic concept which the alliance adopted in April 1999 at its fiftieth anniversary and the progress and scope of its further enlargement.

There is little doubt that NATO's military intervention in Kosovo, justified by humanitarian motivations but without formal approval by either the United Nations Security Council or the OSCE, has substantially reinforced the position of those in the Kremlin who hold that military confrontation in Europe has again become a possible scenario.[23] Thus, Article 1.3 of the new military doctrine states that among the causes of destabilizing the military-political situation are "attempts to weaken existing mechanisms for guaranteeing international security, above all the UN and the OSCE," as well as "military force as a means for conducting humanitarian intervention without the sanction of the UN Security Council"[24] Both assertions, the illegality of a non-UN/OSCE-sanctioned military intervention and the unacceptability of "humanitarian reasons" to justify such intervention, are evidently a response to, and refutation of NATO's military intervention in Kosovo.

We know that Moscow's policy towards the former Yugoslavia in general and Serbia in particular has been, to say the least, highly ambivalent and occasionally contradictory. And yet, its intervention with President Milosevic in the latter stage of the war is considered as having been instrumental in bringing the war to an end.

In Russian eyes the Kosovo intervention is seen, rightly or wrongly, as a further proof of NATO's readiness for actions beyond its defense perimeter and expanding its influence, not in the guise of enlargement, but by way of hardly veiled "unilateral military action." Such outreach would not have been possible without the erstwhile reluctant but then active support of the United States. It offered, as did the Gulf War, a most useful testing-ground for its new military hard- and software. Together with the almost simultaneous bombing of Iraq and surreptitious strategic intrusion in Central Asia such actions could not but vindicate the views of those groups in Moscow (and elsewhere) who see in all this an emerging and evermore self-conscious form of American imperialism. It certainly reveals a temptation to either going it, or deciding central strategic issues, alone. As perceptions matter always more than reality, such views ought to be taken seriously.

Moscow's perception of NATO's "humanitarian intervention" in Kosovo falls into the same category. The idea that an alliance, NATO, would go to war not for reasons of strategic interest but to defend human rights, is either not known in Russian strategic thinking or serves merely as a pretext. It does not, as a knowledgeable expert on Russia phrases it, "exist in Russia's scale of political values (*es kommt nicht am eigenen – russisch-politischen – Horizont vor*)."[25] The conclusion from this may therefore be that, unless the Russian political and military leadership can and will broaden this "value horizon" by way of "Europeanizing" or "Westernizing" it, its full-fledged inclusion into Europe would seem difficult. It will remain "of Europe" but not "in Europe."

Such a conclusion may, however, be both too hasty and too simple. Russia's strategic interests can certainly not be measured by its negative reaction against "humanitarian intervention." This is even less so as many observers, this author included, tend to believe that this highly controversial and far from successful

GASTEYGER

intervention is likely not be repeated soon or not at all. Such an increasingly critical appraisal of NATO's Kosovo intervention is gaining ground particularly in those circles which had the difficult task of carrying it out from the air without the necessary support on the ground. "Far from consolidating a consensus behind the idea that military force can be used successfully against egregious violations of human rights," so says the conclusion of a review of General Clark's book *Waging Modern War: Bosnia, Kosovo, and the Future of Combat,* "the Kosovo war seems in fact to have undermined support for humanitarian intervention, even though it helped bring about the fall of Milosevic." General Clark's own conclusion comes close to that some Russian colleagues of his may hold, namely, "We never want to do this again."[26] The upshot of all this, and events in Macedonia in summer 2001 tend to confirm it, is that NATO's determination to demonstrate its willingness, cohesion, and humanitarian commitment "out of area" has, beyond the undoubtedly welcome assistance to many Albanian refugees, raised many more problems that it proposed to solve.

America's war in Iraq is an entirely different matter. We still can only guess, because the issue in question is still ongoing, the impact it will have on Russian military thinking. Compared to the unending but still basically localized fighting in Chechnya the murderous tragedy in Iraq has almost global implications, both in human and in strategic terms. It would therefore be surprising indeed if Russia and its military establishment – both longtime friends and allies of Iraq and its erstwhile leader, Saddam Hussein – were not watching closely the way the US armed forces perform and the lessons they draw from their tragic mission there.

Perspectives

In the end, Russia's policy towards, and role in the wider Europe will, not surprisingly, remain a function of, first, its internal development; second, of the way Russia sees and identifies its national identity, civic or ethnic; and third, on the way the double enlargement process will be handled by NATO and the EU. All these processes are interlinked and interactive. They can be mutually reenforcing but, if not handled properly, they can also be mutually antagonizing. Thus, if the current U.S. administration's predilection for unilateralism gathers momentum and strength, our forecast for a mutually constructive rapprochement tends to become increasingly cautious.

The agenda of possible misinterpretations or in fact tensions on either side is still fairly long. There is President Bush's project for missile defense in space. There is his intention to develop smaller nuclear weapons for bust-bombing caves in the rocky mountains of Eastern Afghanistan that are suspected to be a hide-out of Bin Laden. Linked too, also under the heading of Bush's increasingly controversial "war against international terrorism," is the U.S. military presence in Central Asia and in Georgia, and the ever more costly war in Iraq. To this can be added Washington's doubts about Russia's all too generous assistance to Iran's civil nuclear program with a potentially military dimension. But perhaps most stinging for Russia's self-esteem is the fact that the United States considers itself as the only world power, which in fact it is, relegating its former rival Russia to the second rank class and thus move from the status of an "indispensable" to that of a partner "à la carte."

The EU in turn poses less of a problem for Russia. As mentioned before, President Putin, torn between the ambition of strategic equality with the United States on the one hand and proximity to Europe and the EU on the other has declared their particular interest in the latter. The EU may be on the way to formulating a somewhat more coherent security and defense policy of its own. It may even be able to set up the institutional framework to carry it out. But all this is still a far cry from becoming a strategic partner of Russia, let alone an alternative to the United States.

Perhaps the most serious obstacle to a mutually fruitful and lasting rapprochement between the two parts of Europe, Russia included, is what is rightly called the "systemic asymmetry" between them.[27] Political systems are emanations of tradition and habits. They constitute a complex mixture of geography, history, mentality, and religion. They evolve and change only slowly. This is precisely what is now under way in Central-Eastern Europe and, partly differently, in Russia itself. It turns out to be a much slower process than anticipated in the heydays after the fall of the Berlin Wall. It need not lead to full reunification but hopefully to new forms of association and cooperation. Nor should it be a one-way road, with its only final destination being either Brussels or Washington. Russia, by being serious and consistent with pursuing reforms at home and constructive in building its relations with its "triple West," has every chance of becoming again an indispensable part of what constitutes both European diversity and unity. Then, and only then, the time-honored concept of "balance of power" will become really redundant because it is counterproductive and stands in the way of a truly pan-European security order.

NOTES TO CHAPTER 9

[1] Quoted after "Die Aktualität vermeintlicher Anachronismen," *Osteuropa* no. 4/5 (2001): 618.

[2] See Assen Ignatov, "Europa im russischen Diskurs," *Die neueste Phase einer alten Debatte, Russland in Europa*, (Köln/Weimar/Wien: Böhlau Verlag, 2000), 25 pp.

[3] See *The Current Digest* 53, no. 13 (2001), quoting the Russian newspaper *Noviye Isvestia*, 24 March 2001. See also Heyward Isham, ed., *Russia's Fate Through Russian Eyes* (Boulder: Westview Press, 2001).

[4] Leaving aside the fact that only a tiny minority of the people interviewed knew that Brussels is the seat of the EU.

[5] Vladimir Baranovsky and Alexei Arbatov, "The Changing Security Perspective in Europe," in A. Arbatov, K. Kaiser, and R. Legvold, eds., *Russia and the West: The 21ˢᵗ Century Security Environment* (Armonk and London: M. E. Sharpe, 1999), 45.

[6] Ibid., 53.

[7] See the introduction to the book, cited in note 5, *Russia and the West*, in which the three editors raise some pertinent questions as to where Russia stands, "in or out" of Europe, how it defines its security, and will it address the challenges connected with it.

[8] S. B. Ivanov, Speech delivered at the Thirty-Seventh Conference on Problems of International Security (Munich), 4 February 2001.

[9] See Renée Nevers, "Russia's Strategic Revolution," *Adelphi Paper*, no. 289 (July 1994): 8.

[10] Regarding the pipeline projects, see "Poland Sides with Ukraine," *Moscow News* no. 12 (21-27 March 2001); T. Bagirov, "Russian Oil & Gas Companies Go Global," *International Affairs* (Moscow) 45, no. 6 (1999): 176-188, especially 179.

[11] "Ukraine's Transition Is Unfinished," *International Herald Tribune*, 4 June 2001, 6.

[12] See Adrian Karatnycky, "Ukraine's Orange Revolution," *Foreign Affairs* 84, no. 2 (March-April 2005): 35-53, especially 39.

[13] *The Economist*, 18 June 2005, 25.

[14] Roman Szporluk, *Russia, Ukraine, and the Break-up of the Soviet Union* (Hoover Institution Press, 2000), as reviewed by Mark L. Von Hagen for *The Harvard Review* 13, nos. 1-2 (April 2001): 30.

[15] See Ludwig Dehio, *Gleichgewicht oder Hegemonie* (1948; reprint Darmstadt: Ludwig Dehio Wissenschaftliche Buchgesellschaft, 2000); Henry A. Kissinger, *A World Restored* (New York: Grosset and Dunlap, 1964); Ulrich Schlier, "Der politische Kosmos als Gleichgewichtssystem," *Neue Zürcher Zeitung* no. 5/6 (May 2001): 79.

[16] See John Roper and Peter van Ham, "Redefining Russia's Role in Europe," in Vladimir Georgievich Baranovskii, ed., *Russia and Europe: The Emerging Security Agenda* (Stockholm: Stockholm International Peace Research Institute, and New York: Oxford University Press, 1997), 505.

[17] See *NATO Handbook 1998*.

[18] See amongst others, Margot Light, John Lowenhardt, and Stephen White, "Russian Perspectives on European Security," *European Foreign Affairs Review* no. 5 (2000): 489-505.

[19] See Andrej Zagorski, "Russia and European Institutions," *Russia and Europe*, 520-540, especially 538; and Heinz Timmerman, "Russland und die internationalen europäischen Strukturen," *Russland in Europa*, 199-213.

[20] See the rather speculative reflections by Daniel Vernet, "George Bush fera-t-il entrer la Russie dans l'OTAN," *Le Monde*, 17 July 2001.

[21] A. Pushkov, "Russia and the New World Order," *International Affairs* (Moscow) 46, no. 6 (2000): 11.

[22] See Frank Walter, "Militär- und rüstungspolitische Aspekte der Moskauer Aussenpolitik," *Osteuropa* No. 4/5 (2001): 377-386.

[23] See the views on the possibility of a "great" or "wide-ranging" war in Europe by Sergei Rogov and Alexei Arbatov, quoted in Frank Walter, "Militärreform in Russland," *Osteuropa* no. 7 (2000): 221-246.

[24] Quoted after *Osteuropa-Archiv* no. 7 (2000): 224.

[25] Gerhard Simon, "Russland – eine Kultur am Rande Europas," in *Russland in Europa*, 3. See also the skeptical appraisal of Russia's future as a "middle power" by Alain Besancon, "Thèses sur la Russie passée et présente," *Commentaire 24* no. 94 (2001): 339-354.

[26] Michael Ignatieff, "Chains of Command" (Review of General Wesley Clark's book *Waging Modern War: Bosnia, Kosovo, and the Future of Combat*) in *The New York Review of Books* 48, no. 12 (19 July 2001): 16-19. See also Serge Sur, "The Use of Force in the Kosovo Affair and International Law," *Les notes de l'IFRI* no. 22 (Paris: n.p., 2001).

[27] Werner Weidenfeld, "Zwischen Anspruch und Wirklichkeit – die europäische Integration nach Nizza," *Nizza in der Analyse* (Gütersloh: Bertelsmann Verlag, 2001), 19-49.

HEARTLAND DREAMS
Russian Geopolitics and Foreign Policy
WILLIAM C. WOHLFORTH

Abstract

The popularity of geopolitics among Russians as well as analysts of the international relations of the former Soviet space is noteworthy in that it contradicts large bodies of scholarship that suggest the declining strategic and economic value of territory, and hence predicts declining analytical payoffs to geopolitical theories. This chapter analyzes the resurgence of geopolitical thinking in Russia and finds: 1) that most geopolitical thinking in Russia accepts some version of the "heartland thesis," which attributes great global strategic significance to Russia's size and location; 2) that this theory is an understandable reaction to Russia's historical experience, although it also has the effect of exaggerating the strategic importance of the only dimension of power in which Russia excels; 3) that the theory is wrong; and 4) that it may have had some deleterious effect on Russian policy, and it has clearly distorted experts' and intellectuals' analysis of Russia's interests and prospects in the near and far abroad.

* * *

Geopolitics is in. From Beijing to Delhi, Berlin and Paris, geopolitics is now widely used by statesmen, political analysts, and scholars alike. The precise meaning of geopolitics can vary greatly. Analysts and journalist are prone to use the term as simply a synonym for power politics. But for most, geopolitics implies a geographical imperative that in some way conditions patterns of national politics and international relations. It suggests at a minimum that the geography of states – size, location, topography, natural conditions, resource endowment, and so on – is critical in determining both their historical evolution and their prospects for future development. In the past, scholars of geopolitics expressed this imperative as simple axioms that were supposed to determine the fates of great states over the long run. Today's geopoliticians are more inclined to be careful, expressing the geographical imperative as multivariate and probabilistic (and therefore less easily falsifiable) propositions. Still, at its root, geopolitics posits that location matters, and matters decisively in the long run.

The resurgence of geopolitical approaches is surprising, especially given intellectual developments in the academic study of international affairs in the United States. After all, the analytical value-added of geopolitics varies inversely with the importance of territory in international politics. Yet today, large theoretical and empirical literatures have produced more reasons than ever to conclude that the importance of territory in international security has declined radically over the last half century. In particular, most scholars of international security agree that deterrence devalues the role of territory in providing security for nuclear-armed states, while the rise of nationalism, the internationalization of production, and the post-industrial revolution all conspire to raise the costs and decrease the benefits of territorial conquest.[1] Moreover, a growing literature in economics, comparative politics and international political economy casts serious doubt on the long-term utility to any state's competitive prospects of attaining control over natural resources. While not buying in to recent globalization hype, there are compelling theoretical reasons, backed up by formidable empirical research, that control over natural resources is irrelevant, or even a hindrance, to the creation of a competitive economy.[2] If the international relations or the political economy literature is right, then the relative analytical importance of geopolitical approaches should be declining, not rising.

Nowhere is the current revival of geopolitics more marked than in Russia. Banned in Soviet times as an imperialist-fascist "false science," geopolitics came back to Russia with a vengeance after 1991. Over the past decade, *geopolitika* has been endorsed in a wide range of reputable academic works in the fields of geography, political science, international affairs, and philosophy. Its academic respectability is ratified, for example, by the creation of a Center for Geopolitical Studies at the Russian Academy of Sciences Institute of Geography. More significantly, it is now a part of popular political discourse. Major political figures – including Communist Party leader Gennady Zyuganov – have written lengthy books emphasizing the importance of geopolitics to Russia's future political destiny.[3] Perhaps predictably, Russia's military brass joined the bandwagon as well. Top policymaking generals have penned tomes on geopolitics, retired generals have formed their own centers for geopolitical analysis, and military academies now include the subject in required courses of instruction.[4] Indeed, the Russian government has made a formal commitment of sorts to geopolitics, through the establishment of a permanent Committee on Geopolitical Affairs under the official auspices of the state Duma – the only such body in the world. Since the mid-1990s, official pronouncements on foreign and security policy

WOHLFORTH

have been larded with geopolitical phrases and ideas.

Russia, therefore, is a good test case of the geopolitical revival. If the Russian geopoliticians are right, then much Western scholarship about international affairs is wrong – at least about Eurasia. If Western academics are right about the relative decline in the strategic significance of territory, then Russian geopolitical thought, to the extent that it has any concrete meaning and influence, has merely contributed to Russians' self-delusions about their country's importance to the world.

In this chapter, I conclude that the latter view is probably right. Although it is hard to demonstrate conclusively that geopolitical ideas have concretely affected Russia's strategic choices, the fact that Moscow's elite discourse has so consistently inflated Russia's real capabilities may owe something to the influence of geopolitical notions. Russians' systematic overemphasis of the importance of territory and location, while understandable, may have slowed their adaptation to decline in the 1990s and hindered their ability to face necessary trade-offs between cherished strategic goals. It is important to stress that this is an argument over degrees of emphasis. Territory obviously matters. Strategy must pay heed to the map, and preferably a good topographical map. But policymakers and analysts must not become transfixed by the map to the exclusion of other factors that bear on strategy, as well as critical technological changes that alter the relative importance of space, natural resources, physical transportation and communication routes, and topography. To the extent that their natural fixation on the vast size of their country and its location in central Eurasia has prevented Russians from coming to terms with their real possibilities, geopolitics has served them ill.

I proceed in four sections. First I document the rise of geopolitical thinking in Russia, and make the case that nearly all Russian geopoliticians to a greater or lesser degree buy into some version of the "heartland" concept. Second, I explain the popularity of geopolitical thinking, which owes much to partially correct but ultimately flawed reading of recent history. The third section evaluates the central proposition of current Russian geopolitics concerning the strategic importance of the Eurasian heartland. Fourth, I assess the influence of geopolitical thinking. A superficial case can be made that this mode thinking affected overall policy; a far stronger case can be made for its influence on analysts and commentators, both within Russia and abroad.

Geopolitics Ascendant

The rise of geopolitics in Russia has attracted considerable scholarly attention, much of which has been devoted to the connection between territory and identity.[5] Often missed in this literature is the fact that geopolitics is not just a theory of state formation but is also, indeed primarily, a theory of international relations and foreign policy. When one focuses on the precise theoretical propositions that various geopolitical thinkers put forward, similarities among seemingly disparate analytical schools become apparent.

Russian geopoliticians can be divided into three types: extremists, mainstream intellectuals, and government officials.[6] The writings of neo-Eurasianists, communists, national-patriots, and other "extreme" geopolitical thinkers have attracted the most attention.[7] For them, it is axiomatic that Russia, still occupying most of Eurasia's heartland, is the key to global stability and the geographical pivot of world politics. This is not to say that today's Eurasian geopoliticans all accept the heartland thesis precisely as spelled out by Sir Halford Mackinder. According to Mackinder, the central Eurasian region constituted the pivot of world history because of its location, size, morphology, and resource abundance. Thus, he postulated, "Who Rules East Europe Rules the Heartland; Who rules the Heartland commands the World-Island [Eurasia]; Who rules the World-Island commands the World."[8] In his view, power emanated from the heartland, as witnessed by the perennially expansionist tendencies of the region's empires, because its location and terrain features allowed expansion in all directions yet it was itself invulnerable to attack. One can accept that technological change has rendered some of Mackinder's argument irrelevant, in particular that nuclear weapons do make the heartland vulnerable to attack, but nonetheless hold that political control over the center of Eurasia's landmass is somehow pivotal to world history. And this, it turns out, is just what Russian geopoliticians of nearly all intellectual stripes do in practice.

For most of these people, Russia's geopolitical centrality does not lie in the classic Mackinderian argument centered on the imperative of territorial conquest. Nevertheless, in the end, these analyses universally posit that Russia is the pivot of world politics, owing almost exclusively to its location and size. Russia, they argue, is the pivot of the global balance of power. Many Russian adherents of geopolitics accept Saul Cohen's concept of two geostrategic regions: the maritime world dependent on trade (with the United States as its core), and the Eurasian continental world (where Russia is the core).[9] They focus on two paramount requisites for the maintenance of world order and stability: establishing a clear boundary between Western sea power and Eurasian land power in Europe; and preserving the unity of the heartland. In their view, the United States, as one of the two geostrategic regions, is now the only remaining superpower chiefly because it has been able to achieve its longstanding objective of weakening Russia's hold on the heartland while keeping Eurasia's major powers from pooling their resources. Thus, the boundary between the West and Eurasia has shifted eastward. To date, this boundary is not properly defined. Russia, which controlled most of the Heartland, has shrunk in terms of territory and is currently unable to play the role of balancer in a geopolitically unstable world. A geopolitically imbalanced Eurasia might provoke a universal re-division of the world with its resources and strategic boundaries. In turn, it could imply a protracted period of turbulence and conflict.

Here, different orientations part ways. The more extreme geopoliticans assume that a global, zero-sum clash between the two worlds is inevitable and argue that policy must be directed at strengthening the positions of the continental powers (under Russia's leadership, of course) in preparation for it. Others argue that the prospect of instability in Eurasia induced by Russia's weakness actually creates a common interest with at least some Western powers (excluding, of course, the United States). To avoid a prolonged time of geopolitical troubles, both Russia and its continental partners in Europe and Asia should make joint efforts to stabilize the post-Soviet space. This could restore Russia's historic mission to be the mediator between the European and Asian rimlands and serve as a safeguard against American attempts at worldwide domination. Echoing Mackinder's three heartland axioms, El'giz Pozdnyakov coined his own geopolitical formula: "He who controls the Heartland can exercise effective control over world politics, above all by maintaining a global geopolitical and power balance, without which lasting peace is unthinkable."[10]

In less stark form, the same emphasis on the heartland concept is evident in the writings of more mainstream intellectual geopoliticians.[11] What makes these writings mainstream is their explicit rejection of territorial expansion or any reacquisition of formal sovereignty over former Soviet states and their greater emphasis on constructive relations with the United States as well as the major continental powers in Europe and Asia. Still, they insist that owing mainly to its size and location, Russia will take a, if not the leading role in the creation of a new world geopolitical order. As Sergei Rogov, director of the Russian Academy of Sciences Institute of the United States and Canada, put it, "the Russian Federation, unlike the Soviet Union, cannot pretend to the role of a superpower. But due to the size of its territory and population, as well as its military and scientific potential, and as a great Eurasian power, it can become a leading participant in a multipolar world, playing an active role in resolving problems in which it has an interest."[12]

Both extreme and mainstream geopolitical thinking made inroads in official discourse throughout the 1990s. Indeed, a consistent pattern emerged over the first ten years after the dissolution of the Soviet Union: the more feedback about the decline of Russia's power and prestige mounted, the more official Russian discourse became dominated by geopolitics. The "new political thinking," an unusually explicit paradigm that replaced the Soviets' old modified Leninist approach to international relations, retired from the political scene with Mikhail Gorbachev in December 1991.[13] It was replaced for a brief two-year period by a clearly articulated liberal worldview, personified by Foreign Minister Andrei Kozyrev, who sought "alliance-like" relations with the West. However, Kozyrev-style Westernism never achieved the hegemonic position formerly occupied by the new thinking. Immediately it contended with powerful intellectual challenges from geopolitical realism and a more nationalistic strain of Realpolitik.[14] By 1993, the liberal paradigm had been officially abandoned by the Foreign Ministry and the Kremlin, replaced by a mildly nationalistic Realpolitik.[15] By the middle of the decade, new thinking's influence matched Gorbachev's, explicit international liberalism was abandoned even by those who took liberal stands on domestic issues, and the overwhelming bulk of the discourse was couched in soft or hard versions of geopolitical realism.

It was the dominance of this discourse that caused many analysts to argue that a consensus on foreign policy had emerged within the Russian elite by the mid-1990s. The impression was strengthened by the appointment of the widely respected and bureaucratically skilled Yevgeny Primakov to replace Andrei Kozyrev as foreign minister, and it was further consolidated during Primakov's tenure as Prime Minster. And, by nearly all accounts, the consensus held during Vladimir Putin's premiership and presidency – at least, that is, until 11 September 2001. Of course, the convergence toward geopolitical language to describe foreign policy hid major differences of emphasis, especially between "old" and "new" security threats. But compared to most other major capitals, the prevalence of geopolitical language in official Moscow remained striking.

While official documents and pronouncements do not explicitly articulate the heartland thesis, they accept its basic premises. In the first six months of his presidency, President Putin signed several documents fundamental to the new Russian state: its official concept of national security, its foreign policy concept, and its defense doctrine.[16] These documents reflected the admixture of old and new. But they were firmly in line with the 1990s consensus in that they furthered the key assumptions that had guided policy since Primakov's heyday:

- Russia is not a regional power. It is a "great Eurasian power" and a temporarily wounded world power. Restoration of Russia's rightful status is a central goal.
- Russia must work to establish a multipolar world in union with China and India and perhaps Germany and France as well. Its location in Eurasia's heartland places it in a central position to counterbalance U.S. power.
- Although the formal sovereignty of the other former Soviet republics should be respected, Russia's interests demand a sphere of influence in the former Soviet territory.

These three central principles of Russian foreign policy are all linked. Russia's claim to be a world power lies mainly in its location and size. Its central role in countering American unipolarity is mainly the result of its position, not its other capabilities. And its dominance in the post-Soviet space is necessary mainly in order to remain a geostrategic, and geoeconomic, bridge between Europe and Asia – the presumed key to its status as global balancer and world power.

Explanation

Whence this Russian fascination with geopolitics? A thousand years of history go a long way toward answering this question. As Dominic Lieven puts it, "The demands of international power politics and of membership of the European and then global system of great powers were of overwhelming importance in Russian history. More probably than any other single factor they determined the history of modern Russia."[17] Muscovy, Russia, and the Soviet Union lived in tough geopolitical neighborhoods, and their chief response to the threatening environments they found themselves in was to acquire and hold territory. The policy worked, though at great cost to Russia. After all, Russia is by some measures the most successful imperial enterprise in history. Surpassed in size only by the British and Mongol empires, Russia and its Soviet successor proved far more durable than either one. It retained its peak territorial extent longer than any other empire, and for most of the last four hundred years it has been the largest polity on earth.[18] Moreover, both St. Petersburg and Moscow were hugely successful as great powers, playing major roles in European and world politics for the three centuries after 1700. For much of Russian and Soviet history, territory did bring prestige and security. The Russian and Soviet states were in some ways bureaucratic machines for the acquisition and retention of land. It is hardly surprising that a people with this history would be attracted to geopolitical modes of thought.

One consequence of Russia's past as a territory-conquering machine is that it remains the world's largest state. Space, location, nuclear weapons, and superpower pedigree are the only plausible sources of Russia's claim to great power status. And only on the geopolitical dimension does Russia truly stand out. This may well help explain the appeal of geopolitical arguments that magnify the global significance of precisely this dimension. Russia is certainly not the first declining state to try to maximize the apparent value of things it still possesses in abundance.

Moreover, the popularity of geopolitics derives in part from superficially plausible lessons that many Russians have drawn from their recent experience. Most of the new players in Moscow's foreign policy game, including Vladimir Putin, experienced the agony of the Soviet Union's last years far from the corridors of power. Nevertheless, many say that they have learned a powerful lesson from the Soviet Union's experience that international politics is a highly competitive realm. Claiming to be pragmatic, unromantic defenders of the national interest, they tend to be critical of Soviet policy in the Cold War for having overextended itself and ultimately weakened the country. However, they are united in the conviction that their Western-oriented predecessors bungled the management of Soviet decline by making far too many concessions based on a mistaken faith in the positive-sum, cooperative nature of contemporary international politics. Their discourse resembles a laundry list of the "myths of empire" excoriated by Western scholars (if not policymakers): belief in the prevalence of bandwagoning in world politics, the possibility of falling dominos, the vital importance of a reputation for power in order to maintain the country's status and internal and external security, and a strongly zero-sum conception of international security and economics.[19] By explicitly rejecting those precepts, and implicitly buying-in to Western academic notions, they argue, Gorbachev allowed himself be taken for a geopolitical ride by less romantic and more savvy Western policymakers.[20]

More specifically, many contemporary Russian geopoliticans contend, the global importance of territory in general and the heartland in particular was demonstrated by the retraction of Soviet power from the river Elbe 1,500 kilometers east to the Eurasian steppe after 1989. From a relatively small economic base, the Soviet Union had formed one of two poles in a bipolar system. Geography is an important port of the explanation for how Moscow managed to pull off this feat. If one measures international prestige by how much attention is paid to a given state, then the Soviet Union obtained immense prestige by virtue of its polar status. And that status was coterminous with the expansion of Soviet power to the Central European portion of Mackinder's heartland after 1945, and its withdrawal after 1989. This shift in territorial sovereignty or suzerainty brought an end to the forty-year-old structure of international political and utterly transformed the strategic desiderata of every major power and many minor ones. The great transformation of world politics after 1989, about which intellectuals have spilt so much ink, is due to the simple fact that the Russians decided not to spill blood to retain control over territory. If ever an event advertised the importance of control over territory to world politics it was the decline and fall of the Soviet Union.

Evaluation

It is not surprising that people who have gone through this experience should think geopolitically. Nor is it any wonder that they tend to see the policies of other states – notably the United States – as guided by geopolitical precepts, especially when prominent Western analysts such as Zbigniew Brzesinki discuss U.S. foreign policy in precisely these terms.[21]

But are the specific geopolitical ideas that are so popular in Russia compelling on analytical grounds? Unfortunately for Russia's current prospects as a world power, the answer is no. The centrality of the Soviet Union's territorial power to the rise and fall of bipolarity does not ratify the heartland thesis that is so central to so much Russian geopolitical thought. The fact that the Soviet Union was the "pivotal" power in the Cold War does not mean that Russia necessarily has a pivotal role to play in creating a new post-Cold War balance of power. For the centrality of the Soviet Union to the Cold War, and its critical role in bringing bipolarity to an end, are explained by standard balance of power theory.

The distinctive feature of the postwar distribution of power was that one state, the Soviet Union, occupied a peacetime position of near-dominance on the Eurasian continent. It was this reality that gave the Cold War its particular cast – the strength, depth, and stability of NATO, as well as the eventual formation of a worldwide coalition of all great powers against the Soviet Union. Balance of power theory predicts that states will take action (building up their power internally or creating alliances) to prevent any state from being able to conquer the rest. When all states are far from posing such a threat, the balance of power imperative is weak, since it is not obvious whom to counterbalance. But when one state is on the verge of attaining military dominance, it will face the opposition of all other major states in the system. This condition was historically only obtained during major wars, except after World War II, which ended with the Red Army in the center of Europe and the Soviet Union plausibly in a position eventually to subdue all the major power centers on the Western and (less likely but still imaginable) the eastern reaches of Eurasia. As a result the Soviet Union soon faced a very tight balance-of-power constraint that shaped world politics until Gorbachev ended it by inadvertently precipitating the Red Army's peaceful decampment from East-Central Europe.

The real lesson from the Soviet Union's Cold War experience, as well as the end of the Cold War, is that the balance of power works in Eurasia.[22] States that acquire the capability to take and hold enough valuable Eurasian territory will scare other states into counterbalancing. Location does matter, in that contiguity enhances the capability to seize territory and eliminate the sovereignty of rivals. Thus, the Soviet Union generated a big counterbalancing effect from a comparatively small economy. The result was truly to make Moscow the center of the Cold War international system, and to create the conditions for the institutionalized presence of American military power on Eurasia's rimlands. But this experience does not ratify Pozdniakov's revision of Mackinder: "He who controls the Heartland can exercise effective control over world politics, above all by maintaining a global geopolitical and power balance, without which lasting peace is unthinkable." That formulation radically overestimates Russian capabilities in today's international system, just as it radically underestimates the difficulty of fashioning a multipolar counterbalance to American power today.

Ironically, geography and balance-of-power theory actually favor U.S. global dominance and a divided Eurasia, the very state of affairs Russian geopoliticians abhor. America's "hyperpower" is offshore, which means that it is less threatening to the sovereign security of other major states. Geography is a material explanation for reduced threat perceptions. As Stephen M. Walt notes, " . . . states that are nearby pose a greater threat than those that are far away. Other things being equal, states are more likely to make their alliance choices in response to nearby powers than in response to those that are distant."[23] Thus, the United States can acquire far more relative material capabilities than the Soviet Union, Russia, or any other Eurasian power ever had, without sparking a counterbalance. All other great powers besides the United States are clustered in and around Eurasia. Distance reduces the salience of American unipolarity, while proximity maximizes salience of the capabilities of the other great powers vis-à-vis each other. They are much more likely to have aspirations and gripes regarding each other than regarding the distant unipolar power. Attempts on the part of individual states to balance via internal efforts are likely to spark local counterbalancing – either through compensatory internal efforts, regional alliances, or alliances with the United States in the classic "checkerboard" pattern – before they substantially constrain the United States.

Effect

The upshot is that Russian geopoliticans' affection for their version of the heartland thesis is misleading simply on standard balance-of-power grounds. The use of old-fashioned territorial power is the *worst* way to try to fashion a Eurasian counterbalance to the United States for it is the most likely to spark strong balance-of-power dynamics in Eurasia, which only favors the current American global position as the security manager of Eurasia's eastern and Western rims. Russia's central location and immense size offer it *no* particular advantage in fashioning a new Eurasian coalition against the United States. On the contrary, its position in the heartland means that overly aggressive efforts on its part will only push the rimland powers closer to each other and/or the United States.

The ideas are wrong, but so what? Have they influenced policy? It is impossible to make this case conclusively even with better evidence than is currently available concerning Russia's strategic choices. The degree to which Moscow has followed a coherent policy at all is debatable. And the degree to which the policies it has adopted have truly been shaped by geopolitical notions is also subject to debate. The case is circumstantial, but it is solid enough to be taken seriously. For one thing, rhetoric does matter, even if subtly. This is especially true if words and deeds match up. In the mid to late 1990s, official speeches, interviews, documents, and – at least superficially – behavior all fitted a geopolitical logic: foster global multipolarity by securing regional dominance.

The overall pattern of policy in the near abroad was superficially consistent with the geopolitical imperative of retaining regional hegemony. Most notable were strategies of geopolitical and geoeconomic denial. The imperative to secure regional unipolarity from a relatively weak economic base appeared to lend Russian policy in the near abroad a strong geopolitical cast. Many analysts viewed Russian policy as guided by a consistent logic of maintaining dominance over strategic affairs, trade and transportation corridors, and, most notably, petroleum resources in the former

Soviet space. Hence, the Kiplingesque geopolitical aims: prevent the Central Asian states from establishing a corridor to the Indian Ocean (the Tedjen-Seraks railway); foil the possible transportation axis connecting Turkmenistan and Uzbekistan via Afghanistan and Pakistan; oppose the Trans-Eurasian Corridor (the restoration of the "Great Silk Road"); undermine the Europe-Caucasus-Central Asia (TRASECA) transportation corridor; and, most notably, oppose the Baku-Ceyhan pipeline project. Russian policy in the near abroad could be seen as being guided by classical geopolitical objectives: to prevent the emergence of a "new rimland" along the southern reaches of the post-Soviet space and in southeastern Europe, which would have the effect of transforming Russia intro a peripheral north-eastern Eurasian state, located off the main trade routes, unable to bring to fruition its full geopolitical potential. A large specialists' literature documents Moscow's costly use of its remaining natural resource and economic assets to purchase regional predominance.[24] In some cases, economic interests appeared to trump geopolitical influence buying, undermining the argument. But in other cases, government officials demonstrated a willingness to exchange potential wealth and/or state rents for influence over neighbors in the near abroad. And Russia showed a periodic willingness to use military power to retain influence over neighbors' strategic choices, Georgia is a prominent example, and retain some access to the Soviet Union's former defense infrastructure.[25]

At the global level, Moscow presented itself as a, if not the key organizer of a "multipolar" coalition to rein-in US power. Primakov's tenure at the helm of Russian foreign policy inaugurated a parade of ostensibly anti-U.S. diplomatic combinations: the "European troika" of France, Germany, and Russia; the "special relationship" between Germany and Russia; the "strategic triangle" of Russia, China and India; and, most recently, the "strategic partnership" between China and Russia.

Even more than in the case of near-abroad policy, it is possible to question the geopolitical impulse behind and ultimate significance of Russia's efforts to foster a multipolar world order. Moscow's real diplomatic behavior bears scant relation to the geopoliticians' dreams of a reordering of the global power structure. The chorus of punditry from the Kosovo crisis in 1999 to the Iraq War in 2003 concerning "counter-alliances," "axes," "ententes," "triangle diplomacy," and "strategic realignments" misses the real news. At most, these diplomatic combinations occasionally succeeded in frustrating U.S. policy initiatives when the expected costs of doing so remain conveniently low. At the same time, Moscow and the other major capitals demonstrated a willingness to cooperate with the United States periodically on strategic matters and especially in the economic realm. This general tendency toward periodic bandwagoning with the United States when doing so meets each country's specific interests was the norm before 9/11 and has only become more pronounced afterwards.

Russia's counterbalancing rhetoric masked a far subtler policy. Even the most pragmatic leaders face incentives to play on anti-unipolar resentment for domestic audiences. And if the main objectives are local, coordination among regional powers can have the attractive potential side benefit of enhancing bargaining power vis-à-vis Washington. It can thus pay to talk up the counterbalancing potential of any prominent coordination effort among major powers that excludes the United States if only as a signal in an ongoing bargaining game. But the strategy of spinning limited regional policy coordination as counterbalancing U.S. hegemony has strict limits. Even before 9/11, no state wanted to volunteer to be the next Soviet Union – that is, to maneuver itself into a situation in which it will have contend with the focused enmity of the United States, whereupon superior resources would largely determine the outcome. At a more subtle level, relying on this strategy has the potential to backfire by reinforcing a country's need for allies and lack of great power status, with potentially harmful consequences domestically, regionally, and in direct dealings with Washington. Russia, like China, wants to remind America that it has other options but not at the cost of talking down their own capabilities or foreclosing a good arrangement with Washington.

Still, Russia's multipolar policy consumed a great deal of the foreign ministry's and the president's energy, most notably during Putin's first year in office. The rhetoric surrounding it was loud and consistent. And the policy of wooing other continental great powers like China, India, France, and Germany was supplemented by a far more controversial strategy of courting regional U.S. adversaries like Iran and Iraq. While the overall policy could be explained partly by reference to a number of potential near-term benefits – a diplomatic bargaining ploy, a popular move with domestic constituencies, a result of incoherent policymaking institutions, an effort driven by commercial interest and the defense-industrial complex – it was consistent enough to suggest a mild version of the geopolitical heartland logic at work. That is, the policy reflected a belief that Russia could serve as a key broker in fashioning policy coalitions, not power-aggregating alliances, among major Eurasian states in opposition to the United States. Although this strategy was a shadow of the strong geopolitical language used to describe it, its outlines did correspond to the geopolitical premises that inform so much recent Russian thinking.

Conclusion

States are always prone to stress the global importance of things in which they stand out. Scandinavians see national greatness in clean streets and generous foreign aid. France stresses culture. China makes much of a large population and growing economy. Russians obsess on vastness and location. The temptation to tout one's advantages is especially great for declining states and empires. But succumbing to that temptation is not without costs. In Russia's case, the geopolitical fixation on territory and location may have fed numerous systematic and ultimately costly biases.

In the near abroad, a growing number of analysts argue that Moscow overestimated the strategic value of political, economic and military predominance, as well as the economic and strategic value of formal control over natural resources, and trade and transportation routes. Geopolitical mindsets may also have helped trick some Russians into seeing weak and unstable local and regional actors as unitary "states" capable of taking decisive action. This may help account for the stress on neighboring regimes' geostrategic orientation as opposed to their chronic weakness and instability, as well as the clearly exaggerated role outside powers like Turkey were once thought capable of and interested in playing in the region.

In the far abroad, the idea that Moscow could take the leading role in fashioning a pan-Eurasian counterbalance to U.S unipolarity, even if viewed as grand policy coordination rather than power aggregation, appears to have reflected an overestimation of Russian capabilities. Seven years after its inauguration, the "Primakov Doctrine" had few identifiable "geopolitical" results in world politics. Moreover, if local hegemony and global multipolarity were each daunting objectives, the combination was formidable indeed. Such an agenda *only* seems plausible if one gazes at a map without consulting other indicators of power. If one thinks of power as economic might, there would be little reason to think that Russia's $500 billion economy should be a linchpin player between America's and the EU's roughly nine trillion dollars each, on the one hand, and Japan's and China's $4.5 trillion apiece, on the other.

Geopolitical terminology also arguably contributed to analysts' hyperbole as well. Describing the scramble for Caspian resources as a new "great game," makes for good copy, but it is highly misleading. Behind the geopolitics of yore was hardheaded thinking about how best to position one's state for a possible great-power war to the finish. Whatever value one might want to attach to the acquisition of ownership or control over the transportation of natural resources today, they can have scant bearing on the outcome of a clash between nuclear-armed states. Describing the efforts of Putin, Jiang, and Chirac to rein-in U.S. unilateralist impulses on missile defense or Iraq in terms of "axes" and "triangles" that will result in a geopolitical shift to "multipolarity" radically misinterprets the real stakes at issue.

Needless to say, excellent scholarly work is being conducted under the rubric of geopolitics, and a necessary reintegration of geography in the study of international security and political economy is underway.[26] But the classics of geopolitics concerned the expansion of territorial states in the industrial era. They are less useful for a declining state in an era of globalization and the information revolution, to use hackneyed but unavoidable phrases.

Vladimir Putin came into office stressing the economic and institutional limits to Russia's power but at the same time he reinvigorated the foreign policy agenda bequeathed to him by his predecessors. He then used 9/11 as a pretext for jettisoning important parts of the old agenda that has been so insistently boosted by Russia's large contingent of geopolicians.[27] The result was minor contribution Russia's reemergence as a more capable great power. Governmental capabilities today reside mainly in the ability to tap money, and lots of it. The Russian government would need a *budget* about the size of the country's current national *economy* to be a kind of global player some Russian geopoliticians imagine it now is. Those kinds of funds do not come from rent-seeking oligarchs or natural resource monopolies. They come from the real resource base for powerful governments today – a large and prosperous middle class. Seeking to counterbalance a country with an economy eighteen times larger and decades more advanced while working feverishly to route oil and gas pipelines and control trade corridors is unlikely to contribute much to the emergence of masses of wealthy Russians to tax. And if Russia's great Eurasian neighbor to the East continues to foster ever more millions of enriched Chinese to tax, Russia's cadre of geopoliticians may have cause to rue the hours spent poring over Mackinder and marveling at the space their country takes on a map of Eurasia.

NOTES TO CHAPTER 10

[1] For concise reviews, see S. G. Brooks, *Producing Security: Multinational Corporations, Globalization and the Changing Calculus of Conflict* (Princeton: Princeton University Press, 2005); Robert Jervis, *American Foreign Policy in a New Era* (London: Routledge, 2005); and Stephen Van Evera, *Causes of War: Structures of Power and the Roots of International Conflict* (Ithaca: Cornell University Press, 1999).

[2] See, for examples of this literature, Leonard Wantchtekon, "Why do Resource Abundant Countries have Authoritarian Governments?" New York University, unpublished manuscript (February 2002); and Adam Pzeworski, et. al., *Democracy and Development: Political Institutions*

and Well-Being in the World, 1950-1990 (Cambridge: Cambridge University Press, 2000).

[3] Gennady A. Ziuganov, *Geografiia pobedy : osnovy rossiiskoi geopolitiki* [The geography of victory: Foundations of Russian geopolitics](Moscow: [s.n.] 1997). Other devotees include LDP leader Vladimir Zhirinovskii, *Geopolitika i russkii vopros* [Geopolitics and the Russian Question](Moskva: Galeriia, 1998), and LDP Duma deputy (and chair of the Duma Committee on Geopolitical Affairs) Aleksei Mitrofanov, *Shagi novoi geopolitiki* [Steps toward a new geopolitics](Moscow: Russkii vestnik, 1997).

[4] A good example is Lt. Gen. Lenoid Ivashov, engineer of the Pristina Airport grab, until recently the defense ministry's director for international co-operation, and currently vice-president of the Academy of Geopolitical Problems. L.G. Ivashov, *Rossiia i mir na poroge novogo tysiacheletiia: global'nye vyzovy, novye realii i starye ugrozy* [Russia and the world on the eve of the new millennium: global challenges, new realities, and old threats] (Moscow: [s.n.] 1997).

[5] See for example, Mark Bassin, "Russia Between Europe and Asia: The Ideological Construction of Geographical Space," *Slavic Review* 50, no. 1 (1991): 1-17.

[6] An excellent overall review is Andrei P. Tsygankov, "Mastering space in Eurasia: Russian Geopolitical Thinking after the Soviet Break-up," *Communist and Post-Communist Studies* 36, no. 1 (2003): 35, 101-127

[7] The best example here is Aleksandr Dugin. See Dugin, *Osnovy geopolitki*, [Fundamentals of geopolitics] fourth ed. (Moscow; Arktogeia, 2000), available at http://arctogaia.com/public/osnovygeo/. For a general discussion, see Andrei Tsygankov, "Hard-line Eurasianism and Russia's Contending Geopolitical Perspectives," *East European Quarterly* 32, no. 2 (1998): 315-334.

[8] Halford J. Mackinder, *Democratic Ideas and Reality: A Study in the Politics of Reconstruction* (New York: Henry Holt, 1919), 186, emphasis omitted.

[9] Saul B. Cohen, *Geography and Politics in a World Divided* (New York: Random House, 1963). See especially, Dugin, *Osnovy geopolitki* [Fundamentals of geopolitics].

[10] El'giz Abdulovich Pozdniakov, *Geopolitika* [Geopolitics](Moscow: Progress, 1995).

[11] For example, Vladimir Razuvayev, *Geopolitika postsovetskogo prostranva* [Geopolitics of the post-Soviet space] (Moscow: Institut Evropy, 1993); V. Kudrov, *Mesto Novoi Rossii v Mire* [New Russia's place in the world](Moscow: Institut Europy, 1994); Konstantin Sorokin, "Geopolitika Sovremennogo Mira i Rossiya," [The geopolitics of the contemporary worls and Russia] *Politicheskie Issledovaniya* [Political studies] no. 1 (1995).

[12] S. Rogov, "Kontory Rossiiskoy geopolitikoi," [Contours of Russian geopoitics] *Nezavisimaia gazeta—stsenarii* [The independent newspaper-scenarios] 3 (1998): 5

[13] A good primary source providing a snapshot of the debate in this period is El'giz A. Pozdniakov, ed., *Natsianl'nye interesy: teoriia i praktika (sobornik statei)* [National interests: theory and practice (collected essays)](Moscow: IMEMO, 1991).

[14] For Kozyrev's views, see "Russia: A Chance for Survival," *Foreign Affairs* (Spring 1992): 1-16; Interviews with *Nezavisimaia gazeta*, 1 April 1992, 1, 4, and *Izvestiia*, 30 June 1992, 3; Kozyrev, "Preobrazhenie ili kafkianskaia metamorfoza?" [Transformation or Kafkaesque metamorphosis?] *Nezavismiaia gazeta* [Independent newspaper], 20 August 1992, 1, 4. A good sampling of the distribution of views in the period is provide by the Foreign Ministry Conference on "A Transformed Russia in a New World," reported in *International Affairs* (Moscow), April-May 1992.

[15] The Foreign Ministry published its revised foreign policy concept in December 1992, and submitted it to the Duma in March 1993. See "Foreign Policy Concept of the Russian Federation," in *Foreign Broadcast Information Service—Daily Report: USSR*: 93-37, 25 March 1993, 1-20.

[16] The most recent drafts of these documents are available at the Security Council's website: http://www.scrf.gov.ru/Documents/Documents.htm.

[17] Dominic Lieven, *Empire: The Russian Empire and its Rivals* (London: John Murray, 2000), ix.

[18] Rein Taagepera, "Expansion and Contraction Patterns of Large Polities: Context for Russia," *International Studies Quarterly* 41, no. 3 (September 1997): 475-504

[19] Jack Snyder, *Myths of Empire: Domestic Politics and International Ambition* (Ithaca: Cornell University Press, 1991), traces such myths to military and industrial elites who profit by expansionism. A comprehensive review of Russia's national interest debate in this period is provided by Hannes Adomeit, "Russia as 'Great Power' in World Affairs: Image and Reality," *International Affairs* (London) 71, no. 1 (1999): 35-68.

[20] For an excellent analysis of this critique, see Vladislav Zubok, "Gorbachev and the End of the Cold War: Different Perspectives on the Historical Personality," in William C. Wohlforth, ed., *Cold War Endgame: Oral History, Analysis, Debates* (University Park: Penn State University Press, 2003).

[21] See Zbigniew Brzezinski, *The Grand Chessboard: American Primacy and its Geostrategic Imperatives* (New York: Basic Books, 1997).

[22] Ibid. Brzezinski actually accepts this view, which is why his use of the terminology of geopolitics is so misleading. He notes that "Geopolitics has moved from the regional to the global dimension, which preponderance over the entire Eurasian continent serving as the central basis for global primacy" (39). This is simply a restatement of standard balance of power theory. For an empirical study that shows that if the balance of power works anywhere, it works against centrally located landpowers like Russia, see Jack S. Levy and William R. Thompson, "Hegemonic Threats and Great-Power Balancing in Europe, 1495-1999," *Security Studies* 14, no. 1 (2005): 1-31.

[23] Stephen Walt, *The Origins of Alliances* (Ithaca: Cornell University Press, 1987), 23.

[24] A superb review is Douglas Blum, "Globalization and the Caspian Region," in *Succession and Long-Term Stability in the Caspian Region* (Cambridge: BCSIA, 2000).

[25] An excellent discussion is Pavel Baev, "Russia Refocuses its Politics in the Southern Caucasus," John F. Kennedy School of Government, Caspian Studies Program, Working Paper No. 1 (2001).

[26] A noteworthy example is the work of sociologist Randall Collins, who used a geopolitical theory to predict the collapse of the Soviet Union in 1980, and the stability of the Russian Federation in 1991. See Randall Collins, *Weberian Sociological Theory* (Cambridge: Cambridge University Press, 1986); and Randall Collins and David Waller, "The Geopolitics of Ethnic Mobilization: Some Theoretical Projections for the Old Soviet Bloc," in George H. Moore ed., *Legacies of the Collapse of Marxism* (Fairfax: George Mason University Press, 1994).

[27] For an analysis, see William C. Wohlforth, "Russia," in Aaron L. Friedberg and Richard J. Ellings, eds., *Strategic Asia 2002-3: Asian Aftershocks* (Seattle: National Bureau of Asian Research, 2003) .

BIBLIOGRAPHY

Abdelal, Rawi. *National Purpose in the World Economy: Post-Soviet States in Comparative Perspective*. Ithaca, NY: Cornell University Press, 2001.

Abernethy, D.A. *The Dynamics of Global Dominance: European Overseas Empires 1415-1980*. New Haven, CT: Yale University Press, 2000.

Ashwin, Sarah and Simon Clarke. *Trade Unions and Industrial Relations in Post-Communist Russia*. New York: Palgrave, 2002.

Åslund, Anders *How Russia Became a Market Economy*. Washington, D.C.: Brookings Institution, 1995.

Barkey, K. and M. von Hagen, eds. *After Empire: Multiethnic Societies and Nation-Building: The Soviet Union and the Russian, Ottoman, and Habsburg Empires*. Boulder, CO: Westview, 1997.

Bermeo, Nancy, ed. *Liberalization and Democratization: Change in the Soviet Union and Eastern Europe*. Baltimore, MD: Johns Hopkins University Press, 1992.

Brovkin, Vladimir. "The Emperor's New Clothes: Continuity of Soviet Political Culture in Contemporary Russia," *Problems of Post-Communism* (March/April 1996): 21-28.

Bunce, Valerie. *Subversive Institutions: The Design and the Destruction of Socialism and the State*. (Cambridge, UK: Cambridge University Press, 1999.

Campos, Nauro F., "Context is Everything: Measuring Institutional Change in Transition Economies." Washington, D.C., World Bank Policy Research Paper No. 2269, January 2000.

Clayton, Anthony. *Frontiersmen: Warfare in Africa since 1950*. London: UCL Press, 1999.

Colton, Timothy J. *Transitional Citizens: Voters and What Influences Them in the New Russia*. Cambridge, MA: Harvard University Press, 2000.

Dawisha, Karen and Bruce Parrott, eds. *The End of Empire? The Transformation of the USSR in Comparative Perspective*. Armonk, NY: M. E. Sharpe, 1997.

Dibb, Paul. *The Soviet Union: The Incomplete Superpower*. Urbana: University of Illinois Press, 1986.

Doyle, Michael. *Empires*. Ithaca, NY: Cornell University Press, 1986.

Duverger, M., ed. *Le Concept d'Empire*. Paris: Presses Universitaires de France, 1980.

Easter, Gerald M. *Reconstructing the State: Personal Networks and Elite Identity in Soviet Russia*. Cambridge, UK: Cambridge University Press, 2000.

Ekiert, Grzegorz and Stephen E. Hanson, eds. *Capitalism and Democracy in Central and Eastern Europe: Assessing the Legacy of Communist Rule.* Cambridge, UK: Cambridge University Press, 2003.

Elster, John, Claus Offe, and Ulrich K. Preuss, *Institutional Design in Post-Communist Societies: Rebuilding the Ship at Sea.* Cambridge, UK: Cambridge University Press, 1998.

European Bank for Reconstruction and Development (EBRD), *Transition Report 1999: Ten Years of Transition.* London: EBRD, November 1999.

Feldbrugge, Ferdinand and Robert Sharlet, eds., *Public Policy and Law in Russia: In Search of a Unified Legal and Political Space.* Leiden, The Netherlands: Martinus Nijhoff, 2005.

Fieldhouse, D.K. *The West and the Third World.* Oxford, UK: Blackwell, 1999.

Fish, M. Steven. *Democracy Derailed in Russia: The Failure of Open Politics.* New York: Cambridge University Press, 2005.

————. *Democracy from Scratch.* Princeton, NJ: Princeton University Press, 1995.

Frye, Timothy. *Brokers and Bureaucrats: Building Market Institutions in Russia.* Ann Arbor: University of Michigan Press, 2000.

Gaddy, Clifford G., and Barry Ickes. "Russia's Virtual Economy," *Foreign Affairs* 77, no. 5 (September/October 1998): 53-67.

Glinski, Dmitri and Peter Reddaway. "What Went Wrong in Russia?: The Ravages of 'Market Bolshevism'," *Journal of Democracy* 10, no. 2 (April 1999): 19-34.

Gritsenko, N. N., V. A. Kadeikina, and E. V. Makukhina, *Istoriya profsoyuzov Rossii (History of the Russian Trade Unions).* Moscow: Akademiya truda i sotsial'nykh otnoshenii, 1999.

Hellman, Joel. "Winners Take All: The Politics of Partial Reform in Postcommunist Transitions," *World Politics* 50, no. 2 (January 1998): 203-234.

Hellman, Joel, Geraint Jones, and Daniel Kaufmann, "'Seize the Day, Seize the State': State Capture, Corruption and Influence in Transition," Policy Research Working Paper No. 2444. Washington, D.C.: World Bank, 2000.

Hendley, Kathryn, ed. *Remaking the Role of Law: Commercial Law in Russia and the CIS.* Huntington, NY: Juris Publishing, 2006.

Herrera, Yoshiko M. *Imagined Economies: The Sources of Russian Regionalism.* Cambridge, UK: Cambridge University Press, 2005.

Hough, Jerry F. and Merle Fainsod. *How the Soviet Union is Governed.* Cambridge, MA: Harvard University Press, 1979.

Huskey, Eugene. *Presidential Power in Russia*. Armonk, NY: M. E. Sharpe, 1999.

International Monetary Fund. *Staff Country Reports on Poland, Russian Federation, and Ukraine*. Washington, D.C.: International Monetary Fund.

Johnson, Juliet. *A Fistful of Rubles: The Rise and Fall of the Russian Banking System*. Ithaca, NY: Cornell University Press, 2000.

Johnson's Russia List.

Jordan, Pamela. *Defending Rights in Russia: Lawyers, the State, and Legal Reform in the Post-Soviet Era*. Vancouver: University of British Columbia Press, 2005.

Kappeler, Andreas. *The Russian Empire*. Harlow: Longman, 2001.

Karatnycky, Adrian, Alexander Motyl, and Charles Graybow, eds. *Nations In Transit 1998: Civil Society, Democracy and Markets in East Central Europe and the Newly Independent States*. Washington, D.C.: Freedom House, 1998.

Klebnikov, Paul. *Godfather of the Kremlin: Boris Berezovsky and the Looting of Russia*. New York: Harcourt, 2000.

Kitschelt, Herbert, Zdenka Mansfeldova, Radoslaw Markowski, and Gábor Tóka, *Post-Communist Party Systems: Competition, Representation and Inter-Party Cooperation*. Cambridge, UK: Cambridge University Press, 1999.

Klugman, Jeni, ed. *Poverty in Russia: Public Policy and Private Responses*. Washington, D.C.: The World Bank, 1997.

Kornai, Janos. *The Socialist System*. Princeton, NJ: Princeton University Press, 1992.

Kornai, Janos and Susan Rose-Ackerman, eds. *Building a Trustworthy State in Post-Socialist Transition*. New York: Palgrave Macmillan, 2004.

Kotkin, Stephen. *Armageddon Averted: The Soviet Collapse, 1970-2000*. Oxford, UK: Oxford University Press, 2001.

Kuchins, Andrew C. *Russia After the Fall*. Washington, D.C.: Carnegie Endowment for International Peace, 2002.

Lieven, Anatol. *Chechnya: Tombstone of Russian Power*. New Haven, CT: Yale University Press, 1999.

Lieven, Dominic. *Empire: The Russian Empire and its Rivals*. London: John Murray, 2000.

Linz, Juan J., and Alfred Stepan. *Problems of Democratic Transition and Consolidation: Southern Europe, South America, and Post-Communist Europe*. Baltimore, MD: Johns Hopkins University Press, 1996.

Lloyd-Jones, Stewart and António Costa Pinto, eds. *The Last Empire: Thirty Years of Portuguese Decolonization*. Bristol, UK: Intellect Books, 2003.

Lukin, Alexander. "What Went Wrong in Russia?: Forcing the Pace of

Democratization," *Journal of Democracy* 10, no. 2 (April 1999): 35-40.

Lustick, Ian. *Unsettled States, Disputed Lands.* Ithaca, NY: Cornell University Press, 1993.

Mann, Michael. *The Dark Side of Democracy: Explaining Ethnic Cleansing.* Cambridge, UK: Cambridge University Press, 2004.

Markova, Ivana, ed. *Trust and Democratic Transition in Post-Communist Europe.* New York: Oxford University Press, 2004.

McFaul, Michael. *Russia's Unfinished Revolution: Political Change from Gorbachev to Putin.* Ithaca, NY: Cornell University Press, 2001.

McFaul, Michael and Kathryn Stoner-Weiss. *After the Collapse of Communism: Comparative Lessons of Transition.* Cambridge, UK: Cambridge University Press, 2004.

Mickiewicz, Ellen. *Changing Channels: Television and the Struggle for Power in Russia.* New York: Oxford University Press, 1997.

Milanovic, Branko. *Income, Inequality, and Poverty during the Transition from Planned to Market Economy.* Washington, D.C.: World Bank, 1998.

Millar, James R. "The De-development of Russia," *Current History* 98, no. 630 (October 1999): 322-327.

Murrell, Peter. "What is Shock Therapy? What Did it Do in Poland and Russia?," *Post-Soviet Affairs* 9, no. 2 (1993): 111-140.

Nunberg, Barbara. *The State After Communism: Administrative Transitions in Central and Eastern Europe.* Washington, D.C.: World Bank, 1999.

Organization for Economic Co-operation and Development, *Country and Regional Reports on Poland, Russia, and Ukraine.* Paris: OECD.

Osterhammel, Jürgen. *Colonialism: A Theoretical Overview.* Princeton, NJ: Marcus Wiener/Ian Randle, 1997.

Pridemore, William, ed. *Ruling Russia: Crime, Law, and Justice in a Changing Society.* London: Rowan and Littlefield, 2005.

Przeworski, Adam. *Democracy and the Market: Political and Economic Reforms in Eastern Europe and Latin America.* Cambridge, UK: Cambridge University Press, 1991.

Reddaway, Peter and Robert Orttung. *The Dynamics of Russian Politics, Volume 1: Putin's Reform of Federal-Regional Relations*, Vols. 1-2. Lanham, MD: Rowman and Littlefield Publishers, 2005.

Remnick, David. *Lenin's Tomb: The Last Days of the Soviet Empire.* New York: Random House, 1993.

Roberts, Cynthia and Thomas Sherlock. "Review Article: Bringing the Russian State Back In: Explanations of the Derailed Transition to Market Democracy," *Comparative Politics* (July 1999): 477-498.

Roeder, Philip G. "Peoples and States after 1989: The Politics Costs of Incomplete National Revolutions," *Slavic Review* 58, no. 4 (Winter 1999): 854-882.

_____. *Red Sunset: The Failure of Soviet Politics*. Princeton, NJ: Princeton University Press, 1993.

Roshwald, Aviel. *Ethnic Nationalism and the Fall of Empires: Central Europe, Russia and the Middle East, 1914-1923*. London: Routledge, 2001.

Rutland, Peter. "The Rocky Road from Plan to Market," in White, Pravda and Gitelman, *Developments in Russian Politics* (1997): 149-168.

Sachs, Jeffrey D. *Poland's Jump to the Market Economy*. Cambridge, MA: MIT Press, 1993.

Shevtsova, Lilia. *Putin's Russia*. Washington, D.C.: Carnegie Endowment for International Peace, 2005.

Slider, Darrell. "Regional and Local Politics," in Stephen White, Alex Pravda and Zvi Gitelman, eds., *Developments in Russian Politics*. Raleigh, NC: Duke University Press, 1997, 251-265.

Solnick, Steven L. "The Political Economy of Russian Federalism: A Framework for Analysis," *Problems of Post-Communism* (November/December 1996): 13-25.

_____. *Stealing the State*. Cambridge, MA: Harvard University Press, 1997.

Solomon, Peter H., Jr., ed. *Reforming Justice in Russia, 1864-1996*. Armonk, NY: M. E. Sharpe, 1997.

Solomon, Peter H., Jr. and Todd S. Foglesong. *Courts and Transition in Russia: The Challenge of Judicial Reform*. Boulder, CO: Westview Press, 2000.

Stark, David and László Bruszt, *Postsocialist Pathways: Transforming Politics and Property in East Central Europe*. Cambridge, UK: Cambridge University Press, 1998.

Stoner-Weiss, Kathryn. "Central Weakness and Provincial Autonomy: Observations on the Devolution Process in Russia," *Post-Soviet Affairs* 15, no. 1 (1999): 87-106.

_____. *Local Heroes: The Political Economy of Russian Regional Governance*. Princeton, NJ: Princeton University Press, 1997.

Stourzh, Gerald. *Vom Reich zur Republik: Studien zur Osterreichsbewusstein im 20 Jahrhundert*. Vienna: ed Atelier, 1990.

Szporluk, Roman. *Russia, Ukraine, and the Breakup of the Soviet Union*. Stanford, CA: Hoover Institution Press, 2000.

Tucker, Joshua A. *Regional Economic Voting: Russia, Poland, Hungary, Slovakia, and the Czech Republic, 1990-1999.* Cambridge, UK: Cambridge University Press, 2006.

Volkov, Vadim. *Violent Entrepreneurs: The Use of Force in the Making of Russian Capitalism.* Ithaca, NY: Cornell University Press, 2002.

Wilson, Andrew. *The Ukrainians: Unexpected Nation.* London: Yale University Press, 2000.

Woodruff, David. *Money Unmade: Barter and the Fate of Russian Capitalism.* Ithaca, NY: Cornell University Press, 1999.

World Bank, *Country and Regional Reports.* Washington, D.C.: The World Bank.

Yeltsin, Boris. *The Struggle for Russia.* New York: Times Books, 1994.

ABOUT THE AUTHORS

RAWI ABDELAL is an associate professor at Harvard Business School. He is the author of *National Purpose in the World Economy: Post-Soviet States in Comparative Perspective*, which won the Marshall Shulman Prize, and the forthcoming *Capital Rules: The Construction of Global Finance*.

SIMON CLARKE is Professor of Sociology at the University of Warwick, U.K., and scientific director of the Institute for Comparative Labor Relations Research (ISITO), Moscow. He has been researching aspects of labor and employment in Russia with local colleagues since 1990 in close collaboration with international trade union and labor organizations (ICFTU, ILO, and GUFs). He is currently engaged in two comparative research projects on "post-socialist trade unions," in collaboration with local research teams, one covering Russia, Belarus, Moldova, Kazakhstan, Kyrgyzstan and Tajikistan, and the other covering Russia, China, and Vietnam. Full details of his Russian research can be found at www.warwick.ac.uk/go/Russia.

RICHARD E. ERICSON is a professor and the Chair of the Department of Economics in Harriot College of East Carolina University. He is the former Director of The Harriman Institute and Professor of Economics at Columbia University. His research has focused on the Soviet and Russian economies and aspects of microeconomic theory related to planning, economic systems, and transition from command to market. He has made frequent visits to the Soviet Union, Russia, and the other successor states, for teaching and research on their economies, and for participation in economics training programs. He has also taught at Harvard, Yale, and NorthWestern University.

MURRAY FESHBACH is a senior scholar at the Woodrow Wilson Center for Scholars, and Research Professor of Demography Emeritus in the School of Foreign Service at Georgetown University. An economist and demographer, he formerly worked in the Foreign Demographic Analysis Division of the U.S. Census Bureau, and has written extensively on demography, health, and the environment in the Soviet Union. His current research focuses on the social impact and policy implications of Russia's current health and demographic crises.

CURT GASTEYGER was Professor for International Relations at the Graduate Institute of International Studies in Geneva from 1974 until 1994, and from 1978 to 1999 was Director of the Graduate Institute's Programme for Strategic and International Security Studies. He is now Professor Emeritus and since October 1999, has been the Director of the Association for the Promotion and Study of International Security.

THANE GUSTAFSON is a professor of government at Georgetown University and a consultant on Russian energy affairs for Cambridge Research Energy Associates. His most recent book is *Capitalism Russian-Style*. He is currently working on a history of the Russian oil and gas industries.

DALE R. HERSPRING, Professor of Political Science at Kansas State University and a member of the Council on Foreign Relations, is the author of ten books and more than eighty articles dealing with U.S., Soviet/Russian, Polish, and German civil-military relations. His last book was *The Pentagon and the Presidency: Civil-Military Relations from FDR to George W. Bush*. His next book, forthcoming in October 2006 is entitled, *The Kremlin and the High Command: The Impact of Presidential Leadership on the Russian Military*.

EUGENE HUSKEY is William R. Kenan, Jr. Professor of Political Science and Russian Studies at Stetson University in Florida. He has written widely on politics and legal affairs in the USSR and the successor states of Russia and Kyrgyzstan. His most recent works include the entry on Kyrgyzstan in Freedom House's "Nations in Transit 2004," and a chapter in *Leading Russia: Putin in Perspective*. He is associate editor of *Russian Review* and a member of the advisory board of *Advokat*, the journal of the Moscow Bar Association.

SIMON KUKES is a director of Amarin Corporation. He worked in major U.S. and Russian oil companies for over twenty-five years, most recently as Chairman and Chief Executive of YUKOS Oil (2003-04), and President and Chief Executive of the Tyumen Oil Company (1998-2003). He has published extensively in the field of international oil company development strategy.

DOMINIC LIEVEN is a professor at the London School of Economics and a fellow of the British Academy. A former Kennedy Scholar at Harvard and Humboldt Fellow, he currently holds a Leverhulme Major Research Fellowship in order to write *War and Peace: the Reality. Russia against Napoleon (1807-14)*. His previous books include *Russia and the Origins of the First World War*, *Russia's Rulers under the Old Regime*, *Aristocracy in Europe*, *Nicholas II*, and *Empire: The Russian Empire and its Rivals*.

PAUL RODZIANKO, Senior Vice President of Access Industries, Inc., also serves as Director of the U.S.-Russia Business Council, Vice Chairman of the U.S.-Kazakhstan Business Association, Director of the Kennan Council of the Woodrow Wilson International Center, and Director of the International Tax and Investment Center. He also serves as Chairman of GreenFuel Technologies Corporation and as Director of Energibolaget i Sverige and Azima Inc. Since 1996, he has been involved extensively with Russia and the former Soviet states holding a variety of corporate positions including Managing Director of Bogatyr Access Komir (1996-97), Director of CNPC-Aktobe in Kazakhstan (2001-02), and Senior Advisor to the President and Chief Executive Officer of the Tyumen Oil Company in Moscow (1999-2002).

WILLIAM C. WOHLFORTH is Professor of Government at Dartmouth College. He is author of *Elusive Balance: Power and Perceptions during the Cold War*, and editor of *Witnesses to the End of the Cold War*, and *Cold War Endgame*. He has published numerous articles on international and strategic affairs and Russian foreign policy. Recent articles include "The Russian-Soviet Empires, 1400-2000: A Test of Neorealism," in *Review of International Studies*; "Revisiting Balance of Power Theory in Central Eurasia;" and, with Stephen G. Brooks, "Hard Times for Soft Balancing," in *International Security*; and "International Relations Theory and the Case Against Unilateralism," in *Perspectives on Politics*.

INDEX

Alternative Trade Union Federations (VKT, KTR) 88

American 10, 23-25, 20, 28, 47, 54, 100, 102, 105, 254-257, 260, 269, 271, 274-275. *see also* United States of America

American Enterprise Institute 107

American imperialism 260

Ammunition 235

Amnesty 105

Ankara 18

Anpilov, Viktor 84

Anschluss 18

Anti-aircraft systems 224

Anti-liberal programs 146

Anti-market foundations 149

Anti-market survival strategies 115

Anti-Russian 212, 214

Anti-Semitism 19-20

Anti-Soviet 24, 212, 214

Apsheron Trend 193

Arable land 102

Arbatov 246-247

Arctic Ocean 192

Armenia 207, 210, 212; Armenian 19; Genocide 19

Armoured equipment 4, 220, 224, 232-233; tank 192, 224, 233, 235; units 222, 226, 229; 42nd Motorized Division 230, 291

Arms 14, 226, 232, 235, 239; Coat of 244

Army 67, 221, 222, 224, 226-230, 232-233, 235-236, 238; Red 259, 274

Article 13 of the Law on Defense 231

Article 49 of the Old Code of Criminal Procedure 49-50

Artillery 224

Assembly of Social Partnership 78

Astrakhan 193-194

Ataturk, Kemal 23

Atlantic 244, 248, 254, 256; Alliance 248, 254

Atomic Industry (Ministry of) 99

Åusland, Anders 122

Austria 19, 22-24; Austrian Republic 9, 18

Austrian-Germans 18-19

Autarchy 122

Authoritarian 8, 21, 72, 143, 243, 251. *see also* autocracy; managed democracy; president

Authority 28, 30, 33, 38-39, 43-44, 52, 66, 69-71, 73, 75, 78, 116-119, 121, 134, 136, 143, 163, 167, 199, 200-204, 206, 208, 211, 224, 231, 238; executive 30, 44, 134, 136; legislative 38; judicial 28, 33, 39, 43-44, 52; moral 121

Autocratic monarchs 11-12. *see also* managed democracy; president

Automotive 138

Axes 276, 279

Azerbaijan 164, 193, 207, 209, 210, 212, 253

Azerbaijan International Oil Consortium (AIOC) 193

Azerbaijani Popular Front 209

Baku 164-165, 193

Baku-Ceyhan Project; Pipeline Project 193, 276

Balkans 259-261

Balance of power 262, 268, 273-276

Baltic 19, 21, 187, 192, 196, 208, 209, 212, 244, 248-250, 256; Sea 244, 255, 256; states 21, 196, 208, 248, 249, 256

Bankruptcy 116, 145, 170, 172, 180-181, 248; judges 116; law 145, 172, 180-181

Baranovsky 246

Barenboim, Petr 51

Barents 183, 256

Barents Europe-Arctic Council 256

Barter 115, 123, 126, 135, 197, 199, 213. *see also* monetary surrogates

Basic inputs 123, 153

Beijing 265

Belarus 24, 194, 198, 207, 210, 212, 214, 244, 248, 249, 250, 255; Belarusian 19, 202; credit 202

Bench 35-37, 40, 47; feminization of 40

Berezovsky, Boris 151

Berlin 251, 262, 265

Beslan 32-33, 237-238, 248

Biokinetic model 103

Bin Laden, Osama 262

Black cash payments 124
Black Sea 192, 194
Black Sea Cooperation Council 256
Blat 119
Bipolarity 273
Borodino 19
Bosnia 251, 261
Branch unions 75, 80, 90
Branch Tariff Agreements 89-91
Bribery 34, 108
Britain 17, 244, 255; British 10-11, 17, 20, 22-24, 107, 271; British Empire 11, 17, 20, 22, 24, 271
British Council 107
British India. *see* India
British Petroleum (BP) 173, 183
Brzesinki, Zbigniew 273
Budapest 256
Budennovsk 223
Budget(ary) 30, 22, 34, 41-42, 50, 53, 72, 90-91, 98, 106, 119, 133, 136, 139, 142-143, 225, 230-233, 279
Bulgaria 188, 248, 254
Bureaucracies 174, 220; bureaucratic 11-13, 15, 67, 73, 80, 85-86, 88, 93, 95, 113, 119, 145, 150-151, 189, 221-222, 225, 227, 270, 272; and management 95. *see also* functionaries
Bureaucrats 124, 152, 199, 220
Burma 17, 20
Bush, George W. 237, 257, 262
Brussels 262
Business 19, 31-33, 42-43, 48, 50-53, 112, 117, 120, 127, 135-137, 140-143, 145, 147-148, 151-152, 163, 165, 172, 174-175, 182, 189-190, 195-196, 200, 211, 235
Bypass 183, 187, 194-195

Capital 5, 31, 108-109, 114-115, 122, 137, 140-141, 145, 164, 169, 174-175, 177, 186, 191; flight 140-141, 153
Capital punishment 32

Capitalism 4, 14, 16, 18, 113, 153, 198; patrimonial 153
Caspian 164-165, 187, 193-196, 278; oil 193; resources 278
Capitalist development 151
Catalytic converters 101
Catering 174
Caucasus 19, 39, 183, 276; North 39, 183
Center-left, coalition 84, 94; opposition 77
Central Asia 19, 196, 226, 257, 260, 262, 276
Central Bank of Russia 197
Central Europe 13, 163, 188, 195, 273-274
Chapayevsk 101
Chechnya 6, 17, 212, 220, 222, 225, 229-230, 237, 248, 256-259, 261
Chechen Hostage Crisis 53, 237. *see also* Beslan Hostage Crisis
Chechen Wars 224, 247
Chekis, Anatolii 67, 87-88
Chernomyrdin, Viktor 78, 203, 205, 224
Chiburayev, V. 103
China 8, 12, 25, 109, 135, 190, 271, 276-278; Chinese 11, 16, 20, 233, 279
Chirac, Jacques 244, 279
Chubais, Anatolii 143, 145
Churchill, Winston 244
Citizenship 9, 17-18
Clark, Wesley 261
Civil practice 48
Civil society 5, 66-96, 118
Civil War (Russian, 1919-1921) 143, 221
Civilian firms 229
Climate 50, 164, 177, 191
Coal 76, 187; and mining 70, 72, 74; regions 70
Cold War 11, 24, 237, 256, 258, 272-274
Collective agreements 70, 73, 75, 92, 94-95
Cologne Summit 256
Commands (*rodi*) 228
Commission on Security and Cooperation in Europe (CSCE) 256
Committee on Geopolitical Affairs 266
Common European economic and social space 256

Macro-economic 4, 30, 53, 77, 112, 126, 127, 133, 136-137

Malaysia 20

Managed democracy 68, 89

Management 66, 70-75, 93, 95-96, 108, 117-118, 127, 137-138, 173-175, 180, 191, 226, 247, 258, 272; culture 6, 163, 174

Managers 72, 112, 124, 137-138, 163, 174-175. *see also* bureaucrats

Manufacturing 100, 126-127, 132, 134, 136, 141, 144, 146, 168, 181

Market, -based 115, 138, 153; decentralized 114; distortion 114, 125, 132, 149, 153; -driven 115, 120, 138; environment 114, 120-121; internal 175; imperial 18, 24; structures 120, 126; value 119, 123, 165

Market clearing level 139

Marketization 51, 119, 127, 188

Mass media 143, 152

Mass protests 77-78, 87

Material 39, 99, 114, 126, 166, 181, 201-202, 208, 211

May Day 73, 84-85

Mayor 84, 92, 171

Mazheikiu refinery 168, 185

Media 143, 151-152

Medical services 228

Mediterranean 192

Metals sector 101-102, 132,135-136, 140

Metropole 9, 23-24; Metropolitan 8, 12, 17

Mexico 125

Middle class 13, 34, 279

Middle East 23, 257

Mikhaylov, Viktor 99

Military 5-8, 53, 106, 109, 127, 146, 168, 199, 212, 220-239, 247, 249-250, 254-255, 258-262, 266-269, 274, 276, 278; coup 24; reform 220-239; regulars 223, 229-230; secrets 44; technology 12, 25

Military-chemical cities 100-101

Military Collegium of the Russian Supreme Court 44

Military-industrial complex 228, 233

Military Sciences, Academy of 237

Milosevic, Slobodan 260-261

Ministry of Foreign Affairs. *see* Foreign Ministry

National and Environmental Health Action Plan (2000) 103
National patriotism 207. *see also* nationalism
National Productivist Project 204
Nationhood 10, 13, 211, 213, 252
Nationalism 8, 9, 13-14, 16, 18, 21, 206-207, 247, 266; democratic 9, 15; ethnic
    8, 16, 23
Natural monopoly 135, 145, 148
Natural resources 98, 179, 181, 183, 247, 266-267, 278-279; Ministry of 98, 179,
    183
Naval Infantry 222
Navy 223-224
Nazarbaev, Nursultan 210
Nazism 14, 18, 19
Neo-Eurasianists 268
Neutral countries 279, 248
New commercial and financial structures (FIGs) 121
New Economic Policy (NEP) 50
New Market Economy 82, 113, 122, 180
New Trade Union Federation 87
New Western Russia 207
New York 237
Nickel-mining 138
Nikitin 100
Non-aligned countries 248
Non-commissioned officers (NCOs) 236
Non-durable goods 122
Non-governmental organizations (NGOs) 68, 99, 100, 150, 152, 261, 271, 277
Non-state education institutions 108
Norm setting 31-32, 45-46, 73, 205, 251, 277
North Atlantic Cooperation Council (NACC) 256
North Atlantic Treaty Organization (NATO) 24, 237, 243, 245, 248, 250-252,
    255-257, 259-261, 273; Information and Documentation Center 251; -
    Russian Permanent Joint Council 256; membership 248, 250, 252, 255, 257,
    259; Secretary-General 250; -Ukraine Charter 251
North Sea 193
Northern Eurasia 8, 10

Real investment 139, 148
Real value 135
Reallocation 137
Recruits 5, 222-223, 230, 235-236
Recruitment 28, 33-34, 73
Refineries 168-169, 171-172, 188, 195
Reforms, economic 6, 28-29, 31, 51, 53, 133, 197-198, 205, 209, 243, 251; legal 28-30, 32-34, 37, 50-53, 173; military 220-239; pension 144; social 142, 144, 148
Reform program 77, 85, 137, 141, 144
Reformist 29, 32, 47
Regional administrations 67, 91-93
Regional agreements 75, 91, 95. *see also* social partnerships
Regional governors 87, 143, 171
Regional legislature 93
Regional trade union 73, 75-76, 83-4, 86, 91-93, 95-96
Registration 77, 92, 145
Regulatory 145; bodies 89, 116; framework 148;
Reintegration 189, 210, 213, 249, 279
Republican 22-23, 42-43, 71
Restructuring 6, 112, 116, 122, 137-142, 145, 148-150, 163, 189, 239
Revenues 72, 98, 143, 150-151, 181, 194-195, 200
Revich, Boris A. 104
Revolution 14, 25, 32-33, 40, 164, 166, 206, 220, 227, 243, 251, 255, 266, 279; Orange 243, 251; Russian 164, 206
Rimland 269, 274-276
Risk 11, 16, 52, 145-146, 172, 196; Russia(n) 178, Western 178
Robertson, George 250-251
Rogov, Sergei 269
Romania 188, 248, 254
Romanov dynasty 206
Rosneft, state oil company 151-152, 171, 180
Rossel, Eduard 92
Rostov oblast 106
Ruble 6, 135, 139, 172, 185, 197, 200, 202-204, 209-210, 213-214; zone 197-198, 201-205, 207-211, 213

Tyumenneftegaz (TNG) 172